DATE DUE

GAYLORD			PRINTED IN U.S.A.

COMMUNICATION

The Process
of
Organizing

COMMUNICATION

The Process
of
Organizing

Bonnie McDaniel Johnson

THE PENNSYLVANIA
STATE UNIVERSITY

ALLYN AND BACON, INC.
BOSTON   LONDON   SYDNEY   TORONTO

Excerpts from " 'Banana Time': Job Satisfaction and Informal
Interaction" by Donald Roy were reproduced by permission of
the Society for Applied Anthropology.

Excerpts from *An Introduction to Interpersonal Communication*
by McCroskey, Larson, and Knapp were reprinted by permission of
Prentice-Hall, Inc.

Excerpts from *Management and Organizational Development* by
Chris Argyris were used with permission of McGraw-Hill Book Co.

Excerpts from *Organizations* by James G. March and Herbert A.
Simon and *The Social Psychology of Organizations* by Daniel Katz
and Robert L. Kahn were reprinted by permission of John
Wiley & Sons, Inc.

LIBRARY OF CONGRESS CATALOGING IN PUBLICATION DATA

Johnson, Bonnie McDaniel, 1944–
    Communication: the process of organizing.

    Includes bibliographical references and index.
    1.   Communication—Social aspects.   2.   Communication
in organizations.   I.   Title.
HM258.J617   301.14   76–57935
ISBN 0–205–05786–1

CONTENTS

PREFACE

The subject of this book is organizing human action. Examples of the process of organizing human action are all around—ball games, cafeteria lines, offices, factories. We recognize the process by the regularity and predictability of people's movements. In a room of office workers, for example, there is a pattern of activity, similarity in the movements of individuals. People do not all do the same thing, but each person seems to act as if he or she knows what each of the others is doing. These people are coordinating their actions and accomplishing common work.

The regularity of coordinated actions suggests the presence of a single "mind" controlling the movements of many people. During the 1920s some social scientists declared that people in groups—mobs in particular—could be controlled through a "group mind." Today, we find descriptions of group minds only in science fiction. Coordinating actions is not a process of magic. Coordinating or organizing human action is a process of communication.

This book is about how people communicate to organize cooperative activities. Many forms of organized action are used as examples. The smallest forms are friendships and families; the largest are corporations and governments. The focus is on how communication functions to make possible those patterns of human action we call "organizations."

The purpose of this book is to help readers learn to become more effective communicators whether they are certified public accountants, production managers, labor union organizers, food coop managers, librarians, or Girl Scout leaders. No one will turn into a "communications expert." Most aren't, nor do they want to be communications experts. People only use communication to survive in and enhance their world.

The book is based on a simple idea—all organizations are created through communication. If people understand communication, then with just a few additional ideas, they can understand how organizations work. Therefore, in this book is presented an organization theory which is developed from a communication theory.

I believe that any theory about how to do something is only as good as the advice one may derive from it. Therefore, I provide here some suggestions about how to do something (communicate and organize) using the theory. At the end of chapters 2, 4, 5, 6, and 7, there are application sections aimed at putting the theories discussed in the chapter into concrete useful practice. These are not cookbook sections. Communicating is such a complex process that no one has yet found a way to write down the recipes. Three of these sections provide the reader with hints about how to analyze communication problems and brainstorm methods for improving situations. The application sections on interviewing (chapter 5) and group problem solving (chapter 6) provide a simple way of conceptualizing the basic tasks to be accomplished in any planned communicative situation. (Actually accomplishing these tasks is far more difficult than it may appear here, of course.)

I had a personal reason for writing this book. I feel I never have enough class time to provide a theory of organizations from a communication perspective through lectures, and to allow the students time to discuss the theory and to develop skills through practice. I felt it would help if the theory could be written down. In writing this book I have sought to provide teachers and students with simple explanations of theory so that valuable class time can be spent in discussion and skill sharpening.

The Introduction and the three unit introductions provide readers with a walking tour of the book. These sections describe the destinations or the goals of the various units, provide a map to what is said, and alert the reader to special attractions along the road. These sections also outline in broad highways the theory which is developed in detail in the individual chapters. You may find it informative to read these sections quickly before proceeding to chapter one.

I have learned a great deal about the process of organizing through a series of "organizing failures" involving coauthors of this project. The original project was to be coauthored by my colleague Richard L. Barton. His ideas had a significant impact on what is here. I thank Dick for convincing me that "consensus" is the key concept in a theory of organizations. He fought vigorously and successfully to persuade me that a theory of organizations which accounts for product-making corporations but says nothing about nursing homes is not much of a theory.

In a new life cycle, Lenard C. Hawes and I planned to coauthor a book on organizational communication. Len persuaded me that goals are retrospective, not prospective, and that I had better rethink my blind faith in systems theory. Len first threw the term "display" at me. It is a central term in this book, though I think my reference for it bears only slight resemblance to how Len uses the term.

Ronald W. Johnson and Larry Spence once agreed to help me write a book on the subject of organizational communication. That project did not work out either, but I thank them for their efforts in stimulating some of the ideas found here. Larry Spence helped me to understand metacommunication in organization. His own research in organizational communication (quoted extensively in the Appendix) helped me to clarify what it means to be a researcher and consultant.

Ronald W. Johnson's contributions to this book extend far beyond any thanks which can be given. He did all the work one lovingly expects of an author's spouse. He proofread; he encouraged; he wiped my tears; he babysat. More importantly, there are critical ideas here which came from him. We have spent hours and hours discussing and observing how decisions are built. His professional specialty being governmental budgeting and policy making, he taught me how to understand budgeting processes as communication processes. Then he checked what I wrote to make sure it was right on paper.

Frank Ruggirello, Associate Editor at Allyn and Bacon, was somewhat understanding through all these changes of personnel and direction. He probably thought he had to be because he persuaded me to undertake the project in the first place. Frank has a talent for writing business letters which are not "documents" (see definition in chapter 7). Sometimes it gets him into trouble. That talent also makes him a fine person to work with.

Diane Addleman, Joyce Diehl, Linda McNerney, and Cheryl Moss are wonderful people. They turned scratched and torn drafts into legible manuscripts.

Gail Whitehead, Patti Lanski, Marilyn Nash, Barbara Pilla, and Lynn Reuter served as the test audience for much of what is here.

One reviewer of an early version of this manuscript described it as "cold." It may still be; but it shouldn't be. I converted enormous amounts of love from many people into insight and energy for writing this book. I could not have done it without them.

B.M.J.

Introduction:
The Organizing Perspective

Communication and Organizational Communi-
    cation
Meaning and Organizational Intelligence
Expectations and Organizational Integration
Messages
Plan of the Book

From the Board of Directors to the first line supervisors, the people who manage a corporation take its existence for granted. Their day-to-day concerns are keeping it in business. When they think of what the organization "is," they think of its capital assets, its stock, its financial statement, its employees, stockholders, and managerial system. All of these "things" are obviously part of a corporation. They make up our common sense reality. They are accomplished "facts" that would prove to anyone the organization does exist. Even the devoted few who work to keep a food coop in operation, despite a lack of funds and commitment from the vast majority of members, tend to take its present existence (if not its future) for granted. The stability of patterns of co-operation directs attention to what is—the organization—rather than how it is created and sustained.

In contrast to this view of organization as taken-for-granted, this book takes an "organizing perspective." That is, the concern here is with creating, sustaining, and changing patterns of coordinated action. The existence of things called organizations is not taken for granted. Rather, the reader is invited to look beyond those features which seem to constitute an "organization"—beyond the money, the buildings, even the people—to examine the subtle and often unnoticed processes or methods by which all kinds of organizations are accomplished.

One common definition of "organizing" is the process which occurs in the beginning of the history of an organization. A labor union "organizer," for example, comes to start a union organization. In this book organizing refers to processes which exist throughout the history of an organization. Organizing is a continual process by which relationships are accomplished. Organizing *is* the organization. Karl Weick defines this view succinctly when he writes: "Assume that there are processes which create, maintain, and dissolve social collectivities, that these processes constitute the work of organizing, but that the ways in which these processes are continually executed are the organization."[1] These continuous processes are the subject of this book.

There are any number of perspectives which might be taken in describing organizing processes. Psychologists describe the ways in which people in organizations develop and change one another's attitudes and perceptions. Industrial engineers talk about designing work flows and incentive structures. Sociologists describe stabilizing social structures through hierarchical positions. Management scientists describe the designing of cost structures and information retrieval systems. Conflict theorists describe processes of coalition formation and negotiation. All of these processes constitute coordination of actions. They are all processes of organizing.

This book examines communication as the process of organizing. The importance of communication within organizations is widely recognized. Almost any textbook on organization devotes some attention to communication within organizations. Keith Davis' statement about the importance of communication is typical:

> Communication is as necessary to an organization as the bloodstream is to a person. Just as a man gets arteriosclerosis, a hardening of the arteries which impairs his efficiency, so may an organization get infosclerosis," a hardening of the communication arteries which produces similar impaired efficiency.[2]

Davis goes on to state that "all management passes through the bottleneck of communication." The focus of his view is that communication is one of a number of processes which happens within an organization. According to this view, communication is the process of transmitting information about other aspects of the organization—planning, designing, and so forth. Quite often, it is viewed as transmission of information from superiors to subordinates, from manager to work-group (often called "communication down the hierarchy").

COMMUNICATION AND ORGANIZATIONAL COMMUNICATION

The term communication is not used here in the same way that Davis uses the term. It does not refer to one of a number of processes which go on within an organization. As the title of this book implies, communication is considered to be the one process. Thus phenomena described by others such as attitudes, incentive structures, hierarchical positions, cost structures, information retrieval systems, coalition formation and negotiation are all described in this book as communicative phenomena. The point is not that these can be seen only as communicative phenomena. There is much to such phenomena which is unrelated to communication. Rather the point is that there is something useful to be learned about organizations when such phenomena are described from a communicative perspective.

What is communication and more particularly what is organizational communication? The commonly used definition in the organizational literature, such as that by Davis quoted above, is that communication is the process of transmitting information and that organizational communication is transmitting information within an organization. One problem with this definition is that it makes it awkward for us to consider things like incentive structures and hierarchical positions from a "communicative perspective." It limits us to thinking of communication as one of a number of processes which occur within organizations. More seriously, this definition takes for granted the existence of organizations. It assumes that organizations exist before communication and that communication occurs only within these organizations. I argue here that the "organizing" of organizations can be examined as communication. Without communication, no organizations exist. Communication is not just something that happens within organizations. Communication is organizing.

At a simple level the title of the book defines communication. Communication is the process of organizing, but that definition is not very informative. If organizing is "the continual process by which relationships are accomplished," then, communication is the continual process of accomplishing relationships. Even this definition somewhat begs the question for it leaves undefined what it means to "accomplish relationships."

In this book communication is defined as the process of constructing meanings and expectations through the exchange of messages. There are thus three critical terms in the definition of communication: meaning, expectations, and messages. Note that this definition specifies both the process and the outcome. The process of communication involves the exchange of messages. This process functions to create two outcomes: meanings and expectations.

Meanings and expectations are outcomes of communication for individual communicators. That is, when I communicate with another, I construct for myself the meaning from messages we are exchanging; I also construct for myself expectations about what I should do and what the other may or should do. I have my meanings and expectations; the other person has his or her meanings and expectations. But if each person has his or her own meanings and expectations, how can we have organization or relationship?

In order to examine communication as an organizing process, two additional terms are needed: organizational intelligence and organizational integration. These terms identify outcomes of communication at the level of a collection of people or an organization. Organizational intelligence is consensual meaning among a group of people who regularly communicate; organizational integration is based in consensual expectations. These two terms represent what is accomplished in the creating of relationship. Figure I.1 shows the relationship of the five key terms of this book: messages, meaning, expectations, organizational intelligence and organizational integration.

When people construct meaning and expectations from an exchange of messages, we say that communication has taken place. When the exchange of messages is patterned over time among a group of

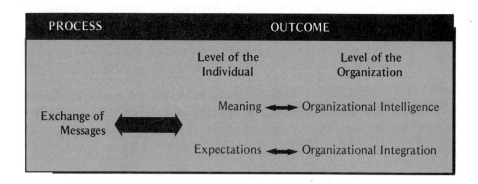

FIGURE I.1
Key Terms in the Definition of Communication as an Organizing Process

people so that they come to "share" meanings and create organizational intelligence and when they create integration from "shared" expectations, then communication is functioning as an organizing process. Organizational communication refers to communication which has certain outcomes (organizational intelligence and integration) rather than communication which takes place within the setting of formal organizations. Figure I.1 lays out in the broadest terms the theory of communication as an organizing process. Let us look at each term a little closer.

MEANING AND ORGANIZATIONAL INTELLIGENCE

The definition of communication as constructing meaning is different from the definition of exchanging information in two ways: "constructing" is different from "exchanging," and "meaning" is different from "information." The reason for the emphasis on construction rather than merely "exchanging" should be clear in light of the focus on organizing.

When communication is defined as the process of "exchanging information" it is tempting to think of information as a set of objective "facts" which can be passed from one person to another and remain the same for all. Few people are naive enough to believe this when they stop and give the idea some thought. It is clear that "giving a person a message" is not the same as "giving the person a pencil." He may get the words (the "message" has been exchanged), but have no idea what the words were intended to mean. But the expression "exchanging information" sometimes beguiles us into confusing information with messages.

The definition of "communication is the process of constructing meaning through the exchange of symbols" allows us to sort "information" into two components. Information has a message component. Messages are exchanged. Messages are what can be sensed—symbols on paper, audio signals, visual signals, but messages are not information, and exchanging messages does not constitute communication. Meaning, the second component of information, must be created. Meaning cannot be exchanged.

When people talk to one another, and/or otherwise throw messages to one another, they are doing more than throwing; they are engaged in a process of creating meaning. The process of meaning goes on within the head of each person, but not totally. Meaning is what we do in our heads to make sense out of the messages we receive. Meaning is a process of relating messages to each other and to other things we know to construct images of what is happening around us, but meaning is not totally within our heads because we learn to construct meaning. We learn to construct meanings in social contexts. This means that we construct meanings similar to the meanings of those people who have taught us how or those with whom we have learned. We are always learning with others how to construct meaning. Therefore, although we construct meanings "in our heads," our meanings tend to be similar to the meanings of people around us.

When people communicate regularly, as in organizations, they come to "share" some meanings. This happens because they are always engaged in a collaborative process of learning to construct meanings. The expression "organizational intelligence" refers to the outcome of this collaborative process of learning. Organizational Intelligence is the complete system of knowledge which permits people to coordinate their activities and work together. It is the totality of what passes for "facts" among a group of people. It is the technical knowledge of how to run machines; it is knowledge about how well the organization is doing; it is grapevine knowledge that Mr. Jones is cross if he is disturbed before his first cup of coffee.

Right now, you may find the idea that communication is the process of creating organizational intelligence rather fuzzy. All of us experience in a concrete sense the "transmission" of stuff we take to be information. It is not unusual for executives to receive a hundred letters, memos, and phone calls in a single day. He or she is likely to "send" that many or more. We do send and receive "messages," but the meaning of these messages cannot be sent or received. It can only be figured out in your head. In this book, you are urged to look beyond what you see and hear and normally take for granted. It urges you to think about how you make meaning from the symbols you send and receive and, in particular, how you have learned with others to make meanings. It urges you then to consider how meanings are related to your coordinated actions in an organization. It urges you to consider how you are engaged in the process of organizing when you are engaged in the process of making meaning.

EXPECTATIONS AND ORGANIZATIONAL INTEGRATION

The definition of organizational communication as communication within an organization presupposes the existence of an organizational structure—usually but not necessarily a hierarchy. This book describes how structures are accomplished. The word generally used here for structure is "integration." Integration is simply a condition or process of people doing things together. We take for granted that people are able to do things together. But how is integration possible? If I am doing my thing and you are doing yours, how can we do a thing together? In part "shared meanings" permit coordination. But sharing knowledge of how to do is not enough.

People can do things together because they are able to take others into account. People can do things together because they have expectations about what others will do and expectations about what others expect of them. Through the exchange of messages people create expectations.

Expectations are attitudes toward action which people presume that other people have. For example, if I expect you to arrive on time for dinner, I am presuming that you have the attitude that arriving on time is a reasonable and proper thing to do. I may or may not even stop to think about the probability of your coming on time. But my actions will be guided by my assumptions, regardless of whether they accurately reflect your attitudes and regardless of whether I stop to think about my assumptions.

When people develop similar or shared expectations, integration is created. Like organizational intelligence, integration is a learned process. People are able to share expectations when they have participated in this learning process together. Chapter 3 describes the learning process by which a group of people develop integration.

The process of learning expectations is as difficult to observe as the process of creating meaning. In this book you are given some tools for looking at this process. You are asked not to take integration for granted. You are urged to think about how you create expectations from the messages you "send" and "receive." Further, you are urged to consider how your expectations permit you to integrate your actions with others. That is, you are asked to think about how you are engaged in organizing when you are developing expectations through communication.

MESSAGES

Messages are what can be sensed—usually visual or auditory stimuli—which represent something else. We use messages to represent or symbolize our meanings and expectations. We sense messages and then interpret what we believe them to mean.

Messages people exchange are constructed in light of the meanings and expectations they have at the time they are constructing these messages. Meaning and expectations are thus constructed within the context of organizational integration and intelligence. Therefore, the arrows in Figure I.1 go both directions. Meaning and expectations are created through a process which involves the exchange of messages. Also messages and expectations are influenced by meanings and expectations which have already been created.

Most organizational theorists do not consider message an important concept in their theories of organization. This is understandable if one is concerned only with messages which shift information around within existing organizations. If one takes for granted the existence of information and organizational structure, then the concept of message is trivial. It is not a trivial concept, however, in the framework presented in Figure I.1 because messages are linked in a causal manner to the bases of organization: organizational intelligence and integration.

In this book the form of organizational messages is a substantial concept. Messages may take one of two forms: displays or documents. These terms are defined and discussed in detail in chapter 3. The theory of organizations in this book proposes that the form of the message has a substantial effect on the accomplishment of organizations. Unit II describes organizations accomplished by display as the message form. Organizations created by display alone are "informal organizations." Unit III describes organizations accomplished with the use of documents as well as displays. Organizations are "formalized" through the use of documents (see Figure I.2).

PLAN OF THE BOOK

This book is divided into three units. At the beginning of each unit there is an introduction to the objectives of the unit and some suggestions for how to read the chapters.

FORM OF MESSAGE EXCHANGED:	TYPE OF ORGANIZATION ACCOMPLISHED:
Display	Informal
Display + Document	Formalized

FIGURE I.2
Messages and Organizations

In unit I, I lay down certain conceptual foundations of a theory of organizational communication. Chapter 1 describes the history of organizational theory. Chapters 2 and 3 describe the theory of communication in which the organization theory is based. Chapter 2 is mostly concerned with the "intelligence" function of communication. Chapter 3 is directed toward the "integration" function of communication.

Unit II is concerned with the informal communication processes which organize any social system. Chapter 4 describes organizing in which people improvise on the basis of taken-for-granted expectations. The result is routine interactions and routine organizations. Chapter 5 describes the process of planning interactions with particular others in order to accomplish particular predetermined goals. In planned interactions people make intrapersonal decisions about how to communicate based on their conscious attention to expectations in particular situations. Chapter 6 describes the process by which a group of people in face-to-face communication produce what they call their "collective decision." In this kind of communication people talk about their expectations for interaction. They talk about how they should integrate for the purpose of producing collective "intelligence."

Unit III is concerned with how formal organizations are created. Chapter 7 describes the creation and interpretation of organizational documents such as budgets, organization charts, and office furnishings. These documents are described as messages which help to create the communication systems we call organizations. Chapter 8 describes how people talk to one another when there are documents which regulate their relationship, in particular, how supervisors and subordinates communicate with one another. Chapter 9 describes the process of collective decision building among groups of people who are formally integrated with one another, but who do not have much opportunity for face-to-face communication.

The conclusion discusses the implications of communication as an organizing process for implementing programs of planned change such as those programs called "organizational development." There is a special appendix which describes methods for researching organizational communication processes.

ENDNOTES

1. Karl Weick, *The Social Psychology of Organizing* (Reading, Mass.: Addison-Wesley, 1969), p. 1.
2. Keith Davis, *Human Behavior at Work* (McGraw-Hill, 1972), p. 379.

UNIT

I

Conceptual Foundations

The Introduction presented several concepts which are the central core of this book: organizing, communication, messages, meaning, expectations, organizational intelligence, organizational integration, and message forms (display and document). The Introduction showed the relationship of these terms in a conception of communication as organizing. The purposes of this first unit are: (1) to define these terms more completely, (2) to provide illustrations and examples, and (3) to show how these terms relate to one another by providing a more complete explanation of communication as an organizing process.

Chapter 1 is a history of organization theory. Although it is presented first, it does not need to be read first. The chapter has three purposes. One purpose is to introduce readers who are not familiar with organizational theory to the most commonly used concepts and terms. A second purpose is to demonstrate from an historical perspective that a theory of organization presupposes a theory of communication. This book presents a theory of organizations developed from a theory of communication. However, one can infer a theory of communication from any theory of organization. Chapter 1 draws inferences about communication and organizing from what others have said about organizations. The third purpose of chapter 1 is to put the concepts of "organizational intelligence" and "organizational integra-

tion" into historical context. The chapter looks at each of four major schools of organization theory and asks: Though they may use different terms, what is "organizational intelligence" and "organizational integration" according to the theorists of this school?

Chapters 2 and 3 should be read together and in the order presented. The reader will probably find them most useful if read before reading the remainder of the book. The concept of "meaning" is the subject of chapter 2; "expectation" is the subject of chapter 3. However, these two phenomena cannot be entirely separated. By understanding how people make meaning, it is easier to understand how people develop expectations. Chapter 3 also contains a detailed differentiation between the message form called "display" and the one called "document." This distinction is critical for understanding the difference between formal and informal organizations presented in Unit III.

Chapter 3 is difficult to read because it presents so many concepts. In addition to the distinction between the two kinds of message forms, there is a three-part explanation of how expectations are developed. There is also a four-part category system for distinguishing kinds of expectations. These kinds are norms, roles, agendas, and motives. This system for interpreting kinds of expectations is used in chapters 4, 5, 6, and 7. By understanding these four kinds of expectations, it will be easier to understand the similarities and differences between the coordination formats described in chapters 4, 5, 6, and 7.

Readers who have read and understood the chapters in Unit I should be able to define each of the terms already described briefly and the four kinds of expectations just mentioned. They should be able to describe the interrelationships among these concepts, and be prepared to look more carefully into how communication functions as an organizing process. Lastly, they should be better prepared to learn how to improve their own communication and organizing efforts.

CHAPTER
1

Images of Organizing

The Classical School: Designing Efficient Machines

The Human Relations School: Motivating Work Families

The Sociotechnical Systems School: Controlling Information Processors

The Contingency School: Playing a Competitive Game

Throughout its brief history, organization theory has focused on issues related to the practical coordination of efforts to achieve common ends. Organization theories have always addressed, at least indirectly, the question: "How can people relate to one another so that they can know some things together so that they can do some things together?" Organization theorists provide us with descriptions or "images" of what organizing processes are and what kinds of relationships are accomplished by these processes. Each theorist has a fairly unique description, but it is convenient to group major theorists into four schools of thought and to discuss these schools in order of historical development. The first school of thought is generally called the "classical school"; the second, the "human relations school"; the third, the "sociotechnical systems school"; and the fourth, the "contingency school."

It is not intended that a complete or detailed account of the history of organization theory be provided here. Rather, the focus is on the central image of the method of organizing which characterizes each school.

For the classical school, organizing was a process of *designing* how work should be done. ("Organizations are like machines.") The ideas of this school are often referred to as a "mechanistic approach." Among human relations theorists, organizing has been described chiefly as *motivating.* ("Organizations are like families.") These theorists provide an "organic approach." Theorists of the sociotechnical school have declared that *controlling* is the essential process in accomplishing organization. ("Organizations are like computers.") For the contingency theorists, organization is playing a game or *gaming.* ("Organizations are like competitive games.")

The classical school and the human relations school proposed universal theories of organizational design. That is, the theorists of these schools proposed what they believed to be the "one right way" to accomplish any organization. For the classical theorists, the right way to design an organization was to make it work like a machine. For the human relations theorists when organizations were run like families, they were run the "right way." The sociotechnical systems school and the contingency schools have provided us with situational theories of organizational design. Early sociotechnical systems theorists proposed a theory of organization which allowed for the possibility of different kinds of organizing. The contingency school is in the process of developing basic ideas about organizing from the systems school into some ways of thinking about how organizations should be different from one another if they are to be effective. The ideas about organizing of the systems theorists and the contingency theorists are largely compatible with the theory of organizing that will be described throughout this book.

The discussion of each school follows the same general pattern. First, there is a description of how the school started. In particular, there is a description of the research used to develop the theories of the school. Next there is a description of "organizational intelligence." In each of the sections on organizational intelligence there is a description of the theory's account of what people in an organization need to know and how they can find out. Then there is a description of integration or how people in an organization relate to one another, in particular how control and motivation are accomplished. Finally, there is a discussion of how the theorists of a particular school describe the function of communication in organizing. The key question here is, to what extent do the theorists see communication as the method by which organizational intelligence and integration are accomplished?

THE CLASSICAL SCHOOL: DESIGNING EFFICIENT MACHINES

Social Science and the Industrial Revolution

The Industrial Revolution provided the principal impetus for the first systematic theories of organization. Prior to that time economic institutions were small; usually they were family enterprises with long histories. Because work relationships were generally family relationships, they were based on traditional lines of authority. Coordination patterns were learned at an early age. Employee-sons did what their employer-fathers told them to do.

Organizing processes, of course, existed prior to the Industrial Revolution, but most organizations were old. Few new organizations were begun. Organizing as a process was invisible because it took place so slowly. We could compare the process to the building of a delta at a river mouth. The delta is built and washed away over hundreds of years. Therefore, during the course of any one lifetime a person is not aware of the process. So too, before the Industrial Revolution there were organizations—families, churches, governments. But there were comparatively few large organizations. People were not aware of the organizing process in which they were engaged because neither organizational intelligence nor organizational relationships were changing rapidly. In *The Organizational Revolution*, Kenneth Boulding observes that in 1852 in America there were no labor unions, practically no trade or professional associations, no important farm associations, no American Legion, and few corporations or large businesses. "National governments absorbed—by present standards—an almost infinitesimal part of the total national product."[1] In short, there was no reason to be concerned with the organizing process because there were so few people in the process of working out new or different cooperative systems.

The mechanization of work made it necessary for strangers to coordinate their activities. Modern organizations are the result of bringing people together who had no traditional norms or accepted standards for relating to one another. Not only large corporations, but also labor unions, trade unions, professional associations, and even farm associations were organized to provide for coordinating the work of strangers. Coordination patterns which served well for such total organizations as families and guilds were not adequate for the less than total involvement of large numbers of strangers in the limited purpose organizations of an industrial society. Common sense ideas about how to coordinate activities have, of course, always existed. The market for organization theory was created when people became conscious of the fact that organizing into cooperative systems was problematic, and that some ways of organizing might be better than others.

The rhetorical process of one person persuading another has long been a subject of philosophical speculation. But theories of the influence process were generally confined to how one person achieves a particular short-term goal through the use of communication forms such as speeches or essays. Philosophers gave little consideration to the use of influence to coordinate the purposeful actions of people in forming continuing relationships. People forming new organizations in the wake of the Industrial Revolution needed a theory to persuade workers day after day to do a particular job; they needed guidance in coordinating the activities of coworkers; and, they needed guidance in methods for creating shared understandings.

Organizational Intelligence

The nineteenth century was the period of the Scientific Revolution as well. Many of the inventions which made the Industrial Revolution possible resulted from experimentation and systematic observation. The goal of the first organization theorists was to apply scientific methods of investigation to the study of human organizing behavior. Even those who performed no experiments described their theories as grounded in "scientific" principles.

For the first organization theorists, those of the classical school, the machines of the Industrial Revolution were not simply the products of the application of experimentation with mechanical force. The machines were the embodiment of scientific thinking. The machines harnessed mechanical energy to work efficiently. Machines were the representations of efficient use of physical energy. To the classical theorists, human organizations of their day were like inefficient machines. The way to improve human machines, they reasoned, was to apply scientific principles of mechanical energy to the design of human coordination. Classical organization theory is the extension of the logic of the machine to human effort. The fascination of the classical theorists with machines led them to believe that coordination is a process of design. Organization theory was a kind of engineering.

The logic of mechanism is a logic of "closed systems." A closed system is a set of discrete particles which move in time and space according to fixed laws. Each particle has a specific set of properties, such as position, mass, and durability. The movement of the particle is determined by the external forces acting on it; particles always move either by being pushed or pulled. It is possible to design a model of a complete system specifying the movement of all the components because the parts can move only in lawful ways. To determine how closed systems work, they are analyzed by reducing the processes which comprise them to irreducible elements or parts. The processes are the result of separate parts acting externally on one another. Classical theorists analyzed organizations by reducing the process of organizing into discrete particles.

Classical theorists whose principal interest was improving the organization of manual work were called "scientific management theorists." They reasoned that by increasing the efficiency of the movement of particles such as fingers, they would necessarily increase the efficiency of the organization. They invented "motion study" which is the minute investigation of the time it takes to complete hand, finger, and sometimes leg motions in physical work. They thereby earned the name "efficiency experts." For them the most important organizational intelligence was information about efficient use of fingers, hands, arms, and feet.

Another group of classical theorists are generally called "administrative theorists." They were interested in improving the organization of white collar workers—public administrators in particular. They too believed that efficiency of an organization may be increased by increasing the efficiency of individual parts. The best way to do this was to design (on paper) an efficient organizational structure. According to classical administrative theorist Henri Fayol, for example, "To organize is to define and set up the general structure of the enterprise with reference to its objective, its means of operation, its future course as determined by planning; . . . It is to give form to the whole and to every detail its place; it is to make the frame and fill it with desired contents."[2] The most important organizational intelligence is a rational paper-and-pencil design of work—an organizational machine.

The first step in building an efficient machine is deciding the purpose the machine is to serve. Only the tinkerer would join metal to metal and then decide, having created a structure, that he or she had produced a reaper or a punch-press. For the classical theorist, the rational approach to organizing human actions must likewise begin by determining the specific purpose of the organization. The next step is to plan the division of work. In summarizing how the classical theorists described organizing, March and Simon write:

> The general problem to which the formal [classical] theory addresses itself is the following: Given a general purpose for an organization, we can identify the unit tasks necessary to achieve that purpose. These tasks will normally include basic productive activities, service activities, coordinative activities, supervisory activities, etc. The problem is to group these tasks into individual jobs, to group the jobs into administrative units, to group

the units into larger units, and finally to establish the top level departments—and to make these groupings in such a way as to minimize the
total costs of carrying out all the activities. In the organizing process each
department is viewed as a definite collection of tasks to be allocated
among, and performed by, the employees of the department. To understand the formal theory, it is important to recognize that *the total set of
tasks is regarded as given in advance*.[3]

The idea that the planner can specify all the tasks to be accomplished and can detail how these tasks are to be done follows from the
analogy of the machine. Typewriters, for example, are designed by
engineers who begin with a precise idea of the purpose of the machine
which they are designing. They have specifications to describe the
desired performance of the resulting machine. In order to create a
machine out of steel and plastic, every part has to be described in detail.
The relationship of the parts has to be shown in the blueprint. Typewriters work only when they function as the planner intended. Typewriters are "closed systems" in that the parts will act in a lawful manner
which can be known to the designer. If the design is good and the parts
are built and assembled according to specifications, the machine will
work as the designer intended.

The people who "need to know" in an organization are those who
create the organizational design. Good typewriter designers need two
kinds of information: information about the mechanical laws by which
the machine will operate, and some general principles for designing
machines like typewriters. To the classical theorists, good organizational designers likewise needed these two kinds of information. Researchers in the classical tradition saw their mission as two-fold: first, to
discover the natural laws of human activity so that organizations might
be "scientifically" designed; second, to catalog universal principles of
organizing so that people creating or improving organizations would
have access to reliable principles on which to base their designs. Thus,
the theorists of the classical school saw their mission as the creation of
knowledge for use by organizational designers.

When the theorists known as scientific managers undertook to discover the natural laws by which organizations operated, their attention
was centered on hand and body movements. In particular, the scientific
managers sought to understand the essential properties of matter.
Their investigations were directed toward discovering human capacity,
speed, and durability as the determinants of motion.

The research method which the scientific managers used to discover
durability is a telling example of dependence on mechanical reasoning.
Their model for human endurance was mental fatigue. Human fatigue,
they proposed was the result of improperly aligned "parts." Humans
become fatigued from the wear of repeated incorrect motions. The re-

searchers began their research on the assumption that if the work is properly designed to meet the physical capacity of the workers, and if they are given properly timed rest periods, fatigue will be avoided. The aim of their research, therefore, was to measure human endurance precisely, to determine the "right" length and number of rest periods, and to discover the least exerting motions. They did not consider boredom to be a significant factor in fatigue—after all machines do not get bored. Therefore, they did not investigate the effects of routinized tasks to fatigue. In their experiments they examined the smallest bits of motion; they timed rest periods to the second and compared the length and time of rest periods directly against daily output.

The classical theorists did not succeed in discovering the rigorous natural laws they sought. They did, however, spell out some useful principles such as that levers, crossbars, and handwheels should be located so that the operator can manipulate them "with the least change in body position and with the greatest mechanical advantage." The cataloging of these principles, often supported by only minimal experimental evidence, rather than the discovery of the natural laws of human activity was the principal outcome of the research activities of the classical theorists.

Cataloging principles for designers was the method by which classical theorists sought to change organizing processes. As writers, they filled their books with explanations of principles; as teachers, they professed their principles; as consultants, or change agents, they grounded their advice in principles. Classical theorists often prefaced their statements of principles with remarks such as, "I shall adopt the term principle whilst disassociating it from any suggestion of rigidity, for there is nothing rigid or absolute in management affairs."[4] Unfortunately, the interpreters of these principles tended to view them rigidly. Principles of administration became organizational intelligence in the form of rules for organizing.

Each theorist, of course, had his or her own set of principles. For some, there were as few as three; for others, fourteen or fifteen; some scientific managers had hundreds. The principles, however, followed the logic of the mechanical engineer. Efficient design was based on the principles of departmentalization, standardization, routing, and control. These principles have become the core of conventional wisdom about how to organize people to do common tasks.

Organizational Integration

According to the classical theory, organizational integration was synonymous with organizational control. Organizational control was achieved by design. If a typewriter is adequately designed, if all the parts are in working condition, then it will type. There is no problem of controlling a machine's behavior beyond adequate design, maintenance, and a routine skill of operation. Human organizations were believed to operate much the same way.

For the scientific managers, human actions could be integrated by the impersonal direction of scientific principles. In his testimony before the House committee investigating scientific management, Frederick Taylor declared confidently that both worker and manager could be "governed by rules and laws . . . developed through hundreds of experiments. . . . Those questions which under other systems are subject to arbitrary judgment and are therefore open to disagreement have under scientific management been the subject of the most minute and careful study . . . and they have been settled to the satisfaction of both sides."[5] The implementation of the rational plan of the organizational designers was accomplished simply by informing the workers. Since the tasks were scientifically determined, reasoned Taylor, it was logical that the supervisors should be people with some scientific training; they should be specialists in particular kinds of tasks. It was possible, therefore, that a single worker might have several supervisors, each a specialist in one kind of task the worker performed.

This notion of specialization of supervisors was called "functional foremanship." It reflects the faith of the scientific managers in the inherent persuasiveness of scientifically determined principles. Supervisors did not need any authority other than the science in which their orders were grounded. Moreover, there was no disputing the orders and there could be no conflict of orders because the scientifically determined procedures represented the "one right way" to perform any task.

Classical theorists outside the Scientific Management tradition such as the administrative theorists had less faith in automatic control of worker activities through scientific determination, though they also believed control to be a function of design. For them, control or integration was assured through designing unitary lines of authority. Hierarchy was the heart of their organization theory. They called hierarchy the "scalar principle" according to which a worker would receive instructions from only one person.

From the scalar principle we derive the practice of constructing organizational charts showing the one person to whom any particular individual in an organization is responsible. For Fayol, the basis for constructing any organization chart was a "scalar chain" which he illustrates as a double ladder (see Figure 1.1). A is the ultimate authority in the organization. A send out orders through the subordinates B and L. In turn these executives communicate to those immediately beneath them. Positions F and P are authorized to communicate only with those

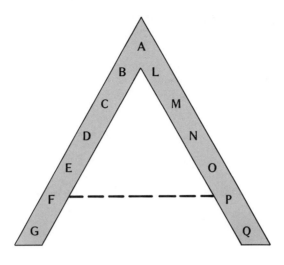

FIGURE 1.1
Scalar Chain

immediately above and beneath them. However, if *F* and *P* need to coordinate some work, they may be authorized to do so directly. According to Fayol, "The scalar principle will be safeguarded if managers *E* and *O* have authorized their respective subordinates *F* and *P* to treat them directly, and the position will be fully regularized if *F* and *P* inform their respective superiors forthwith of what they have agreed upon."[6] Through the scalar principle, control was built into organizational design by centralizing the channels of authority. The scalar chain also "guaranteed" shared information since all information which was shared by *F* and *P* was also known to all their superiors.

One feature of the theory of control which characterized all the classical theorists was the concept of control lying outside the individual person. The parts of a machine are controlled by being pushed or pulled by other parts. The classical theories of motivation are likewise theories of push-pull. Frederick Herzberg calls this method of control the KITA method.[7] He observes that corporation executives want a "quick and practical answer to the question: 'What is the simplest and most direct way of getting someone to do something?'" When Herzberg asks managers how to get someone to do something, he finds that "every audience contains the 'direct action' manager who shouts, 'Kick him!' And this manager is right. The surest and least circumlocuted way of getting someone to do something is to kick him in the pants— give him what might be called the KITA."

Herzberg notes there is a push form of KITA and a pull form: "I have a year-old Schnauzer. When it was a small puppy and I wanted it to move, I kicked it in the rear and it moved. Now that I have finished its obedience training, I hold up a dog biscuit when I want the Schnauzer to move. . . . In this instance all I did was apply KITA frontally; I exerted a pull instead of a push."[8]

KITA was a "science" developed by the classical theorists. Taylor, for example, designed tasks to be accomplished and then paid a worker a bonus each time he succeeded in doing his task in the given time. Thus through proper administration of kicks in the rear—reprimands—or in the front—bonuses—the movements of the worker could be controlled externally by the organizational designer. Thus, integration is accomplished with little or no volition of those people being "integrated."

Function of Communication

Because the process of organizing was a paper and pen activity, classical theorists said little directly about the function of communication in organizing. In the other schools of organization theory, for example, coordination is a communication process. But for the classical theorists, coordination was a counterpart of the division of effort. Coordination was the arranging of separate efforts to produce a predetermined definite end. A few of the classical theorists discussed organizing processes which might be identified as communicative. Two of Gulick's seven elements of organizing were "directing" and "reporting." Directing was making decisions and stating them as orders; reporting referred only to the transmission of information through authoritative channels—up and down the scalar chain.[9]

The definition of communication found in classical organizational theory is the sending of information from superior to worker. The information specifies the method a worker is to use to perform a certain task. This definition assumed that workers receive the same messages that are sent to them. Implicitly, this definition also assumes that the messages sent to the workers will automatically control the worker's actions. All the decisions about how work is performed are made by the designers. This is centralized decision making in its purest form. Some workers might be "defective" and not follow the directions sent to them, but most workers were regarded simply as interchangeable machine parts controlled by the central designers.

Within classical theory there was little attention directed to the problems which arise from workers interpreting instructions or from work groups making independent decisions such as decisions to maintain a certain low production quota. The fact that workers talked to one another on the job was of no significance to the classical theorists. They equated formal structure with organization and ignored the role of communication in coordination. Because they did this, they were criticized both by human relations and sociotechnical systems theorists.

Classical Theory and Conventional Wisdom

The assumptions of the classical theorists seem rather naive today. We are tempted to proclaim that the classical theorists were wrong about the nature of the world. Like other theories, these were ways of constructing an interpretation of what the world is "really like." As an interpretation of reality these theories have influenced what later theorists and organizers have perceived to be essential features of organizations. The classical theorists offered managers ideas which have been used ever since in accomplishing organizations.

Even the theorists themselves proclaimed that their purpose was to influence ideas and not simply to provide techniques of management. Taylor, for example, states that

> scientific management is not an efficiency device . . . not a system of figuring costs, . . . not a piecework system . . . it is not holding a stop watch on a man and writing things down about him, . . . it is not any of the devices which the average man calls to mind when scientific management is spoken of. . . .[10]

Rather, the aim of scientific management was a "great revolution of mental attitude."

The important question to be asked of the classical theorists, therefore, is not whether they were right or wrong, but in what ways did they influence managers' "mental attitudes." Douglas McGregor in outlining the conventional wisdom of managers includes the following three beliefs, all of which were tenets of classical theory:

1. Management is responsible for organizing the elements of productive enterprise—money, materials, people—in the interest of economic ends.
2. With respect to people, this is a process of directing their efforts, motivating them, controlling their actions, modifying their behaviors to fit the needs of the organization.
3. Without this active intervention by management, people would be passive—even resistant—to organizational needs.[11]

The classical theorists provided the first clear rationales for specialization and hierarchy. Organizing became equated with the division of work by specialization and division of authority into hierarchy. Through management texts and schools, the classical theorists' arguments for specialization and hierarchy were conventionalized as the "right way" to manage an organization.

Most organizations are characterized by specialization and hierarchy that these principles are the "one right way" even when their own ex- in a way reminiscent of the classical principles. Some managers believe perience suggests otherwise. Rensis Likert describes an encounter with a person who believed in the classical management practices despite personal evidence that the practices are not necessary. The man was a top manager of a large, highly successful company. He apologized to Likert for the "poor management" of the company: "We are not a 'well-managed' company. We don't do any of the things which we are supposed to do."

Among those things companies are "supposed to" have which his company did not have were an organization chart, a highly functionalized division of tasks, and close control of supervisors of employees. The company did not even have punch clocks for employees in the manufacturing plant. According to Likert, the executives felt that they were not managing the right way; they felt the company should be much better "organized" with more numerous and tighter controls on employees.

The source of these convictions was not evidence that the company was losing money. The company was doing well. At the time of the encounter, however, the only systematic body of literature about how organizations should be operated was the classical theory. Because the company's practices were not consistent with classical principles, the executives believed that their practices were not good ones.[12] The classical theorists' conceptions of what constitutes "proper" organizing methods have greatly influenced our conventional wisdom about how organizations should be managed.

The value of science as an instrument for improving human organizational behavior constitutes another important legacy of the scientific managers. Taylor introduced into conventional wisdom the idea that "incentive wages, threats, and instant dismissal were not sufficient to manage a work force, that it was necessary to select and train workers on the basis of scientific findings."[13] Taylor and others convinced managers of the necessity of using scientific methods to find the "right way" to organize work effort. However, they could not provide the unequivocal methods of coordinating which they promised. Their closed system models did not always produce good predictions of worker behavior. They created a conventional wisdom which supported the value of scientific research as the means to organizational information but they did not succeed in providing an enduring model for conducting that research. The next section discusses how the human relations school emerged as scientists found their closed system models inadequate.

THE HUMAN RELATIONS SCHOOL: MOTIVATING WORK FAMILIES

The Hawthorne Studies

In 1927, Elton Mayo, Professor of Industrial Research at the Harvard Business School, began a study of the productivity of women making telephone assemblies at the Hawthorne Works of the Western Electric Corporation. When he started the research he was operating under the mechanistic assumptions of the classical theorists. In a previous study of labor turnover in the spinning department of a textile mill, he had investigated the effect of rest periods on productivity. He assumed that, with careful control of experimental conditions, he could determine the right timing of rest periods to produce minimal fatigue. The Hawthorne studies were to be follow-up research investigating other correlates of productivity such as wages and lighting. The history of the Hawthorne studies is a story of researchers who found their understanding of the world inadequate to predict the behavior they observed. They were led by successive failures in prediction to change their assumptions about the process of organizing.

The purpose of the first Hawthorne study was to investigate the relationship of the quality and quantity of illumination to the efficiency of workers. Researchers divided workers into a "test group" and a "control group." They first submitted the test group to different intensities of illumination: twenty-four, then forty-six, then seventy foot candles. Production in both the test room and the control room increased at approximately the same rate. Then they decreased the light intensity from ten to three foot candles. Again the output went up in both groups. Next they led workers in the test room to believe that the lighting was being increased, but no increase was actually made. The workers commented favorably on what they thought to be an increase in lighting, but they did not increase their output. Whereupon, the researchers told the workers that the lighting was being dimmed. The workers complained about the poor light (though the actual intensity was the same), but again there was no change in output. Finally, the experimenters lowered the lighting to six hundredths of a foot candle, approximately the intensity of moonlight. Output declined significantly only after the light was this dim.

The researchers' initial assumptions were that the amount of lighting is directly related to the amount of productivity. They were, in Roethlisberger's words, ignoring the "human meaning" of changes in work conditions.[14] The researchers' actions were based on these assumptions, but their understanding or "cognitive map" of the situation did not include the concept that the research subjects were operating on their own cognitive maps of the situation. They thought of their subjects much as one thinks of machines in which a change in one variable (lighting) would directly change another (output). The research subjects constructed interpretations of the world around them differently than the researchers anticipated; therefore, they were behaving in ways which the researchers did not expect. The Hawthorne researchers developed the notion that organizational intelligence is the meaning of the work situation for the workers.

Organizational Intelligence

Another of the Hawthorne studies, this one conducted in the Relay Assembly Test Room, also illustrates how the experimenters developed an understanding of the importance of workers' understandings as organizational intelligence. Again, the purpose of the investigation was to determine how differences in physical conditions affect differences in output. They did recognize, however, that if the workers objected to the experimental treatments they might deliberately hold down production. They wanted to do whatever they could to get the subjects to cooperate. They sought to remove what they presumed to be the extraneous influences on worker cooperation, but, in seeking to remove the features which they defined as irrelevant, they created a whole new work situation for the subjects.

The research subjects in the Relay Assembly Test Room were consulted about changes in work conditions; several plans were abandoned because the subjects disapproved of them. The subjects were "questioned sympathetically" about their reactions to the experimental conditions; many of the conferences about work procedures took place in the superintendent's office. In contrast to the company's usual practice, the subjects were allowed to talk as they worked; they were not required to meet a "bogey" or minimum production. They were consulted about their health, their opinions, their ambitions, their fears.

The experimenters originally thought such changes to be insignificant. Their conceptions about why people act as they do did not include the idea that giving workers more say in how they work could influence them to raise their own production standards. They were ignoring worker talk as a means of creating organizational intelligence.

The changes instituted by the researchers involved workers in decisions about work conditions, but to the researchers, at least initially, the working conditions themselves were the crucial variable; the process by which the conditions were created was not important. The workers' shared understanding of those processes were likewise defined as irrelevant.

As with the illumination studies, the researchers' understanding of the situation failed to predict actual behavior because it did not take into account the subjects' interpretation of the situation. For the first year and a half, researchers consulting with the subjects improved working conditions. They introduced new rest periods and increased the length of rest periods; they gave the subjects Saturday mornings off for a while. According to Roethlisberger:

> The investigators were happy because as conditions of work were being improved, the output rate rose steadily. Here, it appeared, was strong evidence in favor of their preconceived hypothesis that fatigue was the major factor limiting output. . . . But then one investigator—one of those tough-minded fellows—suggested that they restore the original conditions of work, that is, go back to a full forty-eight hour week without rest, lunches and what not. . . . Then the happy state of affairs, when everything was going along as it theoretically should, went sour. Output, instead of taking the expected nose dive, maintained its high level.[15]

The experimenters' mechanical model which predicted that a change in working conditions would necessarily result in a change in output failed to predict the behavior they observed in the Relay Assembly Test Room. Roethlisberger sums up the conclusions the Hawthorne researchers were forced to accept when they abandoned their mechanical notions of causality in human behavior: "If one experiments on a stone, the stone does not know it is being experimented upon—all of which makes it simple for people experimenting on stones. But if a human being is being experimented upon, he is likely to know it. Therefore, his attitudes toward the experiment and toward the experimenters became very important factors in determining his responses to the situation."[16]

Although the Hawthorne studies were conducted almost fifty years ago, they are still of interest to students of organizational behavior. The research methods seem rather crude by today's standards. The specific conclusions of the studies have been questioned because of a lack of sound experimental procedures.[17] In part, the Hawthorne studies are still important because they produced the first clear statement of what is now called the "Hawthorne effect." Simply stated, "If a human being is being experimented upon, he is likely to know it." The Hawthorne effect is the name given to the change in subject's behavior which results from their knowing that they are research subjects, rather than from any particular test conditions to which they are subjected.

Whether or not any particular findings of the research resulted from "valid" experimental procedures, the Hawthorne studies constitute an important contribution to the development of organizing theory. This is because the researchers rejected the classical conception of organizing as simply designing efficient machines. The concept of worker understandings as organizational intelligence became an important idea. The workers' reasons for working—their motivations—became a central concern of organization scientists. The new theory proclaimed that successful motivating is more crucial to organizing than efficient design. The Hawthorne studies introduced the importance of talk into the mainstream of thought about organizing. Although most organization theorists still regard the formal structure (the structure which appears on paper) as important, the formal structure is no longer equated with organization. Mayo and his followers introduced the concept of "informal organization."

The Hawthorne researchers not only dramatized the existence of an informal organization, they also argued convincingly that informal systems are not governed by "logic." The classical theorists maintained that workers would automatically accept logical and methodical systems of behavior. Mayo refuted this position. People, he argued, do not want and will not accept a "blackboard logic" to guide their methods of work and life. Rather, all people want a "method of living in social relationship with other people."

Writing in the early depression years, Mayo traced the breakdown of the economic system to a breakdown in the social systems of factories. Administrators, he said, had become "addicts of specialists who unduly discount social relationships." As a result, factories were organized along formal lines which allowed for little social relationships to develop among workers. The social fabric of society had been destroyed. Workers had been excluded from social participation; the standardization of work had taken away from each person the perception of economic value of his or her individual work. Organizational intelligence is not a "blackboard logic."[18]

Organizational Integration

The metaphor which characterizes patterns of relationships within the human relations school is the traditional family. There are three parallels between families and organizations found in human relations theories. First, to Mayo and later human relations theorists, work relationships were the foundations of society. Work groups functioned like families as "primary units" or "building blocks" of society. Second, workers were described as "totally included" in the organization. Just as one's whole life is the concern of one's family, so an individual's whole life was the concern of the organization for which he or she worked. Worker satisfaction and happiness with his job was a prime goal of human relations theorists because they conceived of work as central to the person's life. Those who worked only for paychecks represented the failure of managers to create happy work families.

Finally, organizations were like traditional families because the human relations theorists conceived of no essential conflict of interest. Conflicts arise in organizations because of break-downs in communication, not, for example, because workers have legitimate interests which differ from their superiors. The similarity of organization to traditional family is illustrated by Amitai Etzioni's description of the "typical human relations training movie":

> We see a happy factory in which the wheels hum steadily and the workers rhythmically serve the machines which smiles on their faces. A truck arrives and unloads large crates containing new machines. A dark type with long sideburns who sweeps the floors in the factory spreads a rumor that mass firing is imminent since the new machines will take over the work of many of the workers. The wheels turn slower; the workers are sad. In the evening they carry their gloom to their suburban homes. The next morning, the reassuring voice of their boss comes over the inter-com. He tells them that the rumor is absolutely false; the machines are to be set up in a new wing and more workers will be hired since the factory is expanding its production. Everybody sighs in relief, smiles return, the machines hum speedily and steadily again. Only the dark floor sweeper is sad. Nobody will listen to his rumors anymore. The moral is clear: had management been careful to communicate its development plans to its workers, the crisis would have been averted. Once it occurred, increase in communication eliminated it like magic.[19]

The "movie" portrays the several tenets of the human relations theorists. The workers' home lives are inseparable from their work lives. There is no essential conflict between worker and management. The conflict in this example is an illusory one which can be merely "communicated away." The movie does not tell what would have happened if the rumors had been correct and a lay-off was imminent. Finally, the workers' productivity was directly related to their happiness. Happy workers were high producers; unhappy workers did not work.

To the human relations theorists organizing was a process of motivating. Theorists of the classical school spent little time speculating about why people do what they do. Taylor, for example, had a very simple view of motivation. He reasoned that most workers were inefficient because they simply did not know better ways of arranging their work. The scientific manager would improve efficiency by informing workers of better methods of doing their jobs. The workers so informed would then be "first class" workers. First class workers receive monetary reward each time they completed the task assigned to them in the specified time. Taylor did admit that some workers might not use the right methods, even if told about them. But he regarded these people as "defective" because they did not respond to the correct application of the bonus. Motivation was not a problem the classical theorists cared to bother about beyond determining the correct wage bonus for each kind of work. Correct knowledge (about how work should be done) led automatically to correct integration patterns.

The Hawthorne researchers found the classical push-pull theory of motivation inadequate. Monetary rewards were not sufficient to guarantee worker motivation in predetermined directions. People do not operate on machine logic or mechanical principles. The theory of motivation which emerged from the Hawthorne studies emphasized the maintenance of human relationships. Healthy relationships mean satisfied workers. Workers who were part of human systems (like families) which made them feel important would produce better than workers separated from one another and treated like machine parts. Roethlisberger described the function of management as the maintenance of "the kind of social organization in which individuals and groups through working together can obtain human satisfactions that will make them willing to contribute their services to the economic objective of co-operation."[20]

The early human relations theorists did not undertake to catalogue human motivations. Their motivational theory was rather abstract because the researchers did not presume that there are universal motivators which could be catalogued. Instead, motivation was a function of the communication skills, primarily the skills of the managers. Roethlisberger and Mayo wrote about the necessity for situational motivation. They told managers to be concerned with "particular human situations" and how they handled them. The outcome of attention to particular individuals and their feelings would be the "exercise of 'control' by understanding and not the ritualistic, verbal practices which address themselves to human nature in general."[21]

Unfortunately, the concern of Roethlisberger and Mayo with organizing particular individuals into particular social relationships was misinterpreted by others. For example, Roethlisberger stated his desire that "the word 'morale' will drop from the vocabulary of administrators and their staff specialists concerned with human situations." Instead, "high morale" became the term characterizing the goal of human relations theorists.[22]

Human relations theorists have been criticized because they could not accurately predict conditions under which morale results in improved work performance. They have been called the "happiness boys" who naively assume that a manager's concern for the well being of an individual worker would encourage that worker to better job performance. Some of this criticism is no doubt justified because the relationship between treating a worker as a "family member" and motivation to work at the organizational task was not adequately mapped out by the early theorists. On the other hand, researchers like Mayo and Roethlisberger with their emphasis on situational motivation had a more complex rationale for understanding the relationship of satisfaction to production than the stereotype "happiness boys" indicates.

In 1965, Raymond Miles proposed the name "Human Resources School" to the group of writers whose theories were based on human relations ideas but who undertook to provide a more complete theory of motivation and to describe the relationship of interpersonal competency to organizational effectiveness and efficiency.[23] Others have called the later theorists "Industrial Humanists." These people are not "happiness boys" who assume that morale automatically leads to increased organizational effectiveness. These writers are referred to here as the "later human relations theorists." The theorists discussed below are of this "later" strain.

The foundation of human relations theory is that correct motivation of organizational members will lead to organizational integration and thus guarantee organizational performance. The major conceptual scheme of motivation found in the writings of human relations theorists was formulated by Abraham Maslow, a clinical psychologist. The conception is called the "Need Hierarchy."[24] Based on his observations of the mentally disturbed clients who came to him for treatment, Maslow proposed that people have five sets of motivators which he called "basic needs" (see Figure 1.2). Classical theorists were concerned with human needs shown at the bottom of the ladder. Maslow admitted that these needs are the "preponent" of all needs:

> What this means specifically is that, in the human being who is missing everything in his life in an extreme fashion, it is most likely that the major motivation would be physiological needs rather than any others. It is quite true that man lives by bread alone—when there is no bread. But what happens to a man's desire when there *is* plenty of bread and when his belly is chronically filled? . . . If hunger is satisfied, it becomes unimportant in the current dynamics of the individual.[25]

Good wages, fringe benefits, and other primary needs are not motivators because they satisfy primary needs only. Once satisfied, these needs ceased to "push" the worker. Motivation for well fed and safe workers depends upon higher order needs. Needs at the highest level such as

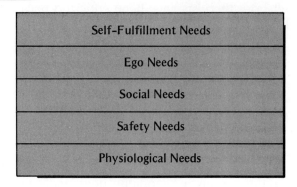

| Self-Fulfillment Needs |
| Ego Needs |
| Social Needs |
| Safety Needs |
| Physiological Needs |

FIGURE 1.2
The Need Hierarchy

self-fulfillment and ego can never be satisfied; we cannot ever get "full" of self-fulfillment and compliments to our ego. Maslow maintained that people may be infinitely motivated toward satisfaction of those needs.

The organization which employs a worker is a primary source of satisfaction for that worker according to human relations theory. Douglas McGregor has extrapolated from Maslow's theory the idea that unless there are opportunities at work to satisfy these higher level needs, people will be "deprived."[26] A person who is not happy on his or her job cannot be a happy person. The work family must be a source of self-fulfillment or the whole worker suffers. Here again is the principle of "total inclusion" of the worker in the organization. According to McGregor, all workers could meaningfully be grouped together with regard to motivation. The hierarchy, with few exceptions, is a universal condition. The concept of universal motivators is a direct contradiction of the early human relations theorists such as Roethlisberger who held that motivation was derived from the meaning which particular workers attributed to particular situations.

The concepts of total inclusion and universal motivators were concepts which Maslow himself eventually spoke out against. In an essay entitled, "Management as a Psychological Experiment,"[27] Maslow outlines how much organizational psychologists *do not know* about what motivates workers. For example, he observed that we do not know "how many people or what proportion of the working population would actually prefer to participate in management decisions, and how many would prefer not to have anything to do with them." In contrast to his interpreters, Maslow himself observed that we do not know "what portion of the population take a job as simply any old kind of job which they must do in order to earn a living, while their interests are definitely centered elsewhere outside the job." He pointed out the limitations of using his conception of motivation to explain the behavior of workers; because his work on motivations came from the clinical study of neurotic people. "The carry-over of this theory to the industrial situation has some support from industrial studies, but certainly I would like to see a lot more studies of this kind before feeling finally convinced that this carry-over from the study of neurosis to the study of labor in factories is legitimate."[28]

The relationship of motivation to integration for the human relations theorists is in fact not as simple as this discussion makes it sound. It is individual motivation mediated by group norms which serves as the basis for integration. The Hawthorne studies provided the first systematic indications of the importance of small group norms in shaping motivation to work. According to Mayo and Roethlisberger, the meaning of particular work situations was not idiosyncratic, but the product of the social consensus of those people who worked together and talked about their common situation. In the experiments in the Bank Wiring Observation Room, the researchers identified four sentiments which the workers used to interpret the meaning of their work and that of others. These sentiments were the norms prescribing the amount of output to be produced by each worker. Roethlisberger explained these sentiments and their impact on output:

> The men were on group piecework, where the more they turned out the more they earned. In such a situation one might have expected that they would have been interested in maintaining total output and that the faster workers would have put pressure on the slower workers to improve their efficiency. But this was not the case. Operating within this group were four basic sentiments, which can be expressed briefly as follows: (1) You should not turn out too much work; if you do, you are a "rate buster." (2) You should not turn out too little work; if you do, you are a "chiseler." (3) You should not say anything to a supervisor which would react to the detriment of one of your associates; if you do, you are a "squealer." (4) You should not be too officious; that is, "if you are an inspector, you should not act like one." To be an accepted member of the group a man had to act in accordance with these standards.[29]

The researchers in the Bank Wiring Room came to understand that the workers were not motivated by any internal driving force or universal motivation other than the desire to maintain a social relationship with others on the job. So-called "motivation" to produce the company product resulted from how the worker interpreted his own actions. The group influenced individual actions by providing each person with a language to interpret his own actions. If a worker produced too much by group standards, then he could be labeled a "rate-buster." If his standing in the group was important to him, he accepted this label for his behavior and he changed his behavior—he produced less. The best-liked person in the group was the one who kept his output exactly where the group agreed it should be; one worker who enjoyed doing what the others disliked was constantly exceeding the group standard.

The Bank Wiring Room research was the beginning of investigations of "group dynamics." Rather than an individual deciding his or her own actions on the basis of rational choices or being directed by commands of authorities, the theorists of group dynamics formulated the concept that individuals' actions become integrated through the force of group pressure. Kurt Lewin and his students conducted a series of experiments to verify whether group pressure generated in discussion groups would result in more change than information transmission alone.

Lewin conducted his most famous experiments during World War II. At that time there was a shortage of conventional cuts of meat; the government wanted to convince people to eat less popular cuts such as brains and sweetbreads. The purpose of Lewin's research was to determine whether group discussion could modify buying habits. The female shoppers who participated as subjects were randomly distributed into two test conditions. One heard lectures about the nutritional value of such foods and learned methods of preparing meat. The other group, in addition to hearing about the value and methods of preparation, also participated in groups where they discussed whether they should buy the meat.

In the follow-up interviews, researchers learned that more of the women who participated in the discussions did in fact purchase the meat than women who heard the information only. Their explanation of this finding was that the women identified strongly with their family role. The possible negative reaction they might receive from their families would counter any cognitive choice they might make based on the information alone. But if a woman had become part of another group—the discussion group—she could be pressured by this group in addition to her own family. The group pressure toward buying the sweetbreads which developed in the discussion groups would be sufficient in many instances to encourage her to buy the sweetbreads and risk disapproval of her family.[30] In other words, the individual's motivation is in large measure the result of the interpersonal pressure of the family. Although the biological family is a primary group, the pressure which the family places on its members is not unique. The same pressure can be generated in other groups; thus, groups in general, not just biological families, are sources of motivational pressure. Information on which people make decisions is influenced by their integration into groups which pressure them into certain actions.

The proposition that group discussions are an effective means of motivating has been tested in real and simulated organizational settings. The pattern for these experiments was set by Lester Coch and John R. P. French.[31] They investigated the use of groups to motivate workers to accept changes in work procedures in the Harwood pajama manufacturing company. The managers of the Harwood company instituted frequent changes in work procedures. The workers reacted to these changes with resistance and hostility. Newly hired workers learned their jobs much faster than workers who were transferred as the result of work changes. The women in highly cohesive work groups with negative attitudes toward the company had much slower relearning rated than those in work groups whose members had favorable attitudes toward management. Coch and French reasoned, therefore, that work groups were critical in the development of worker attitudes toward changes and that worker attitudes were directly related to the success of a change. If the workers could be involved in planning the change through their work group, then resistance might be avoided.

The researchers set up three change conditions to test their theory. One group of workers was subjected to a change of procedures in the usual manner; they were simply informed that a change would take place; the new procedure was explained by a management representative. In a second condition, all the workers met in groups where the need for the change was explained. There was a demonstration of the costs which could be saved with the new procedures. The workers discussed the advisability of the change and approved the plan. The group then selected representatives to be trained in the new procedures. Later these operators trained the others. In the final condition, the meeting and demonstration were held; in addition, all the operators received special training. The operators were asked for suggestions about how the changes should be implemented. They responded with so many suggestions that the stenographer had difficulty recording them.

Workers who were transferred in the usual manner reacted against the change; they were slow in learning the new job; they complained about the piece wage rate of the new procedure; 17 per cent quit within the first forty days. Workers who were allowed to discuss and approve the change in groups had a much faster rate of learning; they filed no grievances about the wage rate, and none quit. Those workers in the third condition, who were even more involved in planning the change, rapidly learned to work at a level 14 per cent above the prechange level. Coch and French concluded that involving work groups in discussing and planning work procedures is an effective means of motivating performance.

This kind of research has laid a foundation for the Human Relation's concept of "participative management" as the "new pattern of management." It also demonstrated the relationship of information (about new procedures) and integration (of people in work groups) as a determinant of organizational performance.

Function of Communication

The concept of commuincation is so predominant in human relations organization theory that one hardly needs to point it out separately. The early human relations theorists stood classical theory on its head. The concepts of formal organizations which absorbed the attention of the classical theorists were largely ignored in human relations theory. Conversely, motivation through interpersonal communication which had been ignored or belittled by the classicists was for the human relations theorists the fundamental process of organizing.

The development of the human relations approach from Elton Mayo to the organizational development movement has been largely a matter of spelling out with increasing precision the necessity of interpersonal communicative competence for achieving organizational purpose. For Mayo and the early theorists the relationship of good communication to organizational effectiveness was so obvious as to need little explanation. Under attack from the neoclassicists, later human relations theorists have developed and investigated elaborate rationales for explaining the relationship.

One of the clearest explanations of the function of communication in human relations has been offered by Chris Argyris.[32] The explanation is summarized in Figure 1.3. Effective organizations are developed (1) through decision-making practices which encourage people to offer all the information they perceive as relevant (instead of withholding information which may reflect badly on their own performance), (2) through creation of social contexts in which people are encouraged to foresee problems rather than wait for crises to make action necessary, and (3) through developing interpersonal relationships which are flexible. Straightjackets of formal regulation and departmentalized structure decrease organizational development. Organizations which are accomplished by people who value norms of rationality and objectivity are largely ineffective because rational values encourage "nonauthentic" communication practices.

In an effort to appear rational and nonemotional, people become overly concerned with their evaluations of themselves and others. They deny their own feelings and the feelings of others; they fail to develop new attitudes and feelings. As a result of such communication practices, there is an increase in conformity, mistrust, and dependence. In such contexts, individuals withhold information; they may wait until

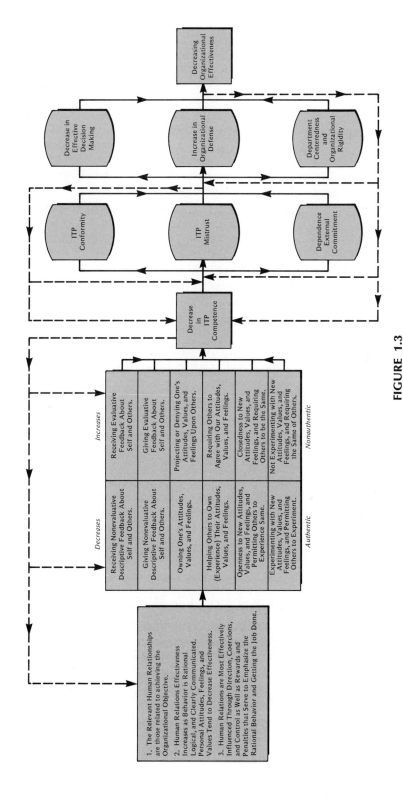

FIGURE 1.3

Impact of Decreasing Interpersonal Competence on Organizations (Reproduced with permission from *Interpersonal and Organizational Effectiveness* by Chris Argyris. Homewood, Ill.: Richard D. Irwin, Inc., Copyright © 1962, p. 43.)

they must act because of a crisis (lest their actions be criticized); they formalize relationships better to defend their position. In effect, by their interpersonal communication habits they accomplish ineffective organizations. Through other communication habits, effective organizations may be accomplished.

Argyris and other human relations theorists use the expression "authentic" to describe what they believe to be effective organizing behaviors. Authentic communication is nonevaluative; it describes rather than renders judgement. The person communicating authentically might say, for example, "Your committee's work helped me to do a much better report and get it finished on time" rather than, "Your committee's work was good." The first statement allows the listener to draw his own conclusion; it provides more information. It allows the second person to be independent of the evaluation of the speaker.

The "authentic" communicator "owns" his or her own feelings and helps others to own theirs. He or she might say, for example, "I get very mad at you when you leave work which I think you had time to finish," rather than, "In the future, finish all your work." In the first comment, the speaker claims his own feelings and permits the other person an opportunity to contribute information to the discussion. It opens the way for problem-solving in which both people will participate. In the second comment, the speaker hides his feelings and disallows the feelings and perceptions of the other.

Finally, "authentic" communication encourages experimentation and development of new ideas, attitudes, and feelings. For example, "It's not easy for me to say this. I am not sure what to do in such cases." By admitting uncertainty the speaker encourages the development of new perspectives on a problem rather than portraying his or her interpretation as the only one possible.

For the human relations theorists, organizations are built through communication. Communication is not simply the transmission of information through formal channels of hierarchy. Human relations theorists were more concerned with face-to-face communications as a method of constructing human relationships and organizational intelligence.

The classical theorists' indictment of organizations was that patterns of work activity were inefficient. The human relations theorists indictment was that patterns of human activity had become overrationalized. Because organizational managers had accepted classical conceptions, they had developed overly simplistic beliefs about organizing. In particular, they had begun to assume that human emotions can be ignored and that if emotions are suppressed organizations will operate more effectively. The human relations theorists refuted these beliefs, arguing that emotional dimensions of human communication are both inevitable and desirable. Organizing is a process of motivating; motivation is primarily non-rational. The successful organizational communicator motivates, by expressing his or her feelings, understanding the feelings of others and encouraging others to be self-expressive.

THE SOCIOTECHNICAL SYSTEMS SCHOOL: CONTROLLING INFORMATION PROCESSORS

World War II and Operations Research

By the time the Human Relations School became popular in the late 1940s and early 1950s, the events which generated the next school of organizational theory had already occurred. The Allied war effort in World War II called for organizing human and machine activities on a larger scale than ever before in history. The military hired engineers, natural scientists, and social scientists and put them to work in teams to solve complex problems of coordination. The result of these "think tanks" of theorists was *operations research* or "O.R." By 1951, non-military organizations had recognized the possibilities for increasing coordination efficiency through operations research. Since that time O.R. has developed into a new school of organization theory called management science.

Operations research is a way of conceptualizing management problems which result from functional division and specialization in organizations. Each unit must be coordinated into the overall objectives of the whole organization. Problems arise in part because unit objectives are often in conflict with one another. In industrial organizations, for example, marketing or sales divisions have a stake in keeping a large inventory so that customers may promptly be served. On the other hand, fiscal control divisions are most successful when they keep investment low which is done in part by keeping inventory low. The management of any organization is charged with resolving such conflicts so that the overall objectives of the company receive priority by all divisions. The objective of O.R. was "to provide managers of the organization with a scientific basis for solving problems involving the interaction of components of the organization in the best interest of the organization as a whole."[33] The aim of operations research is the development of a scheme of integration to maximize the effectiveness of organizational intelligence.

Although the name "operations research" is often used, today the name "systems analysis" is most frequently applied to this same process of problem analysis and problem solving. A "system" is a complex of interrelated parts which function as a whole. The concept of a system was useful to the original operations research teams as a basic scheme for conceptualizing coordination problems. It was obvious to them that the coordination problems they analyzed, for example, air reconnaissance for submarines—involved two kinds of interrelated system components: machine or technical components and human or social components. Hence, organizations were labeled "sociotechnical systems" to indicate the necessity of interrelating humans and machines.

C. West Churchman has described the mythological hero of systems researchers as a creature whose prime defense is the ability to swallow all its enemies. Certainly systems researchers "swallowed" their predecessors. They incorporated the classical notions of planning and organizational design into systems theories. But they also swallowed the human relations theorists conception that organizations are composed of people not simply machines. To the systems analyst, people are the "carriers" of the system. Thus, when the human relations theorists insist that people should not be ignored, the systems theorists reply: "You're right, 'they cannot be ignored because they furnish the sustaining input.' "[34]

People are components of systems. According to system theorists, the exact physical structure of a component is secondary to its function in the larger system. Systems researchers swallow or incorporate seemingly different phenomenon such as humans and machines by concentrating on the similar functions which they serve in maintaining the system. A group of people and an electronic data processing unit are interchangeable if they produce the same product—payroll checks, for example. Systems theorists differ from their scientific management predecessors because they recognize that humans do not function as machines. For example, they recognize that "in human organizations there is the critical problem of motivating the divisions to perform their respective functions."[35] Motivation is one component of a model of a sociotechnical system.

Organizational Intelligence

Systems analysis is the use of systems models to improve organizational intelligence. C. West Churchman has described systems analysis as an "extension of the old-fashioned logic and rhetoric in which the student is trained adequately to think about the world. . . . The systems approach is simply a way of thinking about these total systems and components."[36] The first step is construction of a model for the purpose of analyzing a system to determine the objective or function of the overall system. Churchman uses the example of an automobile. If a person is asked to describe an automobile, he or she may begin with little thought to describe its appearance or structure—"something that has four wheels and is driven by an engine." But for the systems analyst, "the way to describe an automobile is first by thinking about what it is for, about its function, and not the list of items which make up its structure."[37]

Before the systems approach, researchers used one of two ways of approaching the subject of organizational purpose. Classical theorists started their investigations with the formal stated purposes of the founders or directors. Usually these were stated in general terms such as to "maximize profits." This approach was not very helpful as information for predicting actual organizational behavior because the human relationships within an organization are not well characterized by general goal statements. The human relations theorists, on the other hand, assumed that since the general, stated purposes of the organization contributed so little to understanding what actually happens in organizations, the overall objectives could be safely ignored. Instead, they insisted that to understand an organization the research had to understand the human interactions. Systems theorists incorporate both of these ideas into their approach. Katz and Kahn describe the characteristic approach of the systems theorist to modeling an organization:

> The theoretical concepts should begin with the input, output, and functioning of the organization as a system and not with the rational purposes of its leaders. We may want to utilize such purpose notions to lead us to sources of data or as subjects of special study, but not as our theoretical constructs for understanding organizations. . . . All social systems, including organizations, consist of the patterned activities of a number of individuals. Moreover, these patterned activities are complementary or interdependent with respect to some common output or outcome; they are repeated, relatively enduring, and bounded in space and time. If the activity pattern occurs only once or at unpredictable intervals, we could not speak of an organization. The stability or recurrence of activities can be examined in relation to the *energic input* into the system, the *transformation of energies within the system*, and the resulting product or *energic output*. . . . The outcome of renewed cycle. . . . Our two basic criteria for identifying social systems and determining their functions are (1) tracing the pattern of energy exchange or activity of people as it results in some output, and (2) ascertaining how the output is translated into energy which reactivates the pattern. We shall refer to organizational functions or objectives not as the conscious purpose of group leaders or group members but as the outcomes which are the energic source for a maintenance of the same type of outcome.[38]

Thus, the systems approach is a reconceptualization of some principal concepts of its predecessors. Instead of beginning with the stated objectives of the organization's founders or directors, the systems researchers begin by conceptualizing the output of the system. Organizational intelligence is knowledge of how the output is continually accomplished. In explicating this process, systems theorists search for patterns of human and technological relationships.

In the process of constructing a model of a particular system, researchers may interview members of the system or directly observe its operation to gather data about the systems major components and how they are related to one another. From whatever information the researchers obtain, they abstract those patterns of activity which seem best to explain the systems output. They check their final diagram of the process with members of the system to ascertain whether the model has face validity as a picture of the organization. The system model is thus an abstract representation of what happens in the system. In addition to the specific objective of the organization, the systems researcher includes in the model: (1) the system's environment—those constraints over which the decision makers in the system have no control; (2) the resources of the system which the decision makers use to accomplish the system's objectives; (3) the components of the system, and finally, (4) the management of the system. The management consists of those decision makers who generate plans for the whole system (or officially recognized components) and make sure the plans are carried out.

The perspective of the management science consultants influences the form of the model they produce. For the systems analysts to proceed with their work, they need to identify the decision makers of the system. For example, if they have been hired by a municipal government, they might decide that the city manager and council are the decision makers. In this case, the amount of revenue sharing funds flowing into city coffers would be a feature of the environment because the identified decision makers can do little to change the amount. That component of the model must be regarded as fixed from their perspective. If the systems analysts have been hired by an agency of the federal government to study and make recommendations about revenue sharing policy, then the local officials may not be the critical decision makers, though they may decide how the bulk of the money is spent. In this case, Congress might be more appropriately designated by the decision-making unit. The amount of revenue sharing funds is not an environmental or fixed constraint because the decision makers are empowered to change the amount.

In short, the whole model of the system changes when the perspective of who constitutes the decision makers' changes. What is good from one perspective is bad from another. The "information" generated by the model is influenced by the perspective of the information generators. This principle of the relativity of information will be discussed in greater detail in chapter 2. The metaphor which characterizes the systems approach to organizations is the information processor or computer. Organizations "process" information for the purpose of making decisions. The organizational machines of the classical theorists were clockworks which operated in predetermined ways. The components of organizations characterized by computer analogies are decision makers.

Organizational Integration

Integration in the sociotechnical systems school is a process of control. Many classical theorists spoke of control as a fundamental organizational process, but for them, it was a matter of adequate design. The classical theorists overlooked the necessity of checking to ascertain whether the organization procedures are being used and whether these procedures are resulting in the desired outcomes. Within the systems approach, control is the process of checking whether procedures are being followed, comparing the outcomes of the procedures with the goals of the planners, and altering the design when the outcomes are negative. To the systems scientists, the process of organizing is not simply designing coordination of effort, though such planning is important. The essential process of organizing is controlling. Arnold Tannebaum states:

> Characterizing an organization in terms of its pattern of control is to describe an essential and universal aspect of organization which every member must face and to which he must adjust. Organization implies control. A social organization is an ordered arrangement of individual human interactions. Control processes help circumscribe idiosyncratic behaviors and keep them conformant to the rational plan of the organization. . . . It is the function of control to bring about conformance to organizational requirements and achieving of the ultimate purposes of the organization. . . . Control is an inevitable correlate of organization.[39]

The "control cycle" according to Tannebaum and other systems theorists, is the basic unit of organizational integration. Figure 1.4 is Tannebaum's representation of this structure. Note that although there are two "people" in this cycle, only A is portrayed as having intentions. A acts intentionally. A's actions "result in B's behavior." This model ignores the process of intentional choice by B which resulted in B's actions. Of course, Tannebaum admits that B may not do as A wishes: "B may dislike A and refuse to do A's bidding," but Tannebaum goes on to say that "if a cycle breaks down for whatever reason, control cannot be said to exist."

Since control is the essential organizational process, "chronic breakdowns of such cycles imply a breakdown in the organization itself."[40] Although Tannebaum states that control may be reciprocal,

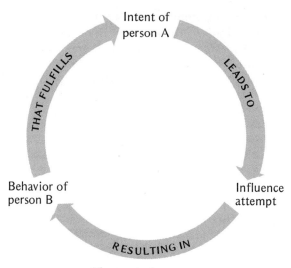

The control process

FIGURE 1.4
The Control Cycle (From *Control in Organizations* by Arnold Tannebaum. Copyright © 1968 by McGraw-Hill, Inc. Used with permission of McGraw-Hill Book Company.)

his "control cycle" portrays only one-way control. The most general use of control models such as this one has been used as a way of conceptualizing the process of assuring that individual behavior is "conformant to the rational plan of the organization." The process of reciprocal control—individual control of the organization—has received little attention.

The control cycle models suggest the use of two procedures which have become synonymous with the systems approach to organizational control. The first procedure is the exact, operational specification of objectives. Objectives are the organization's intentions. Tannebaum points out that "conflicting intents lead to confusing influence attempts and hence to a breakdown in the cycle."[41] If organizations are successfully to influence individual members toward accomplishment of organizational objectives, those objectives must be stated so that their accomplishment may be measured and hence verified. Operationally stated objectives are thus a first prerequisite to systemic control. Researchers have found that workers' performance may be improved if they are given precisely stated objectives (see chapter 8).

A second procedure is the use of "feedback" as a means of checking performance. Feedback is the process of gathering information about the "output" of a systemic process—shown in Figure 1.4 as "behavior of *B*" and checking this information against the intent or objective. Feedback is the third line in the model. If the information fed back indicated that performance matches objectives, decision makers usually assume that the system is operating "properly." In industrial corporations feedback about internal operations may take the form of output per man-hour, yield per ton of material, overhead expense. Such information is relatively simple to obtain and has the appearance of objectivity. Personnel appraisals provide another form of feedback information.

A concept which became popular with the sociotechnical systems school is the dependence of organizations on their environment. Survival is a process of adapting the system to environmental changes. The concept of cybernetic control is premised on the belief that managers must maintain control of organizations which are upset continuously by a turbulent environment. The analogue is a steersman[42] guiding a ship in turbulent waters. Constant correcting is necessary to keep the ship on course. The metaphor of the steersman illustrates the interrelationship of organizational intelligence and integration. Managers of a system are not really like steersmen of ships. The steersman has only a limited set of ways to adapt the ship to the water. The steersman's goal is present, and therefore only the course, not the goal, can be adapted. Organizational members are as likely to change their goals as their methods.

Moreover, only in very small organizations do the decision makers have the direct sensory access to all environmental conditions such as the steersman. In any large organization, the central planners or controllers are several links in a communication channel removed from the people who experience the environment directly. In a state welfare system, for example, the people who are said to "control" the system—who adapt it to meet a changing environment—are in the state capital. The people who experience the changing environment directly—who can see first hand the impact of particular policies—are the welfare case workers. The perceptions of the case workers are translated into reports (whose forms are usually determined by the central planners) which are summarized by several intermediate "information processors" before they reach the central planners.

Thus, any complex system adapts not to the "environment," but to an environment interpreted by people at several levels of hierarchy and across specialties. The adaptation is only as good as the integration-information system which provides the decision maker with data from the environment and provides the system's actors with information about the decisions they are to implement. In an effort to enact the steersman analogy, management scientists direct much of their attention to finding procedures for bringing more information about the environment to the central planners. The redesigning of a management in-formation system, therefore, is the customary outcome of a systems analysis.

Function of Communication

Systems theorists like human relations theorists view "communication" as the fundamental process of organizing; however, they define com-munication differently than those in the human relations school. For the systems theorist, communication is the transferring of information. Information is a commodity which can be measured, transferred, stored, and retrieved. "Good communication" in an organization is obtained by designing the most efficient channels of organizational communica-tion.

For the classical theorists, organizational communications were the directives which a superior gave to subordinates. The classical theorists did not recognize that talk not formally sanctioned could be important in directing organizational activity. For the human relations theorist organizational communication was the process by which people form social relationships. Organizations are created and maintained through communication which inspires organizational members to develop loyalties toward the organization. The nature of the relationship among communicators influences the content of their talk.

For the systems theorist, communication is information transfer. Organizations are created and maintained through the efficient transfer of information among the various functional subsystems of an organiza-tion. Communication is the process of getting accurate, relevant in-formation to decision makers. Not only must information be "accurate" and "relevant," it must be in a language the decision makers can under-stand (a statistical report may need to be summarized in prose), and it must be of sufficient detail to be useful without being so detailed that the receiver does not have time to digest it. Effective organizations, according to systems researchers, need adequately designed and con-trolled information systems.

Thus, problems of communication for the systems scientists are, for the most part, technical problems. When they look at models of organi-zation in order to diagnose coordinating problems they look for sys-temic faults in reception (such as "information collecting too slowly or too fast"), processing ("channels of communication missing, conflicting, overloaded, etc."), and transmission ("no effector feedback").[43]

In corporations and bureaucracies, communication has become largely a matter of data processing which in turn has become the process of managing. Ida R. Hoos has observed:

Information processing, once regarded as an adjunct to the organization, has become a function served by the organization, a factor in its structure, and even a prime criterion by which its overall efficiency is assessed. Armies of workers are employed in the preparation of data and cadres of information experts are required to maintain the system, that is, to keep it working and busy. The management of information has become equated with and is tantamount to the management of the enterprise. In fact, in a strange turnabout, management *of* information has receded from view and management *by* information has become the mode. The science of management is largely the science of managing information. It is also the science of managing by information. The metamorphosis from EDP, once depreciated as nothing more than a fast abacus, to MIS, the Management Information System, nerve center of the organization is complete.[44]

In the later chapters, we discuss management information systems in detail. The argument here is that the computer analogy of organizing is associated with a definition of communication as data processing. For the systems scientist coordinating activities is largely a process of coordinating the reception, processing, and transmission of data.

THE CONTINGENCY SCHOOL: PLAYING A COMPETITIVE GAME

Theorists of the contingency school may also be considered sociotechnical systems theorists, because they accept the major concepts of the systems school. For this reason, and because research of contingency theorists is discussed extensively in later chapters, we will not discuss this school in as much detail as the previous three. The key principle of the contingency school of organization theory is that there is no "one right way" to organize. Rather, organizational effectiveness is maximized when organizations adapt to certain conditions of their environment.

The contingency school began as researchers of the sociotechnical systems schools set out to identify the determinants of organizational effectiveness using techniques developed by operations researchers. In particular they used computers to analyze large amounts of information about organizational processes and outcomes. "Effectiveness" to the classical theorists was no more than increasing the efficiency of individual organizational operations. Human relations theorists assumed that organizational effectiveness would result from worker satisfaction. Only with the development of systems analysis was it possible to measure organizational effectiveness on a large scale as more than the sum of the effectiveness of individual units. Systems researchers became "contingency theorists" when they discovered that no single pattern of organizing is associated with effectiveness.

Some of the first research of the contingency school was done by investigators at the Tavistock Institute in London. T. Burns and G. M. Stalker[45] wanted to know what kind of organizational structure was necessary for successful use of innovation. They investigated organizations in a noninnovative or "stable" industry, and organizations in a highly innovative or "dynamic" industry. They found that successful organizations in the stable industry were organized quite differently from successful organizations in the dynamic industry. The successful organizations in the stable industry relied more on formal rules and procedures. Decisions were made at higher levels of the organizational hierarchy. Spans of supervisory control were narrow. Organizational patterns were consistent with principles of the classical school. By contrast, in the dynamic industry, the successful organizations had few formal rules and procedures, decisions were made at low levels of the hierarchy, the span of control of supervisors was larger so that they could exercise little direct supervision of subordinates. Organizational patterns reflected more ideas of the human relations school.

Joan Woodward[46] and her associates investigated the organizational structure of 100 manufacturing plants in the south of England. They divided the organizations into three groups according to the dominant technology each employed. The first group had a relatively low level of technological sophistication; companies produced according to individual orders of customers. The second group produced large batches at a time using mass production techniques. The third group had a high level of technological sophistication; they were automated to produce on a continuous process basis. She found that successful organizations in these three groups differed significantly from one another. For example, as organizations became more technologically sophisticated, they tended to have more levels of organizational hierarchy (an average of three levels in small order; an average of six levels in continuous process). On the other hand, the ratio of managers and supervisors to hourly paid personnel is comparable for those organizations at each extreme of the technical scale (small order and continuing process) but different from those organizations using large batch or mass production.

The contingency theorists who will be referred to most in this book are Paul R. Lawrence and Jay W. Lorsch of the Harvard Business School. Lawrence and Lorsch premise their contingency theory on a view of an organization as an open system. They state:

> At the most general level we find it useful to view an organization as an open system in which the behaviors of members are themselves interrelated. The behaviors of members of an organization are also interdependent with the formal organization, the tasks to be accomplished,

the personalities of other individuals, and the unwritten rules about appropriate behavior for a member. . . . As systems become large, they differentiate into parts, and the functioning of these separate parts has to be integrated if the entire system is to be viable. . . . An important function of any system is adaptation to what goes on in the world outside. . . . Human systems are very much concerned about dealing with the people and things that make up our external environment.[47]

Thus, Lawrence and Lorsch are specifically concerned with issues discussed throughout this book. At the individual level, they are interested in how members of an organization behave (communicate), and how that behavior is influenced by the formal structure, the tasks, other people who are taken into account and unwritten rules (taken-for-granted expectations) about appropriate ways of behaving. At the level of organization, they are interested in the same two organizing processes which are the focus of this book, namely, how people are integrated into systems and how groups of people acting as a system come to understand its environment or how they develop "organizational intelligence."

A key term in their theory which is important in later chapters is "uncertainty." I describe in the two chapters following how individuals reduce uncertainty *as* they communicate with one another and how individuals must reduce uncertainty if they are to communicate with one another. For Lawrence and Lorsch, "uncertainty" is a quality of the environment of organizations. There are three indicators of uncertainty. An environment is more uncertain if: (1) information about it is unclear (for example, information about how to develop certain new products in the plastics industry is quite unclear); (2) causal relationships are unclear (for example, in the foods industry, it is unclear whether a particular new product will cause a large number of people to purchase it); or (3) there is a long timespan before the organization receives "definitive feedback" about how well it is doing (for example, there is a long period between the time that a research team develops a new product idea and the time that the product hits the market and the organization receives information on how well it is received).[48] Uncertainty is the principal contingency which influences how effective a certain organizational pattern is likely to be. In general, the more uncertain the environment, the looser must be the formal organizational constraints if the organization is to be effective. Decisions must be made at a lower level; personal communications rather than formal rules must be the means of integration.

Unlike Burns and Stalker, who also used "uncertainty" ("stable vs. dynamic") as a predictor of what kind of organizational structure is likely to be effective, Lawrence and Lorsch are not concerned with determining a single environment of a whole organization. Rather, they examine the extent to which an organization is differentiated into units which make differential responses to a complex environment. They have found, for example, that in the plastics industry, the research units exist in a highly uncertain environment while the production units of the same organizations exist in a fairly certain environment.

This means that for the whole organization to be effective, it must be structured so that the research units have a loose structure with low level decision making while the production units are strictly structured with relatively high levels of decision making. In other words, in order for the organization to understand and hence adapt to its environment, the different units must be different from one another. This makes it difficult for the members of the different units to understand one another. (This is discussed in more detail in chapters 8 and 9). Thus, there is a "trade-off" of integration and intelligence. The more integrated a large organization, the more difficult it is to have good intelligence about its environment. The more an organization is structured to obtain good information about its environment, the more difficult it is for members of individual units of that organization to understand one another and thus achieve integration across the differentiated units.

The most successful organizations, according to Lawrence and Lorsch's research, are those which have both differentiation and integration. Successful organizations have conflicts among units, but are also able to mediate those conflicts in appropriate ways. Successful organizations have personnel who are successful conflict resolvers. For Lawrence and Lorsch, organizational communication is conflict resolution. It is in the successful settlement of inevitable organizational conflict that an organization achieves both integration and intelligence. Communication as conflict resolution is achieved by organizational design (formal structuring) and by effective face-to-face communication. They make clear that neither the formal structure nor face-to-face communication skill alone is sufficient for the kind of conflict resolution required for integration and intelligence in complex organizations. (Chapter 8 discusses conflict resolution as an interpersonal skill; chapter 9 discusses conflict resolution as a feature of organizational design).

Organizational conflict is successfully resolved when that unit of the organization with the most information about the most important issue in the industry-wide competition for resources and markets has the most influence in organizational decision making. Lawrence and Lorsch call the most important issue the "major competitive issue." In the plastics industry and the food industry, the major competitive issue is innovation. Thus, the most effective industries in those industries are those in which the research divisions (who have the most knowledge about innovation) have the most influence in organization-wide decisions.

I like to compare this view of organizations to a game of bridge or pinochle. The "major competitive issue" is like the trump suit. The player who most successfully plays that trump suit is likely to win the game. In judging organizational effectiveness, the contingency theorists begin with the premise of competitiveness. Some argue that "an assessment of organizational effectiveness is possible only where some form of competition takes place."[49] Organizing, for the contingency theorists, is playing a competitive game because it is a process of using integration and information as strategies for competing with others who are also using integration and information as strategies to win resources and markets. Those who use the best strategies win the game. This view of organizing is important for those interested in organizational communication because communication is the method of using the strategies of integration and information.

SUMMARY

Four major schools of organization theory have been described. No attempt has been made to cover all theorists of importance or relevance to this book. Instead, the central theme of each school of thought is presented.

Classical theory resulted from the application of early scientific methods to the coordination problems of the industrial revolution. Following a mechanical logic, researchers broke work patterns down into individual units of work or "tasks." Knowledge about how to perform these tasks most efficiently was believed to be the way to improve organizational performance. Classical theorists described universal principles for improving design of human "organizational machines."

Formal organizational design was believed to be the only prerequisite for human integration or cooperation. Planners constructed a logical (mechanical) design and then informed workers of what they were to do in accordance with the formal specifications. Communication was the process of instructing organizational members about their formal responsibilities. Although researchers of the classical school did not succeed in finding universal principles for guaranteeing organizational effectiveness, concepts such as departmentalization and span of control which they introduced have become conventionalized wisdom about the best way to organize. Since the classical theorists there has been widespread acceptance of scientific research as a method for discovering effective organizing patterns.

The human relations school was begun by a team of researchers as the result of their investigations at the Hawthorne plant of the Western

Electric Corporation. They documented for the first time the importance of workers beliefs, attitudes, and social relationships as the basis of performance in the organization. To improve performance required improving worker integration into the organizational family by increasing the workers' motivation. Communication with workers that increases their participation in organizational decision making is a principal means of motivating.

The sociotechnical systems theories were developed by researchers from many disciplines to solve complex logistical problems in World War II. Organizational intelligence is information about how well the whole system is working to produce certain outcomes. Often this information is structured into a model of the system which includes: the system's objective, its environment, resources, components, and management. Integration is achieved through cycles of organizational control. Control begins with the specification of objectives at a control center. Information about objectives and/or strategies is communicated to those who are to accomplish the objectives. Feedback or information about performance is checked against original objectives and future objectives and strategies are determined. Communication as data processing is essential in sociotechnical systems. It is the process of transmitting information relevant to organizational decision making.

The contingency school developed as sociotechnical systems researchers discovered that no single theory of organizational design is sufficient to predict organizational effectiveness. The "best" kind of organizing is contingent on several factors. In particular, it is dependent upon the degree to which the environment is "uncertain." Lawrence and Lorsch's research indicates that the most effective organizations are those in which units are differentiated from one another so that they are most adaptive to particular subsystem environments. Communication is the process of integrating differentiated units into complex systems. Effective communication requires appropriate design of the formal structure and interpersonal skills of those responsible for the integrative function.

ENDNOTES

1. Kenneth Boulding, *The Organizational Revolution* (New York: Quadrangle Books, 1968), p. 3.

2. Henri Fayol, in L. Gulick and L. Urwick, eds., *Papers on the Science of Administration* (New York: Columbia University Press, 1937), p. 103.

3. James G. March and Herbert A. Simon, *Organizations* (New York: John Wiley, 1958), pp. 22–23, italics added.

4. Henri Fayol, *General and Industrial Management,* Constance Sours, trans. (London: Pitman, 1949), p. 19.

5. Frederick Taylor, as quoted in Reinhard Bendix, *Work and Authority in Industry* (New York: Harper Torchbooks, 1956), p. 278.

6. Fayol, *General and Industrial Management,* p. 35.

7. Frederick Herzberg, "One More Time; How Do You Motivate Employees," *Harvard Business Review* 46 (Jan.–Feb. 1968): 53–62. Herzberg's own theory of motivation through job enrichment is not a classical theory of motivation. He discusses classical theory in the introduction to his own theory.

8. Ibid., p. 54.

9. Joseph L. Massie, "Management Theory," in James March, ed., *Handbook of Organization Theory* (Chicago: Rand-McNally, 1965), pp. 387–422.

10. Taylor, in Bendix, *Work and Authority in Industry,* p. 276.

11. Douglas McGregor, *The Professional Manager,* Caroline McGregor and Warren G. Bennis, eds. (New York: McGraw-Hill, 1967), p. 33ff.

12. Rensis Likert, *The Human Organization* (New York: McGraw-Hill, 1967), p. 85.

13. Taylor, in Bendix, *Work and Authority in Industry,* p. 288.

14. Fritz J. Roethlisberger, *Management and Morale* (Cambridge: Harvard University Press, 1941).

15. Ibid., p. 14.

16. Ibid.

17. See for example, Alex Carey, "The Hawthorne Studies: A Radical Criticism," *American Sociological Review* 32 (1967): 403–416.

18. Roethlisburger, *Management and Morale,* pp. 181–183.

19. Amitai Etzioni, *Modern Organizations* (Englwood Cliffs, N.J.: Prentice-Hall, 1964), p. 43.

20. Roethlisberger, *Management and Morale.*

21. Ibid., p. 194.

22. See Raymond Miles, "Keeping Informed—Human Relations or Human Resources?" *Harvard Business Review* 43 (July–August 1965): 148–63.

23. Ibid.

24. Abraham Maslow, "A Theory of Human Motivation" *Psychological Review* 50 (1943): 370–396.

25. Ibid., pp. 373 and 375.

26. McGregor, *The Professional Manager,* p. 56.

27. Abraham Maslow, "Management as a Psychological Experiment," in Walter Nord, ed., *Concepts and Controversy in Organizational Behavior* (Pacific Palisades, Calif.: Goodyear, 1972).

28. Abraham Maslow, *Eupsychian Management* (Homewood, Ill.: Richard Irwin, 1965), pp. 61–62.

29. Roethlisberger, *Management and Morale,* p. 22.

30. Kurt Lewin, Frontiers in Group Dynamics *Human Relations* (1947): 5–42.

31. See Lester Coch and John R. P. French, Jr., "Overcoming Resistance to Change," *Human Relations* 1 (1948): 512–532.

32. Chris Argyris, *Interpersonal Competence and Organizational Effectiveness* (Homewood, Ill.: Richard Irwin, 1962).

33. C. West Churchman, Russell L. Ackoff, and E. Leonard Arnoff, *Introduction to Operations Research* (New York: John Wiley & Sons, Inc., 1957), p. 6.

34. Danield Katz and Robert L. Kahn, *The Social Psychology of Organization* (New York: John Wiley & Sons, Inc., 1966), p. 9.

35. Churchman et al., *Introduction to Operations Research,* p. 7.

36. C. West Churchman, *The Systems Approach* (New York: Dell, 1968), pp. 10–11.

37. Ibid., p. 13.

38. Katz and Kahn, *The Social Psychology of Organization,* pp. 16–18.

39. Arnold S. Tannebaum, *Control in Organizations* (New York: McGraw-Hill, 1968), p. 3.

40. Ibid., p. 7.

41. Ibid.

42. Cybernetic is derived from the Greek word for steersman.

43. Churchman et al., *Introduction to Operations Research,* p. 95.

44. Ida R. Hoos, *Systems Analysis and Public Policy* (Berkeley: University of California Press, 1972), pp. 193–194.

45. See T. Burns and G. M. Stalker, *The Management of Innovation* (London: Tavistock, 1961).

46. See Joan Woodward, *Industrial Organization: Theory and Practice* (London: Oxford University Press, 1965).

47. Paul R. Lawrence and Jay W. Lorsch, *Organization and Environment Managing Differentiation and Integration* (Boston: Harvard University Press, 1967), pp. 6–7.

48. Ibid., p. 90.

49. Ephraim Yuchtman and Stanley E. Searshore, "A System Resource Approach to Organizational Effectiveness," *American Sociological Review* 32 (December 1967): 891–902.

CHAPTER
2

Communication and Meaning

Cognitive Maps
Communication as Process
Constructing Personal Meanings
Constructing Consensus
Metacommunication
APPLICATION: Diagnosing Problems with Meaning

As I sit at my desk, I know where I am. I see before me a window; beyond that some trees; beyond that the red roofs of the campus of Stanford University; beyond them the trees and the roof tops which mark the town of Palo Alto; beyond them the bare golden hills of the Hamilton Range. I know, however, more than I see. Behind me, although I am not looking in that direction, I know there is a window, and beyond that the little campus of the Center for the Advanced Study in the Behavioral Sciences. . . . I am not only located in space and time, I am located in a field of personal relations. I not only know where and when I am, I know to some extent who I am. I am a professor at a great state university. This means that in September I shall go into a classroom and expect to find some students in it and begin to talk to them and nobody will be surprised. I expect, what is perhaps even more agreeable, that regular salary checks will arrive from the university. I expect that when I

*open my mouth on certain occasions people will listen. I am also
located in the world of nature, in a world of how things operate. I
know that when I get into my car there are some things I must do to
start it; some things I must do to back out of the parking lot; some
things I must do to drive home. . . . What I have been talking
about is knowledge. Knowledge, perhaps, is not a good word for
this. Perhaps one would rather say my IMAGE of the world.
Knowledge has an implication of validity, of truth. What I am
talking about is what I believe to be true; my subjective knowledge.
It is this Image that largely governs my behavior.*

Kenneth Boulding, The Image

With these words the economist Kenneth Boulding introduces an essay
on social organization. For Boulding, understanding the process of
organizing requires understanding the relationship of "image" to action
and the formation of "public images." The intent of this chapter is to
explore these two issues: first, the nature of personal images of the
world, and how they relate to individual communicative actions, and
second, how people develop equivalent or "public" images, and how
these relate to collective activity in organization. Public images are
what I have called "organizational intelligence" in the previous chapter.
In this chapter is described the process of communication as it functions
to create "intelligence" (knowledge or images).

COGNITIVE MAPS

We begin our understanding of communication with an understanding
of behavior in general. For this, it is helpful to go to psychologists
whose job is "to make sense out of what people do." As psychologists
Miller, Galanter, and Pribram observe, "What an organism (such as a
person) does depends on what happens around it." But there are two
schools of explanation for this "depending." One school, they term the
"optimists," who claim to find the dependency simple and straightforward." For them, behavior is a simple response to a simple stimulus.
Behavior is reflexive. But, they continue:

Arrayed against the reflex theorists are the pessimists, who think that
living organisms are complicated, devious, poorly designed for research
purposes, and so on. They maintain that the effect an event will have
upon behavior depends on how the event is represented in the organism's picture of itself and its universe. They are quite sure that any
correlations between stimulation and response must be mediated by an
organized representation of the environment, a system of concepts and
relations within which the organism is located. A human being—and
probably other animals as well—builds up an internal representation, a

model of the universe, a schema, a simulacrum, a cognitive map, an Image.[1]

In this book I take the "pessimistic" view of human action. To understand human communicative action we must take into account the way people interpret what they are seeing and hearing. This view of human action is more like that described by Mayo and Roethlisberger as the result of the Hawthorne studies. The view of human action as simply pushed by stimuli is more like that of the classical organization theorists.

This perspective is called "constructivism" by some. According to constructivists, humans are actively "constructing" the world around them and not simply "responding" to it. This perspective in psychology is about as old as psychology itself. In the late 1940s Edward Tolman argued that on the basis of his experiments, even rat behavior is best explained with reference to "cognitive maps": "The stimuli, which are allowed in, are not connected by just simple one-to-one switches to outgoing responses. Rather, the incoming impulses are usually worked over and elaborated in the central control room into a tentative, cognitive map of the environment."[2]

Fritz Heider was one of the first psychologists to relate the notion of cognitive maps to the understanding of human social behavior. In *The Psychology of Interpersonal Relations,* Heider posits three assumptions. First, that understanding social behavior requires description of how people perceive and report their own social world. Like Roethlisberger, Heider claims that to understand a person's behavior, the scientist must understand the subject's interpretation of his world. According to Heider, every person is his or her own psychologist. Each person has theories about how and why people behave. A second assumption is that people want to be able to predict and control their environment. Thus, people use their theories as predictors to guide their own actions in ways which will help them accomplish favorable outcomes.

Finally, Heider claims that there the process of perceiving people is much like the process of perceiving objects. In particular, people believe that human behavior is "caused," and they seek to understand the causes of behavior. Heider's evidence for the second two assumptions is based in part on an experiment[3] in which subjects were shown an animated film of geometric shapes moving around. The subjects described the movement of the shapes as they would the movement of people (the larger shape was "chasing"; the smaller one was "fleeing"). Thus, the subjects were perceiving movements as "caused" and they were perceiving objects as they would people.

Heider's three assumptions have been elaborated by George Kelley in *A Theory of Personality.* Kelley refers to "man-the-scientist" as Heider refers to people-as-psychologists. People are not simply organisms which react to their environment in a predetermined way. People actively "make sense" out of what they perceive:

> Man looks at his world through transparent patterns of templets which he creates and then attempts to fit over the realities of which the world is composed. The fit is not always very good. Yet without such patterns the world appears to be such an undifferentiated homogeneity that man is unable to make any sense out of it. Even a poor fit is more helpful than nothing at all.[4]

The essence of the constructivist perspective, then, is that the world while "real" (its not entirely a fictitious creation), is not essentially sensible. People create for themselves—they construct—the sensibleness of the world they see and hear. Like Boulding, they "know" more than they immediately see and hear. This knowledge is like a "map" which exists in cognitions. We use the map to sort and relate what we are perceiving. The map changes somewhat as we perceive and interpret stimuli. Thus, the map is closely related to our communicative activity.

In the Introduction and chapter 1, I drew a distinction between "intelligence" and "integration" in organizations. That distinction is largely arbitrary since people must "know" certain things in order to integrate, and since knowledge is in part a function of social relationships. There must be some integration to have knowledge, but the distinction is a useful one in clarifying organizing outcomes of communication. We may think of cognitive maps as mapping two kinds of "things": meanings and expectations. Meanings represent the outcome of the intelligence function. Expectations, the subject of chapter 3, are the outcome of the integrative function. In chapter 3, communication is described as the process of constructing relationships.

The remainder of this chapter describes communication as the process of constructing meaning. First, I describe the nature of communication as "process." The intent of this section is to describe the potentials and limitations of communication as the method by which people construct their cognitive maps. The sections following describe the process of constructing meaning; first, at an individual level, then at a "collective" level. At the end of the chapter there is a discussion of six "problems" typically found in organizations because organizing is a process of meaning construction.

COMMUNICATION AS PROCESS

The common sense definition of "process" is readily understood. A process is a sequence of events. The classical theorists looked at organizing as a process in this sense. One event happened, this caused another event which in turn caused another, leading to a conclusion. For example, the process of erecting a building begins with designing the structure, the foundation must be excavated and constructed, the superstructure must be erected, and so forth. The process has a relatively definite beginning and end. There is a fairly regular progression of events. The physical process is deterministic because it is operated by mechanical laws; a nail placed on a wooden board and hit with a hammer will penetrate the board.

By contrast, communication processes are difficult to understand at a common sense level. There are no discrete parts which move according to fixed mechanical laws. In *The Process of Communication*, David Berlo offered the following description of nonmechanical process:

> If we accept the concept of process, we view the events and relationships as dynamic, on-going, ever-changing, continuous. When we label something as a process we also mean that it does not have a beginning, an end, a fixed sequence of events. It is not static, at rest. It is moving. The ingredients within a process interact; each affects all of the others.[5]

Berlo's quotation is very often quoted in explanations of communication as process, probably because it appears to be a clear, succinct description. In fact, it is quite difficult to appreciate the concept of communication Berlo describes. The statement emphasizes the dynamics and relativity of process. It does not describe "parts" in "movement." However, when Berlo elaborated this definition, he described communication as the movement of information over a channel from a speaker to a receiver. He went on to describe four "parts" of communication: speaker, message, channel, and receiver. Berlo's own elaboration of the concept does not appear to meet his criteria for identifying a process.

In part, our *language habits* make it difficult for us to understand the fluid conception of communication in the Berlo quote. Our grammar is based on nouns (parts) and verbs (movement). In part, our senses make it difficult to understand the dynamics and relativity Berlo is talking about because such characteristics cannot be readily observed. We often associate "communication processes" with conversations. Any particular conversation has a fairly definable beginning and conclusion. Thus communications appear to have both beginnings and ends. It is obvious that when people talk to one another, they often change their opinions, but the people talking do not seem to change. The "ingredients" of a communication process which appear to be stable receive more attention than the less apparent features: the dynamics, continuity, and relativity.

Communication Processes Are Dynamic and Relative

To explain the dynamic quality of communication, let us take an illustration that centers on a quotation from a speech. The quotation is "real"; the speech was actually delivered. However, I extrapolate from the quotation, in the manner of historical fiction perhaps, some imaginary communication processes or systems in which the quotation has served as "message."

The speech was delivered by R. L. Frederick, at the time Assistant to the President of the Timken Roller Bearing Company. The occasion for the speech was a conference held by the National Industrial Conference Board in 1959. The stated purpose of the conference was to discuss how industrial corporations inform their employees about events during the negotiation of a labor contract. In the quotation, Frederick describes how his company informs employees about union demands and company offers:

> We put out what is termed *The Daily Negotiation Digest*. This digest is written by the company, disclosing what has happened during the day's negotiations. Its purpose is to inform the employee on a factual basis. We try not to slant it in our favor, as it is a piece of information we are sending out. We are putting our best information foot forward, so to speak, and we certainly should tell the employees the things that are the truth. We find that the truth helps our position. Facts must not be distorted.
>
> Included in the digest are the union demands and our answers and our offers. They are sent to the homes of every one of our employees—not just the foremen. When it arrives the next day, Mrs. Employee can open the letter and read exactly what is going on in her husband's plant.
>
> You would be surprised at the pressure that a woman can place upon her husband if he is considering going out on strike for half a cent an hour or vested rights, or superseniority for the grievance committeeman. Mrs. Employee will often make it clear that she doesn't care for that. We get our information to the home where the employee's family will know what is going on.[6]

We can immediately identify communication systems in which these words may have served as "message." The original conference of corporate executives was one system. Perhaps Frederick sent the president of the company a copy of the address. This was a "supervisor-subordinate" relationship. The speech was first printed in a business journal; it was reprinted in a collection of articles on industrial communication. One part of the speech has now been reprinted in a description of communication as process.

The intentions of "source" and "audience" were different in each system. Frederick's intent, at least his overt intent, in the original speech was to "inform" other businessmen about the success of his company's dealings with the union and the methods to which he attributes that success. In sending a copy to the company president he was saying, "See what a good public relations representative I am." The editors of *Management Record* who first published the words did so presumably to inform a larger group of managers about what the editors thought was sound advice about how to communicate with union members. W. Charles Redding and George Sanborn who reprinted the speech in their collection of readings evidently thought that Frederick's words would help students of industrial communication understand the "vexatious problems which management faces" when communicating about labor relations.[7]

In each system, the source has a different intended message. Managers reading Frederick's words would judge them by how much the words helped them decide how to communicate with employees about labor relations; students of industrial communication would judge the words by their clarity in explaining the role of communication in the process of labor negotiations. I have chosen to reprint some of the message because I feel it can help me demonstrate the meaning of communication as a process. The interpretation of the message is different in each system because the interpretation is relative to other parts of a system.

You read these words not as a manager looking for advice (though you may be a manager and may find the message offers sound advice), not as a student seeking to understand labor relations (though you may be a student and may find the words informative about labor relations), but as a person who is seeking to understand "communication as process." Frederick's words themselves remain the same, but the relationship between the "audience" or reader changes as the intentions of the readers and sources change. Thus the "same words" are not the same because they function in communication processes which are dynamic and relative. The context, the words, the intentions of actors interact with one another. Changes in one part of an interrelated system are reflected in changes in the other. With these changes new meanings are created.

Communication Processes Are Continuous

It is evident that communication is not simply composed of physical ingredients such as people or contexts, though these are most readily identified. Rather communication is a function of an elusive phenomenon called "meaning." Meaning continuously changes; or more specifically, people continuously construct and reconstruct meaning. In this example, the meaning of the words is interpreted differently by different readers. In part, the meaning is different because different readers direct their attention to different parts of the message. In part, there is a difference in meaning because each reader interprets the meaning in light of different past experiences. In part, the meaning is different because readers judge what is being said with different estimates of the future relevance of the words. In other words, different communication, defined as the creation of meaning, is a continuous process.

The beginning of the communication process in our example can never be pinpointed. Seeking the beginning we would have to look into Frederick's experiences in the organization, his schooling, perhaps even how he was treated when he was a small child. Ultimately, we would have to talk about his mother, father, teachers, and a host of others who have influenced him to believe what he does, to act the way he does, and to choose the words he uses. It would be futile to attempt to find the "real" beginning of the communication process symbolized by Frederick's words.

It would be equally futile to speculate about the "end" of the process. What was the ultimate effect of Frederick's words on the people (including Frederick himself) who first heard them, on the people who read them, on you? I am not arguing that the words had any particular effect, quite the contrary. You can assert that you are already forgetting what he said. This is probably true. For the words themselves are not important. The words interact with what you already know; they help you to see the world in different ways. You reinterpret what you "knew" in the past. Your cognitive map changes. The impact of the words is a change in your map, perhaps so subtle a change that you could never consciously identify it. It is in this way that communication processes go on without end.

Let us imagine several possible "effects" of this message. One executive after hearing or reading Frederick's words may decide to institute a newsletter such as the one Frederick describes; another may "forget" the words, but some years later institute a newsletter; still another may condemn the whole idea and hold in scorn corporations who publish such newsletters. All three actions may be described, in part, as the "result" of Frederick's words. The word "result" is in quotation marks to remind us that it is not the words which do anything, rather the "effect" is the reader's interpretation of the words.

Our first hypothetical executive had certain beliefs and attitudes when he read the message. Given this map of beliefs and attitudes his interpretation of the words (that is, the relationship of the words to what he already knew) allowed him to decide that instituting a newsletter would be a reasonable way for him to accomplish certain goals. The second person had different beliefs and values—a different map. The relationship of the message to this person's beliefs and values was not such that instituting a newsletter seemed like a reasonable thing to do at the time. However, the message did result in a change in the person's map relative to the value of communicating with employees. For example, he might never have thought about the influence of wives on husbands during labor disputes in this way before. This change in his map (detailing influence of wife on husband) may have prepared him to be more receptive to the idea of a newsletter of some future date.

The third hypothetical reader may have been a woman executive. Upon reading the passage she might have been annoyed at Frederick's assumption that all union members are men who have wives who stay home and open their mail. This reader's annoyance with one of Frederick's arguments and the manner in which he stated the argument ("You would be surprised at the pressure a woman can place on her husband") generalized into a distaste for his proposal. Later, when visiting a company which has the kind of newsletter Frederick describes, she might criticize it, probably without even remembering that part of her distaste was associated with the sexist arguments one person used to explain the effectiveness of such newsletters. Messages interact with previous experiences, changing one's interpretation of the message and one's map of previous experience. When the map is changed, the interpretation of future events is likely to be affected.

CONSTRUCTING PERSONAL MEANINGS

The term "meaning" is as elusive as "process." One might say it is over-loaded with meanings. Let us examine three important usages and their implications for organizing.

One usage is a "reference" or referential meanings.[8] Some people call this "denotative meanings." These are the meanings which may be found in the dictionary. Using meaning as a reference is like pointing. "When I say 'pot,' I mean this (points to flower pot)." Or, "When I say 'pot,' I mean this (points to marijuana)." Both marijuana and flower pots are references or meanings for the word "pot."

Another usuage is intentional meaning. This is often called connotative meaning. It is more than what is "said." It is the relationship between a thought and the intentions of the thinker. For example, the two sentences, "She will arrive at 9:30" and "She will arrive thirty minutes after everyone else" may forecast the same physical event. Both have the same reference, but they express different attitudes or intentions of the speaker.

A third usage is psychological meaning or a person's response (both verbal and nonverbal) to symbols. Brodbeck uses the following illustration: "Depending upon the circumstances and manner in which it is uttered, the sound 'fire' for instance may mean to Jones either danger or warmth."[9] Psychological meaning changes with a person's knowledge of how a word is used, his perception of the intentions of the person who displayed the symbol, and other circumstances of the context. Another word for psychological meaning is interpretation. The same words have different interpretations to each person in the same context; words have different interpretations to the same person in different contexts. Interpretative meaning like intentional meaning is relative. It is dependent upon circumstance and upon the cognitive map of the interpreter.

For any symbol we can analyze these three levels of meaning. At level one, we can ask to what do the symbols themselves refer. This is the reference meaning. A paycheck is a symbolic message. At level one, we can observe that a particular paycheck can be cashed for $152.00. The paycheck symbolizes the cash and ultimately what may be purchased with the cash. Level one meanings are not very personal.

At level two we must determine the source of the message. We know from the discussion in the previous section that there is no one source for any message. If we are analyzing a paycheck as a message, we may decide that the source-of-interest is the supervisor who sets the hourly rate and allocates overtime. We then observe an event: the paycheck is higher than last week's. Also, the supervisor commented on the worker's excellent performance and said that she deserved a raise. We surmise that the supervisor's intention was to reward the worker. Thus "you're a good worker" is the intended meaning. Intended meanings are personal.

At level three, we can look at the response to the symbol, the psychological meanings. The responder-of-interest in this example is the worker. She may smile. She may find the message to be ego gratifying. She may respond by being "motivated" to do better work to receive even more such ego-gratifying messages. But what if the raise was not as large as she expected? She may be disappointed. She may work even harder to get the usage she feels she deserves. Or she may decide that effort is not really rewarded, so why work hard anyway. She will respond somehow to the "message." The message will have a personal meaning for her.

Whatever her behavioral response, it will be taken as a message by the supervisor. The supervisor may interpret the worker's behavior as an indication that he did the "right thing" in raising her salary. Or he may decide that after she got her raise she began to slough off. The worker's actions interpreted through the supervisor's cognitive map will provide the supervisor with the meaning of his original actions. He will decide whether his action in raising her salary was wise or not.

In this example we can see that because there are different levels of meaning, meaning is both personal and non-personal. A "non personal" meaning is approximately the same from person to person and time to time. "Personal" meaning is different from person to person and time to time. Level one or referent meanings are not particularly personal. Any bank would cash the check and give the worker the same amount of money. Almost anybody recognizes the same referent meaning for a $152.00 check. The meaning is nonpersonal because (1) the cash is observable and (2) there is widespread consensus in this culture on what a paycheck refers to. Dictionaries are possible because people agree to use certain terms to refer to certain things. When the "things" cannot be observed—like "heaven," "anxiety," "superior"—the meaning is more personal. Still, there is a large consensus about the level one meaning of these terms.

Intentional and interpretive meanings are always personal. They vary from person to person and time to time. They can never be put into a dictionary. They include some of the most important "meanings" in our world. When another person says, "I love you," we do not run to the dictionary to look up the meaning of what is said. Even if we know the dictionary meaning, we do not assume that we "know" what the other person means. Instead, we look beyond the symbols to the other person's meanings. We try to figure out what the other person intends when he says, "I love you." What kind of commitment is he symbolizing with those words? Is he sincere? What does he expect from me?

When we examined the Frederick quotation in the previous section we extrapolated some imaginary "systems" in which the quotation might have been a "message." We observed that the intentional and interpreted meaning of the words was different in each system. Level one or reference meaning stayed approximately the same, but intentional and interpretive meaning varied with the intentions of source and receiver. The meaning of any symbol is relative to other parts of the system which provides the context of the symbol. The intentions of sources and receivers are important parts.

Expectations and Meaning

Another important determinant of personal meaning is expectations of communicators. If the worker in the previous example expected a twenty-dollar increase and received only a fifteen-dollar increase, she was probably disappointed. Her prior expectations influenced her interpretation of the message. Researchers have found systematic evidence of the influence of expectations on how people construct personal meaning.

In one study, subjects were asked to evaluate how "deserving of reward" a person was. The subjects in the study were told that after being robbed in the elevator of a parking garage, the person took the elevator to the second floor, watched the thief get into his car, and copied the license number so that the thief was soon apprehended. When the person was identified as a woman, the number of subjects who thought the actions deserved reward was much greater than when the person was identified as a man. The researcher's explanation is that such actions are "expected" of males, but not of females. Therefore, the meaning of the actions is different when they are attributed to females. When people act in an unexpected and positive way, we find their behavior more positive, than if we do expect it. Expectations as elements of our cognitive maps influence how we construct meanings.

Retrospection and Meaning

Meanings must be "personal" because the action of constructing meaning is "retrospective."[10] Karl Weick compares the process of constructing meaning to "a cone of light that spreads backwards from a particular present." He says:

> This light will give definition and contours to portions of lived experience. Since the cone starts in the present, whatever, the ego's attitude or mood is at that moment, the identical mood will carry over to the backward glance. The attitude of the ego toward the ongoing activity determines its attitude toward the past. . . . The meaning, in other words, is the kind of attention directed to the past. . . . Meaning is not something apart from attention, something that exists alongside or above the act of attention for eventual attachment. Instead, the meaning of anything is the way it is attended to and nothing else.[11]

The metaphor of the light indicates the nature of meaning as relative because objects appear differently depending on its direction and intensity. Meanings are different from the perspective of a particular here and now. When we attend to events, we see them as wholes; we look at events as if we know what the outcomes are. We look back and construct meaning retrospectively. Two companies can embark on similar expansion programs. One expansion program leads to more jobs, a better product, and increased earnings. The other leads to financial ruin. The "meaning" of expansion was significantly different in the two instances because the meaning is seen in relation to the outcome of the action.

The construction of meaning is a process, however, and processes do not have beginnings or ends. The "ultimate" result or end can never be known. The company which expanded "successfully" may have been manufacturing explosives. One of the new installations may explode, killing 2,000 people. Members of Congress may be enraged and pass new legislation regulating the manufacturing of explosives and thus saving an estimated 8,000 lives, but the new regulations may force many factories to close down, creating a shortage of explosives used in mining coal. Soon a coal shortage would result in high coal prices. The chain of "resulting" events would go on endlessly.

To say that a person constructs meaning retrospectively means that he or she looks at events from a particular here and now with a particular cognitive map of experiences, expectations, and intentions. Events are seen in relationship to one another. The events included in the meaningful configuration will vary from time to time as other outcomes become apparent, but at any given moment, the process of attending to events, recreating the meaning of those events, involves looking at them as part of a configuration presumed to be complete. Our expectations and intentions allow us to "fill in" the future consequences of actions.

The process of constructing meaning for us as individuals involves interpreting "incoming" symbolic messages. This interpreting process is accomplished with the use of our cognitive maps—our knowledge of what sorts of "things" make up the world, how they operate, and how they relate to one another. The act of interpreting constantly changes the map. The map contains not only our personal record of our past, it also contains our expectations about the future. We interpret the meaning of present events in terms of our fantasies about the future we expect.

CONSTRUCTING CONSENSUS

No two people have identical cognitive maps. No two people can stand in the same place in time and space and thus have identical "perspectives" on the world. Intentional and interpretational meanings must be personal, but obviously people do "understand" one another. Obviously people manage to coordinate their activities. To achieve coordination, meanings must transcend the level of the individual person, but identical meanings are not necessary. Somehow people must learn to "construct meanings together" or construct consensus.

Surprisingly, there has not been very much systematic investigation of how people construct meaning together. Hastorf, Schneider, and Polefka observe that:

> Social psychologists have paid considerable attention to the coordination of behavior but remarkably little to the coordination of meaning. We now know a great deal about how two persons can come to interact and guide each other's behavior so as to accomplish a common task. We do not know nearly enough about how they come to share a common perception of the world. We need to know more about how people get to know one another; *such knowledge would entail the matching of one person's perception of another with the other's perception of himself.*[12]

In the closing part of their statement, they suggest the key concept in understanding the nature of "consensus" or "organizational intelligence." Consensus does not refer to different people all having identical meanings or maps. It is not really "common meanings" we need to understand. Rather, what is required for coordination of meanings is that people understand one another's meanings.

Scheff[13] has described levels of consensus in social systems. Level one is "agreement." At this level people have fairly identical meanings. Person A and person B agree that the sun rises every morning and that the job assigned to person B is "hard." Person A and person B may not *agree* that A should take over some of B's duties, however. On this issue they do not have level one consensus.

Consensus Through Coorientation

A more sophisticated level of consensus, the one referred to in the quotation above, Scheff calls "understanding." A and B have consensus when A is able to understand B's ideas. For example, A knows that B thinks his work is hard because it involves a great exertion of physical effort. B knows that A thinks B's work is not so hard as it would be if it involved making critical decisions.

Theodore Newcomb[14] suggested the term "coorientation" to refer to this process of developing consensus through communication. A is "orienting" his attention both to B and to a subject of discussion X (in this case B's job). At the same time B is "orienting" his attention both to A and to X. Newcomb's schematic representation of this communication process is shown in Figure 2.1.

The process of coorientation takes place when two (or more) people are communicating and each is trying to understand the subject of this discussion as the other person sees it. George Herbert Mead has described a similar process. He called it "imaginatively taking the role of the other."

FIGURE 2.1
Newcomb's Representation of Coorientation

Although I have defined coorientation as taking place when people are "communicating" there are times when we are coorienting with another without simultaneously exchanging messages with them. Such cases might be called imaginatively coorienting. Suppose, for example, that I have been invited to attend a week-long conference in another state. In order to attend, I must be away from home and my classes for a week. In order to decide whether to attend, I must consider not only my own wishes, but also several people whose lives coordinate with mine—my department head, my students, my family.

I have to consider what "message" my going would be for them. Would my department head, for example, interpret my actions as "professional" (I am leaving home for a week to attend to professional business) or will he see it as "unprofessional" (I am deserting my classroom duties for a week of semivacation)? Having observed him respond to similar situations in the past, I can make some informed guesses about how he would respond. (I might also ask him directly. Note, however, that the act of asking will be a message. He might interpret my asking as a sign of lack of initiative.) I have some general expectations about how he will act. I am attempting to orient myself toward the symbolic act of attending a conference as I believe he will orient himself toward that act. The objective is to interpret an act or symbol as nearly as possible to the way the other will interpret it. Past exchanges of messages permit some accuracy in this imagining the other's interpretation.

Coorientation is a learning process. Through watching another's responses, we pick up cues to patterns of responses. The more contact we have with another, the more opportunities for incorrect expectations of that person to be disclosed and corrected. For example, when a new manager comes on the job, there is considerable uncertainty about how he is likely to interpret events. Only after the both managers and subordinates have had an opportunity to talk and to observe one another, do they begin to feel certain about how the other may respond to new situations.

The consensus which is necessary for coordination is not simple agreement. Sometimes that is necessary or helpful, sometimes it is not.

Rather, it is understanding by one person of another's meanings. George Kelley emphasizes this point:

> In order to play a constructive role in relationship to another person one must not only, in some measure, see eye to eye with him but must, in some measure, have an acceptance of him and of his way of seeing things. . . . The person who is to play a constructive role in a social process with another person need not so much construe things as the other person does as *he must effectively construe the other person's outlook.* . . . In order for people to get along harmoniously with each other, each must have some understanding of the other. This is different from saying that each must understand things in the same way as the other.[15]

Kelley's point here is that in order to coordinate activities ("play a constructive role in relationship to another person") each individual's cognitive map must include a representation of the map of the other person, even though that representation may be "minimal, fragmentary, or misguided."[16] This is different from having a map which is identical or similar to the other. Indeed, Kelley points out that if maps are too similar coordination may be impossible. If a psychotherapist identifies too closely with a client, the two will not be able to accomplish a therapeutic relationship. The therapist must be able to subsume the map of the client within his or her own map. He must "understand" the map of the client, but must use his own map to guide his behavior.

Equivalent Meanings

I shall use the term "equivalence" to refer to that kind of consensus or understanding which is required for coordination. The term equivalence comes from the anthropologist Anthony F. C. Wallace. Wallace describes "equivalent meanings" as the minimal requirements for cooperation. He states that through a learning process "individuals learn to predict one another's behaviors." People develop "a set of mutually equivalent (not necessarily identical) learned meanings for stimuli (symbols) which are continuously available during all their transactions, as statements of the boundaries and conditions of their mutual behavior."[17]

Let us consider an example to unravel Wallace's terminology. Suppose I approach you, a stranger in the supermarket, hand you a piece of paper and chalk, and say, "Copy this on the board." I am likely to get only a puzzled look. You will not understand my intentions and, therefore, you can not understand the event. If you are my teaching assistant and I hand you the chalk and use the same words, you will probably do as I intend. You will know what I expect of you. A piece of chalk is not an object that people commonly pass around in the supermarket. In Wallace's terms, it is not "continuously available" during supermarket transactions. It is not recognized as relevant to the "boundaries" or "mutual behavior" of supermarket shoppers. Shoppers have not had the opportunity to learn what one would do with a piece of chalk in a supermarket. A shopper would have no way to represent my map of what to do with chalk in a supermarket.

In analyzing communication and organizing, one needs to look at the stimuli or the symbols which members need to understand to do their work. Learning to coordinate, in part, requires learning what to do with these "props." We can spot a new cashier easily because she or he is somewhat clumsy in handling the merchandise and the cash register. New cashiers do not know whom to ask for help. They have not yet learned the vocabulary or code which facilitates rapid handling of routine situations. Experienced cashiers flip on the P. A. and call out, "Check on two." Other people respond to the summons. The cashier and the responder have equivalent meanings for the symbol "Check on two."

Organizational Intelligence

"Organizational intelligence" is the set of equivalent meanings for events and objects which are "continuously available" to organizational members. Communication as organizing is the process by which this equivalence is developed and changed. Organizational members are constantly answering such (usually) unstated questions as:

What do I need to know? How am I going to find out? How can I "share" what I know?[18]

Stated like this, "knowing" seems to be the problem of individuals. But the activities of individuals as they seek answers to these questions constitute communication which produces organizational intelligence. In relatively certain or routine environments, the answers to such questions are largely taken-for-granted. Supermarket clerks "learn" fast. In highly uncertain environments, such questions are constantly asked; they are asked more explicitly. One feature of the organizational intelligence, therefore, is the extent to which people must devote their energies to making sense—developing a consensus about—what is going on and why.

Organizing is accomplished as people construct consensus. This consensus need not be "agreement." Rather, it is a state of equivalence in which people understand how one other is likely to interpret events and objects typically found in their common environment. Each person is able to represent the map of another in his own cognitive map. The process of learning another's map is called "coorientation." Equivalent meanings constitute consensus or organizational intelligence.

METACOMMUNICATION

Intelligence and integration functions of communication are difficult to keep separated in a discussion of organizing because informative and integrative communications occur simultaneously. Every act of communication contains both a claim about the world or "content" (intelligence function) and a claim about the relationship between sender and receiver (integrative function). Communication theorists Watzlawick, Bevin, and Jackson explain that communication occurs in two dimensions. The content dimension is a "report"; the relationship dimension is a "command." The command dimension, in effect, is a claim that the relationship is of a particular kind. It commands that the relationship be viewed in a certain way and that people behave accordingly. According to Watzlawick, Bevin, and Jackson:

> All such relationship statements are about one or several of the following assertions: 'This is how I see myself . . . this is how I see you . . . this is how I see you seeing me . . .' and so forth in theoretically infinite regress. Thus, for instance, the message, 'It is important to release the clutch gradually and smoothly' and 'Just let the clutch go, it'll ruin the transmission in no time' have approximately the same information content, but they obviously define very different relationships."[19]

Informative and integrative functions of communication are related because content derives meaning from the relationships which provide their context and the content of communication defines the relationship. Take, for example, the words, "Good morning, may I help you?" A phrase such as this is the stock-in-trade of the telephone receptionist. Such a phrase is expected behavior. We expect to hear such a greeting when we phone a corporation. If we heard instead, "Hello, what do you want?" The content would be the same, but our interpretation of the situation would be quite different because the message defines a different relationship. Every message simultaneously contains a claim about the "world" and about the relationship among the communicators.

The "report" or claim about relationships dimension is often called "metacommunication." The prefix "meta" signifies "about." Hence, "metacommunication" refers to communication about communication. Metacommunication is comprised of all those cues which tell us how the other person views the relationship and signals us how to interpret the content of the message. Sometimes we signal to others how to interpret our communication by making aside comments such as, "I'm only kidding." Usually, however, metacommunication occurs simultaneously with report. Our choice of words is an important way in which we communicate to others information about relationship. For example, note the choice of words: "I told you never to do that, Poopsie." We all have pet phrases which signal to others whether we are pleased or unhappy.

Nonverbal communication is more important than words as a means of metacommunication. By nonverbal I mean *all* symbols other than words. Silence, for example, can be nonverbal communication. The inflection of spoken words is also a form of nonverbal communication. A "sarcastic tone of voice" is often a telling signal of the relationship. Eye contact, body position, and gestures are indications of relationship. Such cues help us to interpret the intentional meaning of messages. Proxemics, or the physical stance of one person vis à vis another person, helps communicators to express and interpret their relationship to one another. Clothing and physical surroundings help people to define their relationships and therefore interpret the meaning of message content. The comment, "You are sick," may be interpreted as an insult. It is not an insulting comment if the metacommunicational clues which accompany the message content says, "I am a doctor; you are a patient; this is medical information."

SUMMARY

Communication is a process of constructing meaning. As such communication has several inevitable properties:

1. Communication is dynamic; meanings are constantly changing.
2. Communication is relative; meanings are constructed only in relationship to certain other factors in a system as that system.
3. Communication is continuous; meanings are created in interaction with cognitive maps. By affecting maps their effects have no decisive "end."
4. Communication is somewhat different for messages "sources" and "receivers." Meanings occur at the level of intention and interpretation as well as simply at the level of reference.
5. Communication is dependent on expectations. Meanings are relative to the expectancies of communicators. People's actions tend to confirm their expectations.

6. Communication involves retrospection. People construe events as completed wholes, filling in unknown events with expected events in order to interpret meaning.
7. Communication is not entirely personal. It is consensus seeking.
8. Communication is the process of learning. People learn to represent the cognitive maps of others in their own maps.
9. Communication is a process of knowing. Through communication, people make sense of events and objects necessary for collective work.
10. Communication has both report and command dimensions. These two dimensions function simultaneously to create organizational intelligence and integration.

APPLICATION: *Diagnosing Problems with Meaning*

This is the first of five special sections which describe applications of theoretical content. Applications sections are also found at the end of chapters 4, 5, 6, 7, and 8. The chapters describe communication; the applications sections at the end of the chapters explain how one might use the information. Each application section describes how one might do something to improve organizational communication.

The subject of this chapter has been the creation of meaning. Ten principles or properties of communication have been described; examples of these principles have been given. Yet, no doubt, the principles remain rather vague. A reasonable question to ask is, "So what?" These properties are important because they make certain kinds of communication problems inevitable. These problems may be minimized so that they do not severely affect the functioning of the system, but they cannot be absolutely avoided. Those who seek to improve organizational communication must assess the extent to which the problems plague organizational functioning and then devise strategies or methods for minimizing undesirable consequences. The first step in assessing consequences and devising strategies is diagnosing or recognizing the problem.

In this section I describe six problems with meaning found in organizations: self-fulfilling prophecy, multiple systems, serial transmission, no-exit, concealed distortion, and information overload. The objective is to provide the reader with some fairly concrete categories for seeing the process by which meaning is created in organizations and for diagnosing when the process needs to be changed.

Self-Fulfilling Prophecy Problems

A self-fulfilling prophecy occurs when person A expects person B to behave in manner X. A "sees" B behaving like X and acts as if B is doing X. B is treated as if he is doing X. B learns to do X because others expect that kind of behavior from him. Self-fulfilling prophecies perpetuate stereotypes. When a group of people is labeled "lazy," others treat them as if they are lazy. They learn to be lazy, thus "fulfilling" the expectation. Self-fulfilling prophecies of some kind are inevitable because communication is dependent upon expectations.

Douglas McGregor uses the notion of self-fulfilling prophecy to explain Theory X and Theory Y approaches to managerial style. A manager who assumes that workers are lazy and must be controlled treats his subordinates accordingly. They learn to act as their supervisor expects. Their actions confirm the supervisor's expectations. A manager who assumes that subordinates are self-motivated and work best when permitted independence may similarly encourage independence and self-motivation by workers.

In diagnosing self-fulfilling prophecies from a communication perspective one asks such questions as: (1) What does person (or group) A expect of person (or group) B? (2) With what actions does A think he communicates these expectations? (What are the messages which symbolize the expectations?) (3) What does B think A expects of him or her? (4) What are the actions which B believes to be indications of A's expectations? (5) Are the actions identified in question 2 the same as those identified in question 4? (6) With what actions does B respond to A's expectations? (7) Who are the other people whose expectations influence B? (8) How consistent are expectations of these other people with A's expectations? (9) What actions by B does A think to be important to understanding "what kind of person" B is? These nine questions are only suggestive. Their purpose is to indicate what to look for to determine if there is a self-fulfilling prophecy problem. The questions are centered around mutual perceptions of "person A" and "person B." The analyst using such questions is attempting to understand how the people see each other and how their expectations are related to their actions.

The process of coorientation is a useful strategy for overcoming an undesirable self-fulfilling prophecy. Suppose that a supervisor is dissatisfied with certain actions. The supervisor interprets the actions as incompetence and treats the subordinate as if he is incompetent. (See Figure 4.2 for a more detailed illustration of this point.) Both people are locked into a vicious circle until they can achieve some equivalent meanings for the actions. By each person's talking about what the *actions mean to him, they can learn to take into account the other person's interpretation. There may still be disagreement, but there is increased opportunity for productive coordination.*

Multiple Systems Problems

Whenever we communicate, we adapt what we say to a particular system of receivers and contexts. The intended audience may be as large and undifferentiated as prime time TV viewers or as small and intimate as a lover. We may plan our words to be interpreted in a particular system. What happens when another audience in another "system" sees and hears the message? The interpretation of this second audience is unlikely to be the same as the interpretation of the first audience. I noted earlier that Frederick's words were given different interpretations in each system. As communicators we must continually risk having our messages interpreted by people in different systems.

Communication in large organizations is particularly susceptible to multiple systems. The secretary who types a letter about a forthcoming reorganization of the company is not really part of the system the executive had in mind when the letter was dictated. That secretary will interpret the meaning of the letter differently than the executive to whom it was written. His or her own expectations and intentions will influence the interpretation of the words. The person who wrote the letter adapted the wording to the expectations and intentions of the intended audience. The typists' interpretation can be quite different from the intended interpretation.

When it is impossible to keep messages within a single system—such as when a message is being typed or transmitted—it is useful to bring the outsiders in. This may be done by attempts to provide appropriate contexts for clerks and messengers. Certainly, the union in the Frederick example needed to provide background to the workers and their families.

At the beginning of the Vietnam peace talks nonparticipants in the conference were enraged that people were dying in the war while negotiators squabbled over the shape of the table. After all, a table is a table, isn't it? A table is not simply a table when it acts symbolically as a message in a communication system. The shape of the table, and more particularly how delegates were arranged around the table, symbolized who was to be considered a "legitimate" delegate whose national interests were at stake during the negotiations. The shape of the table had a particular intentional meaning in the negotiators' system. There was no such thing as a "neutral" shape for the table. Every shape communicated some message about how the delegates had a right to be treated, but the symbolic shape of the table was symbolic only in the diplomatic system. For people outside the system who were unaccustomed to diplomatic protocol, the squabbling was "nonsense."

Frederick, in the quotation in the first section, illustrates sending a message to an unintended system as a communicative strategy. The Daily Negotiation Digest takes a message from one system—it prints words which were originally spoken during labor-management negotiation sessions—and "sends the message" into another communication system—the worker's family. Messages about "going out on strike for half a cent an hour," "vested rights," "superseniority for the grievance committeeman," are used with one kind of intention in the bargaining system. Superseniority for the grievance committeeman may be a demand in response to what the union perceives as covert harassment against officials of the union. They may make the demand because of their belief that it is necessary for the continued effective functioning of the union. The intent is to benefit the worker, though indirectly. However, the worker's family has no experience with which to understand the union's perspective on the issue. Family members generally do not have sufficient information to perceive the union's intent. Moreover, the values of family members are concerned, naturally, with more immediate problems such as keeping the pay check coming in regularly so that the mortgage can be paid.

In analyzing possible multiple systems problems, the following kinds of questions might be asked:

(1) How did the source "map" the intended system of the message?
(2) What special adaptations to this system does the message reflect? Special vocabulary? Knowledge of past events?
(3) What expectations and intentions might lead people in another system to interpret the message differently from the intended audience?

The theme of these questions is the relationship between elements of a system as they are mapped by people in the system.

The multiple systems problem is the reason why it makes good sense to keep many meetings closed. The Constitutional Convention is an illustration of a group of people who understood that they were engaged in a communication process in which words would be used and meanings attached to those words which people who were not part of their system could easily misinterpret. Therefore, they insisted upon closed meetings.

Serial Transmission Problems

Serial transmission problems occur when the "same" message is transmitted through several intermediate people. The children's game

"Telephone" is serial transmission. One person whispers a statement into the first child's ear. He then whispers what he thought he heard to the next person. She whispers what she heard to the next, and so forth. The last person announces what she heard, and everybody laughs at how the message changed.

Suppose that the typist in the example above told a friend in the shipping department about what she heard. The shipping inspector told a stock clerk, who told a truck driver. As in the game "Telephone," the "message" is less like the original message each time it is told. In multiple systems problems, the words or symbols remain the same but the interpretation changes with each new audience.

In serial transmission, each audience becomes a message source who sends the message in a slightly different form. The typist read the same words the executive intended for another system. But when the typist told the shipping inspector, the words were not identical to those in the letter. The shipping clerk changed the words somewhat, and so forth. The news of a forthcoming organizational change became a "rumor" as news of it got passed around. Serial transmission problems of some kind are inevitable when there are more than two people involved.

The standard "remedy" for serial transmission problems is to cut down the number of points at which a message must be reinterpreted. Sometimes it is possible to do this. Suppose, for example, a customer representative takes a phone message of a complaint and transmits that to an area representative who, in turn, sends it to the service department. Depending on the function of the second step, it might be possible to eliminate that step and have complaints go directly to service. But there may be some worthwhile organizational function of that step in the communication network. In chapter 9 I describe in more detail the process of sending messages across intraorganizational boundaries. I present some ways of designing information flow to curtail the undesirable problems which may be associated with serial transmission.

No-Exit Problems

No Exit is a play by Jean Paul Sartre. There are three characters in a room with no exit. As the play progresses, the audience realizes that each character is dead and that they have been condemned to be in this room for eternity. The room is hell because they must be constantly in one another's presence. They cannot not communicate with one another. The play is about the binds which we get into with other people and the misery of not being able to escape communication, in this case, cruel communication with others. No-exit problems in organizations appear because any behavior is potentially communicative.

I know one man who suffered considerable psychological pain from his interpretation of company actions. He had been with an expanding gypsum manufacturing company only a few months when he received a general announcement to vacate his office because the building was to be remodeled. He interpreted the message as the first sign that he was about to be fired. He thought the message was a communication about the quality of his work. He stewed a week and still had not heard from his supervisor. He was about to quit, rather than wait to be fired. He finally decided to confront his supervisor about the matter. The supervisor was shocked that my friend thought he was about to be fired. Instead, he was to be in charge of the remodeling. My friend was so pleased with himself that he was almost out the door before he remembered about his office. The supervisor told him to design and build his own office! The point here is that any action may be taken to mean something quite different than what was intended. Any action may be taken as communicative.

No symbol is simply "neutral." Of course, some messages appear to have no strong emotional implications. "I am going to get a drink" apparently means no more than that the speaker intends to secure and imbibe some H_2O. Suppose, however, that two people are engaged in a heated argument and one says, "I am going to get a drink of water" and leaves. The communication here is not "neutral" at all. The message may be interpreted as denying the importance of the conversation and hence of the other person; it will be taken as a command about the relationship. One claims the right to terminate the conversation despite the fact that the other is not ready to stop.

The meaning of the words does not lie in the words themselves, certainly not in the dictionary meaning of the words. Rather, it lies as much in the metacommunication. We "trap" each other because we interpret actions as indicators of relationships. Even "no action" (no content) indicates relationship. No-exit problems are inevitable because all communication has a "command" dimension.

Recognizing no-exit situations is the first step toward escaping the undesirable consequences of such situations. Again coorientation is the key. If two people can see how they are trapping one another with symbols each thinks to be harmless, then they can find other symbols or at least qualify how they are interpreting the symbols in light of what they know of the other's intentions.

Concealed Distortion Problems

It should be clear from the discussion of meanings that all messages are "distorted." There are no perfectly objective facts. Rather, facts are relative to the people constructing and interpreting messages and to the *consensus state the people develop. Concealed distortion problems may arise when people proclaim that their messages represent "facts."*

Frederick makes such a claim in the quotation discussed earlier. Recall that Frederick stated: "This digest is written by the company, disclosing what has happened during the day's negotiations. Its purpose is to inform the employees on a factual basis. We try not to slant it in our favor, as it is a piece of information we are sending out. . . . Facts must not be distorted." Frederick asserts that the newsletter is not persuasion; it is a "piece of information" which is not slanted. However, bear in mind that the newsletter is a digest; *this means that it is a selection from what has happened during the negotiations.*

Those people who make the selections are representatives of the company. The words which are selected are chosen by people who have individual cognitive maps and consensus states. This is always true in any selection process. Researchers who want to be sure that they have an "unbiased" sample of material—for example, a sample of material to be subjected to intensive quality control tests—use a predetermined, random schedule for selecting. If Frederick had used a random schedule to select material for the Digest, *he would have started with transcripts of all the words said during the negotiations. These transcriptions might be a hundred pages per hour. Then he might abstract every twenty-third sentence and print these in the digest without comment. Of course, the digest would be absolutely incomprehensible to anyone.*

Even this "random selection" reflects an intentional decision to limit the digest to verbal comments only. Often in bargaining situations it is what is not said and what is said through nonverbal symbols which is most important in determining the outcome of negotiation. Even a random schedule for selecting messages, then, is a kind of distortion because it reflects a certain perspective.

It is clear that Frederick could not use a "random schedule" for selecting materials to include in the Digest. *Instead, he included those remarks which he believed reflected the "facts." His choice was thus purposeful or intentional. He included those comments which were facts to him. Union officials could insist that their newsletter also presented facts though they represented a different viewpoint. Any display of symbols which we recognize as communicative is produced with some intention. When others interpret symbols—or when we interpret our own symbols—the interpretation is an intentional one.*

If we are motivated to be "objective" we establish certain decision rules for selecting materials and for interpreting the meaning of the materials we have selected. Scientists attempt to establish such rules (for example, random selection) not to make selection and interpretation less "biased" but to make the bias visible to others. When the rules for selecting and interpreting messages are observable, they may be replicated by others; they are not idiosyncratic to particular individuals. Interpretations become less relative in the sense that the interpretations which a person gives to a message may be similar to the interpretations another gives to the same symbols because the two people are using the same rules for interpreting.

Messages which appear to be unbiased "information" rather than frankly biased persuasion may lead people to believe that the information is the fact. In other words, when a message appears to be fact, people may forget that its information is relative and that the message reflects the values and intentions of the source. The situation is probably most deplorable when high-level decision makers and even the scientists themselves forget the relativity of information. The information system of the California criminal justice system illustrates how easily this can happen and how undesirable the consequences may be.[20]

The purpose of the information system was to link "together various agencies of criminal justice" and to permit "evaluating program and system effectiveness through collection, storage, and processing of appropriate data." The system, of course, was based on a definition of crime. In defining "crime" the engineers who developed the system laid down the important selection rule about which acts were to be recorded and stored in the system as "crimes" and which were to be ignored. They chose to define crime as offenses which result in convictions. They calculated their statistics about amount of crime on the basis of convicted offenders. The ultimate objective of the criminal justice system, of course, is to prevent crime. Therefore, the engineers wanted to design an information system to assist in identifying "criminal characteristics." They devised a "neo-Lombrosian"[21] taxonomy for classifying the characteristics of criminals. Data on the sex, age, ethnicity, education, employment status, and geographical location of inhabitants of California penal institutions were fed into the information system. On the basis of analysis of this information, the scientists concluded that there are criminal characteristics which set offenders apart from the population at large. The "major portion of the offenders was found to be male, between 14 and 29 years of age, Negro or Mexican-American, poorly educated, unemployed, and from heavily-populated, low-income geographic areas."

These so-called "criminal characteristics" were isolated as the result of the particular biases of those who selected the information to be fed into the system. Other authorities estimate that arrests are made for only about 25 percent of the known crimes. Thus, the "criminal characteristics" may not be the characteristics of all criminals; they are rather summary descriptions of those who get caught. Hoos observes that what was "really identified in their study was the shared haplessness that *renders certain groups under certain conditions more susceptible to the embrace of the law than others."*

When "criminal characteristics" based on descriptions of arrested offenders become "information" used in making decisions about how to deploy law enforcement officers and, more critically, when they are proclaimed as "indicators of the propensity for a life of crime," the information becomes a self-fulfilling prophesy. There are more police in the ghetto, and therefore, there are more arrests. When the arrest records are examined, they confirm the expectation that more crime will occur in the ghetto. There is more crime because there were more arrests. Since the poorly educated, low-income offenders receive less capable legal defense, they are more often convicted. Their characteristics are entered into the information system which informs later decision making.

Crime is what is interpreted as crime. Crime statistics reflect the way police officers define or construct the meaning of crime—the way they respond to actions by labeling some as "criminal" and others as "noncriminal." Just as criminal justice information systems are dependent upon the judgments of those who designed them and those who feed them information, any information is based upon human interpretations. Information cannot be "objective" or unbiased because it necessarily reflects intentions and values. Meaning is relative to the intentions, values, and perspectives of people who construct it.

In large organizations—such as the state government of California—there need to be regular procedures for collecting and storing information. Management information systems (M.I.S.) is the term usually applied to these procedures. M.I.S. can easily conceal distortion of information. The information stored represents a small proportion of that available to the "eyes and ears" of an organization.

The critical question to be asked of a management information system or any system for collecting and storing "facts" is how these "facts" are used. Do the people who use them as the basis of their actions appreciate the particular "biases" of the information they are using? Does the system include a variety of ways of defining information so that the biases of one way may be compensated by another?

Information Overload Problems

In order to compensate for problems such as serial transmission and concealed distortion, information collectors typically use "redundancy"—more and more messages which say the same thing. The hope is that if the message is repeated enough with enough detail, it will be interpreted as intended.

In one large oil company the main office was receiving two tons of memo paper every day.[22]   Evidently, the assumption here was that more messages will result in more meaning. When more messages are substituted for more meaning, the reason is likely to be poorer coordination.

The Darnell Institute for Business Research surveyed the time 3000 executives spent reading and answering mail. They found an average of two to three hours a day, which adds up to four months a year.[23] We may see here evidence that in an attempt to know enough to manage, managers get stuck just keeping up with what there is to know. The result is "information overload."

Information overload problems result from the consensus-seeking nature of communication and from the fallacy of thinking that if a person is "told" (a message is transmitted to him) then he "knows" (his cognitive map has been affected). Unlike the problems discussed above, information overload is potentially avoidable. Some people may indeed be "underloaded"; they may not receive the messages they need to do their job (though they probably receive too many irrelevant messages.)

There may be nothing in the nature of the communication process itself which makes information overload inevitable, but there is a good deal of evidence that it suggests the universal condition of executives, however. Perhaps our social systems may be designed so that they require more "knowing" at the top levels of a hierarchy than is possible given the properties of communication discussed here. The subject of designing social systems according to information needed for decision making is discussed in chapter 9.

ENDNOTES

1. George A. Miller, Eugene Halanter, and Karl H. Pribram, *Plans and the Structure of Behavior* (New York: Holt, Rinehart, and Winston, 1960), p. 7.

2. Edward Tolman, as quoted by Miller et al., *Plans and the Structure of Behavior*, p. 8.

3. Fritz Heider and M. Simmel, "An Experimental Study of Apparent Behavior," *American Journal of Psychology* 57 (1944): 243–259.

4. George Kelley, *A Theory of Personality* (New York: W. W. Norton, 1963), pp. 8–9.

5. David Berlo, *The Process of Communication* (New York: Holt, Rinehart, and Winston, 1960), p. 24.

6. R. L. Frederick, "How to Keep Your Employees Informed," in Charles W. Redding and George A. Sanborn, eds., *Business and Industrial Communication* (New York: Harper & Row, 1964): 242–247.

7. W. Charles Redding and George A. Sanborn, *Business and Industrial Communication* (New York: Harper & Row, 1964).

8. May Brodbeck, "Meaning and Action," in May Brodbeck, ed., *Readings in the Philosophy of Social Science* (New York: Macmillan, Inc.), pp. 60–66.

9. Ibid., p. 65.

10. Alfred Schutz, *Phenomenology of the Social World* (Evanston, Ill.: Northwestern University Press, 1967).

11. Karl Weick, *The Social Psychology of Organizing* (Reading, Mass.: Addison-Wesley, 1969), p. 67.

12. Albert H. Hostorf et al., *Person Perception* (Reading, Mass.: Addison-Wesley, 1970), italics added.

13. T. Scheff, "Toward a Sociological Model of Consensus," *American Sociological Review* 32 (1967): 32–46.

14. Theodore Newcomb, "An Approach to the Study of Communication," *Psychological Review* 60 (1953): 393–403.

15. Kelley, *A Theory of Personality*, pp. 95–99.

16. Ibid., 98.

17. Anthony F. C. Wallace, "The Psychic Unity of Human Groups," in B. Kaplan, ed., *Studying Personality Cross-Culturally* (Evanston, Ill.: Row, Peterson, 1961), pp. 139–140.

18. This analysis was suggested by Thomas Benson, personal conversation, Feb. 26, 1976.

19. Paul Watzlawick, Janet H. Beavin, and D. C. Jackson, *The Pragmatics of Human Communication* (New York: W. W. Norton & Co., Inc., 1967), p. 52.

20. See example from Ida Hoos, *Systems Analysis and Public Policy* (Berkeley, Calif.: University of California Press, 1972), p. 210ff.

21. Cesare Lombroso, a nineteenth century criminologist, expounded the theory that criminality was a kind of atavism, a throwback to ancestors, and that the inherited traits were identifiable and distinguishable. Recognition of them was, to him, a central factor in controlling crime. See Hoos, *Systems Analysis and Public Policy*, p. 210ff.

22. Eric Webster, "Memo Monia," *Management Review* (September 1967).

23. R. Alec MacKenzie, *The Time Trap* (New York: American Management Association, 1972), p. 72.

CHAPTER
3

Communication and Expectations

Expectations and Integration
Accomplishing Expectations
Interpreting Integrative Patterns
Message Form: Displays and Documents
Coordination Formats
Contingencies and Coordination Formats

Mr. Bono, a mass observer, is making his rounds Tuesday morning, the day for ringing doorbells, assessing tithes, leaving notes for solicitors, and assisting those caught in chancery. A full day's work! Now he calls on Mrs. Dorfman, Apt. 1 in a modest duplex.

"Ring," says his finger.

"Yes?" replies Mrs. Dorfman.

Mr. Bono stands poised and open to all possibilities, his sensory gate ajar, his cognitive throughway green-lighted.

"Yes," he notes aloud, "affirmative."

"If you're looking for Harry," Mrs. Dorfman says, "he's not here."

"Harry," says Mr. Bono and smiles.

The delight of relevancies, the superb pattern of interconnections. A moment ago, Harry was a possibility; now Mr. Bono and Harry are joined in the infinite web of actuality. And Mrs. Dorfman too: a piece of the puzzle, a voice of reassurance, and union in the silent interiors of streets and viaducts. O jacks of selective trades! Artist of mass-construction!

"Mrs. Dorfman," says Mr. Bono, "I congratulate you and Harry too on your contribution to the What of things, the magnificence of mass."

"I'm sorry, we're not Catholics," Mrs. Dorfman replies.

Another line sent tingling into the net of circumstances, a bird for paradise, the innards of creation.

"We are all just men here," quotes Mr. Bono from recent reading.

"You mean the ecumenical thing?" asks Mrs. Dorfman.

"I refer to Leviathan," says Mr. Bono, "the vast summation whose integers we are, whether hidden in homes or conversing al fresco."

"You must have the wrong house," Mrs. Dorfman says, "Nobody by that name lives here."

And closes the door. Mr. Bono makes a notation in his blue notebook, the color of Tuesdays, and turns toward the next house.

> Maurice Natanson, *The Journeying Self: A Study in Philosophy and Social Role*

The philosopher Maurice Natanson[1] provides us with a critical step in the leap from concern with the process of making meaning and constructing consensus to the process of constructing integration. Mrs. Dorfman is interrupted from her routine business by the doorbell. She *expects* that "a caller will state his business, that if he doesn't immediately it may be because of some mistake or confusion, that what he says must make sense in some context, that one does one's best to discover that context."[2]

Thus we see Mrs. Dorfman persistently putting meaning onto the events of which she is a part. At each step her definition of the situation —her construction of meaning—is confused. So, according to Natanson, "if the confusion persists and there seems to be no urgency in the caller's business, it is reasonable to call a halt to the proceedings and suggest that he take up whatever it is with somebody else." Both people are engaged in a process of constructing meaning. They are developing implicit answers to the question: "What do I know?" or "What do we know together?" But they are at the same time, as an integral part of the process of constructing meaning, constructing expectations. That is, each is to some degree answering the question, "How should I act; what should I do?"

Each person is constructing meaning at a different level, and to that extent, Mrs. Dorfman and Mr. Bono are constructing different expectations in this situation. To use Natanson's term, they develop different "recipes" for their interaction. "All action," according to Natanson, "depends on some basic congruency between the recipes of the members of society, the citizens of the everyday world. Mr. Bono, that metaphysical busybody, is an insult to the unity of typifications [expectations], a threat to all recipes. If *everything* is relevant, then nothing can be said."[3] Mr. Bono's actions are confusing for Mrs. Dorfman because each of her mundane statements is found to be meaningful in his own grand schemes. Mrs. Dorfman has only a very limited set of potential recipes. Her interpretation of what is happening (her meanings) do not suggest useful expectations (how she should act). By contrast Mr. Bono has an unlimited set of recipes so that everything is sensible to him. His actions are unconstrained by Mrs. Dorfman's expectations because he recognizes no limitations to her expectations. Result: there is no congruency between the recipes.

In this chapter is described the process by which people construct "congruency between recipes." Recipes are congruent when people have some consensus or equivalence in their expectations about how to act. The first section of this chapter defines the phenomenon called "expectations." The second section provides a systematic explanation of how any group of two or more people develop expectations so that their activity is organized. This section, called "Accomplishing Integration," is concerned with the process by which actions of different people become regularized so that some actions are repetitive and so that actions of one person synchronize or "feed into" the actions of another. The third section, "Interpreting Integrative Patterns," provides a scheme for labeling behavioral regularities. Regularities in human activity are labeled by the kind of expectation which is presumed to underlie them. The four kinds of expectations described are norms, roles, agendas, and motives.

The fourth section distinguishes between two message forms. One form is principally oral; the other is principally written. This section considers some general ways in which organizing via oral communication is different from organizing via written communication. Finally, there are two sections concerned with "coordination formats." A coordination format is a way in which people take others into account. It is the process of people using their expectations to guide their cooperative actions. This discussion of coordination formats serves as an introduction to chapters 4, 5, 6, and 7 in which each of the four coordination formats is discussed in detail.

EXPECTATIONS AND INTEGRATION

Integration is the process of people doing things together. It is a process of people relating their actions to the actions of others. Workers on an assembly line provide an obvious example. Each person is performing a separate task, yet each person's actions feed into the next to form a pattern of related activities. The actions appear to be regularized. In fact, the human movements may be so perfectly tuned to one another that they resemble a machine. A human organization may thus appear mechanistic. But, as we have seen in the previous chapters, a mechanistic interpretation of human coordination is insufficient because it omits a critical process—the process of meaning construction. To understand human integration we must understand how meanings are related to coordinated actions. The term which refers both to cognitions and to actions is expectations.

Taking Others into Account

Max Weber has defined the necessary conditions for human integration or relationship: two parties are socially related when "one party presumes a particular attitude toward him on the part of the other and orients his action to this expectation."[4] One person may "presume" an attitude which another does not have. Nevertheless, it is what person A believes that person B thinks which A uses as a guide to his actions. A may not choose to do what he thinks B wishes, but A's actions are social and integrated with B's to the extent that A takes B into account.

Alfred Schutz provides a useful perspective in understanding the basic attitude of taking others into account. When we take others into account, we anticipate that our intentions will become the reasons for another person's actions and that another's intentions become the reasons for our actions.[5] The supervisor who tells a subordinate to "clean up the storeroom" is anticipating that his intentions (to have the storeroom cleaned) become the reasons for the subordinate's actions (the subordinate cleans the storeroom *because* the supervisor wants it clean.)

We do not usually stop to think about how our intentions affect another's actions and how another's intentions affect our actions. The process of presuming another's attitude is part of a natural ongoing flow of mental activity on the part of all people engaged in a common task. Whether or not people are aware of their assumptions about others, it is these assumptions which make possible human integration. These assumptions are expectations.

In summary, human integration is the connection of action to action. This connection is not mechanical. Rather actions are connected by the process of people taking others into account. We take others into account when we presume (rightly or wrongly) that our intentions are the reasons for their actions and their intentions are the reasons for our actions.

Structuring Uncertainty

Expectations are cognitions (part of our cognitive maps) by which we direct our actions. Expectations help us to know how to act because they provide some constraint or structure to the uncertainty of "What should I do now?" To illustrate this point, let us consider the most primitive form of social organization: the first encounter. A first encounter occurs whenever you meet a person for the first time.

Theoretically, there is a great deal of freedom to say anything you wish in the primitive organization called first encounter. There is much uncertainty in first encounters. The other person has little, if any, knowledge of who you are. If you meet a stranger on a train, you can describe yourself as a prima ballerina or a corporation president. What you say is not limited by past or expected future interaction with that person. The other person has little past history on which to base assumptions about you. There is a great deal of potential uncertainty about what you may talk about.

When you meet a person for the first time there is also great uncertainty about what will happen in the relationship. The next person you meet might eventually marry you or kill you. First encounters then are characterized by a great amount of potential or freedom—freedom to "present yourself" in any way you choose and freedom to develop the encounter into any kind of relationship.

Usually, however, we do not feel comfortable with all that "freedom." When we meet a person for the first time we feel awkward; we do not know what to say. We feel uncomfortable with silence, and are at a loss precisely because of all that freedom.

Lalljie and Cook investigated two communication behaviors in first encounters. They counted the number of "filled pauses" ("ah," "uh," "ugh") and measured how fast the people talked. They found that the longer the conversation between people who began as strangers continued, the fewer the filled pause rate (people used less "uhs") and the faster they spoke. They interpreted their findings as evidence that people are uncertain of what to say when they meet strangers. There is a wide range of possible conversational topics and styles. Therefore, they fill-in with noncontent "uhs." As they learn more about the other through the conversation, they reduce the uncertainty. They sound more confident because they are more certain. They use fewer "uhs" and talk faster.[6]

When people are uncertain about what to say, they stick to the safest topics ("Hot weather we're having today, isn't it?") because these topics are most likely to be the ones on which the other person can talk. They are "safe bets." After two strangers have commented about the weather, they use cues from the situation to suggest what more to say.

To illustrate, on the first day of a large lecture class I tell students to find a person sitting around them whom they have never seen before. They are to talk to that person until I tell them to stop (about five minutes). About 75 percent of the time they talk about the course. About half exchange names, majors, and home towns. Ten percent talk about their plans for the weekend.

In over four hundred such impromptu first encounters, no one has reported discussing existentialism, abortion, or venereal disease (though presumably many of the people are interested in these subjects). In one class, ten dyads reported discussing "dog training." I was flabbergasted until I noticed that one student had a dog sleeping quietly under his chair. The point of this story is that in the most primitive form of human coordinated behavior (the first encounter) people experience too much uncertainty. When they can talk about anything, they do not know what to talk about. They do not know what to expect. So they begin by discussing noncontroversial topics in order to get some hints about more interesting topics of mutual interest and, hence, to generate some more interesting expectations. Here's a typical exchange:

"It sure is hot today."
"Yeah, but not as hot as this time of year in Kansas."
"Are you from Kansas?"
"Yes, I just transferred here from K. U. last term."
"You're kidding. My sister went to K. U. I've been there lots of times. Why did you come here?"

We can predict that these two will discuss relative merits of Penn State vs. K. U., probably "fish" to see if they have common friends, and may even discuss what's new in Kansas! If the second person transferred to be in a different department of music, they might pursue common interests in music. They might find that they are both music majors and are particularly fond of jazz. This could lead to other meetings to hear one another's jazz collection. From a first encounter these two people could build a continuing relationship.

The difference between a first encounter and what I am calling a "continuing relationship" lies in the differences in how uncertainty is structured. In a first encounter expectations about what one might say are very general. People do not adapt content and style to the other as unique individuals. They talk about standard topics such as the weather because anybody can be expected to make some kind of sensible reply to, "Nice day, isn't it?" The immediate situation provides another general "structure" or guide to what to say. In a class, students can talk about the class; at a party, they can talk about the party; at a bus stop, they can talk about when the bus will come, how crowded it may be, etc.

Most first encounters die. They never "go" anywhere because by choice or circumstance the participants never again talk to each other. Some first encounters build into relationships. The process of organizing a relationship from a first encounter involves learning to structure uncertainty about what to say with specialized rather than general expectations about the other person. It thus involves developing expectations about particular people.

Charles Berger and Richard Calabraises observe that when strangers meet, "their primary concern is one of uncertainty reduction or increasing predictability about the behavior of both themselves and others in the interaction." People are attempting to "make sense" out of events.[7] People "make sense" by figuring out what others intend and therefore what is expected of them.

As we shall see in later chapters, patterns of expectations may be conscious or nonconscious. When people join an organization, they usually engage in trying to figure out what is expected of those occupying their position. Even when they are not thinking about "What is he saying?" or "What does he want from me?" they are nonetheless still trying to make sense of their new world. Situations seem sensible when people are reasonably certain about what is happening—what they are doing, what others are doing, and how their intentions become the reasons for the others' actions.

ACCOMPLISHING EXPECTATIONS

Expectations are cognitions which are produced by taking others into account. They function to reduce uncertainty so that people may assume that they know how to act in concert with others. Karl Weick has developed a theory of organizing which is useful as a systematic description of how expectations are created and sustained through communication. According to Weick, organizing is a process similar to sociocultural evolution. Organizing is learning. There are three phases: enactment, selection, and retention. These three phases are helpful in clarifying how actions become expectations and thus provide the basis for choosing future actions. These phases help us to understand how actions come to appear to be regularized.

Enactment

The first phase, enactment, is analogous to the evolutionary phase of "variation." In biology variation is possible through a chance mutation. Weick says, "All forms of behavior we observe in a surviving system, regardless of their apparent value at the present time, were at one time emitted in some more primitive form and then gradually shaped over time into their present form."[8]   Consider the dialogue in the previous section which started out with the weather and led to a discussion of people at the University of Kansas.   One person mentioned Kansas in passing.   The remark was an unlikely variation of talk about the weather. If the respondent had no interest in Kansas, the comment would have had little consequence.   However, the comment (a "primitive form," to use Weick's term) was picked up or elaborated by the other.   Even though the comment was primitive, it was not absolutely unpredictable.

Any comment about the weather is implicitly about the weather at this place.   Thus, a comment about the weather is implicitly about the weather in Pennsylvania (though reference to Pennsylvania is unstated). It invites a comment about other geographical climates such as Kansas. The chance comment about Kansas resulted from one person reflecting on his own experience with hot weather in the context of talking to another in Pennsylvania.   Thus, when we speak of organizing through symbolic evolution (communication) the "variation" stage or mutation is not entirely random.   Even this stage is the product of selection.

What we choose to say is a reflection on our experience.   In this selecting we are creating the environment to which we then respond. Enactment is a function of cognitive maps.   From all the thousands of experiences he might have used to talk about the weather, this person chose to compare Kansas with Pennsylvania.   Thus his comment was not simply a reaction to the weather; it was not simply a random comment thrown out.   It was an adaptation to his perceived environment and at the same time a message which invited the other person's interpretation.

In the enactment phase, people try out ways of relating to one another.   We can think of all enactments as trials.   In the example, the comment about Kansas was a trial which said (implicitly), "I can talk about Kansas, can you?"   The first time a couple kisses is an enactment. The two people are trying out a way of relating to one another.   Kissing behavior is not random.   (Few people kiss every stranger to decide if kissing makes sense as a regular feature of their interaction.)   The decision to kiss is a selection from behavior classified as possible in the cognitive map.   Hence, a kiss is a message to the other, but the first kiss is still a trial.   Depending upon what happens next, kissing may or may not become expected behavior in the relationship.

Selection

In the next phase, certain trials are selected to become part of the developing relationship.   The remark about Kansas was selected for further conversational development. Having kissed once or twice, two people may decide (with or without talking about it) that they prefer to be "just friends." Kissing may not become repetitive behavior in the relationship. The trial was not "selected."

The selection phase consists of developing and applying criteria to make conscious or nonconscious decisions. Criteria about topics of conversation might be "reject controversial topics," "keep unusual topics," "reject ego-threatening topics." Behaviors which are selected become repetitive or habitual. They are retained in the sense that they become expected behaviors. The process of developing and applying criteria takes place through cycles. Essentially, a cycle is a sequence of dependent behaviors. One person acts, this action is accepted, rejected, or modified by a second person. After this, the first person responds to the response of the other. Weick's hypothetical example of how a typical selection phase may be constructed is presented in Table 3.1.

TABLE 3.1
Interactive Cycles in Organizing (From Karl Weick. *The Social Psychology of Organizing*. Reading, Mass.: Addison-Wesley, 1969.)

Act	Interact	Double interact
Action by Person	*Response by Other Person*	*Readjustment by First Person*
1. Isolates a property of the input for closer examination	Accepts or rejects this choice	Abandons, revises, or maintains the property
2. Selects criterion for application to input property	Accepts or rejects criterion	Abandons, revises, or maintains criterion
3. Constructs new selection criterion	Accepts or rejects construction	Abandons, revises, or maintains construction
4. Differentiates an existing criterion, bringing out a new component	Accepts or rejects differentiation	Abandons, revises, or maintains
5. Assembles a set of criteria for application to input	Accepts or rejects assemblage	Abandons, revises, or maintains assemblage
6. Applies assembled criteria to input	Assesses criterion-input fit	Accepts or rejects for retention

Source: Karl Weick, p. 74

Retention

Retention, the final phase, is not simply a process of inert storage. It is not just filing into discrete categories. One kind of behavioral expectation retained influences others. Retention of one kind of behavior may result in a reorganization of the whole retention system. It reorganizes the cognitive map at an individual level. It reorganizes the consensus state at a collective level.

A reorganization of a consensus state took place in a women's group to which I belong. When the group met for the first time in my house, I deliberately did not prepare anything to eat. I had a box of cookies in the cabinet and decided at the last minute to put them out. I was "enacting" a certain preferred environment. I did not want to contribute to the expectation that the meetings were Ladies Wednesday Night Tea Parties. Gradually over six months, the sweets served became more elaborate. A pattern of expectation or a consensus state was selected and retained, to wit, that there should be homemade goodies and specially flavored teas served. I have noticed that this expectation affects my behavior. When I think of the meetings, I think as often of the congenial atmosphere and goodies as of the serious talk which goes on. Goodies are part of my map of the situation. When the meetings are in my home, not only do I bake, I also dust the furniture and vacuum the floor! One element of my map is related to another and to my behavior. I am quite sure that the practice of being a good hostess and being a good guest is not functional for the purposes of this particular group. Being a good guest is quite different behavior from being a good group member.

The expectations have developed through our mutual reinforcing behavior (action, response, response to response). We selected and retained the expectation of serving homemade treats. Our behaviors have constituted messages about what we expect. Along with the treats have developed other expectations about acting as hostess. If an outsider were to observe our organization, he or she would surely report the regularity of the "hostessing" behaviors and consider the implications of these behaviors for our other expectations and values.

I have described very briefly the model of organizing to be elaborated throughout the book. The process is threefold. The first is enactment or creating of trial behaviors. The second is selection which is the developing and use of criteria to choose among trial behaviors those which are in some ways worthwhile. Finally, there is retention which involves the integration of the selected new pattern of expected behaviors with the total pattern of expectations people have for one another. This integration usually means some change in the total pattern.

Each phase of the process is constituted of smaller units of human interaction. One person "acts" and thereby sends a message. Another interprets the intentions of the first. The second responds to those imagined intentions. The first then interprets the responding message of the other. In turn he or she responds to the intentions of the second. This cycle of act-response-response to response is the basic unit of human communicative action.

Figure 3.1 depicts a simplified model of accomplishing or organiz-

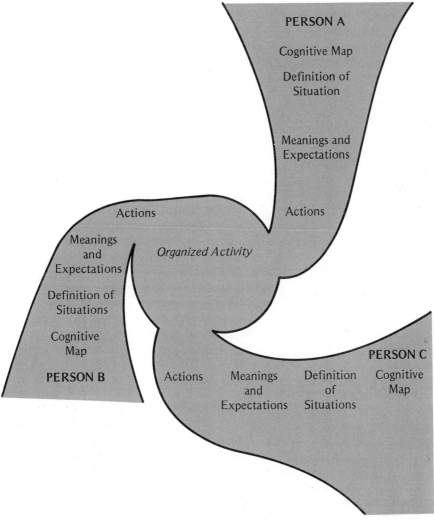

FIGURE 3.1
Developing Organized Activity

ing. There are three people engaged in organizing their actions. Each person has a cognitive map from which he or she constructs a definition of the immediate situation. This definition is composed of the meaning of the situation and the behavioral expectations which are implied by the meaning.

These meanings and expectations are like hypotheses. The people act "as if" the meanings are true. If each person acts as the others expect and each confirms the meanings of the others, "organizing activity" results. If a person does not act as expected or disconfirms the others' meanings, each must construct another definition of the situation using his or her cognitive map of the world as a source for interpretations about about what might be happening. The adequacy of the map is tested in the action-response-action cycles. The most complex organizations are created, maintained, and dissolved through these cycles. People act on their meanings and expectations (enacting their environment) and modify their meanings and expectations as they receive additional information (selection), and, hence, create cooperative activity (retention).

The concept that organization is accomplished through social or communicative actions is widely accepted by social scientists. Also widely accepted is the notion that organization is accomplished through the creation of a system or pattern of expectations. Some words frequently used by organization theorists to refer to expectations are norms, roles, agendas, and motives. When expectations are formalized or are officially communicated by central decision makers, these same four types of expectations are called rules, positions, procedures, and goals. In the following section I describe each of these as categories for interpreting expectations.

INTERPRETING INTEGRATIVE PATTERNS

In the section above I described the process by which behaviors come to be "regularized." Behaviors are regularized when they are repeated and when one person's behavior makes possible another person's behavior. When we observe regularities we assume that people have developed expectations which make those regularities possible. Thus, the concept of "expectation" provides an observer with a way of explaining the regularity he sees in behavior. It is helpful, therefore, to have some terms for sorting kinds of expectations.

People have expectations about *what* kinds of behavior are obligatory for everyone in a group. Social scientists call these expectations "norms." People have expectations about *who* should do what and to whom and with whom it should be done. Social scientists call these expectations "roles." People have expectations about *when* and in what order to do certain things. Social scientists call these expectations "agenda." Finally people have expectations about *why* they engage in certain actions. These expectations are called "motives."

Together this set of kinds of expectations provides a recipe or "social formula" for interaction and integration. Even people who have never heard the terms "norms," "roles," "agendas," and "motives" have expectations about what should happen, by whom and to whom, when, and why. These expectations allow us to make sense out of or define situations. Social scientists who are interpreting social situations use these same concepts to describe the pattern in the interaction they are observing. Let us look at each concept in more detail. These terms will be important in the descriptions of organizing found in the remaining chapters of the book.

Norms

George Homans defined a norm as "an idea in the minds of members of a group, an idea that can be put in the form of a statement specifying what the members or other men should do, ought to do, are expected to do, under given circumstances.[9] According to this definition a norm is not a pattern of behavior. It is not even beliefs about how people do act. Norms are accepted standards about what should be done. Norms represent how people expect people to act because they believe they are obliged to act that way. The sense of obligation is important. Also important is the notion that, if asked, members could articulate norms (though they might not use that term). They would explain their behavior by talking about how they are obliged to act in the situation.

If you asked a student how to act in a classroom, he will probably first tell you the norms or what you are supposed to do. He or she will tell you how others expect you to act. In most relationships, we do not have to be told (in words) what we are supposed to do. We learn norms through a process of informed trial and error. When we join an established group, we behave in ways accepted in similar groups we have been in before. If others respond favorably (they do not frown or shy away from us) we continue those behaviors. If others seem uncomfortable with us, we modify our behavior until it appears to please them.

When we organize new relationships we are engaged in creating a structure of expectations about how people should act toward one another. The process of evolving norms may be largely nonconscious. (For example, a man and woman who develop a serious romantic interest in one another create obligations which constrain each other's actions. They may come to feel that they should not date other people.) The process of creating a formal organization includes deliberate attention to the obligations of members. When these obligations are written down and systematically enforced they are called regulations, or in the case of governments, laws.

Role

The concept of role refers to differential rights and obligations among people in a group. All members of a class are expected to sit in desks (not hang from light fixtures), but those enacting the role of "professor" have different rights and obligations from those who are in the "student" role. The process of organizing involves individuals finding complementary roles or ways of interacting with one another.

Many social scientists consider the concept of role central to understanding organizations because it "is at once the building block of social systems and the summation of the requirements with which the system confronts the individual member."[10] To put it simply a role is how an individual fits into an organization. We engage in different kinds of behaviors in each relationship. The behavior expected of a person in the role of "mother" is different from the behavior expected of the same person in the role of "professor." Organizing or building relationships is a process of creating differential expectations about the behavior of one person which are complementary with expectations for the behavior of others.

The idea that roles are differential and complementary expectations suggests the idea of a "role set." A role set consists of all of the roles which are complementary to a given "focal" role. In Katz and Kahn's example the role set of a press foreman in a manufacturing organization is composed of the nineteen or so other roles—general foreman, superintendent, stock foreman, inspector, shipping foreman, etc.—with whom the press foreman has direct contact. The expectations which constitute the role of press foreman "exist in the minds of members of his role set and represent standards in terms of which they evaluate his performance." But the expectations to be expectations must not simply reside in the minds of others, rather,

> they tend to be communicated in many ways; sometimes as direct instructions, as when a supervisor describes to a subordinate the requirements of his job; sometimes less directly, as when a colleague expresses admiration or disappointment in some behavior. The crucial point is that the activities which define a role are maintained through the expectations of members of the role set, and that these expectations are communicated or "sent" to the focal person.[11]

It is in the concept of role that we find some serious issues related to integration, in particular the issue of role conflict. The possibility—indeed, the inevitability of role conflict—is built into integration. Individuals integrate through roles. Each role, by definition, is interdependent with a number of other roles. This interdependence is accomplished through "sending" expectations. But what happens when the expectations are unclear or contradictory?

The classic case of role conflict is when a person's superiors expect one kind of action and his subordinates expect quite different kinds of actions. There is conflict in the role. In a nationwide survey of male workers, Kahn found that almost one-half experienced role conflict. "Forty-eight reported that from time to time they were caught between two sets of people who wanted different things from them, and 15 percent reported this to be a frequent and serious problem.[12] Thus "accomplishing" organization through role integration is not a simple or straightforward process. The division of people into roles—particularly the division into formal roles as we shall see in chapter 8—also creates differentiation which puts strains on integration.

Agenda

Another kind of expectation is the agenda or time sequencing of events. In informal groups, agendas are not often written down. The "agenda" of two people who date regularly typically includes the expectation that they will "go out" somewhere every Saturday night and that he will call her every night at 11:00. (Note the implied role differentiation: he will call her.) Agendas help people plan their time by knowing when they are obliged to participate actively in a relationship.

The work flow in an office or on an assembly line provides a kind of agenda for workers. Whenever a large group of people need to coordinate their activities to accomplish a particular event by a particular date, a precise agenda is needed. NASA contractors developed Program Evaluation and Review Technique (PERT) as a means of sequencing the hundreds of thousands of events which had to occur before a rocket could be launched. The idea of PERT was to create a system of expectations so that each party would know exactly what he or she was to accomplish and when. In this case, the structure of expected events is planned and written down.

Motives

Finally, motives or intentions are expectations about why we act as we do and why others act as they do. The importance of motives for accomplishing organization is suggested by Karl Weick:

Cognitive theorists have repeatedly demonstrated that when people try to make sense out of events, they are aided most in doing this if they can establish motivational reasons for the actions (e.g. Heider 1958; Schutz 1967). That is, we know more about a person if we can observe him and say, 'Oh, *that's* what he's *trying* to do.' When we say this, we have a plausible motivational explanation of his actions.[13]

The definition of motive implied by Weick's statement may be unfamiliar to the reader. Motive here is not an "internal drive state." Motive, like norm, role, and agenda, is an explanation for a pattern of behavior.

Suppose that we observe a man swinging an ax repeatedly against a large tree, picking up the logs, carrying them into a house. We explain the behavior by referencing a pattern which includes the person's intentions. We say that he is chopping wood in order to build a fire. When we observe human actions, we see not only the movements occurring at the present time, we impute the future or the motive as part of the action.

We see action as directed toward some objective. If we hear a telephone ring and we watch a person get out of her chair and walk toward the phone, we infer that she got up in order to answer the phone. We see not only her behavior, we imagine her intentions. When we explain patterns of behavior, we construct an imagined future which fulfills our imagined picture of her motives. Thus, motives are constructs—elements of cognitive maps—with which people interpret the relationships among actions.

A motivational theory which is consistent with this constructivist perspective is "expectancy theory" developed by Victor Vroom. According to Vroom, motivation cannot be explained with reference to innate "needs." That is, people do not respond automatically to need-stimuli as Maslow's need hierarchy (in chapter 1) might imply. Rather, motivation is a process that governs the selection pattern of employees when faced with alternative forms of activities.[14] We might say that motivation is a function of one's expectations or cognitive maps. An illustration of Vroom's theory is shown in Figure 3.2.

An individual "wants" something. How much he wants it is the "force" or "valence" of his desire for it. Individuals recognize that they have to do things in order to get things. A student, for example, is faced with the possibility of getting an A, B, C, D, or F in each of his courses. The final grade is a "second level" outcome. The final grade is computed from test scores. Test scores are "instrumental" in creating final grades. When a student is considering how much to study for one exam, Vroom's model explains that the relevant dimensions of the student's cognitive map will be:

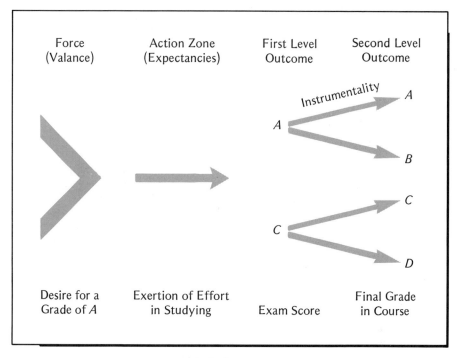

Force (Valance)	Action Zone (Expectancies)	First Level Outcome	Second Level Outcome

Instrumentality

Desire for a Grade of *A*	Exertion of Effort in Studying	Exam Score	Final Grade in Course

FIGURE 3.2
Expectancy Theory of Motivation

(1) His estimation of whether a lot of effort will result in a high test score. (What is his "expectancy" that effort will lead to a successful outcome at level one?)

(2) His estimation of how much the test will contribute to the final score. (How "instrumental" is level one in obtaining his real goal at level two?)

(3) His estimation of how much he wants to get a good grade. (What is the "valence" or force of his desire for a grade of *A*?)

Motivation is an act of interpreting expectations. A student who does not study much may believe that his efforts will be wasted (low expectancy), that the test does not "count" much (low instrumentality), or he may care little about obtaining a good grade (low valence). The way he constructs the situation guides the pattern of his choices. His expectations will constitute his motives.

One implication of this motivational theory is that if one wishes "to motivate" another person, then one should change his meanings and expectations to be more "motivating." But, of course, one person cannot change another's meanings. No part of a person's cognitive map is directly implanted by another. Expectations are learned. To the extent that one learns new expectations, that person may be described as having learned new motivations. In fact, what changes is the regularity of the person's behavioral choices. Then people—the person who has changed and others—will describe the difference as resulting from a change in "motivation." Motives, like norms, roles, and agendas, are concepts used to explain regularities in action.

Motives provide answers to the question of "why" people are engaging in certain activities. Some patterns of action are so common, however, that the motivational question ("Why are they doing that?") simply never comes up. Motivations may be entirely taken-for-granted. Marvin B. Scott and Stanford M. Lyman offer the following examples of intentions which are taken for granted:

> In American Society we do not ordinarily ask why married people engage in sexual intercourse, or why they maintain a home with their children, although the latter question might well be asked if such behavior occurred among Nazars of Malabor. These questions are not asked because they have been settled in advance in our culture and are dictated by the language itself. We learn the meaning of a "married couple" by indicating that they are two people of the opposite sex who have a legitimate right to engage in sexual intercourse and maintain their own children in their own household. When such taken-for-granted phenomena are called into question, the inquirer (if a member of the same cultural group) is regarded as "just fooling around," or perhaps as being sick.[15]

When we understand why a person is acting as he is without asking or even pausing to consider why, then we are assuming the person's intentions or motives. The motives are given as part of the consensual expectations of the situation. They are literally part of the agreed-to definition of the situation. Questions of why are not asked because in Scott and Lyman's terms, they are settled "in advance by the culture."

Vocabulary and Expectations

Taken-for-granted motives are learned as we learn the meaning of symbols. We learn motives which are taken-for-granted in a particular group as we learn the vocabulary of that group or culture. In chapter 2, I used the example of a new cashier. The process of learning to be a cashier is learning to use the vocabulary ("check on two") and the props (the credit card stamper, the tax keys). In learning the meaning of words and objects within the social system, new cashiers learn what is expected of them. In learning the meaning of words and objects, they learn how to interpret the norms of the situation (never leave your machine), the roles (the front supervisor is the only person who can authorize checks), the agendas (always ask first if the purchase is a charge), and the intentions (no one here works for the fun of it!). Thus words and other symbols are means of reducing uncertainty in social relationships. Members of an organization teach newcomers norms, roles, agendas, and intentions as they teach them the special "language" of the organization. As newcomers learn the vocabulary of an organization, they learn what is expected of them. Similarly, in developing a special language people are developing their mutual expectations. This is one sense in which communication is organizing.

We now turn our attention to two other senses in which communication is organizing. Up to this point I have confined my description of organizing to a single model. Whether the organization is a multinational corporation or a coop of fifteen families, the basic process depicted in Figure 3.2 is useful for understanding how organization is accomplished. Obviously, however, there are important differences in organizing processes. The remainder of this chapter is concerned with differences in communication that function to create differences in organization. The following section describes differences in message form that have organizational relevance. The final two sections describe four ways in which people take others into account; these ways are called "coordination formats."

MESSAGE FORM: DISPLAYS AND DOCUMENTS

Organizational theorists are interested in how expectations make some behaviors more probable than others, how expectations develop, and how they may be changed. Organizational communication theorists are interested in these three questions and, in addition, are interested in the messages with which people communicate their expectations. They assume that the form of the message has some influence on the process of developing and changing expectations.

Marshall McLuhan has popularized the concept that the media (the message form) has a primary not secondary importance in explaining what happens in communication. He says, "The medium is the message."[16] If the form of messages influences interpretations, then it must have impact on organizing. This section examines two message forms called displays and documents which have particularly important functions in the organizing process. Organizations which result from exchanges of symbolic displays are different from organizations in which documents are of primary importance. The first kind of organizations are called "informal"; the second are "formalized."

The term "display" refers to acts of speech—not simply the oral words (as some define speech) but all the visual and other stimuli which accompany oral messages. Smiles, frowns, body positioning, distance between people are ways we display our feelings and thoughts. We display our happy feelings as we feel them by smiling, laughing, or touching. Our displays change with our changing mental states.

By contrast, the symbolic forms I call documents are relatively static. Documents refer to written messages. It also refers to any message which has a "permanent" structure. Thus, office furniture is an example of a document. It acts as a nonverbal message about the status of occupants. Documents can be changed, but unlike a smile (nonverbal display), they cannot be changed instantaneously. Documents are tangible; they can be held in the hand as well as in the mind. More important, they are evidence which can be used in the future and substantiate the existence of feelings and thoughts which are occurring now.

"Informal organizations" are those in which people use symbolic displays almost exclusively. In informal organizations, there is nothing written down about how people should relate to one another. Friendships, for example, are this kind of organization. Organizations are "formalized" by documenting how people should relate to one another. Expectations are written down in the form of job descriptions (who does what), organization charts (who has power over whom), budgets (who gets what), organizational goals (where are we going). The larger the organization the more communication takes place through documents (memos, newsletters, etc.) rather than through face-to-face contact.

Electronic recording devices make it difficult to sort all messages into one of two categories. Are tape-recorded messages displays or documents? They are much "richer" in informational content than written words, but tapes can be preserved and shown again and again. They can be used as evidence in the future as Richard Nixon discovered. The development of electronic technology allows us to preserve symbolic displays in documentary form.

What are the implications of the differences between displays and documents for the process of social organizing? There are at least three ways in which they differ which have implications for the creation of human organizations. These ways are:

1. personal richness
2. informativeness
3. potential for editing.

Personal Richness

Any symbolic display is a message constructed by one person and addressed to one or more particular people. For this reason we can say that communication via display is personal. The message is "rich" with the impression of the person. On the other hand, documents such as organization charts, goal statements, budgets, wages, office furnishings, public relations brochures are addressed "to whom it may concern" and signed "the organization."

Documents are impersonal. This does not mean that I cannot be "personally insulted" by some documents. A person may easily be personally offended by his or her position on a newly constructed organization chart. Letters exchanged by friends are personal, but, using the criteria of permanence, they are documents, hence, more impersonal. When I refer to displays as personal, I refer to the following three characteristics which are almost exclusively found in oral communication or symbolic display.

First, in oral communication the speaker's personality "stands with" his or her message.[17] We cannot listen to a person talk without making judgments about the speaker's personality. When we talk face-to-face with another, we experience that other as a person, not as a series of disembodied symbols. When we read letters from a friend we imagine his or her voice as we read. Second, because we "stand with" our symbolic displays, we endow our messages with our own personality. Alfred Schutz observes that for the period of time in which people are in face-to-face communication, they experience "growing old together"; they "live in each other's subjective contexts of meaning."[18] Thus, to be in oral communication with another is to experience the other directly.

Informativeness

Because we experience people not just symbols when we are engaged in oral communication, we get and give a great deal more information than when we communicate with documents. The concept of "meta-communication" (discussed in chapter 2) consists of all the extraverbal cues we use to interpret the intentions of a message. When we see a person, his facial expressions display his intentions. We use eye contact as a clue to sincerity. When he stands very close, we interpret the intentions of messages differently.

Even if we only hear a person, his tone of voice, rate, inflection, and pauses are cues to what he is saying. This point was made clear to me by students in a course in small group research. I wanted them to practice categorizing a discussion I had recorded and transcribed. On the day we were to do this, I accidentally left the recording at home and only had the transcript. We tried for an hour to code the discussion using the written transcript only. It was an easy task for me because I had listened to the tape so many times that when I read the words,

I "heard" the tape-recorded voices. I could understand the intentions of the remarks because the voices contained information which was not on the paper.

After an hour of frustration we gave up and finished the task the next day by listening to the tape. Direct communication with visual and vocal cues provides the other with much more information about the intentions of the source. Even hearing a person is more informative than reading "disembodied" words. This is why the job of a writer is more difficult than that of a speaker because the writer must express in words what the speaker can convey with displays such as inflection, eye contact, tone of voice, and vocal intensity.

Potential for Editing

The task of the writer is more difficult because he or she must depend almost exclusively on words to convey feelings and thoughts. However, writers have one advantage over speakers. Writers can edit their messages. As I write these words I am scratching out and adding words. As a reader of the finished copy, you will never see what has been omitted. You do not know what was added to the original version. Because they can edit, writers have more control over the form of their messages.

Speakers, too, make feeble attempts at editing. When we hear people say, "What I meant to say was," or "Yesterday, no, day before yesterday" we are observing oral editing, but when we are speaking, all of our editing—errors included—is displayed to our listener. I said earlier that we reveal ourselves more when we communicate orally. One reason is that we show the other our "thoughts in process." We reveal ourselves to the other at the same time that we are seeing ourselves. We cannot erase our mistakes from the minds of our audiences.

Lawyers use this principle to the advantage of their clients. For example, a defense lawyer asks a leading question of a witness. The witness answers before the prosecutor can object. When the judge sustains the prosecution's objection, he or she instructs the jury to "disregard" the witness's answer. The court clerk deletes the answer from the trial record (the document), but the witness's symbolic display has been seen and heard by the jury. They have responded to it in some way. The event has happened; its occurrence cannot be withdrawn from history. There is no possibility for a speaker to edit his or her symbols after they have been displayed. At best, the jury members edit by reinterpreting the display in the context of the judge's remark. But the way the display is interpreted is decided by each jury member, not the judge.

This suggests that there is another dimension to the question of editing. If a person does not write down his or her opinions, it is difficult to hold him to account for them. He can always deny them by suggesting that what he said was not accurately reported. Anthony Downs observes that messages passed informally—orally—"can be withdrawn, altered, adjusted, magnified or cancelled without any official record being made."[19] We have more freedom in reinterpreting our past behavior when there is no documented record of that behavior.

This "freedom" of reinterpretation means that relationships created with symbolic displays are more fluid. The relationship changes with the evolving moods of the people. One person cannot point to a document as forcing the other to behave in certain expected ways. Thus people in informal relationships are constantly editing their own images of the relationship. Each person retains memories of the past. These memories are not edited like a script, but they are reinterpreted in retrospect as new events occur.

In this section I have discussed some differences between messages whose form is display and those whose form is documentation. The three differences I have suggested—personal richness, informativeness, and editing—are centered on the theme of rigidity. Displays are more "fluid" than documents. They are constantly changing as our "moods" change, as we adapt to the changing of the other, as we get more information about the other, as we attempt to adjust what we are saying because we are dissatisfied with how it is "coming out."

Those organizations like friendships and families which are created almost totally by "displays" are very fluid. They have a great capacity to adapt because members cannot hold one another to account to behave in accordance with written rules. The expectations underlying interaction are being renegotiated all the time. When members of an organization begin writing down their expectations, they stabilize the patterns of interaction by introducing some rigidity. The message form—the document—stays the same, though, of course, individuals still interpret the same overt messages differently.

COORDINATION FORMATS

Organizational communicators may use either displays or documents as the form for their messages. Through their communication, people are developing patterns or structures of mutual expectations. These are developed through a learning process in which new behaviors are tried out, some are selected and retained as the formula for coordination.

The remainder of this book concerns four "coordination formats," how they function to develop organizations, and how they may be improved. Coordination formats are ways in which people use expectations to coordinate their actions. The first way is through improvisation. When people improvise, they do not think much about what is expected of them or what others should do. If asked why they are doing something, they would typically say that they are doing "what comes naturally." Expectations are simply taken for granted. People's actions are routine. Attention is on the present.

A second format for coordination involves preplanning of interaction. People think about what is expected of them. They fantasize about what they could do. They try to find out the consequences of doing one thing rather than another. Expectations are not taken for granted. People think about future interactions (though the "future" may be only seconds away).

A third kind of coordination is "collective decision building." In this format people are attempting to produce a set of symbols which they can all agree is a collective decision. The audience for the symbolic product of the group ("the decision") may be only the group itself, or it may be outsiders such as others in the organization of which the group is one part. The distinguishing feature of this format is that people talk about their expectations in the process of building a decision. They negotiate expectations directly. They make decisions about who is to do what (roles), what everyone must do (norms), in what order things are to be done (agendas), and why they are talking (motives or goals).

These three formats are alternative forms of coordinated action. In improvising, people act "spontaneously" on their general understandings of the situation and the other people present. They take others into account by acting in ways which are generally expected of them. They proceed on the basis of stereotypes. In planned interaction people think of particular others with whom they must coordinate their actions. They think before they act about how particular others will respond to certain actions. They choose their actions in the hope of securing goals which are somewhat clear to them before they act.

Planned interaction, then, differs from unplanned interaction in that when people are coordinating their actions, they are operating on the basis of a predetermined strategy. This strategy was chosen by considering particular people with whom they would be interacting. In planning an interaction, people make individual or "intrapersonal" decisions by thinking about what individuals might do and what they should do.

In the process of collective or group decision building, the group produces a set of symbols (as simple as "Yeah, let's go to the movies" or as elaborate as the Declaration of Independence) which they agree represents their collective position or attitude about some topic. In building a collective decision, members of a group must explicitly construct a common perspective for interpreting information and then use that perspective in producing a collective message. Decision making is "interpersonal" in that it involves the overt expression and negotiation of expectations and meanings in the attempt to construct the collective perspective necessary to come to a collective conclusion.

A fourth kind of format uses documents. Documented interactions are those in which expectations are based on relatively permanent messages addressed "to whom it may concern" and signed "the organization." They are messages of expectations which may be "official" because they are not personal. We shall consider two kinds of documented interactions. There is the interaction in which the document is the message itself. When a person reads the job description for his position, for example, he is engaged in "documented interaction" with the organization. More common, however, is the interaction in which the document provides a context or a metamessage influencing all communication which takes place. Anytime a supervisor communicates with subordinates, the documents prescribing the role structure of the organization provide a context which the communicators take into account in interpreting what is said and done. Thus, even when documents are not the messages which are being exchanged between members of a formal organization, they sit in the background and influence what is said and what is interpreted as being said.

The four formats are "progressively inclusive" of each other. That is, when people are engaged in planned interaction, only some of the features of that interaction can be planned. It would be impossible to plan all one's actions. Some communicative behaviors are improvised. Likewise, if a group of people are engaged in a process of building a "collective decision," each of the members of the group is planning some of his or her interaction. Each person thinks about expectations which he does not express aloud to others. Also much of the communicative behavior is improvised. In the creation and interpretation of organizational documents, there is improvisation, planned interaction, and collective decision building.

Thus, to classify any particular interaction as "planned interaction" means that some important expectations are attended to by the participants. To classify an interaction as "collective decision making" means that people talked about important expectations they had of one another and that they explicitly verbalized a consensus which they called —or were likely to call—a decision. To say that a relationship is "documented" means that there are documents which people take into account when they engaged in improvisation, planned interaction, or collective decision building.

CONTINGENCIES AND COORDINATION FORMATS

Organizing is the process of structuring uncertainty of both knowledge (thereby creating "meaning") and behavior (thereby creating "expectations"). The process of structuring uncertainty is accomplished through three subprocesses: enactment, selection, and retention. More specifically, there are alternative ways in which people use their meanings and expectations to structure uncertainty. They take their meanings and expectations for granted and simply "improvise" their behavior. They consciously attend to their meanings and expectations and create collective decisions about behavior. They write down their meanings and expectations to document behavior.

Karl Weick provides an important concept for understanding the contingencies which influence the effectiveness of these formats for accomplishing organization. He states that "any process is able to remove [structure] only that amount of equivocality [uncertainty] that is present in the process itself."[20] From this proposition we can make the following prediction: In situations which are relatively stable or certain, coordination formats which do not contain much uncertainty will be sufficient to organize human action. However, in highly uncertain environments, the coordination format used to organize action must itself contain uncertainty.

Improvising and documenting are highly "certain" formats. By definition there are no surprises in improvised behavior. People are able to take their own actions and the actions of others for granted because of the stability of those actions. We saw an instance of an improvisation attempt meeting a highly uncertain environment in the quotation at the beginning of this chapter. Mrs. Dorfman tried to use her taken-for-granted recipe for meeting people at the door to greet Mr. Bono. The recipe was not able to "register" the uncertainty of Mr. Bono's highly unpredictable behavior. If the uncertainty cannot be registered—if it cannot be taken into account—then it surely cannot be structured into a meaningful sequence of behavior.

Documents are likewise rather clumsy methods for handling uncertainty. Documents address situations as well as people "to whom it may concern." Documents deal with classes of situations rather than particular situations. The more uncertain the situations in an environment, the less the situations fit into classes and therefore, the less capably they can be dealt with by formulating laws.

When people are consciously attending to meanings and expectations as in planned interaction they are able to discern particularities which make the situations unique. They are thus able to "register" more uncertainty and make private decisions about what to do in uncertain situations. When people talk about their meanings and their expectations, in collective decision building, they are able to register more uncertainty because they are aware not only of their own private meanings, but they have more information about the situation because they know more about the perceptions of others. Because the collective decision-building process has no predetermined end, it is the most "uncertain" of the coordination formats. Thus, collective decision building should be able to deal most effectively with situations characterized by a good deal of environmental uncertainty.

Although organizational researchers have not investigated coordination formats using these four names, there is evidence from contingency theorists that the effectiveness of integration is achieved by using different coordination formats under different degrees of uncertainty. James Thompson discusses how integration is accomplished in various kinds of environments. In relatively stable and predictable situations, according to Thompson, organizations may use "the creation of rules and procedures to govern the behavior of subsystem members."[21] Rules and procedures are documentary and improvisational formats. However, rules and procedures are not effective for organization in more unstable situations. In these moderately unstable situations, organizations are integrated by "plans," a method which is similar to planned interactions.

In highly unstable environments, integration may only be achieved effectively through "mutual adjustment." Mutual adjustment is substantially similar to the format I call "collective decision building." Thus Thompson, along with Lawrence and Lorsch whose research is discussed in chapters 8 and 9, provide some evidence that the effectiveness of coordination formats in constructing organizing processes will vary with environmental conditions. If organizing is structuring uncertainty, then the most useful method of organizing is a function of the amount of uncertainty to be removed.

SUMMARY

Communication functions to integrate because through communication people develop expectations about behavior which is the basis for integrated activity. The process of constructing expectations in a relationship begins with the first encounter. Thus, a first encounter is a primitive organization.

There is potentially a lot of freedom in how to behave in first encounters. People are not limited by expectations developed in past encounters; there is little direction about where the relationship is going, therefore, expectations about the future constrain present behaviors. But there is also little knowledge about what to talk about and how to relate to one another, so people act in stereotyped ways. They respond to the other in a very general way, one which does not involve much risk. As people communicate, they learn about one another. They learn topics of mutual interest. They develop more specialized expectations about how to relate to each other.

Expectations are learned in a three-phase process of enactment, selection, and retention. In the enactment phases people "try out" ways of relating to one another. These ways are not entirely random but are based on cognitive maps and on definition of situations. Criteria are developed and applied to select those kinds of behaviors which are "good" for the developing relationship. Certain behaviors are "retained" because they become regularized or expected behaviors. The relationship of actions to one another and to cognitive maps is pictured in Figure 3.2. The three processes which build expectations involve cycles of exchanges of symbolic actions. Each cycle has three components: (1) action, (2) response to action, and (3) response to response.

People use expectations to interpret the meaning of one another's behavior. When they see regularity in their own activity and the activity of others they use one or more of four kinds of explanations for that regularity. These kinds of explanations are really kinds of expectations. We may see that people are obliged to act in certain ways. We then say that the action was guided by the "norms" of the situation. We may interpret people as behaving in different but complementary ways with one another. We then say that the action was guided by the "roles" of the group. We may see that there were expectations about what things should happen when. Then we would be describing the "agenda" of the group. Finally, we may see behaviors as based on the actors' notions of why they were acting in the observed way. We would say their actions were guided by what they wanted to accomplish, and we would describe their presumed "motives."

The form of the messages exchanged between people influences the character of the relationship or organization which they create with their messages. Three differences between displays and documents are discussed: (1) displays are richer in the personality of the message source; documents are impersonal; the person "stands with" his or her message of symbolic display; (2) displays are richer in information because there are more metacommunicational clues to interpreting the content of the message; (3) displays cannot be edited; all the behavioral display a person emits is subject to interpretation by others.

The form of the message—whether display or document—influences the kind of expectations people develop for one another and therefore influence the relationships they form with one another. The ways in which people use their expectations to coordinate their actions are called coordination formats.   Coordination formats also influence the development of relationships.   Three formats are briefly described: improvised interactions, planned interactions, and collective decision building.   Each of these three is the subject of a chapter in unit 2.   The fourth format—documentation—and its relationship to the other three are the subject of unit 3.

ENDNOTES

1. Maurice Natanson, *The Journeying Self: A Study in Philosophy and Social Role* (Reading, Mass.: Addison-Wesley, 1970), p. 57.

2. Ibid., p. 58.

3. Ibid.

4. Max Weber as quoted by Alfred Schutz, *Phenomenology of the Social World* (Evanston, Ill.: Northwestern University Press, 1967), p. 152.

5. Schutz, *Phenomenology*, pp. 159–163.

6. Lalljie and Cook, "Uncertainty in First Encounters," *Journal of Personality and Social Psychology* 26 (1973): 137–141.

7. Charles Berger and Richard Calabraises, "Explorations in Initial Interaction," *Harvard Business Review* 1 (1975): 100.

8. Karl Weick, *The Social Psychology of Organization* (Reading, Mass.: Addison-Wesley, 1969), p. 56.

9. George Homans, *The Human Group* (New York: Harcourt, Brace and World, 1950), p. 123.

10. Daniel Katz and Robert L. Kahn, *The Social Psychology of Organizations* (New York: John Wiley & Sons, Inc., 1966), p. 171.

11. Ibid., p. 175.

12. Ibid., p. 186.

13. Karl Weick, *The Social Psychology of Organizing* (Reading, Mass.: Addison-Wesley, 1969), p. 10. The studies Weick refers to are Fritz Heider, *The Psychology of Interpersonal Relations* (New York: John Wiley & Sons, Inc., 1958); and Alfred Schutz, *Phenomenology of the Social World* (Evanston, Ill.: Northwestern University Press, 1967).

14. Victor Vroom, *Work and Motivation* (New York: John Wiley & Sons, 1964).

15. M. B. Scott and S. M. Lyman, "Accounts," *American Sociological Review* 33 (1968): 46–62.

16. Marshall McLuhan, *Understanding Media: Extensions of Man* (New York: McGraw-Hill, 1964).

17. Carroll Arnold, "Oral Rhetoric, Rhetoric, and Literature," *Philosophy and Rhetoric* (Fall, 1968): 191–210.

18. Schutz, *Phenomenology of the Social World*.

19. Anthony Downs, *Inside Bureaucracy* (Boston: Little Brown, 1967), p. 113.

20. Weick, *The Social Psychology of Organizing*, p. 72.

21. James Thompson, *Organizations in Action* (New York: McGraw-Hill, 1967), p. 56.

UNIT

II

Organizing
Social Systems

The chapters in this unit describe three ways of organizing using symbolic displays. The emphasis here is on informal organizing processes rather than the creation and operation of formal systems of authority. The purposes of this second unit are: (1) to describe three different processes of communication or "coordination formats," (2) to describe how organizations which result from these different processes are different, and (3) to draw some implications about how to improve each of these kinds of communication processes.

Chapter 4 describes communication in which people do not stop to plan their goals for a communication situation, or what actions they might take to secure their goals. Most communication has this kind of "improvised" character. In improvising people take their expectations for granted and create routine interactions. The application section at the end describes some undesirable interaction routines and how they might be changed.

Chapter 5 describes communication which is "planned." To plan an interaction is to stop to think about goals and imagine strategies for achieving those goals. There is conscious decision making in this kind of communication, but it is individual decision making. Each person thinks about expectations of the situation and makes personal decisions about how he or she will act in that situation. The application section concentrates on how to develop skill in one kind of planned interaction —interviewing.

Chapter 6 describes how groups of people come to agreements which they announce as their collective decision. In this kind of communication people not only stop to think about their goals and expectations, they talk to one another about them. They actually make collaborative decisions about goals and expectations. The application section is concerned with collective decision building as it occurs in problem-solving committee meetings.

The application sections of chapters 5 and 6 analyze three tasks to be accomplished in any purposeful communication situation. These three are: (1) motivating integration, (2) achieving equivalence of meaning for significant symbols, and (3) achieving purpose. In the Introduction I said that people necessarily achieve integration and organizational intelligence as an outcome of regular communication. In the description of these three tasks I present some methods for achieving more useful integration, intelligence, and ultimately purpose.

After finishing these three chapters readers should be able to distinguish three communication processes (or three coordination formats). They should be able to identify the organizing function of each format. They should also be able to describe some communication methods for achieving improved integration, equivalence of meaning, and purpose.

CHAPTER

4

Improvising Interactions

Prerequisites for Improvising
Improvised Interaction Patterns
Talk in Organizations
Organizing Functions: Stability and Efficiency
APPLICATION: Diagnosing and Changing Dys-
functional Formulas

Everybody has an "automatic pilot." When we drive down a familiar road, we steer, accelerate, and decelerate according to expectations built-up over many times of driving that road or similar roads. Only when the unexpected occurs—a cat crossing in front of us—do our actions become problematic. That is, the question of what actions to take becomes a cause of concern. We confront a "problem" to be solved.

Even then, we may have time only to switch from one automatic sequence (highway driving) to another (emergency stop). We may not have time to weigh the probabilities and consequences of hitting the cat versus being hit in the rear by a car four lengths behind us. We operate on "automatic pilot" when we are not conscious of the reasons and possible consequences of our actions. There is no "problem" toward which we are intentionally directing our attention. We are simply acting "naturally." We have not planned our actions.

Much of our interpersonal behavior is unplanned. It seems "automatic." One example of unplanned interpersonal behavior is greeting a person with "Good morning." Almost always we use such greetings without any thought about alternatives or consequences. We pass by people we know (or think we know) by blurting out an automatic greeting such as "Good morning." Suppose, however, that on Tuesday afternoon you had a loud, emotional argument with a friend. You left his house in a rage. The next morning you see him walking down the sidewalk in your direction. You will have to walk past him in a few seconds. A simple "Good morning" is not a routine action. You must choose (1) to look at him or not, (2) to speak or not, (3) to say "Good morning" and nothing else, or (4) to say something more.

The simplest kind of behavior, which is usually automatic, may become problematic. Saying "Good morning" may be planned activity in that you think about alternatives and consequences in advance. In chapter 5 we will explore this definition of planned activity and planned interaction in some detail. The purpose of the present chapter is to examine nonplanned or routine interactions.

Some routines are so rigid we may call them "rituals." In ritual interaction there are only a few lines which an actor may use. Greetings and leave-takings are examples of these. Other than "Good morning" (or "Good afternoon/evening"), we may say "Hello," "Hi," "How are you?"; there are a very few lines which are generally used by Americans to greet one another. Learning the routine is a matter of learning the lines.

At the Small World Day Care Center every Friday afternoon teachers and kids part company with a jubilant exchange of "Have a good weekend!" The children learn the lines before they learn the constraints upon when the lines are to be used. For two months whenever Neil (age 5) and Jennifer (age 3) left anyplace, or anyone left them, they would smile, wave, and say, "Have a good weekend." After a while they must have figured out when to use the expression because now they only use it on Friday afternoons. Examples like this have suggested to psychologists that we "learn the lines" appropriate to certain social interactions before the lines are meaningful to us. First, we "mimic" and then associate our behavior with certain situations so that it is sensible to us.

Usually, the words appropriate to certain situations are not prescribed. We may learn the lines at first, but there are so many possible lines that we quickly have to learn a kind of "reasoning" behind the lines. Our symbolic display (talk and nonverbal signal) is improvised. The "reasoning" behind the lines is like a social formula. A "social formula" consists of the taken-for-granted expectations in the situation about kinds of "allowed" and "disallowed" talk.

The expression "improvised" is suggested by Leonard Hawes when he compares interpersonal interaction with improvisational jazz:

> Perhaps the best advice to give your friend going on a date is to tell him to "play it by ear," "do what comes naturally," or in short improvise. To introduce a music metaphor, the mutual display of patterned behaviors in the enactment of routines is more like a jam session than a symphony performance. When an orchestra performs, the score is completely written and each musician plays only those notes predetermined in advance. The score is the obligatory sets of rules for the enactment of the symphony. In a jam session, the musicians have no prewritten score. But at the same time they must coordinate their musical outbursts. The notes displayed by the reeds must be interdependent with the rhythm of the percussion section and the notes of the remaining pieces in the group. The musicians may "groove" for several bars and then "fall out." The pattern dissolves and everyone stops to get a fresh start. The history of the jam may change over time as the pattern changes the tempo of enactment.[1]

I shall use the expression "improvising interaction" to refer to that ordinary talk we engage in most of the time. It is ordinary, not because it is unimportant, but because we do it so much we do not stop to think about what we are doing, why we are doing it, or what will happen as a consequence. We take it for granted. But here we shall not take improvised interactions for granted. In the first section of this chapter, I describe the necessary conditions or prerequisites for improvising. I have already stated that improvised interactions are "patterned." Therefore, in the second section I describe the resulting patterns. One kind of pattern is a "theme" or—a repetitive expression of ideas—a kind of mundane organizational intelligence. Another is a "climate" or system of shared feelings—a kind of emotional integration. A third is a "program." A program is the pairing of a simple stimulus with a complex response. It is a routinized pattern in which organizational intelligence and integration are taken for granted. These first two sections, then, explain improvisation by describing "what it takes" to improvise and "what you get" when you improvise.

In the third and fourth sections, I describe improvisation as an organizing process. I describe five vital functions of improvised talk in organizations; defining situations, clarifying relationships, structuring time, motivating, and creating self-esteem. I then describe how organizations in which improvisation is the dominant coordination format differ from other organizations.

In the Application section, I suggest that some social formulas lead to improvised interactions which may be harmful to individuals and organizations. I give examples of these and describe how such dysfunctional formulas might be changed.

PREREQUISITES FOR IMPROVISING

Improvisation is not simply "doing your own thing." Improvisational jazz is music, not noise. It has harmonic structure. The plays of improvisational theater have plots. To use the terminology introduced in the last chapter, uncertainty is structured when people are improvising. The behavior of other people is expected just as musicians have expectations about what each other will play when they are improvising. Improvised interactions are patterns of coordinated behavior. We need to understand here how people coordinate their actions without plans or scripts.

There are two prerequisites to improvising coordinated or structured behaviors. First, actors must be committed to a formula as the basis of their interaction. Second, actors must be monitoring the line of interaction as it is developed.

A "social formula" is a system of interpersonal expectations such as that described in chapter 3. Elements of a social formula are norms, roles, agendas, and motivations. What makes these expectations a "formula" is that they are taken for granted. They are not discussed. They are implicit expectations which are equivalent for all members of the social group.

Improvising takes place in familiar, repetitive situations. In such situations we do not interact with particular other individuals, but with others as stylized roles. We all play "stock characters" in our little improvised plays.

Let us look at an example of improvisational encounter. Jim Smith, Certified Public Accountant, is the first actor. He dresses according to formula (role). He wears a stylish, though not flashy, polyester knit suit, pastel shirt, and striped tie. He carries a leather briefcase and wears glasses. He enters a medium-sized manufacturing corporation accompanied by two younger assistants (also C.P.A.'s). They have come to audit the corporation's books. They have a brief exchange with the receptionist to obtain directions to the comptroller's office.

The three enter the comptroller's reception room. Smith tells the receptionist his name and the purpose of his visit. They are told to be seated, and after a few minutes they are shown into another office. The office is large. At one end there is a mahogany desk. A gold plate on the desk says: Alfred P. Mitchell. The plush carpet matches the drapes hung from ceiling to floor. As they enter a man rises from behind the desk, comes to greet them in the middle of the room. Smith shakes hands with Mitchell. Mitchell then shakes hands with the other two men. He points toward the sofa and chairs near the entrance door; he asks the three men to be seated.

The four men improvise their talk, but the formula is clear. From experience in similar situations, each has learned what behaviors are acceptable in the situation (norms), what behaviors are expected of each of them (roles), the order of major events (agendas), and why each person is there (intentions).

The interaction is routine as long as everyone sticks to the formula. There is no need to "plan" what to do in the situation. The difference between enacting a plan and improvising on a formula is this: When enacting a plan we think about the future, in improvising we attend only to the present. We attend to improvisational conversation merely by nonconsciously checking out or "monitoring" what is happening to make sure that everyone is acting as expected. We do not need to figure out what the other person wants from us because his or her intentions are "given" in the formula. The intentions of the other are taken for granted. The comptroller in the example above takes for granted that the C.P.A. intends to do an honest job of auditing the firm's financial record.

I use the term "monitor" as an analogy to the process of TV technicians monitoring a television show. They monitor the image on the screen to make sure that the equipment is operating as expected. A deviation from the expected signal will throw them into a search for the problem causing the disruption. Monitoring itself is not problem-searching or solving behavior. We monitor our routine interactions as the technician does a TV image.

Any unexpected behavior on the part of one person may cause another to abandon his improvisation. For example, the comptroller, Mitchell, may pick up a hint that Smith is willing to turn in a false report on the finances of the firm. Such a hint would send Mitchell into a "problem-solving" state. He could no longer take Smith's intentions for granted. Instead he would be conscious of his own intentions or goals (for example, to obtain proof that Smith is a crook or intends to dupe the corporation out of some money). Mitchell would then choose among several actions those which seem most likely to secure his goal.

Whenever we pick up unexpected behavioral displays from others, we can no longer improvise our own behavior. We begin to plan our interactions. We start to search for a definition of what is happening. Unexpected behavior is our evidence that our expectations are not equivalent to our partners' expectations. If there's no equivalence, there is no social formula. If there is no social formula, there is no basis for improvising. When we cannot improvise, we have to prepare or plan.

In order to develop an improvised pattern of interaction, therefore, two prerequisites must be met. First, all parties must be committed to the formula. Second, each must monitor the developing interaction line to be satisfied that all parties have minimally equivalent expectations.

The history of an interaction produces an elaboration of the formula. Groups develop special norms. That is, members of the group come to regard certain behavior as obligatory for all group members. The role system becomes elaborated as people gather more information about what to expect from each role incumbent. The agenda becomes special for that group. There is an elaboration of intentions motivating particular actions.

The process of elaborating the routine is a process of increasing complexity, but the increased complexity is not always evident because the formula is for behavior which is "taken for granted." The behavior is mundane and routine. Norms, roles, agendas, and intentions are not questioned. The existence of these expectations must be inferred from the repetitive behavior of the actors in the situation.

IMPROVISED INTERACTION PATTERNS

Themes

If you went into an organization to observe communication you would not "see" the norms, roles, agendas, and intentions. These are terms which observers use to interpret activity. You would see only the repetitive behavior. You would see people talking with one another. After a while you would notice that certain topics are raised repeatedly. You might notice, for example, that when mail carriers are sorting the mail for their routes, they discuss the Pittsburgh Pirates every day. You might notice roles people take (one· person, the "baseball expert"; another, the "Phillie Fan") during the talk. A theme is a topic of conversation which occurs repeatedly among members of an on-going social organization. Theme represents the consensus which emerges through group interaction. Developing a "theme" allows members of a social organization to relate to one another and to relate the past and the future to the present and thus develop a sensible continuity to what they are doing.[2]

Donald Roy's case study of interaction among four unskilled workers in a machine shop illustrates how talk improvised on a social formula develops "themes." The themes of the workers varied from serious subjects to nonsensical chatter ·in no particular consequence. "Serious conversation could suddenly melt into horseplay, and vice versa." He describes how one theme developed:

> I grew almost as sick of a kidding theme which developed from some personal information contributed during a serious conversation on property ownership and high taxes. I dropped a few remarks about two acres

of land which I owned in one of the western states, and from then on I had to listen to questions, advice, and general nonsensical comment in regard to "Danelly's farm." This "farm" soon became stocked with horses, cows, pigs, chickens, ducks, and the various and sundry domesticated beasts so tunefully listed in "Old McDonald Had a Farm." George was a persistent offender with this theme. Where the others seemed to be mainly interested in statistics on livestock, crops, etc., George's teasing centered on a generous offering of help with the household chores while I worked in the fields. He would drone on, *ad nauseam*, "when I come to visit you, you will never have to worry about the housework, Danelly. I'll stay around the house when you go out to dig the potatoes and milk the cows, I'll stay in and peel potatoes and help your wife do the dishes." Danelly always found it difficult to change the subject on George, once the latter started to bear down on the farm theme.[3]

The themes represented the group's consensus about what they were doing and how they were to relate to one another while they worked. The themes were "performed with a system of roles which formed a sort of pecking hierarchy. Horseplay had its initiators and victims, its amplifiers, and its chorus; kidding had its attackers and attacked, its least attacked and its most attacked, its ready acceptors of attack and its strong resistors to attack." All of the group members participated in the developing of themes, "but within the controlling frame of status, a matter of who can say or do what to whom and get away with it."[4]

Integration was achieved and maintained through the development of interaction themes. This was particularly evident in an incident which Roy calls "Black Friday." One of the themes of the group's interaction revolved around George, the oldest group member, who was paid five cents an hour more than the others. The professor theme concerned George's daughter who had recently married the son of a professor at a local college. The theme was elaborated with tales of George going for "walks along the midway" with the professor. Roy calls the professor theme the cream of the verbal interaction. He concluded that George's superior status in the group was associated not so much with his five cents an hour higher wage, as with his role in the professor theme.

On Black Friday, Sammy, the usual recipient of jokes, was not present at work. Roy had an idea for a little fun through elaboration of the professor theme. He whispered to Ike to tell George that he had seen "the professor" teaching in a barber college on Madison Street. Ike thought this one over for a few minutes, and caught the vision of its possibilities. Whereupon Ike informed "the unsuspecting George of his near West Side discovery":

George reacted to this announcement with stony silence. The burden of questioning Ike for further details of his discovery fell upon me. Ike had not elaborated his story very much before we realized that the show was not going over. George kept getting redder in the face, and more tight-lipped; he slammed into his clicking with increased vigor. I made one last weak attempt to keep the play on the road by remarking that barber colleges paid pretty well. George turned to hiss at me, "You'll have to go to Kankakee with Ike!" I dropped the subject, Ike whispered to me, "George is sore!"

George was indeed sore. He didn't say another word the rest of the morning. There was no conversation at lunchtime, nor was there any after lunch. The pale of silence had fallen over the clicker room. . . . For three days, George would not speak to Ike.[5]

For thirteen days there was little interaction among members of the work group. During that time there were emotional attacks on one another, first indirectly and then directly. Finally, George and Ike, for no apparent reason, began some serious congenial conversation. Soon Ike was singing again and "the old themes reappeared as suddenly as the desert flowers in spring." However, the professor theme was never developed again. George never again mentioned Sunday afternoon walks with the professor. Roy describes these events as a process of "reintegration."

Themes represent an implicit consensus among group members about the conditions of their interaction. This consensus is the baseline for improvised talk and hence for integration. In proclaiming that the "professor" taught at a barber college, Roy and Ike were directly attacking the consensus of the theme and therefore attacking George's place in the group's social structure. George responded by withdrawing from the interaction. Suddenly the whole consensus was destroyed and there was no way to "make talk" in the group. Because this was a group integrated through improvisation, when they could not improvise, there was no method for achieving social integration. "Themes" are an important basis for integration. When certain critical themes become inappropriate as a topic of talk, the whole integrative structure of a group may dissolve. Reconstructing integration is not achieved until new themes are developed.

Climates

Sensitive observers of any group will soon realize that there is a pattern of how people talk to one another as well as of what people talk about. This is the climate of the organization. Themes are easier to observe than climates. To discover a theme requires sensitive listening for ideas which are repeatedly discussed and elaborated. The "climate" is feeling. I may experience a "hostile climate" and yet have difficulty verbalizing to others why I believe that the climate is hostile.

Words such as "tense," "friendly," "supportive," "defensive," "open," "warm," and "cold" are often used to express how we feel in a group. How we feel in a group is a response to the climate of the group. This response is a complex of behavioral displays which reflects the climate. We smile, grimace, withdraw, sit down, grit our teeth. When a person is in a group which seems "friendly," that person is likely to act differently than if the person is in a group which seems "tense." When we feel tension, we respond with tension. Thus, the climate of a group is self-sustaining. A person in a group which is tense responds with tension. His tension then contributes to the climate of the group to which others respond. One cannot say therefore that a climate is "caused" by the actions of any one individual. Producing a climate, like producing a theme, requires some participation of all involved. Therefore, climates reflect assumptions of participants. In particular they reflect assumptions about roles and motivations. McCroskey, Larson, and Knapp discuss three kinds of climates typically found in large, bureaucratic organizations.[6] Their typology illustrates the relationship between expectations and the resulting improvised patterns called climates.

The first climate they call "dehumanized." The assumptions underlying this climate resemble those of classical organization theorists (see chapter 1). Actors in a situation assume that others are lazy and have no interest in the organization's objectives. They assume that the superior's role is to direct and manipulate which the subordinate's role is to shirk responsibility and to do only that work which is absolutely required. To say that a climate must be "felt" does not mean that there are not observable behaviors which indicate the existence of the climate. They illustrate this with a list of reciprocal behaviors typically found in dehumanized climates (see Table 4.1). In the left column are supervisory actions. In the right column are subordinate responses. Note that the behavior of each actor confirms the expectations of the other. The actors in the situation have developed equivalent definitions of their social situation. Each party acts as the other expects him to do.

The steelworker doing manual labor may also be in a dehumanized climate. In the following description of his work situation, a steelworker tells us what it is like to work in a dehumanized climate.

It's hard to take pride in a bridge you're never gonna cross, in a door you're never gonna open. . . . In a steel mill . . . you don't see where nothing goes. I got chewed out by my foreman once. He said, "Mike, you're a good worker but you have a bad attitude." My attitude is that I don't get excited about my job. I do my work, but I don't say whoopee-doo. The day I get excited about my job is the day I go to a head shrinker. How are you gonna get excited about pullin' steel? . . . It's not just the work. . . . It's the non-recognition by other people.[7]

TABLE 4.1
Reciprocal Behaviors of Supervisor and Subordinate in a Dehumanized Climate (From James C. McCroskey, Carl E. Larson, and Mark L. Knapp, *An Introduction to Interpersonal Communication* © 1971, p. 43. Reprinted by permission of Prentice-Hall, Inc., Englewood Cliffs, New Jersey.)

Supervisor	Subordinate
1. I withhold information from you. After all, I'm the boss and have integrity. Confidential information is perfectly safe with me, but not with you.	Since I don't share information with you, you become quite ingenious at ferreting out secrets. Now, of course, a secret is of no status unless you can use it to prove to someone that you are "in the know." This is how we get leaks, and this is how you, my subordinate, "prove" to me that you have no integrity.
2. I not only tell you what to do, but I quite often tell you how and when to do it. If I'm smart I may use a little participation as a gimmick, but the end result is the same.	Since I tell you what to do and quite often how and when to do it, you don't reach for new work. Thus, you "prove" your laziness and dislike for responsibility.
3. I write all the important letters or I have you write them for me and I sign them. In some cases I may even have all the incoming mail delivered to me so that in my superior wisdom I can screen it.	You learn to communicate as I do, but not as yourself. And since I do the communicating, you learn very little about the other parts of the business or even very much about your own sphere of endeavor. Thus, you "prove" your indifference to organizational needs.
4. I'll do all the upward and lateral communicating. If I think your idea is good, I'll handle it myself. If I don't think it's any good, I'll kill it right now because there is no point in bothering other people with harebrained ideas.	Since I either kill your ideas when they come to me or carry them upstairs myself, you stop generating new ideas and thus "prove" your lack of desire to achieve.
5. I'll ask you to study a problem and give me a recommendation. If you haven't been able to guess what's acceptable to me, I'll tell you to change the recommendation. Again, of course, I am using participation as a gimmick.	You don't bother to study the problem—it's much more practical to study me and anticipate what I'll buy in the way of a recommendation or solution. By this you "prove" that you prefer to be directed.
6. What I do communicate within the department, I'll communicate with each of you individually to keep you all competing for my favor, and also	Since I don't communicate with you as a group, you and your fellow subordinates use woodshed communication and form an informal

to insure that I'll be the only one who has all the information. 7. If somebody is interested in having you work for him, I'll decide whether I want to let you go or not, and I will cut the deal then and there. If I decide that you are my property, you'll never know anyone else was interested in you.	but very effective alliance to keep me off your backs. This simply "proves" you are incapable of controlling your own behavior. Since you never have to make any career decisions—I make them all for you—you never develop the reliance on self or the spirit of risk taking that comes only with the experience of making decisions, thus "proving" that you avoid decisions.

A dehumanized climate is created when people do not allow one another to be human, to build their self-esteem. In the case of the steelworker, he is not given any recognition for the value of his work. In the case of the office worker, he is not allowed to make any decisions. In such a climate, people begin to act as if they are not people. They improvise on a social formula in which their intentions are for money alone and their role is to have minimum compliance with organizational rules.

A second kind of organizational climate McCroskey, Larson, and Knapp call "Happiness for Lunch Bunch." There is a taken-for-granted expectation of equality of status among different roles. The obligation of the members is to "be nice" to one another. Conflict and tension are not permitted by the norms. People are assumed to want acceptance by all others at all times. The resulting climate is one in which conflicts cannot be resolved because the norms of the group do not allow for expression of conflict. Individuals may be unable to express concern for the group's task because the unstated, but common assumption is that individuals are primarily together for social interaction and that sociality is in conflict with task accomplishment.

Irving Janis provides an example of a group with a "happiness for lunch bunch" climate. The group consisted of a group of smokers, twelve middle-class men and two women. They were participating in a clinic whose *stated* purpose was to help people quit smoking. Janis records the following indications of the "happiness" climate: "At every meeting, the members were amiable, reasserted their warm feelings of solidarity, and sought complete concurrence on every important topic, with no reappearance of the unpleasant bickering that would spoil the cozy atmosphere." He offers the following evidence that the maintenance of a "happy climate" was more important to members than the goal of quitting smoking.

At the second meeting . . . two of the most dominant members took the position that heavy smoking was an almost incurable addiction. The majority of the others soon agreed that no one could be expected to cut down drastically. One heavy smoker, a middle-aged business executive, took issue with this consensus, arguing that by using will power he had stopped smoking since joining the group and that everyone else could do the same. His declaration was followed by a heated discussion, which continued in the halls of the building after the formal meeting adjourned. Most of the others ganged up against the man who was deviating from the group consensus. Then, at the beginning of the next meeting, the deviant announced that he had made an important decision. "When I joined," he said, "I agreed to follow the two main rules required by the clinic—to make a conscientious effort to stop smoking and to attend every meeting. But I have learned from experience in this group that you can only follow one of the rules, you can't follow both. And so, I have decided that I will continue to attend every meeting but I have gone back to smoking again until after the last meeting." Whereupon the other members beamed at him and applauded enthusiastically, welcoming him back to the fold. No one commented on the fact that the whole point of the meetings was to help each individual cut down on smoking as rapidly as possible. As a psychological consultant to the group, I tried to call this to the members' attention . . . but during that meeting the members managed to ignore our comments and reiterated their consensus that heavy smoking was an addiction from which no one would be cured except by cutting down very gradually over a long period of time.[8]

The group Janis described developed a theme: "Smoking is an addiction which requires gradual removal." This theme constituted the group consensus or "organizational intelligence." It also developed a "cozy atmosphere" (climate) among members in which the norm would not permit statements which might engender conflict among members. Theme and climate were closely related. The result, of course, was that members of the group would not quit smoking. The group's overt purpose was readily sacrificed to obtain the pleasures of a nonconflicting climate.

The descriptions of "dehumanized" and "happiness" climates are exaggerations of typical climates of groups. These exaggerated climates are found in some organizations, as the words of the steelworkers testify. In most groups, however, the climate is a mixture of the two. There is more concern for people than in the "dehumanized" and more concern for the task than in the "happiness," but in any group there is usually a relatively constant set of expectations which lead to relatively stable feelings among interactants.

A third climate is called "situational." The norm here is that people should be "adapting." The roles are worked out by participants in the interaction. The agenda is highly flexible. People are assumed to have intentions which are different from one another and which change from time to time. The key concept in this "kind" of climate is change.

People are presumed to be changeable and therefore the interpersonal climates which encourage some behaviors and discourage others are changeable. McCroskey, Larson, and Knapp explain:

> By definition, the situational approach attempts to elicit the "appropriate" responses for a given situation. When it is necessary to use a strict uncompromising type of discipline, it is used; when it is necessary to spend time in structuring experiences for a person's self-development, it is done. . . . It is clear we are still dealing with human judgments. . . . Such a climate also demands a constant awareness that there will be differences in such things as the amount of time, patience, skill and commitment demonstrated by the workers in this climate.[9]

Note the emphasis on judgment and awareness in this statement. It seems that situational climates do not result from improvised interactions. Rather a situational climate refers to patterns of planned interactions. It is only when we are conscious of uniqueness of the present situation, of our purposes, and of the people with whom we are talking that we can adapt our behavior. Before we can conclude that people should always plan their interaction in order to construct a desirable situation climate we must consider whether all interaction can be planned interaction.

Is it possible to have the kind of flexible, adaptive interactions typical of situational climates by avoiding the practice of improvising on social formulas? If so, at what cost? To answer this question, we shall examine the function of improvisation in organizations. However, first let us consider the third kind of interactive pattern, the "program."

Programs

A program can be seen in the relationship of one person's action to the response by another. James March and Herbert Simon define the term "program" as a simple stimulus followed by an immediate and highly complex response. They illustrate:

> The sounding of the alarm going in a fire station initiates such a program. So does the appearance of a relief applicant at a social worker's desk. So does the appearance of an automobile chassis in front of the work station of a worker on the assmbley line. Situations in which a relatively simple stimulus sets off an elaborate program of activity without any apparent interval of search, problem-solving, or choice are not rare. They account for a very large part of the behavior of all persons, and for almost all of the behavior of persons in relatively routine positions. Most behavior, and particularly most behavior in organizations, is governed by performance programs.[10]

A program is observed when one sees an elaborate response to a simple stimulus. The response follows immediately and appears to be automatic. From this, one infers that there was no intervening period of search or problem solving.

A program is organizational intelligence and integration reduced to a kind of "printed circuit." What a person needs to know is (1) how to recognize the stimulus to invoke his program, and (2) what specific actions are to be carried out in the program and in what order the actions are to occur. If the person recognizes the stimulus and runs the correct program of responding action, then integration is achieved.

But if actions are so routinized, how can we say they are "improvised?" They are improvised because they are not planned. At some point in the past, the actors or some organizational decision makers may have planned the actions. But now the actors no longer think about the expectations which lead to their actions. The warehouse clerk routinely checks people out of the warehouse without stopping to think, "What does this person want from me when he appears before my desk?" You can put a stack of books in front of the librarian at the charge-out desk and he will stamp them and hand them to you. Every action is "spontaneous" in that the librarian does not stop to plan them. The interactive sequence of events is routine because it is similar to hundreds of other interactions. It is interaction based upon "performance programs" or rigid formulas prescribing the expectations of the situation. People take for granted what behaviors are expected (norms), who is to do what (roles), in what order (agendas), and why (motives).

In this section, I have discussed three observable regularities of action. Themes, climate, and programs are patterns which can be found by watching and listening to a group of people communicating regularly with one another. I have suggested in passing that these regularities are associated with organizational intelligence and integration. Now we look more directly at how improvised interaction patterns function to create and maintain human organizations.

TALK IN ORGANIZATIONS

Some talk is planned; some is collective decision building. But most of our talk is improvised, and for this reason, this section on talk is put into this chapter. The section which follows describes some of the functions of improvised talk which are different from functions of other coordination formats.

Before proceeding with a description of the functions of talk, the term "function" should be clarified. In chapter 1 several sections referred to the function of communication in different schools of organizational theory. "Function" meant the use or role which communication was seen as performing in organizing according to the various theories. The definition of function in chapters 2 and 3 as well as this chapter is somewhat different than that. A succinct definition of function is provided by Dance and Larson:

> Function is different from purpose. A function happens as an inevitable and natural result of something, while a purpose is that which can be done with something. For example, the production of heat is the inevitable result of the dissipation of energy. Therefore, the production of heat is a function of the dissipation of energy. The heat thus created can be used for a multitude of purposes: for creating personal warmth, as a source of energy. . . .[11]

Chapter 2 described "intelligence" or consensus on meaning as a function—an inevitable and natural result—of communication. Chapter 3 described "integration" as a function of communication. Now I examine particular functions of talk. These functions are not the deliberate purposes of talk. Rather, they take place because the talk takes place. They are the inevitable and natural results through which organizing happens. Improvised talk is not "purposeful," though people may see in retrospect that their talk accomplished some purpose.

The existence of talk in organizations was "discovered" by the early human relations theorists.[12] The Hawthorne researchers found that the talk which goes on among coworkers influences how much production they are willing to turn out. It's difficult to talk about talk. In fact, it's almost a miracle that it was discovered at all. (Historically, talk in organizations was "discovered" no sooner than the capability to produce the atom bomb.) Discovering talk is rather like a fish discovering water. Its constant presence and constant influence obscure its existence. Talk is taken for granted.

When we talk to one another we develop the social formulas which are the basis of organizing. Not only are expectations necessary for communication. Through communication, we inevitably develop or elaborate those expectations. To be specific: Norms are a basis for interaction; the corollary is that through talk we "define situations." Roles are a basis for interaction; the corollary is that through talk we "clarify relationships." Agendas are a basis for interaction; the corollary is that through talk we "structure time." Motives are a basis of interaction; the corollary is that through talk we "motivate" ourselves and others. In addition to these four dimensions of constructing organizations (situations, relationships, time structures, and motivations), I discuss in the last subsection the function of talk in developing individual self-esteem in organized settings.

Although I use the term "talk" in the discussion, I am referring not simply to verbal communication. I mean all "displaying" of symbols. (See distinction in chapter 3.) Some groups engage in oral, verbal interaction almost continuously. They have elaborated verbal-codes—extensive vocabularies and the norms which encourage "talking things over." Other groups have more restricted vocabularies. Members of these groups do not talk as much. A factory in which the noise level is high and the people are not positioned close to one another discourages verbal communication, but if the workers can see one another, they are still influencing one another. By intently concentrating on their work they display to themselves and all who can see that this is the "proper" conduct. In their silence, they are still "talking" to one another. But the "talk" is limited. To the extent that oral communication is limited, the process of organizing may be somewhat restricted.

Talk and Defining Situations

A repetitive theme of this book is that people do not respond to an "objective world." Rather they respond to a "constructed" world. People respond to situations as defined in terms of their cognitive map. Through talk, people construct equivalent definitions of their situation. The talk among members of a group helps each person understand what he or she is doing in the situation and how "important" the individual and collective work are. A definition of a situation provides norms about obligatory behavior.

The construction of a situational definition takes place as people display, through symbols, their taken-for-granted assumptions about the norms of interaction and the character of the situation. A proofreader quoted in Terkel's *Working* exemplifies nicely how people use their talk to define their situation.

> I noticed somebody talking on the phone the other day, one of the older guys. He said he was at the office. It dawned on me when a guy says, "I'm at the office," it means, "I'm a white-collar worker." It means "I don't dirty my hands." He wasn't at work, he was "at the office."[13]

Through talk we define our situation. Even from what people do not say we learn to interpret what we are doing. We learn that we are "at the office." The phrase signifies more than a room with desks and chairs. It signifies status, life style, and obligatory behaviors.

Talk and Clarifying Relationships

In order to coordinate our behavior with others we need to know how to act with others. This means having an image of our relationships with others. Like the process of defining a situation, clarifying relationships is done with words. Again, however, what is not said is important. Fred Katz has studied the process by which medical pathologists are coordinated into hospital organizations. Katz relates the story of how one pathologist "learned" about his relationship with others in the hospital:

> There is the case of the old-time pathologist, a leader in the field. One day the administrator of the hospital called him and told him that he planned to have pictures taken of the heads of all departments at two o'clock that afternoon in a certain room, and would he come. When the pathologist arrived at two, he found assembled there the chief janitor, chief linen service man, etc. He thought the administrator lacked tact; he would have preferred to have his picture taken with the chief of surgery.[14]

We clarify our relationships with other people by "acting out" our images of what those relationships are. In Weick's terms, we "enact" the relationship. If we act in ways which another takes to be improper or unsatisfactory we can usually tell by their response to our actions. Enacting the image of a relationship need not be as "graphic" as the example above. Whenever we act, in fact, we are displaying to others our image of the relationship we have with them.

Katz provides a more typical example of how we enact our images of relationships. He is illustrating the pathologist's role as "doctor's doctor." The following exchange took place in a pathologist's office. A surgeon came in to ask about the analysis of tissue he had removed from a female patient the day before. The pathologist and a resident in pathology told him the tissue indicated advanced cancer. This conversation followed:

Surgeon: She's had symptoms for five years, but not seen a doctor. I delivered this woman ten years ago, and she hasn't seen a doctor since.
Resident: Did you ask her why she waited so long?
Surgeon: (Mimicking patient) "I was scared, doctor" . . . makes you mad . . .
Resident: What are you going to do?
Surgeon: Tell her she has advanced cancer. Tell her husband her chances of recovery are about nil; we'll try deep X-ray and radium treatment, if she can stand it, and if they have any plans for the two of them, they should carry them out now. (Then after asking the pathologist, "You don't mind if I use your phone, old boy?" the surgeon called the husband of the patient.)
Surgeon: (to patient's husband) . . . we've got the microscopic report; it's as I

told you the other day; your wife has very very extensive cancer, with it at this stage our only treatment is X-ray therapy; it'll eliminate her functions, no more chances of pregnancy—you know she's always afraid of pregnancy; well, there won't be any more danger of that. . . .[15]

The conversation is interesting not because it is unusual, but precisely because it is typical of how the people enact for one another their taken-for-granted roles. The surgeon is adapting to the husband's expectations. The doctor-patient relationship does not permit the doctor to express the anger (and other strong emotions) he feels. The resident, being a "learner" in this situation, is asking expected questions. Moreover, the surgeon has taken the liberty of expressing his emotions in the presence of the resident and pathologist. Erving Goffman would call this "backstage" behavior.[16] The doctors are a team. They present a performance to an audience, the patient. They signal one another that they are both members of a performing team when they communicate ideas and feelings to one another which are "closed" to the audience.

Thus, we work out our relationships with each other by what we say and do not say. This process of "clarifying relationships" is hardly noticed in most interactions. It is taken for granted. Only when a relationship is undergoing rapid change may we be aware of what a person is telling us, and how a person is telling us about our relationship. Of course, we can talk about our relations. But most of the information about our roles vis-à-vis one another we learn by enacting our expectations and monitoring how others respond to us. Again, the words are important, but the "talk" by which we clarify relationships goes beyond the words.

Talk and Structuring Time

By talking with others we not only construct a social reality of the world and form relationships with other people, we also construct agendas which permit work to be done. Structuring time is functional for individuals and for organizations. The term "structuring time" comes from Eric Berne. He defines the concept in *Games People Play:*

In everyday terms, what can people do after they have exchanged greetings consisting of a collegiate "Hi!" or an Oriental ritual lasting several hours? After stimulus hunger and recognition hunger comes structure hunger. The perennial problem of adolescents is: "What do you say to her (him) then?" . . . The eternal problem of the human being is how to structure his waking hours . . . The function of all social living is to lend mutual assistance for this project.[17]

Through structuring our time we avoid boredom. Talk is the most common means by which people structure their time.

Charles R. Walker discusses work, talk, and boredom in his study of social changes associated with the installation of automated machinery for making pipe in a U.S. Steel Mill.[18] Mill 4 was the first automated mill. Most of the crew came from Mill 1. The workers were located at stations farther apart than in the old mill. A public address (P.A.) system was installed so that they could signal one another about when their machine broke down, or give information necessary to keep the work flow going. At first the men resented the new procedures:

> It's not as good as the old mill. I can't talk with the fellows. I'm on the stand alone. I don't use the P. A. system because I don't talk good.

> Most of the time I work by myself just looking into the furnace. There's no chance to get away and talk to the fellows. You do and something happens and you get into trouble. One Number 1 we were close and could talk to each other.

> In Number 1 we used to have a lot of fun—those on the furnace, anyhow. Over here in Number 4 there is too much tension . . . You work alone on Number 4.

> It's against the rules for anybody to talk to me while I'm operating. On Number 1 there was a group of us on the furnace. We got to know each other good.

The workers resented the rules, the distance, and the necessity to watch their work so closely that they could not talk. Because they could not structure their time with talk, it dragged:

> Time seems to go better when you have somebody to talk to.

> Talking helps to pass the time away.

Some felt they would produce more pipe if they could talk to one another:

> You may think it's a funny thing, but when the men are fooling around and talking to one another and having a lot of fun, then you'll really see production moving.

As might be expected, rules or no rules, the men found a way to talk. They reconstituted their cognitive maps. The P.A. system, which had at first intimidated them, was incorporated into the formula for their interaction. They developed a new meaning for it.

> We use the P. A. system on the job all the time. It helps in two ways. If something goes wrong on the mill we can let the piercer operator or someone else know about it probably quicker than we could any other

way. Like I said before, we do a lot of talking and kidding around, and that helps, too.

That P. A. system is really nice. You get quick action. Now I got so I know just who is talking and just where it's coming from.

That (P.A.) system they have helps out quite a lot. If there's trouble some place in the mill, a man can yell over the system and tell just what's wrong. Then we all know what to do. Also, when things are going along good why the fellows like to use it to razz each other and fool around. It helps the time go by.

Walker and Guest found the same function of talk on automobile assembly lines. According to one worker: "We have a lot of fun and talk all the time," and "If it weren't for the talking and fooling, you'd go nuts."[19]

Donald Roy describes the agenda of workers in the machine shop he studied as composed of "times": coffee time, peach time, banana time, fish time, coke time, and of course, lunch time. "Banana time" occurred about the same hour every morning. Ike would sneak over to Sammy's lunch box and remove a banana. He would then call out "Banana time!" and gulp it down while Sammy protested the theft. Afterward the other two group members would join in talk about the theft. During Roy's whole stay with the work group, not once did Sammy get to eat his own banana at lunch, though he brought one every day. Roy describes the function of these "times":

> As phases of the daily series, they occurred almost hourly, and so short were they in duration that they disrupted work activity only slightly. Their significance lay not so much in their function as rest pauses, although it cannot be denied that physical refreshment was involved. Nor did their chief importance lie in the accentuation of progress points in the passage of time, although they could perform that function. . . . The major significance of the interactional interruptions lay in such a carryover of interest. The physical interplay which momentarily halted work activity would initiate verbal exchanges and thought processes to occupy group members until the next interruption. The group interactions thus not only marked off the time; they gave it content and hurried it along.[20]

Thus, by "structuring time" talk provides job satisfaction and at least the potential for what is generally called "motivation."

Talk and Motivation

The classical theorists took motivation for granted. It was not until the Human Relations theorists discovered the importance of talk in organizing that theorists became interested in motivation as a problem. It is not simply coincidence that organizational theorists became interested in motivation at the same time that they became interested in talk. For the classical theorists, people worked if they were rewarded (in money) for their effort. If a person did not work, he or she was not paid. Likewise, workers were to be paid on the basis of the amount they produced. The Hawthorne researchers found that workers being paid on a piece rate did not produce as much as they could. Instead, each person produced what was considered by the work group to be an "honest day's work." In other words, the members of a work group had a definition of their situation which included how much production was to be done. Individual workers constructed their motivation within the group's definition of the work situation. Rather than motivation being an internal "drive," it is in part the result of the talk which goes on among a member's group.

The Hawthorne researchers found that workers frequently used terms such as "rate buster" (a person who produces too much) and "chiseler" (a person who produces too little). Such symbols are the means by which a group influences the behavior of individuals. These terms become the themes of talk in a group. The group uses them to describe an individual's actions. Likewise, they are the language which the group provides individuals to interpret their own actions. Thus, they constitute the display of consensus of the group.

If a person's motivation is constituted using a group's definition of the situation, then there should be similarity in motivation among people working together. At the same time, there should be different patterns of motivation among groups which are related to the differences in talk themes among various groups. Gouldner foud this to be the case in a gypsum factory. In the factory, there were two kinds of workers: gypsum miners and the surface workers who made the gypsum into wall board. Gouldner found significant differences between motivation on "top" (surface workers) and "bottom" (miners). Gouldner describes motivation in the gypsum factory with words and expressions characteristically applied to the two groups and their work. "The Miners Work Hard" was a theme found in the talk of miners and their supervisors. One miner put it this way:

> The miners make a lot of money, but they deserve it. *They work hard* and under a dangerous roof.

Miners did not report that they worked hard because they were paid well, however. Instead they claimed to work hard to produce quality. "Skill" and "quality-work" were themes in the miners' talk. Miners felt that surface workers valued only "seniority" because only seniority was the basis for their promotion:

One time when they posted a job, it was more than seniority that counted. Quality counted, too. It's still that way down here. On top, I guess it's getting to be just seniority.

Coordinated with the presence of themes describing the miners as "hard working" was a climate in which the miners were relatively "free" to establish their own work rules. The gypsum miners were not punished for absenteeism as the surface workers were. One mining supervisor describes the work climate of the miners:

> I think they should be given the chance to show initiative. Here in the mine we give the man a job to do and he does it without being watched. . . . The men have a job to do themselves. They're not controlled.

Gouldner does not report how the surface workers described their work and themselves. He says that promotion to management positions came almost exclusively from the ranks of surface workers. He says that there was little informal solidarity among them and they were willing to "squeal" on one another. From his description, we can surmise that there were no themes of worker talk which promoted "quality" job performance. No doubt "promotion" was valued, but promotion is accomplished only by individuals, not work groups.

Miners coopted their supervisors into their work groups. They described their foremen as "chums." Surface workers, on the other hand, described ideal supervisors as impartial but distant:

> [A good foreman is] very level-headed and doesn't get excited when a guy makes a mistake; if the foreman is nice and friendly, *but not* too friendly, he's good.

> The idea is not to be too sociable with the foreman. Just get your work done and get out.

The work climate on the surface is reflected by differences in themes of talk. Gouldner describes the surface supervisors as "distant" from the workers. One theme of the foremen's talk was that their workers are "lazy":

> You have to watch the men; some of them would sneak away and go to sleep if you let them.

> One fellow wanted to sleep quite a bit. I talked to him two or three times and told him finally that he'd change or else it meant his job.

Here then are two different patterns of motivation. The miners went about their work "quickly." They "worked hard." But they refused to come to work whenever they did not want to come. The surface workers, in general, were "lazy"; they slept whenever they could sneak away. But they obeyed the no absentee rule. Gouldner explains why there was such a difference in motivation: "Definition of the mining situation as particularly perilous permitted miners legitimate resistance to authority and disciplined control." Because there was a consensus among miners, management, and surface workers that the miners' work was dangerous, miners were permitted, if not encouraged, to be idiosyncratic. As one painter on the surface put it:

> They can't stop the miners taking off. The men get their pay and take off. Hell, it's no fun working in the mine. Too much danger. I don't blame them.

Working in a climate in which they were autonomous from the control of the management, the miners used themes to define their work as important. There were few external controls in a dangerous situation where close coordination was necessary to the workers. Therefore, through their informal talk, the miners established their own norms, roles, agendas, and motivations without much intervention from management. Some of their norms meant higher production; some resulted in lower production. The difference between motivation among miners and surface workers is evidence of the importance of talk in motivating organizational performance.

Talk and Self-Esteem

Talk not only functions to develop cooperative activity, it also is the method by which individuals construct their self-esteem. There are two reasons for discussing individual needs in a book on organizing. First, to understand how organizations "work," you should understand how organizations affect members as people. Therefore, I describe how expectations influence the development of self-esteem. Second, organizations are constructed by people. Therefore, I describe how a person's self-esteem is related to his or her participation in collective tasks.

Before proceeding, however, let us observe that self-esteem is both valuable and complex. Eric Berne has called the presumed need for self-esteem "recognition hunger." It is not a simple hunger. The need for food is biological. Although people have different food preferences, presumably, biologists can establish the minimum daily requirements (M.D.R.) for human food consumption without paying much attention to cultural and personality differences. (For M.D.R., see listing on the side of your favorite cereal box.)

No one has yet established the M.D.R. to satisfy recognition hunger. Berne says that "strokes" are the necessary "food" but a "movie star may require a hundred strokes a week from anonymous and undifferentiated admirers . . . while a scientist may keep physically and mentally healthy on one stroke a year from a respected master."[21] Recognition or self-esteem is a symbolic construction. As with any symbol, each individual has his or her own meaning, but there is equivalence of meaning within groups. Each movie star has an individual definition of what it means to be "successful." But movie stars, in general, define "success" differently than scientists.

Berne observes that the process of growing up involves switching from the pleasures of physical strokes to symbolic strokes. Ernest Becker makes this same point: "The entire early training period of the child is one in which he learns to *switch modes* of maintaining self-esteem. . . . His vital sense of self-value no longer derives from mother's milk, but from mother's mouth. It comes to be derived from symbols."[22]

As the child grows up and learns to participate in formal organizations, he learns to construct his self-esteem from his roles in these organizations. As Ernest Becker puts it:

> Finally, in the twenties one comes to earn his self-esteem by performing in the roles that society provides: doctor, lawyer, corporation man, teacher, engineer, and so on. Then we get our vital sense of inner worth by repeating, "I am a good doctor, . . . lawyer . . . engineer. . . . Look at the operation I performed, the business deal I pulled off, the way that beautiful girl looks at me . . ." and so on. Almost all of one's inner life, when he is not absorbed in some active task, is a traffic in images of self-worth.
>
> If our first reaction is to shrug off this as an exaggeration, let us try to be honest and admit to ourselves what we do most of the time. We run what I like to call an "inner-newsreel" that passes in constant review the symbols that give self-esteem, make us feel important and good. We are constantly testing and rehearsing whether we *really* are somebody, in a scenario where the most minor events are recorded, and the most subtle gradations assume an immense importance. After all, the self-esteem is symbolic, and the main characteristic of symbols is that they cut reality very fine. Anthony Quinn in his great role in *Requiem for a Heavyweight* earned his inner sense of self-value by constantly reminding himself and others that he was the *"fifth*-ranking contender for the heavyweight crown." This made him really *somebody*, gave him continual nourishment, allowed him to hold his head high in the shabbiest circumstances. Academic intellectuals have their own fine gradations of worth: a six-hour teaching load, with *no* undergraduate teaching, in an Ivy-League school; versus a three-hour teaching load, with only *one* undergraduate course, in an *almost* Ivy-League school. How these balance in the scale of self-worth can cause agonizing life decisions.[23]

There are two important things to remember in what Becker says here. First, self-esteem is most important to us. We spend a great deal of our time constructing our image of our own worth. Becker describes self-esteem as a prime motivator. By this he means that we do things which are consistent with our image of "who" we are. The gypsum miners identified themselves as "hard-working"; their foremen and even the surface workers concurred with this definition. Their actions were motivated by this definition of self-worth.

A second important observation of Becker's is that adults construct self-esteem largely within the context of their work roles. The gypsum factory gave miners considerable autonomy within which they could define themselves as important.[24] Studs Terkel in the introduction to *Working* says that his book "is about a search . . . for daily meaning as well as daily bread, for recognition as well as cash, for astonishment rather than torpor; in short, for a sort of life rather than a Monday through Friday sort of dying." He describes some people who find self-esteem through their work. The stone mason, the piano tuner, the bookbinder find "a meaning to their work well over and beyond the reward of the paycheck." Terkel describes people who find their organizational roles so rewarding that they always "play" their role. For example:

> At a public unveiling of a celebrated statue in Chicago, a lawyer, after a deep study, mused, "I accept Mr. Picasso in good faith. But if you look at the height of the slope on top and the propensity of children who will play on it, I have a feeling that some child may fall and be hurt and the county be sued."[25]

This lawyer is a lawyer even when he is judging art!

In contrast to these people who find so much self-esteem in their work that they are always working, there are some who "live" just for quitting time. What kind of self-esteem do these people find in their organization role? They describe themselves as "machines," "mules," "monkeys," "less than a farm implement," "objects," and "robots." A young accountant trying to describe his work, concludes in frustration, "There is nothing to talk about." These people must act to protect their self-esteem from the definition offered by their organization. How do they do it? According to a union leader at an automotive plant:

> Occasionally, one of the guys will let a car go by. At that point he's made a decision, "Aw, fuck it. It's only a car! It's more important just to stand there and rap. With us, it becomes a human thing. It's the most enjoyable part of my job, that moment. I love it!"[26]

Here is a man constructing self-esteem within the context of an organization, but he is doing it by opposing the regulations of the organization. In much the same way, the gypsum miners defined the no absentee rule as a sign of their independence. Note that the man describes his action as a decision. The organization offers him a program for his behavior, but he decides not to act in the manner officially expected by the organization. It is defiance of an official expectation which is dehumanizing. But not all routine expectations are dehumanizing; quite the contrary, most of our self-esteem is constructed from our accomplishment of taken-for-granted actions. According to Becker it is through our routine interactions that we develop our self-esteem:

> Usually we think of man's life in society as a rather routine thing, people going about their business so that the work can be done, saying what they have to say on the job or at the union hall. Even if we know about roles and statuses, how they structure social life, we tend to consider the whole thing as matter-of-fact; there shouldn't be much at stake in social encounters, since everything is fairly well pre-coded and automatic. So many of us may think—and we would be wrong. . . . In the social encounter each member exposes for public scrutiny, and possible intolerable undermining, the one thing he needs most: the positive self-valuation he has so laboriously fashioned. With stakes of this magnitude there can be nothing routine about social life. Each social encounter is a hallowed event.[27]

Through routine interaction we expose and build our self-esteem. If our self-esteem is to be thus exposed we need conventions for handling self-esteem. Berne points out that people who pass each other each day often develop a norm of exchanging one stroke, "Hi!"; "Good morning."[28] The implicit consensus is not to ignore the other person's brief greeting (and thereby implicitly deny the other's worth).

Erving Goffman's *Behavior in Public Places* and *Presentation of Self in Everyday Life* are detailed accounts of the rules by which people in middle-class American cultures regulate their routine exchanges. The fundamental norm is that "any individual who possesses certain social characteristics has a moral right to expect that others will value and treat him in a correspondingly appropriate way . . . he automatically exerts a moral demand upon others, obliging them to value him."[29]

Thus, we are obliged to be sensitive to the enacted status of other people. We must go beyond the golden rule of treating another's status as we would have him treat ours. We are enjoined to treat others as they claim they should be treated. The man who displays the signs of a "grocer" should be treated as a grocer. The person who displays the signs of a "lawyer" should be treated as a lawyer.

In an attempt to lay claim to higher status, people embellish themselves through their dress and the job through the title.

> The salesman in the advertising agency is an account executive. "I feel a little downgraded if people think I'm a salesman. Account executive—that describes my job. It has more prestige than just saying, I'm a salesman." A title, like clothes, may not make a man or woman, but it helps

in a world of peers—and certainly impresses strangers. "We're all vice presidents," laughs the copy chief. "Clients like to deal with vice presidents."[30]

When a person is titled an account executive or a vice-president, he is given the right to claim the appropriate status in an interpersonal transaction. The client who receives personal attention from a person of such high standing is complimented. Each person accords self-esteem to the other. Through such manipulation of symbols we handle and enhance our self-esteem, and that of others. Through interaction based upon social formulas we build the meaning of ourselves through "meaningful" coordination with others. As Becker puts it:

> By verbally setting the tone for action by the proper ritual formula, we permit complementary action. That is, the ability to use formulas with facility actually implies the power to manipulate others indirectly by providing the symbolic context for their action.[31]

The social formula as the basis of coordinated activity, is the means by which individuals construct a meaningful collective situation. Only within situations which are meaningful, can an individual's action be meaningful. Becker uses a transaction between a private in the Army and a sergeant to illustrate this point:

> The delight with which young recruits learn all the military jargon testifies to the pervasive feeling of power that accompanies proper definition of the situation for action: "Private Johnson reporting, sir!" not only creates the context for action, but at the same time provides the motivation to act. We sustain one another with properly placed verbal formulas.
>
> The actor can feel himself an object of primary value, motivated to act in a mutually meaningful situation. "Private Johnson reporting, sir!" affirms the self, the proper motivation, and the life meaning which forever is. And when we permit (the other) as well as ourself to act in a fabric of shared meaning, we provide him with the possibility of self-validation. As we act meaningfully in pursuit of agreed goals we exercise our self-powers as only they can be exercised. This is vitally important. It is easy to see the reverse side of the same coin: namely, that if we bungle the verbal context for action, if we deliver the wrong lines at the wrong times, we frustrate the possibility of meaningful action and unquestioned motivation. "P-P-P-P-Private Johnson, reporting, s-s-sir!" not only arrests all movement on stage but also undermines word power. Unflinching mastery of the lines actually serves to create meaning by providing an unequivocal context for action. The leader who after a short whispered outline of attack, shouts, "Let's go men!" with proper gravity and conviction, says much more than simply that. He implies that of all times and all places, this is the situation that man should want most to be in: and that "to go" into the attack is unquestionably the greatest, most meaningful act that one could hope to perform.[32]

If the officer were to bungle his lines, all present might begin to question why they are there. The social formula in this situation contains motives which are taken for granted. If someone flubs the lines, then the whole formula may be up for grabs. People may start to ask why they are doing what they are doing (motives), who they are (roles), what they should do next (agendas). Convincing improvisation on the social formula displays to everyone that the person is confident of the formula. It reinforces the legitimacy of the formula. To flub one's performance, or to question openly who you are or what you are doing may destroy a group's consensual definition of its situation. Social formulas are like the "emperor's new clothes"; they exist only so long as people act as if they exist. They are fragile, but they are not often questioned (and hence destroyed) because most of the time we follow credo: "Let us all protect each other so that we can carry on the business of living."[33]

ORGANIZING FUNCTIONS: STABILITY AND EFFICIENCY

As people talk they elaborate and detail expectations which are the bases of coordinated action. Organizational intelligence and integration are created through consensual definitions of situations, relationships, time structures, and motivations. Some of the talk which functions to create organizations is planned; some is collective decision building. In this section, we examine the organizing functions of improvised interactions. There are similar sections in the next three chapters which describe organizing functions associated with the other formats.

Organizational stability is the first function of improvising. To engage in improvising is to engage in rather conventional behavior. This is because the standards of "how shall I act" are generated from what has just happened or from what has happened in similar situations in the past. We find improvising in familiar, repetitive situations. We interact not with particular other individuals, but with others as stylized roles or "stock characters." Stock characters act in quite predictable ways. The more predictable people are, the more stable their interactions.

When people are improvising on a well known formula for interaction, they tend to create interactions which are like their previous interactions (hence "stable"), even when they think they are creating new patterns of interaction. Seymour B. Sarason illustrates this stabilizing influence of taken-for-granted expectations among people who create new organizations:

> From time to time I have asked a class of my students to imagine that they want to start a new school for children. . . . They come up with all kinds of ideas and plans but they invariably have one thing in common: in the new school all the children are in one place. When I point this out to them with the statement that one could imagine a school in which different groups of children were in very different locations, the response is usually one of puzzlement or surprise. The point is not that I could or do seriously justify such a plan but that the characteristic common to their plans is a reflection of their previous experience with the existing organization we call school. (New relationships are related to old ones, but the relationship is not obvious.) It is not obvious in the same way that categories of thought are not obvious; they are the unquestioned, even unverbalized aspects of thinking that insure that the new will have some of the features of the old.[34]

To say that interaction improvised on social formulas is "stable" means that we construct new situations using expectations we have learned in similar situations. We are seldom aware of these. They are, to use Sarason's words, "categories of thought" which are unquestioned. The more a relationship is constructed on the basis of unquestioned assumptions, the more conservative or stable it is likely to be. This accounts for the regularity of first encounters we spoke of in chapter 3. It also helps to explain why improvised interactions are not sufficient for structuring highly uncertain environments. Such interactions are not adaptable to differing constraints of an uncertain environment.

Improvising on taken-for-granted expectations is efficient in stable environments. Programs permit people to act without stopping to reflect and choose what they are to do. The assembly line worker does not have to decide what to do when the auto chassis reaches his work station. The decisions about what parts are to be attached at that station have already been made (in an earlier period of enactment and selection).

Think of the expectations which exist in the relationship of a man and a woman who have been married thirteen years. The two leave the house for work each morning. They approach the car. Nine mornings out of ten the same person goes to the driver's side of the car. There is no discussion; there is no need for discussion. The expectations prescribe which one is the customary driver. If the routine is disrupted—for example, they do not have their usual destination—then they have to stop and think about who should drive. They have to choose by thinking of the consequences of each person's driving. They enact in their minds the action of each person as driver. They think about the future. They invoke selection rules such as "the person who is going farthest should drive" or, "if one is sick, the one who feels better should drive." When the situation is routine, it is time-consuming to stop and choose who should drive each day. It is more efficient to have a formula in which one takes for granted the role of the driver and the other takes for granted the role of passenger.

The process of decision making is "costly." At the very least, it consumes time. In larger organizations where many people perform the same task, it is usually valuable to have some standardization of what is done. Formulas or expectations for interaction are, therefore, substituted for decision-making processes whenever possible. When action is based on a formula, it may be done faster than if it must be chosen and there can be more consistency among people doing the same job.

An earlier section on organizational climate described a "situational climate" and raised the question of how practical such a climate might be in the everyday operation of any organization. In a situational climate, there is a good deal of problem solving rather than improvising. Improvising is more economical in the short run than is the search behavior required for adaptation. If we went around in a problem-solving state all the time, attempting to adapt what we said to each person as an individual in an individual situation, we would soon grow tired. So we "run a program" for much of our interaction and engage in planned interaction when there is no equivalence of expectations or when we want to change expectations.

Organizations which are constructed largely through interactions improvised on rigid social formulas may appear to be machinelike, for they tend to be stable and efficient. But unlike machines, they may not be the product of design. In fact, they are never totally the product of rational design. A social formula is a system of taken-for-granted expectations. Expectations cannot be mandated by an individual or group of organizational planners. Their creation is a process of reciprocal influence among all the people in the group. Planners cannot control any behavior which is based on unstated assumptions. Activities can be controlled only to the extent that they can be described, hence, observed and supervised.[35]

Organizational planners, therefore, can plan or design changes in an organization only by changing expressed expectations. Planners in the classical school, as you may recall from chapter 1, believed that with sufficient research all organizational tasks could be specified and thereby subjected to central control. The prevalence of automated assembly lines today is testimony of the extent to which organizational planners have succeeded in specifying activities exactly and creating machines to perform the work. However, when people perform even the most routine tasks described in procedures manuals, they embed their "controlled" actions in activity governed by social formulas which are not controlled by organizational planners.

William M. Jones's study of decision making in the Department of Defense illustrates this interweaving of the formal expectations with the subformal expectations.

> The introduction of the new budgeting procedure in the Department of Defense is an excellent case study that demonstrates some of the difficulties. Without describing either the prior procedure or commenting on their merits and failings, one can simply observe that there was a sharp change in the formal organizational arrangements for handling this (budgeting) pattern of organization and communication at the subformal level. The sharp change in the formal system shattered many of the subformal arrangements and necessitated a rather unpleasant period of adjustment. [The personnel in charge of budget proposals] knew [the personnel] with whom they should interact in an attempt to "sell" their package. Without suggesting that they were always pleased with the results of such interactions, it can be noted they generally understood the subformal operations they had to perform in the attempt to accomplish their job. With the advent of the new system this knowledge of operations was removed and a period of trial and error, false starts, and general confusion ensued. It is worth noting that the pace with which the new system gained operating efficiency has been closely related to (and in the view of this writer, dependent upon) the rate at which a new subformal pattern has developed.[36]

Personnel in the Department of Defense had established social formulas ("subformal patterns") for accomplishing the budgeting process. They knew whom to contact for certain kinds of information. When they received information, they knew to whom it might be useful. They had norms of interpersonal conduct. They knew what kinds of questions they might ask others and what kinds would be regarded as "out of line." They understood what kinds of materials would constitute "support" for their budget request. The new budgeting system was imposed upon the personnel from above. The new expectations written in procedures documents were too incomplete to serve as sufficient behavioral guides to all the activity necessary to produce budget requests. The personnel had to learn to contact different people with whom they had no established norms of contact. Their sources of information had been changed. The kind of information now required was different.

The concept of "metacommunication" (communication about communication) helps to explain how the learning took place. In order for information to be understood there must be "metacommunication" which helps receivers understand the source's intent in providing information. In this example, information was offered and demanded, but there were no stable patterns of expectations with which people could understand what to do with the information. There was an "intelligence" problem because of the integration problem. The new procedures were not "meaningful" to participants in the budgeting process until they had sufficient interaction to create for themselves a new context of interpersonal expectations. Through interaction with one another they created a social reality for interpreting the budgeting system. They developed equivalent definitions of what was to be done and what to expect from one another. They developed a social formula within which the new information procedures were meaningful. This was accomplished largely through "metacommunicational" messages.

Along with the confusion in the process of developing the social formula, there was some predictable hostility toward the imposed procedures. An employee of the Department of Education in Pennsylvania expressed similar hostilities to a new budgeting procedure recently imposed upon his office. When asked if the procedure would result in more meaningful information for legislators, he responded, emphatically, "No, it just means a longer budget number." Instead of the procedures name, P.P.B.S., he called it PP-*BS* (emphasis on the last two letters).

One conclusion from this example is a familiar one to organizational theorists. It is that formal organizations are "incomplete." Organizations' planners cannot describe (and thereby prescribe) all the activity required to accomplish an organization's objectives. There are limits to organizational control. Therefore, if there is to be organization, individuals must develop through their interaction the social formulas which make coordination of their behavior possible and which promote efficiency by reducing the need for decisions. All organizations are dependent upon the unstated but equivalent assumptions of individual members.

Beyond serving to "complete" the organization, social formulas are the source of autonomy of groups within the overall organizational structure. Organizations are not control structures in which all decisions made "at the top" are mindlessly implemented "at the bottom." Rather groups of organizational members, through their interaction (largely through their talk), create the social reality within which they interpret the meaning both of their common task and the documents written to control their behavior.

Alvin Gouldner, in his study of a gypsum mine and manufacturing company, provides an example of this. Gouldner describes how informal networks of talk and cohesion among workers give them some autonomy from company rules.

The miners' solidarity provided them with an effective agency for defeating innovations which they disliked. . . . In an effort to reduce absenteeism in the mine, for example, management had decreed that those who were absent without permission, or a "good excuse," would be laid off for the same number of days that they had taken. Far from inhibiting absenteeism, this rule actually encouraged it in the mine, for the miners took the regulation as a direct challenge. When several miners had been penalized in the specified way, others would deliberately take off without excuses. The result was usual, and the team would be unable to function. Clearly the success of this resistance rested on the coordinated action of the miners, their mutual and solidarity in the face of Company action.[37]

The network of social interactions woven by unstated social formulations is necessary for the existence of any social system. The most elaborate code of formal regulations will not be sufficient for the coordination necessary in any human organization. You simply cannot write down enough instructions for a person to know everything he needs to know in order to act. The informal networks are influenced by the regulations of the formal system (as seen in the Defense Department example), but it is beyond the direct control and often in opposition to the formal organization (as seen in the miners' example). Therefore, improvising functions to create autonomy for individual work groups as well as to create stability and efficiency for the organization as a whole.

SUMMARY

This chapter examines "ordinary talk." Ordinary talk is improvised; it is patterned, but communicators "make up" the pattern as they go along. Improvised interaction is different from the coordination formats discussed in the following two chapters because when improvising people do not stop to think about what they are doing, why they are doing it, or what will happen as a consequence.

Coordination in an improvised pattern is possible when there is a consensus on expectations. When such a consensus exists we say there is a "social formula." People do not need to be conscious of particular expectations of particular others. The social formula is constructed with the participation of all interactants, even though some may not seem to contribute much to what is going on. All people contribute because expectations are not constructed verbally; they are constructed by people acting as if their expectations are shared by others.

When people are improvising they are attending to the present. This attention process I have called "monitoring." Monitoring is not problem solving, though it is a kind of low level or nonconscious decision making. It is the process of continuously "checking" to make sure that events are occurring "according to formula." Through monitoring people maintain cybernetic control of the developing pattern of interaction. But events are not checked against predetermined goals or plans, rather they are "checked" against general expectations.

Patterns of interaction have three more or less distinguishable elements. First, patterns have repeated content called themes. Themes are the ideas which are elaborated in discussion. They represent consensual meaning or "intelligence." Second, patterns have an intentional or feeling quality called "climate." A climate is a quality of integration among group members, their intentions, and their actions. Third, actions are linked directly to one another so that a simple action by one person calls forth an elaborate yet predictable response or program from another.

Improvised interactions function to construct cooperative systems because they have the following four necessary and inevitable results. Through talk people define their common situations (construct norms), clarify their relationships (create roles), structure time (create agendas), and motivate one another (create motives). Talk also is the method by which individuals create their self-esteem. This is important from an organizational perspective because self-esteem influences participation in cooperative activity.

From the perspective of an on-going organization, the two most important functions of improvised interactions are stability and efficiency. Improvised interactions are highly predictable, creating a basis for stability. They also avoid "costs" associated with search and problem solving, thus, they are a source of "efficiency." But improvised interactions cannot be completely controlled by central decision makers. Hence these interactions are a source of autonomy for individual organizational members and for groups within larger organizations.

APPLICATION: Diagnosing and Changing Dysfunctional Formulas

To say that a set of expectations or formulas is "dysfunctional" means that those expectations lead to disintegration or ineffectiveness of a social system. When people interact on the basis of a dysfunctional social formula, they create relationships which are not as good as they could be. To say that something is "not as good as it could be" implies that we have some standard for judging what "good" is. I shall not attempt here to describe standards which are good for all systems. Judgment is a matter of perspective. Behavior which is functional in a fraternity may be dysfunctional among an airline crew. In order to judge whether a particular pattern of behavior is dysfunctional in a particular relationship, you need to observe the relationship closely.

However, I can illustrate formulas that you might look for as possibly disruptive. There are some characteristics which are often dysfunctional because they are destructive of self-esteem and suppress information needed for collective decisionmaking. Some of these are norms of super-rationality, impoverished roles, ecocentric roles, hidden agendas, and impoverished motivations. Two typical outcomes of these formulas are defensive climates and destructive themes.

Norms of Superrationality

According to human relations theorists, organizations may be improved by training people to avoid a norm of superrationality in communication. Rationality is valuable in any social system. It is desirable to have people communicating as "adults." Our rational self or "adult ego state" is our information processor.[38] It is necessary to act "rationally" in order to get tasks accomplished. Because of the obvious necessity to have people acting as adults in organizations, adult behavior is often rewarded so that people are unwilling (literally unable) to express their emotions. The following three values become the basis for expectations about how you and others should communicate:

1. *The significant human relationships are the ones which have to do with achieving the organization's objectives.*
2. *People are most effective when they are rational. They are least effective when they express feelings or emotions.*
3. *Human relationships are most effectively influenced through unilateral direction, coercion, and control, as well as rewards and penalties that sanction all three values.[39]*

These three values become the basis for norms of superrationality.

How can you recognize when norms of superrationality have developed? Since norms are expectations, you can ask what kinds of behavior you expect to see and hear. Argyris found the following communicative patterns in systems operating on norms of superrationality. He categorized 45,802 units of behavior in 163 different meetings.

> *75 percent of the talk consisted of people stating their own ideas, expressing concern for ideas, or conforming to the ideas of others.*

20 percent of the talk consisted of people stating their opposition to ideas, reasserting their individuality, and expressing antagonism to the ideas of others.

Rarely observed were individuals helping each other own up to, be open toward, and experiment with ideas or feelings.

People rarely said what they believed about important issues if they perceived them to be potentially threatening to any member.[40]

Norms of superrationality are dysfunctional when they prevent people from expressing their beliefs because they cannot justify them on rational grounds. Note that these norms do not prevent people from holding "irrational" beliefs. I may harbor a secret grudge against a person because I heard that he said something bad about me two weeks ago. I will not say anything to him about it because I cannot prove that he said it, but I will still mistrust him, and I will act accordingly. Because I can only communicate what is "rational," he will not know why I do not trust him (though he will figure out from my behavior that I do not like him). The basis of my attitudes toward him will not be discussed, and possibly errors corrected, because I am unwilling to express my "irrational" anger.

The impact of withholding so-called "irrational" ideas and feelings is that people are denied access to information which others in the group are using to make decisions. A study by Argyris documents this. He investigated 199 "important influence attempts" among twenty executives over a one year period—134 failed; 65 succeeded. In only two of the 134 cases of failure was honest feedback given. "In all other cases the individual was assured that he had succeeded when, in fact, he had not. Of successes (65), 54 represented influence attempts made by the president." Despite the fact that the president "succeeded" in getting his message across, in 48 cases the subordinates reported to the researchers that they felt hostility toward him over the matter. None communicated their hostile feelings to the president.

Norms of superrationality function to organize irrational social systems. Individuals make influence attempts (they enact certain behavior); their attempts are rejected, but they do not know it. They are led to believe that they are successful. The result is that behavior which is not influential on others is retained as their habitual behavior. The result is a parody of coordination in which people learn only that they cannot trust one another because they do not know what to expect.

Norms of superrationality are stifling because they make it difficult to experiment. If people expect to be challenged to defend the rationality of every suggestion they make, they refrain from making suggestions. The result is that groups have few ideas to discuss. In order to encourage people to contribute more ideas in problem-solving groups, some groups adapt a "brainstorming" procedure. In a brain-storming session the objective is to produce a lot of ideas. Ideas are not evaluated as they are given. People are instructed to say anything which comes to their head, regardless of how irrational it may appear.

We have seen here that one dysfunctional social formula includes norms of superrationality. These norms prevent people from express-ing ideas and feelings which they think will be viewed as irrational. The norms may be stated colloquially as, "We are all adults here." The result is that people suppress information (including information about their feelings). Without such information, people cannot de-velop equivalence of meaning which I have described as necessary for adaptive and enduring social systems.

Impoverished Roles

You know that your social formula contains impoverished roles when you say to yourself, "I'm nobody." We build our self-esteem largely through our improvised interactions. But what if the formula does not permit us to see ourselves as worthwhile? We may lose our motivation for everything.

Egocentric Roles and Hidden Agendas

These two terms refer to group patterns in which individuals are com-mitted to their private interests at the expense of cooperative activity. You know that these characterize the social formula of a system when you feel like the proper attitude is "you do unto others as they do unto you, but do it first."

Our mothers taught us that it is nice to "share." Sharing is not only nice, it is necessary. To the extent that I "hoard" my self—my information and my feelings—I make it impossible for others to co-ordinate their efforts with mine. If I "share" my information and feel-ings, but do not allow others to share themselves with me, I am playing an egocentric role. Argyris describes the interactive nature of desirable communication:

> Note that it is not recommended that an individual be completely open, or show complete trust. The key is for A, for example, to be open to the extent that it also permits B to be open. Openness, therefore, is not something in an individual. True openness or trust exists only in inter-personal relationships. One asks, therefore, how open the relationship is between A and B; not how open A or B is. This implies that A adjusts his degree of openness to how he believes he will be heard most accu-rately and completely. If A believes that B is not open to as much rele-vant information as A has, then A can explore the issue with B as to how

to widen the channels of communication. To say what you believe is to be honest; to say what you believe in such a way that the other can do the same is to be authentic.[41]

Social formulas which allow each person to "do whatever he wants" are not desirable. There are two dimensions of openness: what you say and do, and what your behavior encourages the other person to say and do. In order to learn about ourselves (build self-esteem) and to organize cooperative activity we need social formulas in which all participants are permitted openness.

Rigid Agendas

Assembly lines are rigid agendas. Every action must be made in a prescribed sequence. People need time structuring. Organizations need routines for accomplishing sequential tasks, but rigid agendas become boring because there is no surprise. Organizing is structuring uncertainty. Agendas must be kept flexible enough that people can recognize uncertainty and can act to reduce it.

Impoverished Motives

Impoverished roles lead to impoverished motives. Impoverished motivations exist when people are committed only to their role, not to the relationship. Couples who divorce after twenty years of marriage may talk about their marriages becoming "meaningless." Men become committed to being husbands; they cease to be committed to the relationship. Women become wives for the sake of being wives. Workers become assemblers, foremen, and managers for the sake of their roles, not for the sake of the satisfaction of taking part in the collective effort.

You know you have impoverished motives when you say to yourself, "I'm doing this because this is what (mothers, husbands, sisters, foremen, presidents) are supposed to do." Impoverished motives lead to dry rot of organizations. The facade of cooperation remains, but the satisfactions are no longer there. When people discover their behavior produces no satisfactions, they get out of the system if they can. If they cannot, then they do as little as they can get away with.

Changing Formulas

I have now developed the idea that sets of expectations called social formulas are the basis for improvising human interaction. Without such formulas coordinated behavior would be impossible. And yet, some formulas are destructive. They rot organizations. They deper-sonalize people. How can they be changed?

A simple model for change in human behavior was formulated by Kurt Lewin. Lewin's model stipulates that the old pattern must first be broken. He used the term "unfreezing." We can think of this un-freezing as the introduction of uncertainty into a system. New behaviors may then be learned as people attempt to cope with the new un-certainties. As people learn (select and retain new behaviors), they construct a new set of expectations which serves as the basis for a re-stabilizing of behavior. Figure 4.1 shows cooperative output during this period of change.

Lewin's model is fine for an overview of change processes. But it is not much help in knowing specifically how to change a dysfunctional social formula. The model does remind us to expect confusion during a change as people learn to expect new kinds of behavior from one another. It warns that things will get worse (no formula) before they get better (new formula).

In thinking of how to change social formulas, remember that for-mulas are taken-for-granted, implicit expectations. Formulas are the basis for habitual patterns of behavior enacted in routine situations. With this in mind, I outline five ways to change formulas:

1. Wait for conditions to change. This is the passive way; you do not try to change. Instead you tell yourself that patterns of behavior are responses to situations. You wait for unforeseen circumstances to intro-duce uncertainty. You wait for the routine situation to become un-routine. This method "works." Social formulas are reconstructed. In fact, they are constantly being slightly reconstructed.

One problem, of course, is that if you have an impoverished role in an office with rigid agenda of clerical work, the probability of an earth-quake disrupting the routine is slim. Circumstances may change, but will seldom change very much. You cannot count on it.

Moreover, we do not simply "react" to an external environment.

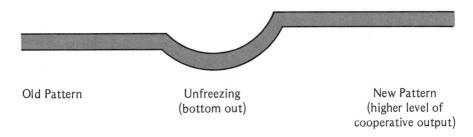

| Old Pattern | Unfreezing (bottom out) | New Pattern (higher level of cooperative output) |

FIGURE 4.1
Changing Patterns of Interaction

We interpret our situation. Our expectations condition what we see. We act "as if" things stay the same. In doing so, we act to keep things the same.

2. Be conscious; plan interactions. *In situations where other people are improvising their routines, you can be conscious of your goals and choose your behavior. Salesmen do this. They go to parties where everyone is improvising. They pick out likely sales targets and choose their communicative strategies to get what they want. When a communicative partner recognizes that you are after something not taken for granted in the formula ("Hey, this guy's not making small talk, he's trying to sell me something!"), he or she will be more conscious of the interaction and his own motives. He or she will start to respond to you by planning his own communication. The social formula then is up for renegotiation. Each person is analyzing and adapting to the other.*

A book which describes changing social formulas through the process of planned interaction is Saul Alinsky's Rules for Radicals: A Practical Primer for Realistic Radicals. *The book describes principles and methods for changing social systems where you are deprived, impoverished, and dehumanized. The method is essentially this: analyze the other (enemy) members of the system, change your behavior in selected ways, and they will have to change theirs. In other words, be tactical. Alinsky defines tactics:*

> Tactics means doing what you can with what you have. Tactics are those consciously deliberate acts by which human beings live with each other and with the world around them. In the world of give and take, tactics is the art of how to take and how to give.[42]

The important words for us are "consciously deliberate." To be tactical, to plan interaction, means that you no longer take behavior for granted. You choose what to do on the basis of what you want (though you may not be clear about what you want) and what you have (though you may not know everything you have). Alinsky illustrates the choosing of ways to communicate:

> For an elementary illustration of tactics, take parts of your face as the point of reference; your eyes, your ears, and your nose. First, the eyes; if you have organized a vast, mass-based people's organization, you can parade it visibly before the enemy and openly show your power. Second, the ears; if your organization is small in numbers, then do what Gideon did: conceal the members in the dark, but raise a din and clamor that will make the listener believe that your organization numbers many more than it does. Third, the nose; if your organization is too tiny even for noise, stink up the place. Always remember the first rule of power tactics: Power is not only what you have but what the enemy thinks you have.[43]

In the last sentence Alinsky emphasizes another important point about planning interactions: when planning an interaction you must think about what the other person might be thinking. Improvised behavior takes the intentions of the other for granted, but if you want a new formula, the other person must act in a different way. That means he, she, or they must learn to define the situation differently. In the following chapter, I discuss planned interactions in detail. Suffice to point out here that formulas can be changed when only one person is aware of the formula and plots to undermine it.

3. Make a collective decision to change the formula. Because a social formula requires the participation of all interactants, one person can stimulate renegotiation of the contract. One person can force others to treat him differently, but he cannot always force them to treat him in some particular way. If a group of people want a new social formula, they can explicitly—in words—attempt to renegotiate that formula together.

An interesting book which describes how to change a social formula through collective decision is Nena O'Neill and George O'Neill's Open Marriage: A New Life Style for Couples. They describe the routine established by a newly married couple during the first week of their marriage. They conclude this description by stating: "John and Sue, without so much as a word of discussion, have . . . set the pattern for a contract that will govern their interaction for as long as they are married. Sue does the cooking and housework, John carries the laundry to and from the laundromat. . . ." The change strategy which O'Neill and O'Neill propose for a marriage formula (which they call an unconscious contract) is for the marriage partners to discuss their assumptions and explicitly to renegotiate the contract:

> Instead of surrendering to the hidden clauses of the old, closed contract, you can write your own, individual open contract. You can agree to look honestly and openly at what you are doing and why you are doing it— whether you are going to get married today or have been married ten years. The power of the hidden clauses of the old contract to constrict your marriage lies in the very fact that they are hidden. . . . Look at your own marriage. Get the hidden clauses out into the open. Then you can begin to rewrite your contract as you go along starting new, from scratch, today.[44]

Of course, rewriting the hidden assumptions about who should do what in a relationship is not a simple matter. The dishes get dirty every day. It is a routine occurrence. It is efficient to have a general assumption about who will do them. Few people want to spend the effort to do collective decision-making every time the dishes need washing. It is harder to change a social formula than to quit smoking. In chapter 6, I discuss collective decision building in detail. The section on "Decision-Building As Organizing" discusses the on-going process of modifying formulas through intentional and collective choices of the interactants.

4. Change the written rules. Executives in formal organizations try to change formulas by changing the rules for behavior. The executives in the gypsum plant described by Gouldner attempted to change the work absentee practices. They successfully stopped surface workers' absences; miners' habits were not changed. In Unit III I discuss how formal rules influence the change of social formulas.

5. Bring in an outsider. Interpersonal patterns of behavior are difficult to change because they are self-sustaining. The behavior of each reinforces the expectations of the others. Expectations operate below the threshold of awareness of the individuals. People may be unable to figure out hidden assumptions guiding their behavior. Often systems seek a change agent.

The role of the change agent or "interventionist" is to help members of the system (1) become conscious of their assumptions, (2) to clarify the goals of their interaction, (3) to experiment with new modes of behavior, and (4) to interpret the consequences of the experimental behavior. Psychotherapists intervene in peoples' lives to help them learn how to live with others. Marriage counselors act as change agents. Some educational organizations employ "educational development officers" to assist teachers in developing new patterns of interaction with students. Businesses often hire consultants to help their managers and workers develop new patterns of communicating. In the conclusion of this book, I describe the process of change through intervention as a means of organizing.

ENDNOTES

1. Leonard C. Hawes, "Interpersonal Communication: The Enactment of Routines," in John J. Makay, ed., *Exploration in Speech Communication* (Columbus, Ohio: Charles E. Merrill Publishing Co., 1973), pp. 84–85.

2. Peter McHugh, *The Definition of the Situation: The Organization of Meaning in Social Interaction* (Indianapolis: Bobbs-Merrill, 1968).

3. Donald Roy, " 'Banana Time': Job Satisfaction and Informal Interaction," *Human Organization* 18 (Winter 1959–60): 163–4.

4. Ibid., 167.

5. Ibid., 165.

6. James C. McCroskey, Carl E. Larson, and Mark L. Knapp, *An Introduction to Interpersonal Communication* (Englewood Cliffs: Prentice-Hall, 1971).

7. Ibid.

8. Irving Janis, *Victims of Groupthink* (Boston: Houghton Mifflin, 1972), pp. 8–9.

9. McCroskey et al., *An Introduction to Interpersonal Communication*, p. 202.

10. James G. March and Herbert A. Simon, *Organizations* (New York: John Wiley & Sons, Inc., 1958), pp. 141–142.

11. Frank E. X. Dance and Carl E. Larson, *Speech Communication Concepts and Behavior* (New York: Holt, Rinehart, & Winston, Inc., 1972).

12. Talk was "discovered" in the same sense that Columbus discovered America. Some people knew it there all along. But those people who put its existence into a book are credited with "discovering" it. We discover something when we no longer take it for granted, when we think it is worth writing about.

13. Studs Terkel, *Working: People Talk About What They Do All Day and How They Feel About What They Do* (New York: Pantheon Books, Random House, Inc., 1974), p. 589.

14. Fred E. Katz, *Autonomy and Organization: The Limits of Social Control* (New York: Random House, Inc., 1968), p. 115.

15. Ibid., p. 126.

16. Erving Goffman, *Presentation of Self in Everyday Life* (Garden City: Doubleday, 1959).

17. Eric Berne, *Games People Play* (New York: Grove Press, 1964), pp. 15–16.

18. Charles R. Walker, *Toward the Automated Factory: A Case Study of Men and Machines* (London: Oxford University Press, 1957), pp. 39–47.

19. Charles R. Walker and Robert H. Guest, *The Man on the Assembly Line* (Cambridge: Harvard University Press, 1952), pp. 68, 77.

20. Roy, " 'Banana Time': Job Satisfaction and Information Interaction," p. 162.

21. Berne, *Games People Play*, p. 15.

22. Ernest Becker, *The Birth and Death of Meaning* (New York: Free Press, 1971), p. 67.

23. Ibid., p. 68.

24. It should be noted that the upper level management considered the production of wallboard, not the mining of gypsum, as the plant's vital function. One administrator stated: "The board plant brings in the money . . . we can and do have board plants without mines" (pp. 147–48). The point here is not that self-esteem comes from what central administrators define as important, rather, that miners had sufficient control over their situation to establish their own definition.

25. Terkel, *Working*, p. xix.

26. Ibid., xviii.

27. Becker, *The Birth and Death of Meaning*, p.88.

28. Berne, *Games People Play*, p. 38.

29. Erving Goffman, *Presentation of Self in Everyday Life* (Garden City, N.Y.: Doubleday, 1959), p. 13.

30. Terkel, *Working*, p. xx.

31. Becker, *The Birth and Death of Meaning*, p. 97.

32. Ibid., pp. 97–98.

33. Ibid., p. 99.

34. Seymour B. Sarason, *The Creation of Settings and the Future Societies* (San Francisco: Jossey-Bass, Inc., 1972), p. 35.

35. March and Simon, *Organizations*, p. 145.

36. William M. Jones, *On Decision-Making in Large Organizations* (Santa Monica: The Rand Corporation, 1964), p. 7.

37. Alvin Gouldner, Patterns of Industrial Bureaucracy (New York: The Free Press, 1954), p. 151.

38. Berne, *Games People Play*.

39. Chris Argyris, *Management and Organizational Development* (New York: McGraw-Hill, 1971), p. 11.

40. Ibid., p. 13.

41. Ibid., p. 18.

42. Saul Alinsky, *Rules for Radicals: A Practical Primer for Realistic Radicals* (New York: Random House, Inc., 1971), p. 126.

43. Ibid., pp. 126–7.

44. O'Neill and O'Neill, *Open Marriage* (New York: Avon Books, 1972), p. 70.

CHAPTER
5

Planned Interactions

Nature of Plans
Interactions as Objects of Plans
Accomplishing Planned Relationships
Organizing Functions: Predictability and Purpose
**APPLICATION: Interviews as Planned Inter-
    actions**

*And has the reader never asked himself what kind of mental fact is
his intention of saying a thing before he has said it? It is an entirely
definite intention, distinct from all other intentions, an absolutely
distinct state of consciousness, therefore; and yet how much of it
consists of definite sensorial images, either of words or of things?
Hardly anything! Linger, and the words and things come into the
mind; the anticipatory intention, the divination is there no more.
But as the words that replace it arrive, it welcomes them successively
and calls them right if they agree with it, it rejects them and calls
them wrong if they do not. . . . One may admit that a good third
of our psychic life consists in these rapid premonitory perspective
views of schemes of thought not yet articulated.*

William James, *Principles of Psychology*

"Anticipatory intention" was James's term for that period of time when
individuals "linger" in order to consider what to say and how to say it.
Anticipatory intention is when intention is filled out with words and

things to become purpose. This chapter examines purposeful communicative transactions in which people are not operating on programs, but rather are thinking consciously about their interactions before engaging in them. The period of "before" might be as much as weeks, as when a speaker is preparing for an important address, or it might be as little as an instant, as when a subordinate is deciding how to respond to his supervisor's questions. James's estimation is that one-third of our psychic life is spent in these planning periods in which we devise "schemes of thought not yet articulated." In this chapter I discuss the nature of planned interactions and how they function as organizing processes. At the conclusion of the chapter there is a lengthy application of these ideas to interview situations.

NATURE OF PLANS

In chapter 2, I described the importance of cognitive maps in human activity. Cognitive maps are organized sets of "knowledge" which an organism has concerning itself and the world. In the last chapter we saw one way in which the knowledge in the map is translated into action in the world. That "way" is through interaction formulae. In improvising on a formula an individual is directing his or her actions according to learned expectations. Miller, Galanter, and Pribram use the term "plan" to refer to the process which relates map to action. They define a plan as a "process in the organism that can control the order in which a sequence of operations is to be performed."[1] To them a plan is not necessarily a deliberate, conscious process. A plan could be deliberate, but it could also be what I have called a formula.

I use the term "plans" to refer to those processes by which individuals control their actions deliberately with the intent of achieving predetermined purposes. A plan is thus like a formula in that it connects map to action. Further, planned action is typically "improvised." Even a person reading a prepared speech is improvising gestures, but the behavior is not truly impromptu because the general behavior has been rehearsed mentally prior to the interaction. Thus, planned interactions differ from interactions improvised on a formula because planned interactions are "controlled" by specific images or decisions created prior to the interaction.

In chapter 6, collective decision making is discussed as a third form of coordinated action. Collective decision making is a process in which individuals discuss reasons for preferring one course of action over another. In these cases communication precedes decisions; communication between people makes collective decision making possible. The subject of this chapter is the intrapersonal decisions which precede communicative actions. Planned interactions result from individual decisions.

The assertion that communicative events result from personal decisions rests on three assumptions. First, no person communicates all (or even most) of her or his thoughts. Second, there are innumerable ways in which any thought may be displayed to others. Third, any given set of symbolic displays may be interpreted in various ways by the same receiver. Thus communicative interaction involves choosing or deciding on the part of the individuals who engage in it.

All communicative processes may be seen in retrospect to involve acts of choosing. As actors, we see our choices when we look back on what we might have done. The angry husband who storms out of the house may realize before he reaches the car that he had no "rational" grounds for his action and that he could have chosen to carry on the argument with his wife rather than leave. We can say that he improvised his behavior on the spur of the moment without considering its consequences. He might say that he was simply doing what he "felt like" doing at the time. From our perspective, and from his perspective in retrospect, the situation was one in which he "chose" to act in a particular manner, but "choice" is an observer's construct used after the fact to explain the action by fantasizing alternative actions.

In this chapter our concern is with those times when actors are consciously aware of some communicative choices before acting. If the husband in the example above (1) deliberates about the possible effects of leaving or not leaving on his future relationship with his wife, (2) thinks about how he might justify his actions, and (3) uses those imagined consequences and justifications to decide whether to leave, he is engaged in a process of "planning" interaction. The characteristic which distinguishes planning interaction from improvising interaction is the conscious consideration of imagined futures. In "planning" an interaction, an individual consciously attends to expectations of a future interaction. The interaction may be a speech to be given the next week, or a question to be answered in the next fifteen seconds. Both are in the future. Thus, the distinction between improvising and planning interactions is: in improvising, people take expectations for granted and they attend to the present; in planning, people are conscious of expectations, and they attend to the future as well as the present.

The process of planning is the imaginative projection of consequences and justifications. Intrapersonal planning is displaying imagined futures to oneself. Planning is part of the process by which people make conscious choices. As I have said, the term "choice" may be applied to actions even when there is no planning. Actions may be routinized or programmed so that the "choice" is obscure; actors may seem to make choices even when they are unaware of alternatives.

For example, the executive who calls a staff meeting every Monday afternoon regards such meetings as routine. He or she may have chosen to hold the meetings during a period of rapid change. After a while the meeting time becomes filled with mundane announcements which could be made through other channels. An observer could conclude that the "choice" to hold the meeting on November 5th was a poor one. The executive and staff probably would be unaware when and why they "chose" to hold the meeting. Holding staff meetings is part of their interaction program. The actions are no longer planned; they are programmed. It is not a conscious choice on the part of the interactants, but an observer, by considering alternatives, could consider the action the result of "choice."

"Planning," unlike "choice," is not a concept which an observer may use to describe another's nonconscious behavior. By definition planning is always deliberative, or conscious. We can say, indeed, that to plan is to be conscious. The philosopher Alfred Schutz distinguishes conscious "action" from nondeliberative "behavior" in a way which helps us understand the nature of planned interactions and how they differ from programmed interactions in organizations:

> An action is conscious in the sense that, before we carry it out, we have a picture in our mind of what we are going to do. This is the "projected act." Then as we proceed to action, we are either continuously holding the picture before our inner eye, or we are from time to time recalling it to mind. The total experience of action is a very complex one, consisting of experiences of the activity as it occurs, the various kinds of attention to that activity, retention of the projected act, reproduction of the projected act, and so on. This "map-consulting" is what we are referring to when we call the action conscious. Behavior without the map or picture is unconscious. . . . Our actions are conscious if we have previously mapped them out "in the future perfect tense."[2]

Several ideas in Schutz's statement warrant elaboration. First, he equates what I am calling "planning" with consciousness when he insists that conscious action is guided by a "picture in the mind." This picture is formulated before the action. People often turn routine conversations into planned interactions in process. That is, they begin to imagine possible future actions of a conversation which they had been improvising on a program. Planned interactions may be woven into conversations which are largely routine. Most conversations, in fact, begin and end with interaction rituals; greetings and leave-takings are generally unplanned. In the process of conducting a programmed conversation it may become more than routine. Actors begin to consider their own words and those of others before the words are spoken. When this occurs, the casual or routine conversation becomes "planned interaction."

Schutz's description of conscious action also helps us to understand the nature of plans. One common-sense understanding of "plan" is a step-by-step, how-to-do-it guide to construction. "Plans" for constructing furniture are examples of this kind. However, the construction of human relationships is not analogous to the construction of physical objects. Interaction plans are not step-by-step guides. Schutz uses the term "projected act" to describe plans for human encounters. A projected act is "the goal of the action . . . which is brought into being by the action." He insists that "only the completed act can be pictured in phantasy" because it is only the total or completed act which is meaningful.

The kind of plan I am describing is a fantasized picture of completed human action. The meaning of any action can only be seen in retrospect. What then of actions which are not yet completed? Even incompleted actions are pictured as completed acts. We are able to imagine justifications and consequences of actions as if we had completed them. Through our imagination we "look back on" what we have not yet done. We think of possibilities in the future perfect tense (for example, I will have done it).

To say, then, that an interaction is "planned" means that at least one party has an image of the completed interaction. The plan is this imagined future state. Precisely because it is imagined, the plan is vague. It necessarily lacks significant details. Plans are symbolic representations of the future. They are "displays in the mind." They are dynamic, fluid, and abstract. As such they can never be realized. The feeling of unfulfilled expectations is a common one to all of us. We anticipate "what it will be like when. . . ." We have pictures of what it will be like to have graduated, to be working on a new job, or to live in a new house. Most important, we picture what human interactions will have been like. When the actions and interactions we plan actually come into existence, the lived experience is never exactly as we had thought it would be.

INTERACTIONS AS OBJECTS OF PLANS

Interactions as objects of plans are unique because they concern interactions—that is, they are the product of the actions of more than one person. If a person plans her solitary actions, she can be reasonably confident of the projected outcome though the experience will be different from the projected image. If she notices that it is time to change the oil in her car, she may plan her actions beginning with buying the new oil and ending with discarding the oil she has drained from the crankcase. Any number of unanticipated events may intrude to motivate a change of plans—the store may be out of oil or she may fall and break an arm, but such accidents would literally be intrusions into a sequence of events which would otherwise be predictable.

The events would be predictable because they are solitary actions; they do not require much active participation by others. Once we begin to speak of participation of others—interaction rather than action—we must confront the fact that others have plans of their own. We cannot predict interactions as we can solitary actions because the actions of others are relatively unpredictable. Unpredictable events are accidental intrusions into our planned actions. But unpredictable events are the very substance of our interactions regardless of how well we "plan." If a person unscrews a crankcase plug she can be sure that oil will flow out. The oil is subject to the law of gravity. If a wife plans to convince her husband that he should change the oil, the results are characteristically uncertain.

Whenever we speak of a planned interaction, then, it is proper to ask "whose plan?" The existence of multiple plans for interaction means that no one plan will be enacted. Instead of the metaphor of building construction guided by visual plans, a more appropriate metaphor is a game in which each opposing party has plans for the mutual interaction, and each person's plan must take into account the plans and actions of the other. Seen in light of this metaphor, plans are strategies. Planned interaction is what Erving Goffman calls "strategic interaction." The game metaphor helps us to understand the role of "the other" in the planning process—in other words, how planning an interaction is different than planning an action. It also helps to explain how people enact their plans through interactions in which others are simultaneously enacting their plans.

To explain the features of a "game situation," Goffman uses a series of scenarios involving a fictitious hero named Harry. The first scenario is of a planned action. Harry is a forest ranger who is caught in a brush fire. He perceives that to his right there is a tall tree that he might climb and maybe survive the flames. To his left there is a high bridge which is already beginning to burn. Harry plans out in his mind four possible courses of action: make for the bridge, make for the tree, call on the gods to save him, vacillate in an attempt to think of other escapes.

Using the language of the game, it is Harry's "turn," the opportunity for choice is his. The action he decides upon is his "move." To take a rational, game-like approach or to "plan his action" Harry would list all the possibilities, attach a success probability to each one, and solve his problem by selecting which one seems to offer his best chance for survival. He has got to figure whether the bridge will burn before he gets across or whether he has a better chance to survive the high fall into the water. This is a complicated situation, but Harry is planning only his solitary actions. The tree will not move itself in anticipation of Harry's climbing it.

The situation is different when Harry must plan an interaction. Contrast the planning of action with Goffman's scenario of planning interaction:

> Harry, the native spearman, having strayed from the territory populated by his tribesmen, comes into a small clearing to find that another spearman from a hostile tribe is facing him from what would otherwise be the safe side. Since each finds himself backed by the other's territory, retreat is cut off. Only by incapacitating the other can either safely cross the clearing and escape into his own part of the forest.
>
> Now the game. If there were no chance of missing a throw, then the first spearman to throw would win. However, the likelihood of missing a fixed target increases with the distance of the throw. In addition, a throw, as a move, involves a spear easily seen to be on its way by the target. And the target itself isn't quite fixed. It is able to dodge and will certainly try to do so. The greater the distance of the throw, the more time to dodge and the greater the chance of doing so. And to miss a throw while the other still has his spear allows the other to approach at will for an easy win. Thus, each player begins at a point where it does not pay to chance a throw and presumably approaches a point where it does not pay not to. And each player, in deciding what to do, must decide knowing the other is engaged in exactly the same sort of decision, and knowing that they both appreciate this.[3]

The crucial process involved in planning interaction which distinguishes it from planning action is figuring out the intentions on which the others will base their actions. This is done by starting with what we see (for example, an enemy with a spear blocking the path home). We then imagine what we would do if we were he. We attempt consciously to "take the role of the other." In effect we imagine what our goal would be in the situation and project the presumed goal of the other as if it were our own. Then we imagine what actions we would take if that presumed goal of the other were our goal. We may do this by remembering what we actually have done in situations we think to be comparable. We then use these pictures of imagined consequences as information in deciding what we should do. Or as Goffman explains: "Once Harry sees the need to assess his apparent view of the situation, game theory gives him a way of being systematic. He should exhaustively enumerate the distinctively different courses of action open to the opponent as a response to each of his own moves, and in light of these settle on his best course of action."[4]

We can now see that a plan for interaction is a strategy: "A framework of different courses of action each linked in advance to a possible choice of the opponent." A plan is a complex picture of "if-then-if-then" relationships. If I do "A," then he will do "B." But the "if's" and the "then's" which constitute strategies or plans for interaction, are vague guesses of what the future will be like. We have incomplete pictures of what others will do in response to our actions. We cannot possibly think of all the alternatives and calculate probabilities. We cannot even know what our own actions will be like until we actually do them.

ACCOMPLISHING PLANNED RELATIONSHIPS

Goffman's language may suggest to some that in planning interaction an individual must take an "I win—you lose" attitude. Some writers state that acting "strategically" is inevitably undesirable for communicators and that to accomplish "genuine" relationships people must communicate with one another spontaneously.[5] The concept of "spontaneous interaction" is a bit misleading if one accepts the idea that human behavior is chosen and that behavioral choices are made with reference to one's map of the world.

Planned interactions may be used to seek selfish purpose to the harm of another person, but there is no reason why planned interactions may not be used to seek unselfish purpose for the mutual benefit of communicators. Goffman's example of the native tribesman trapped in enemy territory is a good illustration of a situation in which strategy is necessary for the mutual benefit of communicators. The "spontaneous" thing for the tribesmen to do is to kill one another. If they are both to live they must plan how they can get around one another. By consciously attending to the intentions of a specific other, they can construct together an interaction which is mutually beneficial. The alternative to strategy in this case is a clumsy interaction in which both perish.

The process thinking about specific others, their values and intentions, and their cognitive maps, is a distinctly human process. Planning interaction is almost sure to be desirable from a humanistic perspective, but it is possible to plan an action in regard to another person without planning an interaction with that person. In planning an action the other is viewed as an object to be manipulated. (Even the word "manipulated" comes from the Latin *manus* which means hand. To "manipulate" is literally to move with the hand as one would an object.) Planning an interaction means thinking about the other as an actor (not an object) with plans of his own.

The most obvious example of a planned interaction is a speech. The speaker is invited to address a group of people on a particular topic. He is told approximately how long to speak. The speaker then plans what he will say. The speaker who is planning an interaction begins with imagining what kinds of people will be in the audience. What will they expect of him? What will they be interested in hearing? Then he formulates an exact purpose for his talk. He does this by deciding, in light of the audience's expectations, what he wants the audience to know or to do after he has finished.

He then considers alternative ideas which could be discussed. He cannot say everything; he must choose what to say. Then he chooses how to say what he intends—the ordering and the wording of important themes. He prepares some kind of notes. These may be as brief as a few words on an old envelope or as complete as a written text. Regardless of how complete the preparation, enacting the plan will be done in interaction with the audience. The speaker with a few notes picks up cues from the audience's reactions and either expands or cuts off discussion of particular ideas. Even good speakers who read from a text look at their audience and adapt their gestures, inflection, and rate to the responses they are getting. We have all had the experience of having to sit through lectures or speeches in which the speaker did not respond adequately to the audience's reactions. For example, often speakers will continue with their talk long after the audience has signaled, "That's enough; quit now." Such speakers are enacting action plans, not interaction plans. We are irritated because we are being treated as objects of their plans rather than people who are cooperating in a communication process.

Enacting interaction plans is a matter of attitude and action. It is being simultaneously committed to a plan which was constructed by taking into account particular people and committed to the interaction. The skillful communicator balances his or her concern for plan and for interaction so that neither one suffers disastrously. In a public speaking situation this means that the speaker is committed to the theme and purpose of the speech he came to give (the plan) and equally committed to members of the audience as active cooperators in creating a communication process (the interaction).

It is fairly easy to understand public speaking as enacting an interaction plan. The same principles, however, apply to other forms of communication. Roderick P. Hart and Don M. Burks[6] have described five attitudes and appropriate actions of "rhetorically sensitive" people, people who are enacting interaction plans to build relationships through interpersonal communication. Though they use different words, they are essentially saying that good interpersonal relationships are constructed by communicators who are simultaneously committed to their plans and to the interaction. The five attitudes they describe are helpful in understanding interaction plans in informal communication.

The first attitude is that role-taking is a part of the human condition. People who are planning their interactions (not just actions) are not attempting to find their "true selves" and express that self whatever the situation. According to Hart and Burks, "Man is by nature a role-taker. His most common existential choice is not one of playing or not playing a role but one of selecting among roles available to him."[7] The person enacting an interaction plan is map-consulting. The part of his or her choice of "how to get there" involves choosing the roles he will show to others in interaction. The mother who wants to get her screaming three-year-old out of the store quickly chooses between showing herself as a brute, as her child's pawn, as "Ms. Efficiency," or as a briber. The office worker who comes to work an hour late must decide how he wishes others to "see" him—as lacking in ambition, as scatterbrained, or as incompetent at mechanical tasks (such as changing tires). Our choices take the others into consideration. This is what makes enacting interaction plans a form of cooperative activity.

A second attitude and action of people enacting plans is that they "avoid stylized verbal behavior"; they do not attempt to play the same role on all occasions. Interpersonal situations are complex. We choose different roles not simply because situations are different but because we want to influence situations and people differently. Our purposes change and so does our behavior. Hart and Burks describe this process:

> While the individual himself is complex, an even higher order of complexity, and hence uncertainty, results when two or more communicators come together in an interpersonal transaction. . . . During an interaction both participants are making introspective decisions relating to role-selection and role-manifestation and simultaneously are trying to solve the more immediate problems of what to say and how to say it.[8]

We may desire to be seen as "tough-minded." We may enter into communication planning to act that role, but we only know the consequences of our actions as we are enacting the plan. The consequences which actually result from our actions may not be what we anticipated. The person who is engaged in a "planned interaction" may find himself acting in quite inconsistent ways. This is because he is attending to the actual, on-going consequences of his actions and planning new strategies as those consequences become evident.

The third attitude follows from this reasoning. People enacting plans must be "willing to undergo the strain of adaptation." They are acting purposefully to influence the direction and content of their interactions. The only "plans" which are realized are those which are altered in process to take account of the plans and actions of others. Therefore they are adapting themselves and their plans.

The last two attitudes concern choices. People enacting plans (1) "distinguish between all information and information acceptable for communication," and (2) attend to how they communicate as well as what. A plan for communication concerns what you will say (and not say). You choose content. It also is a projection of how you will say it. You choose language, tone, gestures.

Constructing human relations through planned interaction is a "cybernetic" process. It involves checking the theme of the developing relationship against a plan worked out in advance in one's imagination. Unlike mechanical cybernetic control, however, people make choices about whether to change their plans or their behaviors as they go along. No "plan" is a fixed guide to our communication.

ORGANIZING FUNCTIONS: PREDICTABILITY AND PURPOSE

We have seen that interaction plans are a communicative method for accomplishing integration of human relationship. We now consider what kind of relationship may be constructed. We examine how planned interactions function as organizing processes.

One function of planned interactions is predictability. Routine or programmed interactions tend to produce stable systems, but routines are constantly being disrupted. When the routines which provide stability are disrupted we still seek security and order. Plans function to simplify the complexity of the world so that we maintain at least a fiction of predictability even during times of transition.

Ernest Becker has observed that "the problem of 'what will the next person be like?' is at the core of human adaptation, because self-preservation depends upon it. 'How are they going to act next?' allows one to frame an adequate response based on a reasonable inference."[9] Human behavior is theoretically unpredictable (Becker's example: "The person with whom one has lived for years with mathematical dependability may one day calmly slaughter a brood of children"[10]).

At the same time, the existence of expectations permits reasonably accurate planning of interactions even when those expectations have been disrupted. Even when social roles, for example, are not taken-for-granted guides to action, they still serve as information to ourselves about how we should behave and how other people might behave. They still serve as categories within which to lump complex human actions. As Becker puts it, "When one is dealing with massively undependable human objects, dependable cues for inference are not easy to come by. Therefore, man is given to stereotyping in the interests of his own security. . . . Any clue is a port in a storm."[11]

The fantasies about the future which I call "plans for interaction" thus serve a vital function of making us feel more secure about the future. In saying that plans make us feel more secure by providing the fiction of predictability, I do not mean to imply that making plans is analogous to giving a woman a toy gun so that she will feel safe in a neighborhood noted for a high frequency of rapes. The toy gun in no way prepares her for an attack. It provides only a fictitious security. Plans, on the other hand, do provide some real security, though the image of the future they represent is fictitious. They function to provide security because they give us a scheme with which to interpret what is happening to us.

The most important function of plans is purposefulness. Plans are the method by which we simplify complex phenomena and relate it to desired futures. Planned interactions are rhetorical. They proceed from prior planning periods (reflection) in which actors clarify their goals (by imagining them as completed states) and imagine alternative communicative methods for accomplishing the goals. During the planning period alternatives are tested in the mind until a satisfactory one is chosen. The interaction is characterized by "plan consulting" in which people modify their actions (and/or their plans) in light of unfolding contingencies.

Without the ability to plan interactions there could be no human organization as we know it. Without individual purposefulness, there could be no collective purposefulness. Many human routines would not occur without plans because routines often begin as plans.

It should be clear that our ability to set goals that require the co-operation of others, and then choose actions with the hope of securing the help of others, is useful in the process of organizing. We can speculate about the formation of the very first informal organization. We have a mythical first person who has encountered a problem—a tree fell over the entrance to her cave. It was a big tree and she could not move it by herself. Her friend Joe was busy inventing an arrowhead and did not come over routinely to assist her. In fact, everyone around was engaged in their own personal tasks. If she was ever to get into that cave again, she had to do several things: she needed to secure commitment from other people to help her accomplish her goal; she needed to design a plan to coordinate each person's contribution to the common effort; she needed to inform each person of the job he or she was to do; and, she needed to monitor the whole operation to make sure that individuals were doing their assigned jobs and that the effort was working out as planned—the tree was actually moving away from the door. Thus, an "organization" of some sort arises out of a goal which cannot be met by the efforts of a single individual. Planned interaction occurs as people secure cooperation, draw up collective goals, assign tasks, and assess progress toward the collective goals.

Of course, cooperation does not spring automatically from one person's plan. The existence of routines for cooperation must have existed before one person got an idea about using cooperation to accomplish predetermined goals. Thus, while many routines begin as plans, many plans begin (are based on) preexisting routines. Our sense of what we can do is based on what we have seen done. Even when we plan new ways of relating, our plans take into account routine expectations. The process of organizing, then, involves planning, enacting plans, and routinizing actions. Because human interaction and organizational environment is complex, routine situations are constantly becoming novel, thus calling for new plans. The plans people construct are based in part on the expectations which make situations routine.

SUMMARY

Interaction plans and social routines both serve the same general function: they relate cognitive maps to behavioral choices. However, routines control behavior without deliberate or conscious thought by the actor. Plans are the processes by which individuals control their actions deliberately with the intent of achieving predetermined purposes. In planning people are aware of expectations; they are attending to the future as well as the present.

Plans are pictures in the mind. They are images of the future as if the future were the present. When people plan, they imagine the future in the future perfect tense (*i.e.,* "I will have done it"). Plans are displays in the mind. They are dynamic and abstract. They change as the imagined future becomes the reality of the present.

Plans for interaction are more fanciful than plans for action because they involve unpredictability of others' behavior. Interaction plans must take into account the plans of others; thus, an interaction can never be "constructed by a plan" as a chair may be.

Planned interaction may be called "strategic interaction." A plan is a "framework of different courses of action each linked in advance to a possible choice" of other people. Though plans may be thought of as "battle plans" (i.e., "I win, you lose"), planning interaction is a distinctly humanistic endeavor. When people plan interactions, they take others into account as people (who have plans of their own), not as objects. In enacting interaction plans, people are adjusting the developing theme of discourse to create mutually satisfying relationships.

Interaction plans function to create predictability in human systems. Systems characterized by a high degree of planned interactions rather than improvised or routine interaction are not as "stable." They are constantly changing. Information about the purpose and expectations of the actors, however, provides a reasonable basis for predicting the direction of the change.

Interaction plans function to create genuine purposefulness in a social system. In reflection (the planning period) individuals clarify their goals and choose actions with the intent of influencing others to act to accomplish specified goals. Without such actions by individuals there could be no deliberate, collective purposefulness.

APPLICATION: *Interviews as Planned Interactions*

Planning, or the conscious deliberation in advance of action, allows us freedom in social situations. Because we can "plan," our behavior is not automatic or routine. The purpose of this section is to examine the application of ideas about "planned interaction" to one kind of situation—the interview. I choose to discuss interviewing here for two reasons. First, interviewing is a fairly frequent kind of organizational communication. As such, it deserves attention in a book of this kind. More importantly, however, interviewing represents a paradigm or an "ideal example" of what I mean by planned interactions. In discussing how to improvise this kind of planned interaction I hope to clarify, by example, how to improvise all kinds of planned interactions.

It is useful to begin our discussion by defining the term "interview." Robert Kahn and Charles Cannell have defined an interview as "a specialized pattern of verbal interaction initiated for a specific purpose and focused on some, specific content area, with a subsequent elimination of extraneous material."[12] There are three key concepts in this definition. First, an interview is a specialized pattern of verbal interaction. All verbal interaction is "patterned," responses are never random. To say that the pattern is specialized indicates not only that it is relatively unique or not routine, but also that expertise is called for. There are talents which make some individuals "good conversationalists" while others are bores. With training, people who lack talent in improvising a social conversation may improve. But for the most part, the ability to carry on a casual conversation does not require specific training or expertise. On the other hand, because interviewing is a specialized rather than routine pattern it requires specialized skill. A journalist may have to develop this skill largely on his own by experimenting and observing the effect of his questions on others. Nonetheless, most effective interviewers are conscious of their technique because they have developed them by conscious attention.

A second key term in Kahn and Cannell's definition is "initiated for some specific purpose." The interviewer always wants something from the respondent. He may want information; he may want to entertain an audience; he may want to sell an idea or a product to the respondent. All interviews are planned for a purpose. Interviewers often write out statements of purpose to clarify for themselves their intent.

Finally, interviews are "focused on some specific content area, with a subsequent elimination of extraneous material." The key term here is "focused." Two people enjoying a friendly chat may allow their conversation to range over many topics. There is little effort made to explore fully any particular idea if another, more interesting topic is brought up. Any topics may be considered appropriate.

In an interview the purpose is used as a criteria for deciding which topics should be discussed and which should not. This does not mean that extraneous topics never occur in interviews. When a job interviewer learns that the applicant is a brother in his old fraternity, neither may be able to resist the temptation to exchange brotherhood stories or discuss the state of repair of the fraternity house. But usually the interviewer will suddenly become aware that the conversation has "strayed" a bit too far from the purpose and will clear his throat and say, "Well, I guess we'd better talk about some of your other interests." Each person has an image of the topics which should be discussed to accomplish a predetermined purpose.

One problem with Kahn and Cannell's definition is that it does not allow us to distinguish between interviews and other forms of planned interaction such as public speeches. Charles Stewart and William Cash have offered the following, more complete definition: "a process of dyadic communication with a predetermined and serious purpose designed to interchange behaviors and usually involving the asking and answering of questions."[13] Let us consider the key terms in this definition.

First, interviewing is a "process of dyadic communication." To say that an interview is a process is to emphasize dynamics, continuity, and relativity. Dyadic means that it takes place between two parties. Sometimes interviews are conducted by teams; but in this case, one "party" consists of more than one person. Communication in a dyad is between one party and another.

Like Kahn and Cannell, Stewart and Cash emphasize purpose as a central defining characteristic of an interview, but they specify that the purpose must be predetermined. This is a useful specification. All communication transactions may be seen as purposive in retrospect.

Looking back on a two-hour conversation with a friend, you may conclude that the purpose of the conversation was to avoid doing some unpleasant work, but that purpose was not a conscious or predetermined one. The use of the term "predetermined" emphasizes rationality involved in the planning process.

Next, they observe that an interview is "designed to interchange behaviors." When parties in an interview "interchange behaviors" they enter into a mutual (though often unstated) agreement. They agree to assist one another in achieving acceptable questions and the other responds, in some way, to the questions.[14]

Finally, an interview involves "the asking and answering of questions." At this point Stewart and Cash emphasize that the use of questions is not merely a matter of form. "The mere mouthing of questions and responses is inadequate for successful interviewing."[15] Questions and answers are the means by which participants share experiences symbolically with one another. They allow one person to direct purposefully the talk of another.

Drawing comparisons with other forms of interaction, we could describe an interview as a speech, planned and managed by the "audience"; a two-party discussion with one person leading and another doing most of the talking; a planned dyadic conversation.

Planning Interviews

Throughout these definitions of interviewing I have emphasized planning. Planning an interaction is visualizing or imagining a future and then using that image as a guide to deciding how to act. This suggests that if people wish to improve their ability to plan, they must improve their ability to visualize or imagine. A person who wants to conduct better interviews needs a system for better imagining the expectations in an interview situation.

The ancient Greeks were probably the first people to devise a system for improving imagination. Aristotle invented a system of topoi or "topics" to help speakers think of things to say. Today planning experts use elaborate computer-based models to improve their scenarios or images of the future. A systematic way of thinking improves one's ability to imagine details. To plan an interview, it is helpful to have a systematic way of thinking about an interview as a communicative system. The idea is to think of the whole interview as a completed act with as much detail as can be imagined. In order to think of details, we can picture the interaction as based on the kinds of expectations discussed in the preceding chapters: motives, roles, norms, and agendas. I shall discuss each of these separately and suggest how to use each as a way of imagining interviews.

INTENTIONS AND GOALS. In both of the definitions of interviewing discussed above, the concept of purpose or motive was central. In improvising interactions, we are not aware of specific purposes. If asked why we are doing what we are doing, we may use a motivational explanation—"I'm here to have a good time"; "I'm here to learn more about myself"; "I'm doing this to make money." When we engage in planning, we turn implicit motives into exact purposes. I use the term "goal" to refer to a statement of a purpose. The term "objective" (as in "management-by-objectives") is also frequently used in management theory to refer to a precise, stated purpose.

Clear purposes or goals allow people to conduct interviews more efficiently. If we wish to construct anything useful, we need to have some idea of its intended use. The clearer our image of its use, the more efficiently we can design the structure. Although planning an interaction is different from planning the construction of physical objects, the metaphor is informative. The clearer our goals for an interview the more efficient we can be at planning the interaction because the more precisely we know what kind of information we want to get or to give.

In thinking of the goal of an interview, think of what you want to accomplish. Describe for yourself outcomes with which you would be pleased. We can sort possible outcomes according to interview types because types are but general ways of classifying purposes. Three of the most common types of interviews in organizational settings are information-giving interviews, selection (job) interviews, and information-gathering interviews. Let us examine the planning considerations in formulating a statement of purpose for each of these types.

If you are planning an information-giving interview such as an orientation interview or if you are planning how to instruct a person in the operation of a new machine, think of what that person should know at the end of the interaction. Think in the future perfect tense. Imagine what the person will have to be able to do on the job or with the machine. List everything you can think of. Then ask yourself, if a person knew all this (could do all this) would I say that he had been successfully "oriented" or "instructed"? If not, think of what he would need to know in addition.

Add to this list until you are satisfied that all the information is as complete as you can make it. Now you have an image of the goal of the interaction—the imagined completed state the interview is to achieve. Do not be alarmed that you discover additional information the other needs to know or that you find some information to be irrelevant as you are conducting the interview. Goals can never simulate all the detail of the completed act.

Selection or job interviews have as their general purpose the matching of people and tasks. For placement interviewers to specify the goal of their interviews they need to clarify for themselves the requirements of the positions they hope to fill. Planning the job interview means first imagining the job and what a person would have to be (friendly? strong? quick-witted?) and to do (type 80 wpm? teach spelling? allocate scarce resources among various departments?). The placement interviewer first learns as much as possible and practical about the position and then "fills in" a description of what the appropriate person might be like.

The interviewer's description probably starts with vague adjectives such as "ambitious" or "polite." In planning the interview, though, the interviewer must go beyond fuzzy adjectives to think about specific indicators of those qualities. What would one look for as an indication of "ambition"? What would a person do from which one might infer that he or she is likely to be "polite" on the job? In planning a selection interview, the interviewer should think concretely about the nature of the position and the behaviors which predict success in that position. Applicants or interviewees must also plan. They must imagine what they are looking for in a job. What would the company have to be like? How will they recognize these qualities from what the interviewer says and does or from the materials the interviewer provides?

An interview is never conducted for its own sake. Interviews conducted in an organization have some purpose in that organization. In order to specify the purpose of the interview itself, therefore, you have to know what is supposed to happen in an organization as the result of the interview. Information-giving interviews are typically supposed to result in knowledge about how to do a job; job interviews are supposed to result in competent people hired for positions.

To determine the purpose of an information-gathering interview, you need to know the purpose of the "research project" of which the interview is a part. What I call a "research project" may be a very formal occasion for gathering information. For example, a company may send out a couple of people to find out, "why #9 breaks down more often than any other assembly line." In addition to examining the machinery, the "researchers" (representatives of the production manager) interview the line workers.

Charles R. Walker's study of the installation of a continuous seamless pipe mill at U.S. Steel in 1949 illustrates a research project on a larger scale. The study was supported by the Institute of Human Relations of Yale University. Members of the Yale Institute were interested in the "psychological and social effects of technical change" in general and of automation in particular. The study took place over a four-year period, 1949–1952. In over fifty visits to the mill, the researchers observed the actual manufacturing process and talked casually with the men as they worked. Most of the research, however, involved "three *carefully prepared rounds of interviews . . . conducted with all members of the three mill crews in their homes."*

Walker identifies the goal of these interviews: "This organized series of interviews was specifically designed to examine the major points at which the technological revolution impinged on the worker's lives and to record their changes in attitude over time."[16] The major points investigated were: motivation, "the job," automatics, relations with workers, working conditions, relations with supervisors, incentive and promotion, and the Union. Questions were planned which addressed this topic directly and indirectly.

The goal of an information-gathering interview cannot be as precise as the goal of an information-giving interview. The information giver knows what information he or she wants to "give"; the selection interviewer can know fairly precisely the qualifications for a position. At best information-gathering interviewers know the kinds of information they need relative to a specific research purpose. To plan the goal of an information-gathering interview one needs to know what kinds of information are necessary in the larger research project of which the interview is a part. The more precise the research hypotheses being investigated, the more specific the goals of the interviews may be.

ROLES. Participants are performing roles. The existence of social roles makes possible the planning of interactions. When you are preparing to be interviewed for a job, you have some ideas about how the interviewer will act because you know he will be performing a fairly standard role. Planning to be interviewed involves imagining the likely role behaviors of the other and possible responses you might make. You engage in "if-then thinking": "If he does . . . then I will do. . . ." The "ifs and thens," however, are pictured as images of completed acts.

Interviews are almost always "first encounters." We usually interview and are interviewed by people we are meeting for the first time. Since we do not know people as individuals, we respond to them initially as stereotyped roles. A placement interviewer for U. S. Steel whose name is R. M. Jones will be seen by a job applicant more as a "placement interviewer for U. S. Steel" than as a "person named R. M. Jones." The job applicant will be treated and will act like a job applicant. The actors are in part improvising an "interview routine." As the interview progresses, however, each person will begin to recognize the individual characteristics of the other. The "first encounter" reactions to a standard role will progressively become responses to a particular person as each person learns more about the other. Each begins to plan interaction in view of likely responses of a person they know.

Some communication researchers insist that "the single most important element in interpersonal communication is source credibility."[17] Credibility is what one person thinks of another. In interviews, for example, the credibility of an interviewee is the extent to which the interviewer is inclined to believe what the interviewee says because the interviewee said it. Credibility is important for both interviewers and interviewees. An interviewer who tells a respondent that answers will be kept confidential wants to be believed. In a performance appraisal, an interviewee who reports that his machine does not run well wants to be believed.

When planning an interview, you need to think about the methods by which you can establish your credibility. Since you will first be seen as a standard role, your initial credibility will be only as good as the credibility of the organization you represent. A job applicant with a good scholastic record from a prestigious university will have more credibility than one from a school without a very good reputation. Once into the interview, however, a person can either enhance his or her personal credibility or damage the credibility of the organization by his or her communication. Although communication researchers agree on the importance of credibility, they are less unanimous on how one goes about establishing it. Three dimensions are frequently discussed: competence, intention, dynamism.

The first dimension is "competence." People tend to believe those who appear to be competent. Suppose that you are conducting a research project for a College of Business Administration to determine student attitudes on the required courses. Because of the random sample of all students, you are interviewing a sophomore who has not yet had any of the required courses. He tells you that the courses are worthless. His opinion is not very credible with you unless he can convince you that he is competent to judge. If you learned that he had conducted a random selection series of interviews on his own and has concluded they are worthless, he would appear more credible.

The interviewer who begins without any prior information on a topic is sure to end up with a poor interview. The most obvious reason why this happens is that the interviewer does not even know what kinds of information he needs. He cannot distinguish the important information which should be pursued from the less important information. Beyond its direct effect, an interviewer's lack of information influences the way the interviewee sees him.

Charles Stewart and William Cash observe that "the interviewer's credibility is judged by what he knows about the topic."[18] A poorly prepared interviewer has difficulty motivating the respondent to be interested in the interview. He must somehow overcome the handicap of a lack of credibility. An uninformed interviewer may fall into a pattern of overtly agreeing with everything the respondent is telling him or her. As a result, the interviewer may be unintentionally "conditioning" the respondent to continue a line of answers because the respondent is receiving agreement with the opinions he or she is expressing. In the process of building an impression of competence, an interviewer may ruin his chances of getting valid information. In planning an interview, both interviewees and interviewers need to consider how they can convince the other that they are competent without undermining the purpose of the interview.

Kenneth D. Frandsen[19] explains the dimensions of credibility with the example of a sales pitch for a vacuum cleaner (such a salestalk we might call a "persuasive interview"). We judge the credibility of the salesperson when we ask ourselves two questions: "Does he or she have accurate information about the machine, its quality, and performance?" And, "How much of what the seller is saying is influenced by his or her desire to sell me the machine?" The first question relates to the dimension of "competence". The second question is concerned with the second dimension of credibility: "intention."

We judge as less credible those people who seek to promote their own interests rather than ours. The answers of most competent and honest people will be influenced by their knowing that the purpose of your interview is to evaluate their job performance. You doubt their credibility because of your perception of their intentions. If you, as an interviewer, try to hide the purpose of your interview, you may arouse the interviewee's suspicions about your intentions. You could lose credibility. In planning an interview, both interviewers and interviewees need to consider how they can convince the other that they are motivated toward common, not selfish goals.

A third dimension often ascribed to credibility is "dynamism." We think of dynamic individuals as forceful and emphatic. Some research has suggested that dynamic individuals are more credible than less dynamic ones. Others have disputed the claim. If dynamism is a dimension of credibility, it may be because dynamism is a way of indicating interest. The dynamic interviewer displays an attitude of concern for the topic of the interview and the other person. He or she thus helps the other person define the situation as one in which display of interest is an appropriate behavior. The interviewee is likely to respond to the interviewer who displays interest and enthusiasm for the interview.

NORMS. Most of us operate on social norms which prevent us from disclosing personal information to strangers. In first encounters we stick to "safe topics." Stewart and Cash[20] describe three "safety levels of inquiry" which interviewers should consider. Level One is the norm appropriate to most first encounters. The questioner asks about a "safe" topic: "How do you feel about your education at Purdue?" The interviewee responds with a socially acceptable or superficial answer: "Well, I think I got as good an education as I could have somewhere else." Such a response does not say very much, but because the response is so obviously a "socially acceptable" one, the respondent may be just saying what she thinks the interviewer wants to hear.

Level Two responses are more revealing. Stewart and Cash's example is: Interviewer: "Tell me, really, how do you feel about your education at Purdue?" Interviewee: "Well, I think I am probably well prepared in accounting, but my basic preparation in other areas is weak." Notice here that the interviewer interjects "really" into his question to show enthusiasm and to invite a more revealing response. The respondent's answer is more informative than at Level One. The respondent is indicating how she divides up and evaluates parts of her world. We know from her answer that she differentiates business education from other education (such as science). She differentiates accounting from other business training. From this answer an interviewer can proceed to probe more specific areas.

Stewart and Cash characterize Level Three as "more ideal than real—providing maximum self-disclosure on the part of both parties in the interview." The Kinsey studies of sex behavior come to mind as an instance of when researchers sought Level Three information. It is helpful to think about what level of response you are seeking or are willing to give when planning any interview. Asking a person to reveal personal information is likely to be a violation of a conversational norm. The problem for interviewers and interviewees is to create norms within the interview situation which permit both parties to ask and answer questions required by the purpose of the interview. In planning an interview, one needs to think about what can be done in the interview situation to create these special norms.

AGENDA. The agenda of an interview is typically called the interview schedule. It is the ordering of questions and answers. A highly scheduled interview is one in which all questions are written in advance. One half of the interview conversation is thus completely planned. The interviewer does no more than read a questionnaire to the respondent and write down the answers. At the opposite extreme is a nonscheduled interview. Here the interviewer knows the goal and major topics to be covered, but improvises the wording and the ordering of the questions as the interview progresses. Most interviews fall somewhere along the continuum between completely scheduled and nonscheduled.

There are several questions which can guide you in deciding how rigid the schedule should be:

1. How many people will be conducting the interviews? *In general, the more people, the more rigid the schedule. The schedule of questions can provide consistency among interviews.*
2. How knowledgeable are the interviewers? *A large corporation may have a hundred placement interviewers who use relatively non-structured schedules. Each person, however, knows the company well and has specific information about the kinds of people being sought. Moreover, the people are experienced in conducting interviews. They know how to move from topic to topic without wandering from the goal of the interview. In general, the more knowledgeable the interviewers about the goal and the more experienced they are conducting interviews, the more the wording and ordering of questions can be left to their discretion during the interview.*
3. Do I know enough about this topic to detail specific questions or do I expect to learn what to ask as the interview progresses? *A good background knowledge of the subject is essential for planning and conducting any interview, but often it is impossible to know enough to write out all the questions in advance. In general, when conducting a large number of interviews, it is better to pretest or practice with a nonscheduled or semischeduled interview format. For example, the flexibility of a relatively free schedule will let you learn the language respondents are likely to use. You can then use that language in formulating questions for the large-scale interviews.*
4. Will specific, direct questions encourage the interviewee to give me information he might not have given? *The more rigid the schedule, the less the interviewer can follow up or probe the answers he receives. This means that the questions in a highly scheduled interview are general and less adapted to the opinions of a particular respondent. In general, the more reluctant a respondent to give information, the less rigid the interview schedule should be. A freer schedule will allow the interviewer to follow up on general responses with specific questions to encourage more information.*

Planning an interview schedule or agenda involves first deciding how rigid the schedule should be. In a rigid schedule, the wording of all the questions is planned or predetermined and the sequencing of questions is planned.

Types of Questions. Planned questions can range on a continuum from open to closed. Open questions are broad. They allow the interviewee considerable freedom in answering. Examples of open questions are:

What do you think about working conditions at your company?

How do you think our school system might be improved?

How do you feel about the 55-mile-an-hour highway speed limits?

Questions which ask, "What do you think?" and "How do you feel?" about broad topics allow the respondents to choose what they will talk about as well as what evaluation they will give.

In responding to the question about a school system, a person might talk about teachers' salaries, busing children for racial balance, renovating old buildings, or selecting textbooks. A respondent's choice of what to talk about first may be as revealing of his beliefs as what he says. Another reason for using open questions is that it is easier to detect if a respondent does not understand a question than if he is asked to answer with yes or no or some other brief answer. Also, using the language of the respondent is not as important when using a brief question to elicit a long answer.

There are some problems with open questions. The most obvious one is that the interviewer has much less control of what is said. A respondent may spend a long time telling "war stories" which are largely irrelevant to the goal of the interview. Answers to open-ended questions can be difficult to write down. If the interviewer uses a tape recorder, then answers must be transcribed or coded from the tape. Both transcribing and coding are time-consuming processes. Time usually means money.

Recording the answers to closed questions is easy because respondents are asked to choose from a narrow range of possible responses. For this reason it is easier for inexperienced interviewers to use closed questions. Asking for an answer of "yes" or "no" is the most closed form, but an interview with only closed questions is likely to miss some important information because the respondent has no opportunity to offer unsolicited information.

All but the most highly structured interview schedules have unplanned as well as planned questions. Unplanned questions occur spontaneously to the interviewer. They are used to follow up on interesting responses. Most unplanned questions are called probes. The interviewer using a probe asks the respondent (rather directly) to explain something he or she has said, or to extend the answer further.

A mirror question is an indirect form of probing. The interviewer simply restates part of the response, perhaps using a raised inflection toward the end. This invites the respondent to expand or clarify.

Another kind of probe is a verifier. Verifiers are extended mirrors. For example, an interviewer after listening to a response to an open question may say, "I hear you saying that you are opposed to the proposed policy because it may produce long-term unemployment. Is that correct?" The interviewer has summarized a long answer and has drawn out the evaluation which the respondent seemed to imply. The respondent now has an opportunity to verify the interviewer's perceptions before his answer is coded. The respondent may reply, "Yes, that's right" or "No, I'm not totally opposed. I just think we need to investigate the potential impact on employment before we proceed further on the idea."

Probes, mirrors, and verifiers cannot be planned in advance. However, the interviewer can plan to use these follow-up questions. Planning to use unplanned questions means imagining some possible responses to the planned questions and thinking of possible follow-ups. More important, the novice interviewer needs to tell himself or herself (about 100 times) that a list of planned questions (no matter how carefully prepared) will not necessarily produce a good interview. The greatest mistake made by inexperienced interviewers is that they rely too much on planned questions. They think of too many questions before the interview. While conducting the interview, they become more concerned with getting all their questions asked than with listening to the responses they are getting and probing and verifying what they think they hear. Planning to use unplanned questions therefore is a matter of not overplanning the allotted time with too many questions.

Sequence of Questions. Because an interview is a developing process, the order in which the planned questions are asked may influence the responses. Four commonly used sequences are the funnel, inverted funnel, quintamensional design, and tunnel. Table 5.1 describes each of these sequences.

The agenda of an interview must be partly planned in advance. The interviewer, or interviewing director (if there are many interviewers), determines what questions will be asked of all respondents and the order of the questions. In this section I have outlined some of the factors which need to be considered in making this decision. The principal questions are:

1. How rigidly structured is the schedule to be? (How much time should be left for unplanned questions?)
2. How many planned questions will be open; how many should be closed?
3. How should the planned questions be sequenced?

In addition to the goals, roles, norms, and agenda of an interview, some consideration should be given to the context and the setting of an interview. Both can affect intended and interpreted messages.

TABLE 5.1
Sequencing Questions in Interviews (From Charles J. Stewart and William B. Cash. *Interviewing Principles and Practices.* Dubuque, Iowa: Wm. C. Brown Co., 1974, pp. 64–66.)

Funnel Sequence	Begins with broad, open-ended questions and proceeds with ever more restricted questions. Appropriate when the respondent knows the topic well and feels free to talk about it or when the respondent is in an emotionally charged situation and would like to express her feelings.
Inverted Funnel	Begins with closed questions and gradually proceeds toward open-ended questions. Useful when you need to motivate the interviewee to respond freely.
Quintamensional Design	Questions follow a five-step sequence: (1) awareness, (2) uninfluenced attitudes, (3) specific attitudes, (4) reasons why, (5) intensity of attitudes. Used by George Gallup and others to determine intensity of attitude held by an individual.
Tunnel Sequence	Series of similar questions—all open or all closed—and usually allows for little probing. Useful for getting reactions toward persons or ideas when the interviewer wants to quantify data.

CONTEXT. The context of an interview consists of those events of the present and past which influence how participants interpret what they are talking about. The first time Nelson Rockefeller was "interviewed" by the House Judiciary Committee deliberating his appointment to the Vice Presidency he was asked "polite" questions. His confirmation seemed assured. In the course of later investigations several scandals appeared. Rockefeller owed a million dollars in back taxes. His brother had been accused of financing an unethical political brochure. Rockefeller had given money to several politicians for undisclosed reasons. Events such as these changed the context of Rockefeller's second appearance before the House Committee. The questions were more probing, if not more hostile, because the contextual events of the recent past had changed the questioners' minds about the advisability of Governor Rockefeller's nomination.

Another example of the influence of the context is described by Charles Walker in his study of the steel automation discussed earlier. Walker was interested in the workers' attitudes toward the wage incentive system which accompanied the change to automated machinery. During the second interview round, interviewers asked several questions about the system. One question asked: "Some men say the bonus system on Number 4 (automated mill) is a better system than on Number 1 (old mill). Others say that it is not. What would you say?"

Most of the men said that the new system was not as good. However, this round of interviews took place soon after the system had been installed. The union had opposed the system. A series of mechanical failures and other unanticipated events had led to decreased earnings. Between the second and third round of interviews production increased greatly. The men were earning 35 percent more than their base pay. This had a great effect on how the men viewed the merits of pay incentive and automation in general. As one worker put it:

> Well, I've got to admit when I saw you last time I didn't think the incentive was any good. . . . But during the past year, why it's worked out pretty well and we made a lot more than we thought we could, and we made a lot more than the engineers thought we could.[21]

In order to put these remarks "in context" the interviewer had to know that the system was only recently put into effect during the first round of interviews, that the union had opposed the system, and that there were unforeseen mechanical failures which resulted in lower pay just when the system should have been raising the workers' pay. The increase in amount of pay prior to interview rounds two and three changed not only the workers' attitudes toward the incentive plan, it indirectly changed their attitudes toward other aspects of their work. The change in the frequency of mechanical breakdowns and similar events influenced the meaning the workers attributed to "incentive pay" and to "teamwork." For the interviewers to understand what they were being told, they had to understand the effect of the context on what the respondents were discussing.

SETTING.   The setting is what can be seen (heard or felt) during the interview. It provides participants with information they use in defining their situation. It also can influence the mood of both interviewer and respondent.

The decor of a room can influence behavior which takes place within it. For example, it can affect evaluations of people. Researchers Maslow and Mintz[22] gave people photographs of faces and asked them to rate the attractiveness of the faces. One third of the subjects were in "ugly" rooms resembling janitors' closets. One third were in "beautiful" rooms decorated with carpeting and drapes. The subjects in the beautiful rooms gave much higher ratings to the same pictures than did the subjects in the ugly rooms. Those in the beautiful rooms reported feeling comfort, importance, and energy.

The arrangement of furnishings can also influence how people feel during an interview, and presumably therefore, affect what they say. "Barriers" between interviewers and respondents may have a significant effect. One study investigated the effect of a desk between a doctor and patient during a medical interview. Only 10 percent of patients felt "at ease" when separated from the doctor by a desk. In interviews without the desk barrier 55 percent of the patients felt at ease.[23]

Another element of the scene of an interview is created by the appearance of the participants. Several studies have confirmed the importance of clothing as a means of communication. In summarizing some of this research, Mark L. Knapp has observed: "To make a list of the things invariably communicated by clothes would be impossible. . . . Some of the potential personal attributes which may be communicated by dress include: sex, age, nationality, relationship to the opposite sex, socio-economic status, identification with a specific group, occupational or official status, mood, personality, attitudes, interests, and values.[24]

The appearance of one person in an interview provides cues to his or her social role and attitude about the situation. The clothes of actors in interviews set the scene for their own actions. In describing the general effects of clothing on an actor's behavior, Knapp observes that "self-consciousness often results from wearing an 'inappropriate' outfit. By dressing for a particular role we provide assurance to ourselves that we are competent to enact that role. Thus, graduate students wear "professional" clothes (suits, dresses) to identify themselves as teachers. Their clothing gives them confidence in dealing with students,[25] because they look the part of the role they play. Job applicants dress in such a way that they tell themselves they are qualified for the job. The dress of the interviewer (whether "loud" or ultraconservative) provides clues to the interviewees about the work environment of the organization.

The acts which constitute interviews are the acts of constructing meaning. In the preceding subsections I have identified the elements in interviews which affect how people interpret the meaning of what's happening. Actors' intentions and goals lead them to attend to some potential messages and not to others. Each person's perception of himself (and his role) and of the actors in the situation influence what he thinks is happening. The agenda in the form of types of questions and their ordering affect how participants interpret meaning. The context and setting affect the construction of meaning. The goals, roles, norms, agendas, context, and setting can all be anticipated or planned to some extent.

Skillful interviewers plan in order to encourage a communication situation in which they can understand as much as possible the meanings of respondents. They imagine their role and respondents' roles and try to devise ways to encourage relationships between themselves and others which will facilitate meaning.

Fred Blum describes how he "planned" interviews with packinghouse workers. The object of his research was "to understand the ways in which these workers are related to the industrial and social process."[26] Blum attempted to establish a relationship with the workers based on frankness. He did this, in part, by revealing to them his role and the goals of his project. He quotes his typical introduction:

> Ideally, we should just talk, but in order to write one story from all the stories I hear, I must have comparable stories. It would take too long to get such stories without following a definite schedule. That's why I am going to ask you a series of questions. . . . If you do not feel like answering some of these feel free to tell me. . . . I have no desire to pry into personal matters, but I have to ask you all kinds of things in order to get to know you. . . . There is nothing I am going to ask you that I am not willing to answer myself. . . . You are entitled to know as much about my life as I want to know about yours. After I have asked you a series of questions about your younger years, I will tell you on my own what I have been doing during these years. . . . Other things you may want to know about me you have to ask on your own initiative.

He thus told the respondents about his own life as they told him about theirs. He observes that "this departure from the regular interview procedures led to a notable change in atmosphere and a greater facility in obtaining information." The effect was to create a feeling or expectation of "reciprocity" between the two participants in the interview.

Cline and Johnson[27] found that respondents in interviews in which the interviewer kept all attention directed on them reacted defensively to direct verbal attention away from their personal lives. In interviews in which the interviewers talked about themselves, the respondents reciprocally told more about themselves.

Blum allowed the workers to choose their own setting for the interview. When they preferred their own homes, he used what he saw in their homes as information pertinent to his project:

> Those workers who were asked to cooperate on the project by spending some time with me outside the plant, and who accepted this invitation, were given a choice of whether they wanted to come to my apartment or talk to me in their homes. Practically all preferred the latter, a choice which I welcomed because it gave me a good opportunity to meet the worker's family.

He attempted to obtain information about the context within which the workers were speaking by asking about their family and educational background, their relationship to other workers and to the supervisors.

In addition, Blum worked with the men in the factory so that he could observe the nature of the work directly and thus better judge the contextual scene of his interviews. Blum's purpose in conducting the interviews was to be able to describe how workers constructed for themselves the meaning of their own worlds. Therefore, he needed to get workers to talk about what was important to them and to talk in such a way that Blum could reconstruct for himself the meaning the worker had for important events in his life. The successful interviewer plans the interaction. As Blum suggests, he plans the agenda—the questions and their ordering, he plans the setting. He also "plans" the role relationship between himself and the other actor.

How one plans an interview is dependent upon the purpose of the interview. If you are instructing a person about how to perform a new job, you would not make the kind of choices Blum made about agenda and setting, but the fundamental point would still be valid, however. You would "plan" the role relationship of the actors, the setting, the norms. The process of the interview would still be the creation of meaning.

We now turn our attention from the kinds of things a person thinks about in preparing for an interview to a description of what happens during interviews. The intent of the following section is to spell out the implications of the concept of interviewing developed here for conducting interviews.

Enacting the Interview

Interviews are guided by some kind of interaction plan. The plan may be as rigid as a highly structured series of questions which constrain the respondent to choose answers from among a few alternatives. Or it may be as loose as a few ideas which the interviewer wants to discuss. Regardless of how rigidly he or she has planned the interview, the interviewer faces three problems in enacting that plan:

1. Motivating integration.
2. Achieving equivalent meanings for central symbols.
3. Achieving the goal.

Below I discuss what happens in an interview by discussing strategies and techniques employed to meet these three problems.

MOTIVATING INTEGRATION. Participation in an interview is not guaranteed by the physical presence of people, or even by the talking which takes place. Particularly in formal organizations, there are a number of means which can be used to force a person to present himself to be interviewed. An organizational regulation requiring annual appraisal interviews is almost always sufficient to "motivate" the presence of workers and supervisors, usually with a good deal of apprehension on the part of both parties.

Such regulations can force minimal compliance, but they do not guarantee any commitment or integration of the people. When people are integrated fully into a communication system they are actively pursuing goals and trying to understand the meanings of others. If you are "talking" with another, but you do not care to understand what he is saying or to be understood by him, then you are merely mouthing words. You are not integrated into the conversational system.

Motivation to participate in an interview is like motivation to participate in any organized activity. Frederick Herzberg's[28] system for explaining job motivation can help us understand the interviewer's task in motivating a respondent's integration. The core of Herzberg's scheme is the notion that satisfaction and dissatisfaction are not polar opposites. Individuals seek to avoid discomfort. If factors such as policy, interpersonal relationships, working conditions, and salary are unsatisfactory to members, there will be little or no integration into organizational activity.

The existence of satisfaction with these factors (Herzberg calls them "hygiene factors"), however, is not by itself sufficient to motivate participation. A worker may be paid an adequate salary and still not want to do anything beyond what is required by the supervisor. Motivation, Herzberg says, results from factors intrinsic to the job itself. Recognition of achievement, responsibility, the content of the job itself are the sources of rewards for employees. It is acts seeking these internal rewards that constitute a person's true integration. In this discussion of motivating integration, I make a similar distinction between satisfiers (factors internal to the interview) and dissatisfiers (failure to provide basic rewards which are necessary but do not motivate a respondent).

Motivating a person's integration into an interview begins with the opening. Interviewers must attend to this process throughout the interview, but the specific purpose of the opening is encouraging participation. The interviewer must secure at least a minimum commitment of the respondent before the interview can proceed.

Stewart and Cash observe the following about opening information-gathering interviews:

> The function of the opening is to make the interviewee ready to communicate freely and accurately during the remainder of the interview. This readiness is accomplished by establishing rapport—creating a feeling of trust and good will between R and E [the interviewer and the interviewee]—and by orienting the interviewee—explaining the purpose and nature of the study, what will be expected of him, how this information

will be used, why we selected him as an interviewee, and perhaps how long the interview will take.[29]

As Stewart and Cash are using the term here, rapport is an "hygienic factor" in an interview. If the interviewee does not have some minimum attraction to or liking for the interviewer, it is unlikely that he will commit to begin the interview. He will be dissatisfied. But goodwill for the interviewer is not sufficient for motivation to participate. A young, attractive interviewer may have no trouble securing the attention of a respondent, but may find that the respondent is more interested in enjoying the rapport itself than in giving or receiving information pertinent to the purpose of the interview.

Sometimes money or other material goods are offered to respondents to compensate them for the time they spend in the interview. As with rapport, material compensation does not by itself motivate participation. A person may be unwilling to participate unless compensated. But compensation is only for the time (the presence) of the respondent. It guarantees only the minimum. A respondent may or may not feel "obliged" to participate because he or she is paid for his time. Stewart and Cash pointed out that there may even be a disadvantage to informing a respondent in the opening that he or she is to be paid. Salesmen typically offer gifts to encourage people to listen to their salespitches. "If you start with such [an offer], you may never convince the respondent that you are not a salesman pretending to be an informational interviewer."[30]

The interviewer's attempts to orient respondents to the purpose of the interview are his or her chief satisfiers or motivators in the beginning of an interview. Typical ways of orienting include:

1. Summarizing the problem on which the interview will be focused.
2. Describing how you (the interviewer) became interested in the problem.
3. Describing how the interviewee will benefit from participation. (I am referring here to intrinsic benefits which result from the interviewer's accomplishment of purpose, not to compensation of the respondent for his time. Stewart and Cash use the following example: "Good Morning, Mrs. Williams. I am conducting a survey of attitudes on current meat prices. My study might result in a stabilizing of meat prices in the area.")

All three ways attempt to secure the respondent's commitment to the purpose of the interview. If the respondent sees that his or her participation will be valuable, he is more likely to want to participate. The idea behind these suggestions is to get the interviewee committed to the goal of the interview. Motivation throughout the interview depends upon the respondent being committed to the goal more than he or she (1) wants to secure self-centered needs (such as ego satisfaction), or (2) wants to please the interviewer (for example, by giving answers he thinks the interviewer wants to hear).

Successful interviewers, of course, avoid dissatisfiers. These may include biased terms which would annoy a respondent, questions which violate the norms of the situation, insulting or threatening questions.

ACHIEVING EQUIVALENCE OF MEANING. Novice interviewers who are intent on asking all their planned questions are usually sacrificing their possibilities for developing equivalent meanings with their respondents. They obtain a list of "answers" to their questions, but they may not have understood what the respondent meant when he said that he was "only working for the money." (Did he think the money was exceptionally good? Did he mean it was the only job he could get? Did he mean he was about to quit?) Unless both interviewer and interviewee have developed equivalent meanings for the important symbols they are displaying to one another, then both have wasted their time.

As in any conmmunication, people achieve equivalence through co-orientation. Let us examine some methods of coorientation in interview situations. Note that these methods may be used in any kind of planned interaction where communicators do about the same amount of talking.

Participants in an interview can concretize what they are talking about through the use of unplanned questions. Both the interviewer and the interviewee can ask the other to be less abstract. In particular, they can ask for examples.

A "living example" is even better than an abstract one. We may more easily achieve equivalent meaning with others when we can see them actually doing what they are talking about. This gives us a better sense of the context within which they are choosing what they are saying and how they are saying it. Alvin Gouldner describes the importance of such observations as a means of interpreting information gathered in interviews with gypsum plant workers.

> We spent a good deal of time just walking around, or standing with a worker and talking with him casually as he worked. The small size of the plant enabled us to "see" it as a whole fairly quickly. We quickly became immersed in the plant's "atmosphere" and got the feel of it by walking through the massive heat of the kiln, breathing in the dry gypsum dust, climbing the catwalks high above the plant, poking around the tops of the enormous mill vats, riding the rough gypsum cars, lighting cigarettes as we sat exhausted on full cases of dynamite in the mine—a practice which miners insisted was safe, though they were always addicted to broad humor. Aside from simply having a wonderful time—a factor of not little

motivational significance—this total immersion helped our interviewing considerably. It helped us to talk, with some degree of fluency, about the complicated mechanical environment that surrounds the worker. We did not have to ask the workers, say, how the mix was beaten up, unless we deliberately wanted to play 'possum,' for we had seen it.[31]

The interviewers were better able to understand what the workers meant when they talked about the heat in the factory because they had experienced it themselves. It was a concrete experience they shared. Beyond the concreteness, the interviewers gained a sense of the "world" in which the workers lived and were better able to interpret what workers say from the perspective of how they lived. Such experiences thus make it easier for us to coorient our interpretations with those of others.

Of course, not all interviewers can walk around and see the world with those they interview. They must depend upon what can be said in the interview itself. The use of verifiers can help participants in an interview to coorient themselves to the meanings of the other. The verifier (discussed in a previous section) says in effect, "This is what I hear when you say that." By exposing our interpretation of a speaker's words to the speaker, we give the other some sense of how we are interpreting what another intended; it also gives the other some clues about how to phrase what he wants to say so that we may interpret it more easily.

If you are interviewing a person and you hear what you think to be an inconsistency in the person's responses, you should suspect that you may not have equivalent meanings for some important concepts. For example, you may interpret one response as indicating that the person is against school busing for racial balance and later hear him speaking in favor of it. The information from the interview will not be worth much unless this seeming inconsistency is probed. This probing is done by verifying the speaker's intended meaning.

Another verbal device for facilitating coorientation is the transition. When an interviewer wishes to switch from one line of questioning to another, he summarizes his perception of the central theme of what has just been discussed and then mentions the central idea of the line of questioning to follow. For example, "We have been talking about the availability of new homes in this area. Another major factor in determining the number of home purchases is mortgage availability. Let me ask you some questions about this. First . . . ." Note that there are three parts to this transition: a summary of the last theme, a summary of the new theme, and a statement of the relationship between the two themes. Such a transition allows both participants to switch gears—mental sets in this case—at about the same time.

Sticking to relevant issues is another way of keeping mental gears meshing together. It is tempting to probe side issues. Often a respondent must be allowed to tell stories of little apparent relevance to the goal of the interview. The stories may turn out to be relevant after all. Or they may give the interviewer a better view of the respondent's world, thus helping the interviewer to orient himself or herself to the perspective of the other. There is also, of course, the necessity to be polite. An interviewer who seems too pushy in getting only information he or she wants to hear is likely to encourage the respondent to say nothing. The successful interviewer carefully guides the conversation so that both people constantly perceive that what they are talking about is relevant to the goal of the interviewer.

In chapter 2 I said that equivalence results when people are acting within the expectations of one another. For example, Person A may not like the way Person B does his job, but he knows fairly well how B does his job and he expects B to do it that way. Coorientation has taken place and both parties have developed stable expectations about what is happening. Verbal methods such as verifiers, transitions, and sticking to the goal of the interview help create similar definitions of the situation so that the parties have stable expectations as well as equivalent meanings.

ACHIEVING THE GOAL. Motivating integration and achieving equivalence are essential to a successful interview, but alone they do not guarantee success. Interviews have predetermined goals. The goal of the interview must also be accomplished.

In the previous subsection I emphasized the importance of both parties achieving equivalence of meaning. One way to think of the goal of an interview is to think of whose meanings are to be learned by the other. In an information-giving interview (such as job instructions) the interviewer is the teacher and the interviewee is the learner. Both people take the responsibility of shaping the interviewee's ideas to be equivalent to those of the interviewer. In an information-gathering interview the interviewer is the principal learner and the interviewee is the teacher. The interviewer should "change" more during the interview than the interviewee. In a selection interview both parties may be learners. The interviewer must learn the applicant's qualifications; the interviewee must learn the opportunities provided by the company.

In the interview conversation, of course, both people will learn and will change to some extent. One person is not like a "mold" which forms a piece of clay into its shape. Good interviews are those in which both people are actively learning. However, consider the problems which may occur if the parties are not attending to whose learning is most relevant to the goal. In an information-giving interview the interviewee may insist on describing his or her abilities and/or problems in such detail that the interviewer learns about the person, but the interviewee does not learn how to do the job.

In an information-gathering interview the wording of questions may be unfamiliar to the respondent. He may have to struggle so to fit his answers to the vocabulary of the interviewer that his answers do not reflect his own perceptions of the world. Or consider the job interviewer who spends so much time learning about an applicant that the applicant has no opportunity to learn about the company. When he or she is offered a job, it gets turned down. In each of these cases, the parties may have been motivated and may have developed equivalent meanings, but the meanings were inappropriate to the purpose. The information-gatherer, for example, must be more concerned with learning the respondent's vocabulary than the respondent is with learning the interviewer's vocabulary.

Skill in Planned Interaction

The intent of this "applications" section is to exemplify planned interactions in general as well as to discuss interviews. The planning period gives communicators a "choice" about what to say and how to say it that they do not have when they are improvising. Because of this "choice," we can speak of skills of planned interaction. Skills cannot be learned by reading about them in books. Miller, Galanter, and Pribram make the following observation about the relationship of "plan" to "skill":

> When people have time to develop the skill themselves, that is to say, when they form a Plan to guide the gross actions—even an inefficient plan—they find for themselves the interposed elements that produce the skill. Finding these elements is essentially a test of the adequacy of the strategy. Once the strategy has been developed, alternative modes of action become possible, and we say that the person "understands" the job he is to do.[32]

Skill in planned interactions such as interviews is not an inherent trait. It must be learned. Learning is a matter of developing your ability to plan. You may learn to plan "nonconsciously" by watching a skilled interviewer. You may also learn through conscious attention to the kinds of considerations discussed here in combination with practice and judgments about how successful you are.

This section has offered a systematic method of thinking about an interview. I have suggested that these are six considerations that are helpful in planning any kind of interaction: speech, casual conversation, conference. The six are:

1. *The goal* (*How can it be stated as exactly as possible?*)
2. *The roles* (*How do I want to be seen by the other? How does he want me to see him?*)
3. *The norms* (*What is appropriate in this situation? What kinds of actions need to be seen as appropriate for me to meet my objective?*)
4. *The agenda* (*What questions or statements shall I use in what order?*)
5. *The context* (*What events are influencing how actors are interpreting messages?*)
6. *The setting* (*How are physical surroundings affecting communication? How can the setting be changed to facilitate the purpose of the interaction?*)

I have also suggested that participants in interviews have three tasks. These three tasks are also common to all planned interactions. They are: integration, achieving equivalence of meaning, and achieving goals of the interview. Successful interviews depend upon finding methods in particular situations to met each of these criteria. These same considerations and tasks provide useful framework for constructing any kind of interaction plan. Public speakers must plan their speeches by attending to expectations relevant to goals, roles, norms, agendas, context, and setting. Speakers must plan ways to achieve integration, equivalence of meaning, and purpose.

Of course, the methods used in different forms of planned interaction are different but the general process is the same. These tasks must be accomplished by the guy who goes in to ask his boss for a raise. He must plan the interaction by thinking about goals, roles, agendas, context, and setting. He faces the tasks of achieving integration, equivalence, and purpose. These considerations provide a universal framework for planning interactions. Becoming a skilled communicator involves developing one's own methods to "fill in" the framework.

ENDNOTES

1. George A. Miller, Eugene Galanter, and Karl H. Pribram, *Plans and the Structure of Behavior* (New York: Holt, Rinehart, and Winston, 1960), p. 16.
2. Alfred Schutz, *Phenomenology of the Social World* (Evanston, Ill.: Northwestern University Press, 1967).
3. Erving Goffman, *Strategic Interaction* (Philadelphia: The University of Pennsylvania, 1969), pp. 93–94.
4. Ibid., p. 100.
5. For example, see Jack Gibb, "Defensive Communication," *Journal of Communication* 11 (1961): 141–148.
6. Roderick P. Hart and Don M. Burks, "Rhetorical Sensitivity and Social Interaction," *Speech Monographs* 39 (1972): 75–91.

7. Ibid., p. 77.

8. Ibid., p. 79.

9. Ernest Becker, *The Birth and Death of Meaning* (New York: The Free Press, 1971), p. 84.

10. Ibid., p. 84.

11. Ibid., p. 84.

12. Robert Kahn and Charles Cannell, *The Dynamics of Interviewing* (New York: John Wiley & Sons, Inc., 1957), p. 16.

13. Ibid.

14. Charles Stewart and William Cash, *Interviewing Principles and Practices* (Dubuque, Iowa: Wm. C. Brown Co., 1974), pp. 6–7.

15. Ibid., p. 7.

16. Charles R. Walker, *Toward the Automated Factory: A Case Study of Men and Machines* (London: Oxford University Press, 1957), p. 23.

17. James C. McCroskey, Carl E. Larson, and Mark L. Knapp, *An Introduction to Interpersonal Communication* (Englewood Cliffs: Prentice-Hall, Inc., 1971), p. 80.

18. Stewart and Cash, *Interviewing Principles and Practices*, p. 73.

19. Kenneth D. Frandsen in a personal conversation, July 1975.

20. Stewart and Cash, *Interviewing Principles and Practices*, p. 10.

21. Walker, *Toward the Automated Factory*, p. 80.

22. A. H. Maslow and N. L. Mintz, "Effects of Esthetic Surroundings," *Journal of Psychology* 41 (1956): 247–54.

23. A. G. White, "The Patient Sits Down: A Clinical Note," *Psychosomatic Medicine* 15 (1953): 256–257.

24. Mark L. Knapp, *Nonverbal Communication in Human Interaction* (New York: Holt, Rinehart and Winston, 1972), p. 84.

25. Ibid.

26. Fred Blum, "Getting Individuals to Give Information to the Outsider," *Journal of Social Issues* 8 (1970): 83.

27. Rebecca J. Cline and Bonnie McDaniel Johnson, "The Verbal Stare: Focus of Attention in Conversation," *Communication Monographs* 43 (1976): 1–10.

28. Frederick Herzberg, "One More Time; How Do You Motivate Employees?" *Harvard Business Review* 46 (Jan.–Feb. 1968): 53–62.

29. Stewart and Cash, *Interviewing Principles and Practices*, pp. 77–78.

30. Ibid., p. 79.

31. Alvin Gouldner, *Patterns of Industrial Bureaucracy* (New York: The Free Press, 1954), p. 250.

32. Miller et al., *Plans and the Structure of Behavior*, p. 85.

CHAPTER

6

Collective Decision Building

Collective Decisions
Classical Approaches to Decision Making
Integration in Task-Oriented Groups
Phases of Decision Building
Characteristics of Effective Decision Building
Organizing Functions: Commitment and Change
APPLICATION: Problem-Solving Discussion

The subject of this chapter is the process by which small, informal groups of people produce a set of symbols they call a "group decision." The focus is on understanding the process and developing a framework for improving it. The kinds of coordination formats discussed in the preceding chapters are involved in the process of making a collective decision. That is, people are in part improvising on formulas; they are in part enacting their private interaction plans. Beyond this, however, they are making collective decisions about what they shall do.

In the first section I discuss the nature of "collective decisions." I then describe some "classical approaches" to understanding the process of decision making. The "classical approaches" are mainly concerned with the development of a collective intelligence among a group of people. I then discuss the character of integration in task-oriented groups. The following sections on "Phases of Decision Building" and

"Characteristics of Effective Decision Building" describe interrelationships of intelligence and integrative functions. These sections provide
the framework for understanding decision building and how it might
be improved. In the concluding application section, I describe some
methods for improving problem-solving group discussions which are
suggested by the theoretical framework developed in the first sections
of the chapter.

COLLECTIVE DECISIONS

Some people argue that "collective decisions" do not exist. They say
that committees, for example, do not make decisions. Instead, "decisions" are made by committee members. Groups do not decide.
Only people (as individuals) can decide because deciding is thinking,
and groups cannot think. I use the term "collective decision building"
to distinguish the collective process from the individual decision making
or planning discussed in the previous chapters.

There are two distinguishing features of this coordination format.
First, a group of people deliberately construct a set of symbols and
announce this to be their "decision." A group of people engaged in
improvising may be interpreted by others (or by the members themselves in retrospect) as having made decisions. Our concern here is
with people who are consciously making decisions which they announce
as "theirs." The decisions are announced as collective decisions and
not as individual decisions.

A second feature of this format is that the people talk about their
expectations. In planned interaction people are aware of their expectations, but general discussion of expectations is not part of the agenda
of discourse. In collective decision building, people talk, and even
reach decisions, about what they are to expect from one another. They
talk about their norms, their roles, their agenda, and their intentions.

Planned interaction is deliberately purposeful. It involves an individual choosing his or her goals and then directing behavior toward
those goals. Collective decision building involves collective goal setting. Group members talk about what they want to accomplish together. There may be no agreement on a single goal. Certainly individuals have some goals which are quite far apart from the collective
goals. Clarity in goals may not be (typically is not) apparent until after a
group has accomplished one or more of its goals, for goal setting even at
a "collective" level is largely restrospective. Nonetheless, the process of
collective decision building involves seeking consensual goals. Those
goals are expressed somehow in the talk of group members. The ful-

fillment of the goals entails, in part, the "announcing" of decisions by the group.

Announced decisions of informal groups usually take the form of symbolic displays. After some bickering about where they'll eat, one guy says, "McDonald's is closer. Let's go there." Several others shout out: "Yeah"; "I'm in a hurry anyway." All five move in the direction of McDonald's. Individual decisions have been made, but also, a collective decision has been made. The evidence or symbolic display of the decision are the words and movements of the group members. They intended to "decide together." Their actions fulfill that intention. Such symbolic actions constitute the minimum announcement of a collective decision.

In formal organizations collective decisions are more easy to identify. They are made by officially designated groups. They are made in the name of the whole organization. When AT&T declares its stock dividend, the decision is a collective one no matter how influential any single individual might have been in the decision process. When John Kennedy decided to block shipping to Cuba, the whole United States government "decided." The decision was "collective" because it was made by the formally recognized representation in the name of the whole organization. Decisions made by formal organizations usually are symbolized or communicated to others in the form of a symbolic document. Such symbolic actions constitute the maximum announcement of a collective decision.

One important characteristic of a collective decision, then, is that it is "announced." Informal groups may announce their decisions to others or only to themselves. Their "announcing" may be in the form of their actions. In walking toward McDonald's the guys announce to themselves their "collective decision." Formal groups usually announce their decisions to outsiders as well. Even formal groups, however, may decide not to announce publicly. Even here there is a displaying to one another that they have come to an agreement.

Because they are necessarily "announced," collective decisions are symbolic messages. They are "collective" in the same way that any symbol is shared collectively. Any announced "collective decision" provides a focus for individual interpretations of the meaning of that decision. But it is not simply the words a group uses in announcing a decision that constitute that decision. Words without other actions do not constitute decisions. Without the announcement, however, there could not be any change of action. Announcement is part of a continuing process of decision building. The symbols serve as guides which individuals use in making individual decisions about how to act. Collective decisions are the actions of people (perhaps several, perhaps millions) which are motivated in part by a set of symbols devised and announced by a group of people. The total process includes both methods by which a group produces an "announced decision" and the methods by which people interpret the symbols in action.

The more conventional term for this process is "decision making." When we think of decisions, there is a tendency to think of discrete acts. For example, Chrysler Corporation "decided" to close most of its auto manufacturing plants for the month of December, 1974. We think of categories of decisions such as volume of output, prices, wages, location of new plants. We also think of discrete acts which are presumed to follow automatically from verbal announcements (closing a plant, raising a price). The word "decide" is derived from the Latin expression "to cut away." Deciding, then, might be thought of as "slicing." Before the "slice" there is confusion and uncertainty; after the slice there is "decision." But decisions are not discrete acts; decision building is not "slicing."

There is no time at which there is total uncertainty followed instantaneously by a time of perfect certainty. Decision building is a process of uncertainty reduction, or structuring. As such it is cumulative. It is often helpful to identify phases (such as the phase of decision announcement). The concept of phase will be discussed later. Use of the term "decision building" rather than the more conventional "decision making" emphasizes on-going, cumulative activity. At minimum, the process involves a group of people engaged in collective decision building who construct symbols which they agree represent their collective "position" on an issue. Decision building also involves the process of interpreting through actions the meaning of those symbols which constitute the announced decision.

In producing an announced decision, informal groups discuss some of their expectations. Unlike improvising and planned interactions, in collective decision building important expectations for interaction among group members are stated. Decisions about whether smoking is to be allowed in a particular place illustrate the distinction I am making between unstated and stated expectations. Few people smoke in church sanctuaries. The social formula provides an unstated injunction against smoking. In committee rooms there is typically widespread smoking. People expect when they are sitting around a conference table that a norm of "smoking permitted" is operative. At a meeting I attended recently a group of us "nonsmokers" brought the matter up for a collective decision. We all discussed the problem of providing for the comfort of all committee members. The result was a collective decision about expectations. We decided that no one person would smoke more than two cigarettes during the meeting (which was to last several hours). Thus a taken-for-granted permission to smoke became the object of a collective decision.

Collective decision building is an activity most of us are involved in every day because it blends with improvisation and planning. We can identify decision-building activity because it is focused on the explicit or unstated question: "What shall we do?" One example of everyday decision building is a group of professors who eat together almost all the time. The pattern of eating together has become what I have called a social routine. Each day they expect to eat together. Around noon they gather in the hall and walk together in the general direction of town.

Most of the lunch talk is improvised. There are some standard formula topics: "the state of the profession," "places I've been," "interesting people I've met." Some of the lunch talk is planned interaction. Some individuals have agendas. They come to lunch intending to discuss with one another or with a group some departmental matter. One may want some advice from a student's advisor about whether to be lenient in giving that student a deferred grade. The lunches provide an informal setting in which people can learn what others are doing, tell what they are doing, get information and advice. The talk is important because it directly and indirectly helps people coordinate their actions in the department.

This "group" also makes collective decisions. They decide collectively each day where they will eat and what they will eat. The norm is that they all order the same food. They all look at the menu. Then someone says, "the Reuben sandwich special looks good." Another concurs, "Fine with me." There is often at least one dissenter, "Anyone interested in pastrami?" The Reuben special contingent will put the matter to vote. The collective decision is announced: five-to-one for Reuben. The pastrami advocate must then make an individual decision: shall he or she follow the group norm though his stomach cries for pastrami?

The point of this story is not that these lunch time collective decisions have any direct impact on how the department functions. The six people who order Reuben sandwiches may nonconsciously regard this collective decision as evidence of their solidarity as a group. Announcing their decision to the waiter might serve as a symbolic display of their commitment to each other. I shall not argue this point too vigorously, however, for I have little proof. The point is that even the most casual collection of people engage in collective decision building. Anytime we are with other people we "risk" having our individual decisions influenced by the collective position of the group. If you go to lunch with this lunch-bunch, you risk being influenced to have a Reuben special instead of a pastrami.

To begin examination of the process of collective decisionbuilding, let us consider the "classical theories" of decisionmaking. These theories purport to tell us how decisions should be made. Then we shall consider some descriptions of how decisions are made.

CLASSICAL APPROACHES TO DECISION MAKING

There are two kinds of decision theories: normative theories and empirical theories. A normative theory describes how decisions *should* be made. An empirical theory describes how decisions *are* made. Classical approaches to decision making are normative theories. They are also theories which are concerned with the intelligence rather than integrative function of communication. The classical theory of informal group decision making is called "reflective thinking." In formal organization theory, the classical approach is called "rational" or "optimal" decision theory. "Reflective thinking" and "optimal decision" theories are based on similar assumptions and describe similar "steps" leading to decision.

Harold Zelko's description of decision making in *The Business Conference* illustrates the classical approach to decision making in small problem-solving groups. In this approach "rationality" is accomplished through the use of a series of largely discrete "steps" which may be known to all group members in advance of their discussion. Others have called these steps the "standard agenda."[1] Zelko states:

> There is a series of steps to be followed in systematic decision making in groups. But it would be a mistake to assume that these are rigid or that they represent a formal procedure. Actually, it is best to avoid procedure in a formal sense, yet it is important to use a sequence that is logical and clear. And it is necessary for the group to know the sequence and to be aware of which state it is in at a given time. The leader should indicate each phase clearly, make sharp transitions and make internal summaries frequently.[2]

Expressions such as "it is important," "it is necessary," and "the leader should" signal us that the writer is presenting a normative theory. He is telling us how decisions should be made. He is telling us how collective intelligence is best developed. The steps are summarized in Figure 6.1.

Two features of this procedure warrant careful attention. First, proposals are not supposed to be made until after the "facts" are gathered. Zelko states, "It is foolhearty to move toward solutions before all the necessary information is obtained." Second, alternative proposals are supposed to be considered simultaneously. Zelko suggests that prior to discussing the proposals, the group (or the leader for the

TOPIC INTRODUCED	PROBLEM	POSSIBLE SOLUTIONS	BEST SOLUTION	ACTION
Orientation to Subject	Information and Facts Furnished	Free Period Offering Solutions	Critical Analysis Establishment of Criteria Selection of Facts	Decision Making

FIGURE 6.1
Steps in Reflective Decision Making (From Harold Zelko. *The Business Conference.* New York: McGraw-Hill, 1969.)

group) decide upon the order in which the proposed solutions will be considered. He implies that it is preferable that group members concur on criteria they will use to judge the proposals before they begin considering specific proposals.

This approach to decision making is like judging livestock at the county fair. Before beginning deliberations about who gets the blue ribbon, all the judges know the criteria they are to use. They can have all the information. Their options are limited. (They cannot award a ribbon to a cow which has not been entered in the contest). Their decisions, therefore, are relatively straightforward. They examine the livestock and weigh the merits of one against another. The cow which comes closest to the ideal standard is awarded the prize.

Anyone who has ever judged livestock will protest that it is by no means a simple task. The judge has to decide whether an excellent hindquarter on a cow that is a bit small is better than a less perfect hindquarter on a cow of standard size. My point is that theories of small group decision making such as shown in Figure 6.1 involve only judgments about which one of a limited number of possible choices best fits a set of predetermined criteria agreed upon by all members. Decision making in such situations is not necessarily easy, but these situations allow for more rationality because the situations themselves are "well-structured." When decision theorists describe problem situations as "well-structured," they mean that there is one best solution. The problem is to identify which decision is best.

The "optimal" decision-making theories of the classical organization theorists are also best applied to well-structured problems. James G. March and Herbert A. Simon describe the classical theory of decision making:

The rational man of economics and statistical decision theory makes "optimal" choices in a highly specified and clearly defined environment: When we first encounter him in the decision-making situation, he already has laid out before him the whole set of alternatives from which he will choose his action. . . . To each alternative is attached a set of consequences that will ensue if that particular alternative is chosen. . . . At the outset the decision maker has a "utility function" or a "preference ordering" that ranks all sets of consequences from the most preferred to the least preferred. The decision maker selects the alternative leading to the preferred set of consequences.[3]

The classical approaches to decision making—"reflective thinking" in small groups or "optimizing" in formal organizations—make three important assumptions:

(1) all the alternatives of choice are known;
(2) all the consequences attached to each alternative are known; and,
(3) decision makers know their preferences; they know what consequences they will prefer over others.

Given such a well-structured situation, it is possible to make decisions by considering alternative proposals simultaneously. The merits of particular proposals may be considered simultaneously. Rationality is possible because much of the situation is not very complex. People make choices from known alternatives according to predetermined values and information.

As normative theory, the classical approaches are not without merit. They set a standard or goal to be sought for, if one realizes that no group could actually make decisions in the way described by these theories. The theories have unrealistic assumptions about capacities and processes of "knowing." If a well-intentioned teacher or group leader insists that a group consider all the information or write down all the solution alternatives early in the discussion, the most likely consequence will be a stumped group. No one can know all the information. Many (probably most) good solutions come up as modifications of proposals to what is being discussed. The steps in so-called rational decision making are not natural to the process of developing collective intelligence in most decision-building situations.

Any human being's and certainly any group's potential for behaving rationally is "bounded." As we saw in chapter 2, there are finite limits on knowledge and hence on rationality. There are limitations on the degree to which a person can know what alternatives are available to him, the degree to which a person can know the consequences of alternative actions, and the degree to which he can know his own values. People make decisions on the basis of what they "know." But no person sees the "real world," rather, each of us sees but a simplified version of the world in the form of a "definition of the situation," or more broadly a cognitive map. March and Simon observe:

> An individual can attend to only a limited number of things at a time. The basic reason why the actors' definition of the situation differs greatly from the objective situation is that the latter is far too complex to be handled in all its detail. Rational behavior involves substituting for the complex reality a model of reality that is sufficiently simple to be handled by problem-solving processes.[4]

Our capacity for rationality is limited because our perception is always filtered. The way people see a situation is somewhat dependent on their motivations to see a situation in one way rather than another. A study conducted by Dearborn and Simon illustrates one source of bias in perception and its possible influence on collective decision building. They tested the general hypothesis that, "presented with a complex stimulus, the subject perceives in it what he is 'ready' to perceive; the more complex or ambiguous the stimulus, the more the perception is determined by what is already 'in' the subject and the less by what is in the stimulus."[5]

The study involved executives of a large manufacturing firm. All were enrolled in a company-sponsored training program. They were asked to read the "Castengo Steel Company Case." The description of approximately 10,000 words was written with concrete facts and almost no interpretation. Subjects then wrote a brief statement of what they considered to be the most pressing problem of the company. They were told to assume the role of the top executive. The subjects were drawn from the different divisions. The results are summarized in Figure 6.2.

DEPARTMENT OF SUBJECT	TOTAL NUMBER	NUMBER WHO MENTIONED AS PRINCIPAL PROBLEM		
		Sales	"Clarify Organization"	Human Relations
Sales	6	5	1	0
Production	5	1	4	0
Accounting	4	3	0	0
Miscellaneous	8	1	3	3
	23	10	8	3

FIGURE 6.2
Relationship of Organizational Position to
Perception of an Organizational Problem

Note that the people from the sales division perceived sales problems in the organization five times as often as they saw other problems. Moreover, executives from sales comprised only about 25 percent of the total but accounted for 50 percent of those who reported sales to be the chief problem. All the accountants who reported sales as the problem were involved in analysis of product profitability. Organizational problems were mentioned by four of the five production executives. The public relations, industrial relations, and medical executive all mentioned human relations as the problem. People perceived the problem in terms of their experiences.

The normative model of rational decision making is based on assumptions of perfect information about alternatives, consequences, and values. But the information we act on is that which we perceive. Since we perceive selectively, there are finite limits on our ability to make rational decisions. The purpose of collective decision building is to compensate for the biases of any particular person so that collectively the group "knows more" than any person in it. Increased rationality in the form of more information and differing perspectives on information is thus a goal of collective decision building. Descriptions of rationality do not provide a very realistic approach to understanding the process of developing collective intelligence.

INTEGRATION IN TASK-ORIENTED GROUPS

The "intelligence" function is analogous to what small group researchers refer to as "task" dimension of group interaction. The integrative function is generally called the "socioemotional" dimension in a group. The task dimension is the relationship of group members to the work they are to do. Since we are only concerned here with groups which produce a symbolic product (a decision rather than a house or car), the task dimension is the relationship of group members to the symbols they are producing. The process of producing the symbols is coordination.

As members talk to produce a set of symbols which they announce as their decision, they construct a pattern of talk which I called "theme" in chapter 4. The thematic pattern in a decision-building group constitutes that group's emerging consensus on: (1) choices available to the group, (2) consequences associated with each choice, and (3) the values or preferences of group members for the various consequences.

As the group members develop a theme around these questions, they develop the "intelligence" of the group. We saw in the previous section that answers to these questions are not simple. Only in highly structured situations is there any one "right" answer. The answers to these questions are dependent upon the attitudes and values which individual members bring to the group, the communication skills of various members of the group, and the extent to which the members of the group are willing to verbalize their ideas and values. Since a cataloguing of attitudes and values relevant to collective decision building is outside the scope of this book, we shall concentrate on communication skills for relating group members in the constructing of decisions.

A group engaged in the process of constructing a collective decision is somewhat like a machine. (Remember that there are also VAST differences). The essence of the similarity is this: like machines, groups must be "maintained" if they are to do the task expected of them. For small group researchers, "maintaining" a group is the task of the socioemotional dimension of group talk. If a group of people are to stay together and continue to produce collective decisions, then group members must attend to the climate as well as the theme of the group. But how do group members know if their climate is being maintained? Researchers have provided several systems for observing group interaction. A significant feature of many of these systems is that they provide "categories of talk" for observing the ways in which group members attend to their task or their socioemotional climate.

One such scheme was developed by Robert Bales. He called it the system for "interaction process analysis" (IPA).[6] Table 6.1 presents the Bales scheme for analyzing the talk of a group. The middle six

TABLE 6.1
Bales Categories for Interaction Process Analysis

Shows SOLIDARITY, raises other's status, gives help
Shows TENSION RELEASE, jokes, laughs, shows satisfaction
AGREES, shows passive acceptance, understands
GIVES SUGGESTION, direction
GIVES OPINION, expresses feelings, wishes
GIVES ORIENTATION, information, repeats, clarifies, confirms
ASKS FOR ORIENTATION, information, repetition, confirmation
ASKS FOR OPINION, evaluation, analysis, expression of feeling
ASKS FOR SUGGESTION, shows passive rejection, formality
DISAGREES, shows passive rejection
SHOWS TENSION, asks for help, withdraws
SHOWS ANTAGONISM, deflates another's status, defends or asserts self
UNCODED REMARKS

categories are task talk. When group members use that kind of talk they are bringing information into the group and evaluating it. The outer six categories are "emotional talk" by group members. They are the methods by which group members reward (show solidarity) and punish (show antagonism toward) each other. They are also the way they "release" emotions (emotion release; shows tension) and thus maintain the balance of the "decision-building machine."

Another early scheme for classifying talk in a group was developed by Kenneth Benne and Paul Sheats.[7] They were interested in the characteristic talk by individual group members through which each person was differentiated from others and at the same time complementary to one another. They called their scheme a classification of roles. Table 6.2 shows the original Benne and Sheats list of group roles.

Classifications similar to that of Benne and Sheats have been developed to provide group members with a language for observing their own typical behaviors in groups and for talking with one another about what roles are and are not being played. The idea that a classification scheme is a language is important. In collective decision building people talk about their expectations. They talk about what kind of agenda should be followed to develop the best decision. They talk about the norms of their interactions. They set collective goals for their interaction. Classification schemes such as the one above provide group members with a means of talking about their role expectations.

Seldom will you find in a group members who have not had communication training saying, "Why don't you be more encouraging, John?" When group members are trained to produce better decisions,

TABLE 6.2
Benne and Sheats Classification of Group Roles

Group Task Roles	Group Building and Maintenance Roles	Individual Roles
Initiator	Encourager	Aggressor
Information-seeker	Harmonizer	Blocker
Opinion-seeker	Compromiser	Recognition-seeker
Information-giver	Gate-keeper	Self-confessor
Elaborator	Group observer and	Playboy
Coordinator	commentator	Dominator
Orienter	Follower	Help-seeker
Evaluator-critic		Special interest-seeker
Energizer		
Procedural-technician		
Recorder		

they are taught to use these terms so that they can talk more directly about role expectations. By talking about what roles are and are not being performed, groups can more easily work out a balance of participation by making sure that important roles are being performed.

Although such classification schemes provide a necessary language for talking about expectations, they may be misinterpreted as suggesting that task and socioemotional functions are separate. The two processes occur simultaneously. Aubrey Fisher, for example, notes with respect to the Bales categories: "Common sense should tell us that a comment such as 'Aw, you don't know what you're talking about!' implies not only an outright rejection of a contributed idea (a task comment) but an impact as well on the social relationship of at least two members."[8] In Fisher's example we can see both a content or idea level and a meta-communicational or relational level. The process of building decisions occurs at both levels simultaneously.

In the discussion below task and socioemotional processes are discussed together though the emphasis in each section is different. The section immediately following considers the chronological pattern of developing a decision. Thus its emphasis is on theme, task, or collective intelligence. The next section considers "characteristics" of effective decision building. Most of the characteristics discussed there refer to feeling states. Thus its emphasis is on climate, socioemotional, or integrative considerations.

PHASES OF DECISION BUILDING

When Robert Bales wrote *Interaction Process Analysis* in 1951, he observed that the process of human interaction in groups had largely been ignored. Instead of looking at what people say to one another, researchers had been content to relate personality traits of individual members to outcomes of the group process such as the quality of decisions. His research was among the first to investigate how people actually communicate in the process of deciding. This section presents four descriptions of the phases which groups go through in building decisions. Unlike the normative theories presented in a previous section, these theories of decision building are empirical. They are theories of how groups have been observed to decide; they do not prescribe how groups should decide.

Bales's Three-Phase Process

Using the classification scheme shown in Table 6.1, Bales and Strodbeck[9] observed several hundred groups. They found that the category of talk varied by time. Early in the discussion people tend to give and ask for orientation. They called this first phase the "orientation phase." Then the conversation shifts and most of the talk involves the giving and asking of opinions. This constitutes the "evaluation phase." Finally, people begin to give and receive suggestions. They called this the "control phase." They also found patterns of positive and negative reactions. In the control phase, for example, negative reactions characterize the beginning; positive reactions characterize the end. This analysis of three phases of group development was one of the first descriptions of how people actually do solve problems.

Janis's Cumulative Process

Irving Janis, in his study *Victims of Groupthink,* approached the task of describing group decision making in a different way. His intent was not simply to describe how groups decide. Rather, he sought to describe how integrative processes—especially pressures to conform—can affect decision making. His claim is that "The more amiability and esprit de corps among the members of a policy-making in-group, the greater danger that independent critical thinking will be replaced by groupthink."[10] Groupthink refers to a mode of thinking in which members, strivings for unanimity override their motivation to realistically appraise alternative courses of action.

In the process of describing the manifestations of groupthink, Janis indirectly presents a description of how any group builds decisions. Although his concern is not with "phases," he is concerned with the chronological development of ideas or "themes" in a discussion. The description following is largely my abstraction and extrapolation of ideas about group decision building from Janis's description of groupthink.

The process of reaching a final decision involves many subdecisions. Group members explicitly or implicitly decide upon what kinds of information are relevant and valid. Group members decide which "experts" are credible and relevant to the problem at hand. They arrive at some kind of consensus to be used to evaluate proposed decisions. Any group member who criticizes the group's assumptions about information, criteria, or possible proposals risks censure and exclusion. The process of excluding a person may happen so subtly that group members do not realize what they are doing. When members of a group fall into the groupthink syndrome, they simply censure their own comments to avoid the risk of group censure. They refrain from making remarks contrary to commonly held assumptions of the members. Janis describes the kind of group process which results from groupthink:

1. The group's discussions are limited to a few alternative courses of action (often only two) without a survey of a full range of alternatives.
2. The group fails to reexamine the course of action initially preferred by the majority of members from the standpoint of non-obvious risks and drawbacks that had not been considered when it was originally evaluated.
3. The members neglect courses of action initially evaluated as unsatisfactory by the majority of the group. They spend little or no time discussing whether they have overlooked non-obvious gains or whether there are ways of reducing the seemingly prohibitive costs that had made the alternatives seem undesirable.
4. Members make little or no attempt to obtain information from experts who can supply sound estimates of losses and gains to be expected from alternative courses of action.
5. Selective bias is shown in the way the group reacts to factual information . . . Members show interest in facts and opinions that support their initially preferred policy and take up time in meetings to discuss them, but they tend to ignore facts and opinions that do not support their initially preferred policy.
6. Members spend little time deliberating about how their chosen policy might be hindered by bureaucratic inertia, sabotaged by political opponents or temporarily derailed by common accidents that happen to the best of well-laid plans. Consequently, they fail to work out contingency plans.[11]

Implicit in this description of the groupthink syndrome are four behavioral tendencies of people engaged in decision building. Janis was concerned with "faulty" decision methods. The principles discussed below must be inferred from what he says. I have labeled the four principles:

> The Rabbit in the Hat Principle: Version 1
> The Rabbit in the Hat Principle: Version 2
> The Rich Get Richer Principle
> The Ala Kazam! Principle

The *Rabbit in the Hat Principle* reminds us that problem solvers are not magicians. Unlike magicians, the only rabbits which problem solvers can pull out of a hat are those which they put into the hat. Version 1 states that a group chooses its solution to a problem from among those alternatives it discusses. This means that people in the group must communicate the ideas they have to others. Groups do not choose from among all possible alternatives. Before a possible alternative becomes an actual possibility in a discussion, it must first occur to a member of the group. Furthermore, the person to whom it occurs must risk describing the proposal to others. Any number of interpersonal factors such as "groupthink" may cause an individual to be unwilling to risk offering a particular proposal for consideration. Limitation of group discussion to only a few alternatives results from such individual members censuring their own ideas.

Version 2 of the Rabbit in the Hat reminds us that problem solvers do not use all relevant information to solve a problem. The only information they use is what they obtain and perceive to be important. Thus, the quality of group solutions depends on the aggressiveness of members in searching for information. (Again, information is not a rabbit which appears by magic. Rather, it must be searched out and then shared.)

The *Rich Get Richer Principle* states that ideas are not "born equal" or given equal consideration. Ideas initially preferred by the majority, as Janis observes, are given preferential treatment throughout the discussion process. Information which confirms the majority's original position is more likely to be considered by the group than information which reflects badly on the majority's position. Likewise, ideas originally frowned upon by the majority are disadvantaged. When a group member offers a proposal, the initial reactions (though often unreflective) result in a biased treatment of the proposal. Group members selectively interpret information in favor of proposals which they initially found attractive. The "rich get richer."

The final principle is concerned with the nature of the group "product." In the beginning of this chapter, I stated that group decisions are always announced. I distinguish between the announcement of a decision (which is a set of symbolic displays and/or documents) and the actions which people take in interpreting the announcement. Implementation of a decision is part of the decision itself because it is the interpretation of the announcement in the form of actions. When group members think of desirable "products" of their deciding process, therefore, they must think of implementation as well as announcement.

The *Ala Kazam! Principle* is concerned with the confusion of implementation and announcement which characterizes much decision building. In Janis's words, "group members spend little time deliberating about how the chosen policy might be hindered by bureaucratic inertia, sabotaged by political opponents, or temporarily derailed by common accidents." The process of deciding is inevitably directed toward producing some kind of message (announcement) as the solution. Decision building is symbolic activity (talk). The only direct output of symbolic activity is symbols. Decision-building groups therefore can directly produce only symbols. But the goal of such groups is seldom to produce only symbols. They want to have an impact on the problems they discuss.

The Ala Kazam! Principle states that a group in producing a symbolic message (statement of a solution) does not ipso facto solve the problem. The solution can result only from actions taken in interpreting the message. This principle can result only from actions taken in interpreting the message. This principle obviously has implications for how groups should go about building decisions.

Underlying Janis's conceptions of how people decide collectively, there is the notion of decision building as a cumulative process. Decisions are built as ideas occur to people, as they share ideas, evaluate ideas, announce decisions, and implement decisions in action. The talk which occurs at each phase influences what happens in the next. The expectations of a group—the roles, norms, agenda, and intention—can either encourage or discourage unusual ideas and frank evaluation of ideas in a group.

Scheidel and Crowell's Spiral Model

Thomas Scheidel and Laura Crowell have developed a "spiral model" to describe the process of decision building.[12] They criticize classical models such as reflective thinking as grossly "inaccurate in portraying the reasoning process in small groups." The reflective thinking model insists that for rational thinking to take place group members must proceed in a linear fashion. Members "complete" one step and then proceed to the next. The model of reflective thinking presented earlier in Figure 6.1 illustrates this linearity.

Scheidel and Crowell support their argument that ideas are not developed in a linear fashion with analysis of talk from several small groups. Their data indicated that only 22 percent of all talk in sample groups was devoted to the initiation, extension, modification, and synthesis of an idea. By contrast, 33 percent of the talk was spent substantiating and accepting an idea already under discussion. They interpret this to mean that:

> Group-thought seems to move forward with a "reach-test" type of motion, that is, one participant reaches forth with an inference which seems to be elaborated at length with movements of clarification, substantiation, and verbalized acceptance. Little wonder that group thinking often proceeds slowly when the anchoring of thought takes up practically half of the time.[13]

The spiral model of idea development suggests that when people collaborate to build decisions, one person "moves" the discussion to a "higher" level and then the talk of several people solidifies group consensus about that idea. The "movement" comments are those which initiate, modify, and synthesize ideas. The solidifying comments accept and substantiate. A spiral is a good metaphor for the "building" of decisions. It emphasizes the cumulation of group consensus through a process of "anchoring" thought. The announced decision results from a group's resolving its position on many lesser ideas.

Fisher's Four Phases of Decision Emergence

B. Aubrey Fisher in his theory of "decision emergence" combined features of the spiral model and models of "phases" of decision making into a more sophisticated conception of decision building. According to Fisher, there are four phases in "decision emergence." These phases can be identified by the kinds of talk which people engage in. The first phase is orientation. Much of the talk in this phase is "clarifying" and "agreement." People are trying to understand what each other is saying. The talk is generally "first encounter style"; people stick to safe topics, so there is little disagreement.

The second phase is conflict. After members of a group have talked enough to get to know one another, there are attempts to confront their differences. When this happens, conflicting opinions are voiced. People feel freer to respond unfavorably to ideas they do not like. Also there are more comments which are intended to substantiate an idea being debated. In groups such as those described by Janis, the conflict phase is brief. Groupthink suppresses conflict. In other groups, the conflict may be so bitter that the group dissolves before any decision emerges. According to Fisher, however, most groups move from conflict to a phase which he calls emergence.

The emergence phase is characterized by: (1) a decline in the proportion of unfavorable comments, (2) an increase in comments which modify the speaker's previously dissenting opinion, and (3) an increase in the proportion of comments indicating some change in stance toward what proposals should be accepted. Fisher says that during this phase people emphasize differences of opinion. They use their talk to make clear their individual points of view. In order for a group of people to agree to a common set of symbols as their "decision," they typically begin to describe their position in more general terms.

For example, two people may be in conflict because a particular proposal would cause immediate benefit to one and immediate harm to the other. During the conflict phase they argue strongly the pro and con of the proposal. As they realize that they must come to an agreement, they search for alternative ways to define the problem as well as for alternative proposals. They find that if the proposal is modified slightly, it will serve the long-run interests of both. Thus, they redefine the nature of the problem in light of a desirable solution. (Note that this is in contrast to the linear description of problem solving in Figure 6.1 where the problem is defined only at the beginning.) They say that "after all" the immediate costs will not be so great. By concentrating on the ambiguous "long-run" and by talking about mutual benefits, each is able to get out of being locked into his or her conflicting positions. Each saves face. A collective decision is possible. In the emergence phase, talk becomes more ambiguous, proposals get modified, and people modify their objections.

The final phase is reinforcement. The comments of group members are more favorable; typically there is little or no dissent. People talk about their unity and how "really good" their decision is. In the emergence phase, people modify proposals being considered. In the reinforcement phase, people recognize that they have reached agreement on how to solve the problem being discussed. Fisher describes the building of decisions like this:

> A specific point in time at which decisions are made is not apt to be found. In fact, the emergence process presupposes that groups achieve consensus on their decisions *after* those decisions appear to have been made. The very final stage of interaction then fulfills the purpose of procuring members' public commitment, the essence of consensus, to decisions already reached.[14]

In earlier chapters I described goals as "retrospective." This means that while we have some idea about what we want, we do not have a very clear idea until after we get it. This same idea applies to Fisher's description of how groups solve problems. Members of a group have some general ideas about what they want to accomplish. They can set down in the beginning of a discussion some general criteria which any solution to a problem must meet, but specific criteria become evident and agreed upon during the discussion. Only during the final, or reinforcement phase, can the goals be made explicit. In the process of telling one another what is "good" about the decision, group members are practicing how to sell the idea to others, and they are convincing themselves that it is a good idea. They are "announcing" the decision to themselves.

CHARACTERISTICS OF EFFECTIVE DECISION BUILDING

Empirical theories of how groups solve problems such as the four discussed above are helpful in understanding the general process of decision building. They suggest the cumulative nature of the decision-building process. They point to the role of talk in constructing the set of symbols which is the "collective decision," but for those of us who have sat through hours of unproductive conferences, empirical theories do not seem to be of much immediate benefit. What we want to know is how can we improve our meetings, not simply what is likely to happen in these meetings.

Empirical theories are not directly informative about what people should do. For example, if an investigator finds that in most groups there is a concentration of disagreement in the middle of a discussion, what are the pragmatic implications? We cannot conclude that talk should be concentrated in the middle. We would hardly want to train people not to make any statements of disagreement until one third of the discussion is completed.

Some researchers have investigated factors in group discussions which seem to be related to more effective decision building. Jay Hall suggests that group effectiveness results from four factors: commitment, conflict, creativity, and consensus.[15] Note that the first three refer to feeling states or climates. I describe each factor and its relationship to decision construction in informal groups below.

Commitment

Commitment, according to Hall, is a feeling of "attraction, belonging, and ownership of the group ethos"; it is the "unifying force which holds the group together."[16] Commitment is what some people call motivation because it is a personal feeling which leads people to take actions because they want to do so. People who are committed to a group are actively involved in the talk which goes into the announced decision and then actively attempt to translate the words into actions.

In the group decision phase which Bales and Fisher have called "orientation" members attempt to secure commitment of people to one another and to the common task. Fisher says that there is a high proportion of talk classified as "clarifying" and "agreeing." Clarifying talk enables people to understand what is happening. When people state their agreements with one another, they build some foundation for commitment to one another.

The need for commitment is not concentrated in the opening of a discussion, though it is necessary throughout the decision-building process. We have all been in groups in which people seemed highly committed at first. All the members were actively participating; all were looking at one another; no one was doodling or engaging in other activities "on the side." Then as the discussion progressed, one by one people "dropped out." Most of them stayed in their seats, but only two or three people did the talking. Some of the nontalkers still watched. Occasionally, one would attempt unsuccessfully to break into the conversation. Some others seemed not to listen to what was being said. Members of such a group have lost their commitment. They display their lack of commitment by their failure to participate actively in what is happening.

Hall investigated the relationship of acts of verbal participation and feelings of involvement. His study involved approximately four hundred people participating in small group discussions. About two-thirds of the people reported they were "active participators" in the discussion. Hall instructed one hundred people (one or two in each group) to remain silent throughout the discussion unless someone extended to them a direct invitation to participate. About forty people who had not been so instructed reported that they were largely silent during the discussion. After the discussion, the people completed questionnaires which asked them to describe their feelings about the group and its decisions. Figure 6.3 shows the comparison among the three groups.

Items three and four are of particular importance here. Item three asked, "How much responsibility for making the decision work would you feel?" Notice that those who perceived themselves as active participators felt much more responsible for the decision they helped to construct than those who felt they did not participate. The relationship of commitment to participation is also evident in answers to question four: "How committed do you feel to the decision your group made?" Those who reported high participation also reported feeling committed to the decision. Notice, however, that members who did not participate rated the *quality* of the decision about as high as those who did participate (Item 6).

According to Hall, this rating indicates that nonparticipators may be silently saying to the others: "We have heard your arguments, and they are sound. On the basis of facts—which we all heard and assessed—the decision you reached is a good one. But don't expect me to be satisfied with it, feel responsible for its success, or be committed to it." Hall continues: "The feeling tones associated with noninvolvement would seem to overshadow the logical appeal of decision content. The data from this exercise clearly reveals a paradox of human systems. What may be logically acceptable is not necessarily psychologically acceptable."[17]

In other words, decisions we "accept" in the sense that we are willing to take action are those decisions we feel we have helped to create. The most logical decision created by other people is their decision. Let them do what is necessary to make it work! Securing commitment, then, is a continuing problem of all decision-building groups. Special attempts are made during the first few minutes of a discussion to secure initial commitment, but initial commitment does

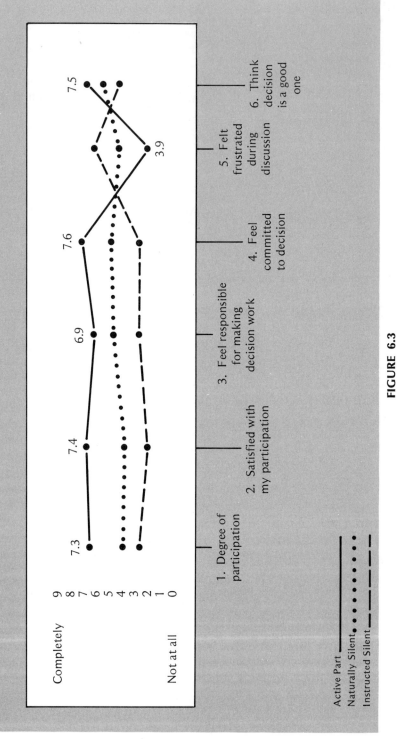

FIGURE 6.3
Relationship of Participation to Commitment

not insure its continuation. People must be motivated to participate throughout the discussion. In this sense, the task of group members is analogous to that of interviewers or public speakers. All must secure initial commitment and then continuously motivate integration of all members of the group. After discussing three other factors related to effective decision building, I shall discuss methods for improvising effectiveness. The first set of methods is for motivating integration, and thus seeking commitment.

Conflict

Conflict is Fisher's term for the second phase of decision emergence. After an initial period in which group members stick to safe topics about which they can agree, they begin to offer proposals for solving the problem. Because these proposals are usually controversial, conflict ensues. Janis stresses that conflict is essential to the effective functioning of a decision-making group. According to Janis, those groups who develop norms which suppress conflict are not capable of critically evaluating ideas presented to the group. As the result, they are led toward poorer decisions.

It is not simply the presence or absence of conflict, but the meaning of a conflict situation which distinguishes ineffective from effective groups. According to Hall, members of ineffective groups tend to believe that conflict is necessarily unhealthy. He states: "The earmark of the ineffective group is often the unarticulated feeling that speedy resolution of task demands is the sine qua non of effective functioning, and that anything, particularly dissenting points of view, which frustrates closure is seen as detrimental to the group."

Conflicts are seen as impeding the "efficiency" of a group. When people voice disagreeing opinions it means that others must take time to answer the objections. It is easier to agree on a solution if people do not voice their objections. When people define their job as getting to a group decision as quickly as possible, anything which slows them down must be seen as bad. Conflict, then, is necessarily defined as a bothersome disturbance. Conflict can also cause hard feelings among group members. Members of ineffective groups tend to view interpersonal relationships as fragile. People must like one another if the group is to do its job. Therefore, they tend to define conflict as bad because it may damage the good interpersonal relations among group members.

Maier and Hoffman investigated the relationship of a discussion leader's attitude toward a dissenting member and the quality of the decision constructed by the group.[18] Some leaders reported that they appreciated the contributions of the dissenter. The dissenter reminded the group of risks they had overlooked. He or she made members explain the logic of their position. In short, for some leaders, the dissenter was a positive force helping the group construct a better decision. For other leaders, dissenters were "troublemakers" who did not really care about the group. Dissenters kept the group from being more effective.

Maier and Hoffman found that those groups led by people who saw dissenters as positive contributors were much more effective than the other groups. Their decisions were better than the other groups. The researchers conclude that the leader's perceptions have a powerful influence on how group members define their situation. Leaders who see dissenters as troublemakers create (with others' help) a set of expectations in which people are reluctant to disagree. Leaders who see the value of conflict subtly reward people for disagreeing and thus contribute to a norm which encourages open expression of doubts and disagreements. Thus, the meaning which the leader has is related to the meaning the group adopts to define conflict.

In effective groups, according to Hall, conflict means that

> there is less than optimal sharing of the group frame of reference; conflict is treated as a symptom of unarticulated rationales or latent feelings from which, once they are verbalized, the group may be able to profit. Getting to the bottom of conflicts, drawing out deviant opinions so that they may be tested for feasibility, and seriously attending to far-out member insights have more often than not sparked a reappraisal of group thinking to such an extent that group positions are revised and performance enhanced. . . . Differences are encouraged and handled by the effective group in a "clearing the air" working-through manner which increases the likelihood that end products will reflect the contributions of all.[19]

People act in a situation according to how they define it. Groups who establish a collective definition of conflict as detrimental not only develop expectations which discourage conflict, they also develop methods for suppressing and circumventing those conflicts which do arise. In some groups, one or more people develop the role of "peace maker." People learn to acquiesce to the compromises suggested by this person. Other groups use majority rule to prevent open conflict. Whenever a conflict arises, the matter is immediately put to a vote. Those in the minority are expected to remain silent.

Another method might be called "reciprocal payoffs." It is the expectation that if a person "gives in" on one issue, he should be allowed to win on a later issue regardless of how unreasonable an argument he presents. Conflict is avoided because people simply take turns in influencing what the collective decision will be. It is like two people deciding about a vacation. One wants to go a thousand miles away and fly. The other wants to go two hundred miles and drive. They compromise. They go a thousand miles and drive!

A final method groups use to avoid controversy is changing the subject. When debate over an issue gets under way, one person brings up an issue which may be largely unrelated to the debate. Group members drop the controversial topic; everyone then speaks in favor of (or opposed to) the new idea and the appearance of agreement is maintained.

Successful handling of group conflict is not easily achieved. People must express their doubts and disagreements. In order for this to happen, they must expect that others will try to understand their position. The expectation that others will try to understand does not mean that others will agree. The terms "understand" and "agree" are used here as they are in chapter 2. Successful handling of conflicts results in people developing equivalent meanings for common symbols (and symbolic actions). It is a process of coorientation. Some specific techniques which may be used to achieve equivalence in conflict situations are discussed in the *Application* at the end of this chapter.

Creativity

According to Hall, creativity is dependent upon conflict. Groups without conflict over ideas are not as likely to produce "creative" ideas as those who must talk out differing opinions in order to reach a collective decision. In order to measure the creativity of discussion groups, Hall had research subjects list possible solutions to a problem before engaging in a discussion. These prediscussion judgments were rated for quality. The higher their quality, the higher the group's "average resources" for problem solving. After the group discussion, the collective decision was rated for quality and also to determine whether one or more group members had listed it as a suggested answer prior to discussion. Decisions which had not been suggested by anyone were termed "emergent."

Hall found that those groups in which the prediscussion suggestions were diverse more often produced emergent decisions. He calls this the "high conflict condition"; there is little initial agreement on what must be done, and therefore, people must present and discuss differing ideas. These groups were more creative because they had to do more than merely accept a decision which several people felt to be best before the discussion began.

All emergent decisions are not equally "creative." Hall found a difference in quality between groups of strangers meeting for a brief period only (ad hoc groups) and established groups.[20] The collective decisions of *ad hoc* groups were consistently inferior to the members' average predecision judgment under conflict conditions. However, the emergent decisions of established groups were vastly superior to their prediscussion judgments. One inference from these findings is that the established groups had more stable procedures for handling conflicts when they arose. Groups of strangers are unlikely to have worked out consensual expectations for managing conflict. Their relationship is more fragile than relationships in established groups. They are more uncertain about how to talk to one another when there is conflict.

Hall states two ways in which conflict, if adequately managed through supporting group norms, can facilitate creativity. First, "one effect of conflict in groups may be to achieve a more tentative opinion stating among members which, in turn, facilitates decision flexibility of the type needed for creativity."[21] This reason is similar to Fisher's description of what happens in the "conflict" and "emergent" phases of discussion. Group members state opinions and disagreement ensues. This disagreement is followed by more ambiguous, or in Hall's words, "tentative" statements of opinions. Group members become more flexible. It is this flexibility or ambiguity which allows group members to find creative decisions. A second way in which conflict facilitates creativity is through subjecting ideas to examination and modification. Hall states:

> Effective groups seem to recognize intuitively that where there is a conflict there is a need for both more data and a closer examination of existing inputs. Out of such additions and re-examinations frequently come those "aha" kind of insights which not only have a compelling quality of logic once articulated, but which underlie and lead to creativity as well.[22]

Creativity, then, is a third factor in group effectiveness. Creativity results when group members question one anothers' assumptions (often their unrealized assumptions). When disagreements force people to justify their ideas to one another; when people thus force one another out of comfortable paths of thought, they may hit upon less obvious but better solutions to problems. They may construct decisions more acceptable to everyone. If the norms and roles of a group allow the expression of conflict without personal defensiveness, the result can be collective decisions which are better than the best individual judgments.

Consensus

According to G. M. Phillips consensus is the distinguishing characteristic of small groups.[23] Consensus is often thought of as perfect agreement, but as we saw in chapter 2, consensus does not mean that everyone in a group holds the same values or sees the world the same way. When a small group reaches a "consensus," it means that every person in the group accepts the collective decision as his or her own with understanding of what the decision means to others.   Any person might have really preferred another decision, but all people feel committed to the group decision.

Hall explains consensus as both a set of expectations which constitutes a "decision rule" and a performance goal for which members strive. As a performance goal, consensus is the idea shared by group members that their final collective position or decision will reflect (at least) the tacit approval of every member.   "Tacit approval" is not disgruntled silence.   All members must "say"—in words or silent symbolic displays —"Yes, I can live with that decision."

Consensus as a decision rule means that all members actively seek out the opinions of other members.   The job of constructing a collective decision is one of putting together many smaller decisions.   At each decision point members of a group operating under a decision rule of consensus ask one another to express opinions.

I saw consensus work best as a decision rule with a group of "Outreach Workers" employed by metropolitan New York City Y.M.C.A. The group's task was to suggest some organizational goals.   The discussion lasted several hours before they produced a set of goals on which they could all agree.   In the process, however, they scrupulously attended to each others' attitudes and feelings.   The most common comments I heard them use were questions to one another such as, "What do you think about that idea?"   "Are we all agreed?"   "How would that go in your district?"   "You're not saying anything, what's the matter?"   Thus, they not only reached consensus on their announced decision in the end, they secured consensus on the validity of each idea they discussed.   They would not proceed until everyone agreed he understood what was being said at that time and until they all had an equivalent sense of how relevant the issue was to the decision they were constructing.

Consensus as a decision rule is a means for accomplishing group effectiveness through commitment, conflict, and creativity.   When group members' opinions are actively sought, they are more likely to participate, and therefore to feel commitment.   By insisting on consensus, those who disagree are invited to express their opinions and feelings.

Consider the expectations of people who have learned that consensus is a decision rule in their group.   First, they expect to be supported when they raise objections.   Being "supported" does not mean others will necessarily agree with their ideas.   Rather, it means that they will not be personally censured as a troublemaker for having said them. Everyone's opinions will be seen as contributing to a better decision in the end.   Also, group members can expect that regardless of how much conflict there is over ideas, they will resolve the conflict. A person does not have to worry that in introducing conflict he may be destroying the group because the expectation is that people will talk about their disagreements until a consensus is reached. Such expectations are sure to lead to people being more willing to disagree and more able to sustain conversation until a creative solution is found.

I have now described in a general way four characteristics of effective decision building in small groups: commitment, conflict, creativity, and consensus. These terms describe qualities found in the discussions of groups which produce high quality decisions. They result from the discussions of groups which produce high quality decisions. They result from the interaction patterns which people learn. For example, some groups learn to be creative, others learn to be uncreative. In chapter 3 I described the process of learning or developing an interaction pattern as having three phases: enactment, selection, and retention. We should expect, then, that effective groups are those which experiment with different ways of relating to one another; select those relationship patterns which seem to result in commitment, conflict, creativity, and consensus; and then retain those patterns as consensual expectations for their interaction. They learn to expect one another to act in ways which produce the pattern.

Because commitment, conflict, creativity, and consensus are learned interaction patterns, members of a group cannot simply decide they will be "creative" (for example) and then automatically be creative. They must learn methods of relating to one another which allow them—with all the unique constraints of their situation—to be creative. The methods which facilitate creativity among a group of jazz musicians may be totally unsuccessful among a group of car salesmen, but there are some general methods for improving group effectiveness which are worth trying in decision-building groups. I discuss some of these in the applications section. I present them to suggest how members of a group can experiment with their interaction patterns. After trying out these methods, their effectiveness should be evaluated and those which suit the personality and purposes of the group retained as expectations for interaction. Note that I am suggesting here that a group's expectations can become the object of discussion and collective decision by the group.

ORGANIZING FUNCTIONS: COMMITMENT AND CHANGE

I have now described the process of decision building in face-to-face or discussion groups. I have suggested four characteristics—commitment, conflict, creativity, and consensus—which seem to distinguish effective from ineffective groups. The examples I have used have mostly concerned "conference-type" problem-solving discussions. These are discussions in which people sit down at an appointed time, usually with some kind of agenda, and discuss a problem area with the specified intent of producing a "decision."

Conferences of this type take place in all kinds of organizations. They may be called board meetings, committee meetings, employees meetings, or family conferences. In such meetings, "organizational policy" is arrived at and announced. People sit down to discuss "what we should do." The outcome is an agreement on a policy statement in which it is announced, "We shall do . . ." But decision building as an organizing process does not stop with the announcement of a decision. The phase which is often called implementation of the decision is really a continuation of considering what "we shall do."

There are good reasons for considering decision making (policy making) and implementation all part of a continuing process of decision building. When members of a policy-making discussion group sit down to find a solution to a problem, they are not free to do whatever they think is best. They are in an environment created by the decisions as well as the routines and plans of other people. Any impact of the announced decision will be in that environment. It will, in short, depend upon how people interpret the "policy decision" in terms of their routines and their personal and collective decisions. Katz and Kahn emphasize this point: "Policy is also created by day-to-day decisions, often made on an ad hoc basis and often made by administrators rather than by designated policy makers."[24] They exemplify interrelatedness in the process of decision building:

At the Baltimore shipyards during World War II, management took action to slow the production of Liberty ships and to start the production of invasion barges in response to changing military requirements. The novelty which this change introduced into plant operations was not fully anticipated when the decision was made. Technological changes had been foreseen but the impact on the social system of the workers had not been anticipated. Skilled workers saw their most valuable personal assets, experience and skill in building big ships, suddenly devalued and liquidated. Workers who had identified with the product of their work on Liberty ships took no pride in producing "row boats." Since the purpose of these barges was labeled classified information, workers could not be told they were turning out the craft to be used in the invasion of the European continent. In the absence of information about these technological and threatening changes, the shipyard became a rumor factory, morale and productivity declined, and a disastrous strike was narrowly averted.[25]

The "decision builders" in this case were not only the managers who "decided" to build the invasion barges. Workers made decisions of their own—individually and collectively. The lesson for those who conduct discussions which produce "policy decisions" is that they must consider their task as part of a cumulative process. The decisions will not implement themselves (the Ala Kazam principle). The members of a discussion group must, therefore, bring the historical past and the imagined future into their talk. The methods for improving group discussion presented later are ways others have found useful in generating talk which considers both the past and the future in realistic terms.

This example also suggests the most important function of decision building as an organizing process. Collective decision building facilitates change. The more people are involved in all phases of the decision-building process, the greater the change capacity of the organizational system. In the shipyard example, the workers were ordered via documents to change. The workers' actions were a necessary part of the decision building, but they had no knowledge of the motivations behind a change of work procedures. The change did not "make sense" from their perspective because they had not been part of the discussion in which the rationale for the change was created.

The work of early human relations theorists (for example the Lewin and the Coch and French experiments discussed in chapter 1) demonstrated that when the people involved in implementing a decision are part of early decision phases, there is more success in changing work procedures. Hall's research cited earlier in this chapter demonstrates that the more committed people feel to an announced decision (because they have participated in it), the more likely they are to participate in turning the symbolic decision into action. Thus, it appears that one function of collective decision building is facilitating change in a social system, through increased commitment on the part of system members.

Collective decision building facilitates change because it involves talk about expectations. Once expectations are verbalized they become objects of attention. Of course, expectations do not automatically change because people say they should change. But expressed consensus to change encourages commitment to change and permits the possibility of individuals supporting one another in their attempts to change.

Early human relations theorists promoted "participation" by work group members in organizational decisions as the principal method for improving organizations. We can now understand that participation is not a universal solution to organizational ills. Collective decision building becomes useful under two conditions. It is essential in organized settings which are highly unstable or uncertain. Where there is no basis for stable routine, then people must continually make decisions about what they are expecting of one another and what they should be doing together. Even in relatively routine situations, however, collective decision building may occasionally be necessary. When expectations become undesirable, for example, if norms of superrationality or dehumanized climates emerge as the result of interaction, then group members need to talk and make collective decisions about what they are expecting of one another. This is talk about their expectations. Its function is to introduce some uncertainty into the stable situation, thus disrupting the routine. Through making some collective decisions about expectations, members of a group can act purposefully to change their expectations.

SUMMARY

There are two characteristics which distinguish collective decision building from the process of organizing discussed in chapters 4 and 5. First, group members have a conscious intent to produce a collective decision; part of the act of producing that decision is symbolizing it in an announcement. This announcement may be directed only to the members of the group. Second, the "planning" process is interpersonal; rather than just thinking about expectations, group members discuss their interactions with one another. Implementing collective decisions takes the form of actions which are motivated in part by a set of symbols devised and announced by the group of people. The total process of decision building includes both methods by which a group produces an "announced decision" and the methods by which people interpret the symbols in action. This chapter has largely focused on the process by which a group of people through face-to-face communication construct an announced decision.

Classical approaches to decision making are normative. They purport to tell people how to make decisions, but they are based on unrealistic assumptions about how people can know and how they develop collective knowledge through communication. In particular, it is impossible in most cases for people to know all alternatives, to know all consequences attached to each alternative, and to know their own values or preferences. The process of developing "knowledge" about each of these issues is an interpersonal process. It is limited by our capacity to perceive information and our willingness to state our ideas.

Researchers of small group communication have given us category systems for talking about the task and socioemotional content of decision-building processes. The chief advantage of such category systems is that they provide members of groups with vocabulary for talking about their role expectations. However, such systems may unrealistically suggest that task (or "intelligence functions") in groups may be separated from socioemotional (or "integrative functions") in a group.

Phases of building collective decisions are concerned principally with the development of ideas (intelligence or task functions), but most give some attention to the influence of integrative functions. For example, according to Janis, amicability and esprit de corps among group members (part of the integrative dimension) greatly influence the group's ability to engage in critical thinking (intelligence dimension). Four empirical theories of how people build collective decisions are described.

Four characteristics of effective decision building are principally concerned with the climate of talk in a group. Effective groups contain people who talk to encourage participation and hence commitment to the common task. They do not allow individual members to become disgusted and drop out of the discussion. While maintaining a friendly atmosphere of participation, however, effective groups do not avoid necessary conflict. Rather, there is a consensus in effective groups that conflict is essential for healthy groups. Effective groups have procedures for handling conflict. Effective groups are creative largely because they do not rush to the easiest or first solution.

Finally, effective groups seek consensus as a "decision rule." They encourage everyone to express their feelings as well as their ideas so that members can know each others' perspective. The resulting decisions are not always the first choice of each group member, but decisions are made with full understanding of what they mean to each member. Each group member states that he or she can "live with" the decision.

Collective decision building in face-to-face groups is not the best method of integration in all organizations, but it is most effective in organizations where there is a need for change. Collective decision making functions to create commitment on the part of organizational members. Because it involves people talking about their expectations, it is also useful as a method of changing dysfunctional social formulas.

APPLICATION: Problem-Solving Discussion

Problem-solving discussions take place among a small number of people (usually three to ten). The people may be related to one another through formal organizational roles; for example, the members of an "executive committee" or "advisory committee" may be "full pro-

fessors," "middle managers," or "department heads." Although members of a small group may have formal organizational roles in the larger organization, typically members of small groups do not have formally designated roles. At best there may be a "chairperson" and "recorder." The influence of formal organizational roles on behavior in dyads and small groups is taken up in chapters 8 and 9. Here we are concerned only with only how decisions are "built" by small groups of people. I shall largely ignore for the time being the influence of a person's formal or organizational role on his or her behavior in the small group.

There are several reasons for using the process of problem solving in small informal groups as an application of decision building in general. First, problem-solving discussions are particularly well suited to illustrate the influence of interpersonal processes in decision building. People in discussion groups are using the exchange of symbolic displays to organize their cooperative behavior. More important the problem-solving task provides convenient boundaries around a "whole" process of decision construction. The decision building takes place at a single "sitting." People come to a meeting with a problem to be solved. When they leave, they have decided on a solution.

Another reason for describing problem-solving discussion is that it constitutes an important form of organizational communication. Problem-solving discussions which take place in organizations are often called "conferences." Harold Zelko states that the average members of middle and higher management spend fifty to ninety percent of their days in conference.[26] Improving organizational communication, therefore, means in large part improving the process of problem solving in small groups.

The basic tasks of problem-solving groups are analogous to those of interviewing dyads. Group members must (1) motivate each other's participation or integration in the collective task, (2) achieve equivalent meanings for the important symbols and procedures used in the discussion, and (3) achieve the purpose of the discussion. Although these basic tasks are like those faced by interview participants, the methods are different when the situation involves a group of people building collective decisions.

Motivating Integration

The task of motivating integration or participation is a two-fold one. First, "dissatisfiers" must be prevented or minimized. When people are unhappy with what is happening in a group, they are unlikely to be interested in active participation. The absence of dissatisfiers such as annoyance and frustration, however, will not guarantee the positive forces of motivation. The principal source of motivation to participate *in a problem-solving group is identification with the goal or the need to solve a particular problem.*

Identifying with the Problem

The initial phase of a group discussion should secure some identification of group members with the need to solve a problem. This is analogous to an interviewer attempting to motivate respondents by informing them of the purpose of the interview and convincing them of the importance of the purpose. Often, if a small group has a formally designated leader, that person will open the discussion with a brief statement of the purpose of the group.

In a general sense, the purpose of any problem-solving group is to find a solution to a problem. Here arises a major difficulty with many groups: the leader and members believe that they know what the problem is without any need to discuss it. A typical opening line by a leader is: "Now, you all know the problem. The problem is. . . ." More likely than not, people do not "know what the problem is." Each person may think that he or she knows what it is. After twenty minutes it may occur to people that they all have a different idea of what the problem "really" is. In this case the lack of a clear, mutually agreed upon definition of the problem acts as a dissatisfier which discourages integration.

Taking time to hash out varying opinions about the nature of the problem facing the group, members can establish the strongest basis for motivation—identification with the need for a solution. There are two points here to remember: First, people are likely to think that they know what the problem is without even talking about it. It is unlikely, however, that without discussing the definition of the problem, members will, in fact, have equivalent definitions. The need to discuss the definition of problems as a necessary condition for participation should be recognized by group members. This does not mean that the group defines a problem once and for all at the beginning of a discussion. After discussing a problem for a while, members may realize that they need to redefine the problem. Even as they are choosing among alternatives, they may reinterpret what the problem "really is."

A second point about the relationship of the definition of a problem and the task of motivation is that although there are many ways in which a problem might be defined, some ways are more likely than others to facilitate participation as well as to result in a feasible solution. Norman Maier's research suggests several guidelines or principles to use in stating a problem. If these are followed, a group is more likely to achieve integration in the form of people's motivation to participation in the discussion and commitment to the solution agreed upon.[27] Maier suggests that:

1. Problems should be stated in situational rather than behavioral terms.
2. A problem statement should encourage freedom of thought. To imply a solution or suggest alternatives restricts freedom.
3. A mutual interest of all discussants should be apparent in the statement of the problem.
4. Only one objective should be clearly specified.
5. The statement should be brief.

The first principle is of particular motivational importance. One of Maier's examples is of two statements describing a problem with use of a company telephone for personal business. A behavioral statement of the problem is: "How can we best stop people from using the company phone for personal matters?" A situational statement would be: "What would be a fair goal to set for personal calls?" Note that in the first statement the problem-solving group becomes a punishing group. In order to meet its purpose (stated this way) it will need to reprimand people for their behavior. That is not a very appealing task. The statement of the problem implies that some people are in the wrong. People who are discussing the problem may think that their own behavior is being censured. In this case they are sure to act defensively. The situational statement of the problem is more likely to encourage integration in the group because people will not be required to punish others, nor will they be implicitly accused of wrongdoing. Rather, they will be considering how to change a situational factor (such as a company policy). Situations are typically easier to change than people.

Principles two and three suggest that the discussants' freedom to discuss an issue be left as broad as possible, and that the problem must be one in which they are interested. It is easy to see how these two suggestions are related to integration. People are likely to be frustrated if they feel constrained to give yes/no answers instead of discussing many possible solutions and then selecting the best solution. On the other hand, when people have latitude to discuss and propose any solution they think suitable, they are more likely to involve themselves in the discussion to come up with the best solution they can.

According to Maier, failure to conceptualize problems in terms of mutual interests is a common problem with groups in formal organizations. A problem is often seen as "their" problem (management's problem, the union's problem, etc.) by the people discussing it. As a result people are not motivated to find a workable solution because, after all, "if it is their problem, let them handle it!"

Principles five and six insist that a problem be stated briefly with only one objective. These principles can help a group "get together" on what the problem is because they have a clear statement which everyone can understand. Thus, frustration over "what are we doing, anyway?" may be avoided. By having only one clear objective people are more likely to achieve integration than if they are left with several vague objectives.

A good definition of the problem to be solved with the collective decision can help all group members see the value of their contribution to the group and to themselves. If the group process is working well in the initial or "orientation" phase, all group members will make a commitment to the collective task, but motivating integration is a task which continues throughout the life of the group. Members must continuously orient one another to the discussion and provide motivation to participate.

GATEKEEPING. The method by which every member attempts to encourage participation is called "gatekeeping." According to Hall, gatekeeping is

> *the assumption of responsibility for others' levels of participation; it is the active solicitation of contributions from other members and it is the providing support and reinforcement, as well as the creating of openings, for others to become involved.*[28]

The key concept here is "responsibility for others' levels of participation." Thus, gatekeeping is an attitude which group members have.

There are, of course, actions which accompany this attitude. One action is watching others' responses. In Hall's words, the gatekeeper is a "participant-observer" who not only attends to the content of the discussion, but also attends to the process of who is saying what (and who is not saying anything). The skilled gatekeeper follows hunches and invites people to respond to ideas. For example, "That's your department, John, what do you think?" or "Didn't you try something like this a few years ago? How'd it work out?" Note that in these examples the gatekeeper is not simply saying, "Tell us what is on your mind." The silent person may not have anything particular on his mind. Rather, the gatekeeper both provides the quiet person with an entrée into discussion and suggests a background from which the person can talk ("That's your department"; "you've had some experience with that," etc.) Gatekeepers do not assume they know what another person is thinking, but they do follow hunches about who wants encouragement to get into the conversation.

Gatekeeping, then, is a method of watching the process of group discussion and taking responsibility for encouraging all members to participate. The encouragement may involve asking specific people for opinions, asking for the opinions of "those we haven't heard from," giving eye contact to signal a person whose trying to "break in" that you are listening to what he has to say.

RELEASING FRUSTRATIONS. Frustrated emotions are a common dissatisfier. When people have strong feelings about an issue and the norms of the group do not allow them to express those emotions, they may easily become apathetic toward the collective task. I have stressed the importance of conflict in producing better collective decisions; the emotions associated with conflict must be handled skillfully or people will drop out of participation.

Maier suggests several methods for handling conflict constructively. First, be alert for "guarded expressions of resentment." Direct expressions of dislike and distrust are usually "out of bounds" according to the social formula of most problem-solving groups. When people are confronting real problems, they usually have hostilities and distrust. So they express these feelings indirectly. The result is that the feeling is bottled up. We signal others our feelings indirectly, and typically they ignore our signals. Maier suggests that people should take time to uncover hostile feelings when they appear in disguised form and convert unstated feelings into stated feelings. Disguised feelings are often unclear even to the person expressing them. When people invite others to express their emotions, the frustration can be relieved and the relevance of the emotion to the collective task can be clarified.

A second guideline is similar to the first. Not only must expression of feelings be invited, they must be accepted after they are expressed. If the person who expresses his or her feelings must suffer while others describe those feelings as absurd or unfounded, he or she is unlikely to express feelings again. This does not mean the person will not experience the feelings. He will still feel, but he will not discuss his feelings with others. He may drop out of the discussion altogether, or he may lead the group into irrelevant issues because he cannot express his real objections.

Accepting the feelings of another does not mean agreeing with them. Suppose Al says that he objects to a proposal being considered because he does not trust a particular contractor to live up to the proposed contract. I do not have to agree that the contractor is untrustworthy. However, I do need to be accepting of Al's feelings—that is, I should believe that Al has a legitimate right to feel as he does. If I tell Al he's foolish to distrust the contractor, I will not convince him. If I ask for a detailed explanation of why he distrusts the contractor, my actions may be a message that I distrust Al. My message to Al needs to be, "I understand that you distrust this contractor. Can we think of ways to insure that, in this case, he will live up to the bargain?" Here I am accepting Al's feelings (Al finds him untrustworthy) but not Al's conclusion that the contract should not be offered. I am inviting Al to offer information which can lead the group to making a better decision. I am telling him that his feelings and his ideas are important to the group. We can thus achieve consensus or equivalence of meaning about the contractor.

People can seldom explain their feelings. One person can explain why he feels a certain way and another will be totally unable to understand. To ask people to offer rational grounds for emotions may put them in a "no-exit" situation. If they cannot explain the rational grounds for their feelings, the presumption is that those feelings are not relevant to the decision being made. Asking a person to explain feelings is asking something which by definition is impossible. If feelings were rational, we would not call them feelings.

AVOIDING PSEUDOPARTICIPATION. Another common dissatisfier might be called "pseudoparticipation." Take the manager of a small manufacturing outfit just back from a training session in "human relations." Mr. Smith has seen the evidence that people are more committed to a decision in which they participate. So, he decides to try a participative managerial style. "Line Sixteen" is always breaking down. The workers on that line are pretty rough on the machinery. Smith would like them to stop carelessly banging pipes into the machines. He decides to try "participation."

Smith selects five workers who also seem concerned about the breakdowns. He presents them with the problem: "hundreds of dollars a year in unnecessary repairs." He informs them that he would like their suggestions on how to encourage people to be less careless. No one says anything. He repeats his request for suggestions. When everyone remains quiet (looking at the floor), he asks Harry for his opinion. The "discussion" proceeds wtih Smith making every other comment. After twenty minutes, Smith dismisses the group. He is pleased that they have suggested most of the ideas he had already thought of. After two months, however, Smith's enthusiasm for participative decision-making fades. The suggestions from the workers did not work out much better than if Smith had implemented them on his own. The workers were not committed to the suggestions.

This example is "pseudoparticipation" because the manager deludes himself into thinking that he is involving the workers in decisions which affect them. In fact, he is making all the decisions. The situation is planned interaction, not collective decision building. He calls the meeting; he chooses who will attend; he presents the problem to them in such a manner that they cannot discuss their beliefs about what constitutes the problem. Then, he controls who will speak; he evaluates the contribution of each ("That's a good idea, Harry." "I'm not sure that's a practical suggestion, Louise.") Thus, the leader encourages people to say what he wants to hear.

The discussion becomes little more than his ideas coming from their mouths. The expectations constructed by the group manager and the workers do not encourage the workers to offer their own ideas. Some of these expectations may not be questioned. That is, the formal organizational structure provides that Smith is the manager. His leadership, in a formal sense, has been decided outside the group. Subordinates will give deference to Smith because of his formalized role; but Smith's actions, however, accentuate the impact of his formal role, turning the workers' deference into pseudoparticipation. Consider how Smith could have motivated integration by his choice of messages:

1. He could have conceptualized the problems on Line Sixteen in situational rather than behavioral terms. Instead of: "workers are being careless," he could have thought that "Line Sixteen is out of order more often than other assembly lines."
2. He could have invited workers to select representatives to discuss whether anything could be done to improve working conditions on Line Sixteen.
3. He could have let workers discuss the nature of the problem. (Perhaps the repair crew is overworked and does not attend to regular maintenance of that line as often as other lines. Perhaps excessive heat at that end of the building causes fatigue in workers and affects proper functioning of the machinery). The chief advantage of involving workers in a decision is to open channels for information which they have but management may not. It defeats this purpose to tell them what the problem is. When they believe the problem to be something other than what they are told, telling them the problem acts as a dissatisfier preventing motivation to participate.
4. During the discussion, Smith could have kept his own opinions to himself. There are several methods for doing this. He might have left after a brief introduction to the purpose of the meeting. Even if he decided to stay, he could have asked someone else to preside. Or he could have refrained from calling on people and commenting on the ideas of each. For example, if other procedures had been followed (more open description of the problem, etc.), there would probably not have been silence after the opening remark. But a chairperson who is insistent on genuine (not pseudo) participation is not afraid of silence. Smith could have remained quiet until

someone spoke. In this way, the formal leader displays his insistence on group members taking responsibility for participation. When the leader calls on people to talk, an interaction pattern like the one in Figure 6.4 is produced. Such an interaction pattern is not a discussion at all. It is more like a group interrogation. To encourage participation, the chairperson must let people remain silent if they choose.

5. Smith called on people when they were staring at the floor. Calling on particular people is sometimes needed as a gatekeeping technique, but usually people are nonverbally signaling that they want to speak. Also calling on people should only be used as a technique for spreading participation. To call on people routinely to speak discourages participation. Maier observes that this practice threatens individuals. It may cause those not called on to wonder why certain individuals are given this 'special treatment'; it suggests to all that spontaneous responses are not in order, and leads to people planning a ready response instead of thinking about the problem under discussion.[29]

The task of motivating integration in collective decision building is similar to motivating integration in any other organizing activity. The task has two dimensions: dissatisfiers must be prevented and positive motivators must be provided.[30] The methods of accomplishing motivation in a small decision-building group are, of course, somewhat different. I have described briefly here two methods of motivating: first, achieving identity with the common problem the decision is to remedy, and second, "gatekeeping" as attitudes and actions through which members involve one another in the talk. I have also described two dissatisfiers and suggested how they may be avoided. The first was frustrated feelings; the second was pseudoparticipation. We now turn

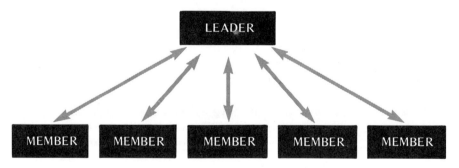

FIGURE 6.4
Channels of Communication in Pseudoparticipation Groups

to methods of accomplishing a second task—equivalence of meaning for important symbols and procedures.

Achieving Equivalence of Meaning

In any group discussion each person is displaying a set of symbols which makes sense to him or her. Each hopes that those symbols will make sense to the others in the group. But, of course, no one can understand exactly what another is saying. At best we can build equivalent images of what another is saying. Maier uses an illustration to introduce this problem to students:

> A man had a window in his garage that was twelve inches high and twelve inches wide. It was too small, so he sawed around it and made the window twice as large. He then measured the window and found it to be twelve inches high and twelve inches wide.[31]

I have used this illustration in classes on group discussions many times. The responses from students are pretty much the same every time. At first, they squirm in their seats and stare at me in puzzled silence. Then someone says, "Repeat that." After I repeat the description, someone says "Twelve high and wide both before and after the cutting?" Someone speculates that the man cut a second window. I insist that the second was cut around the first, so that at the end only one window remained. At this point, people are really frustrated. They squirm more and shake their heads. Some even begin to act somewhat hostile toward me. They accuse me of lying in an effort to trick them. I then ask someone to draw the window they are thinking of on the board. They draw B in Figure 6.5. That is what the window looked like after cutting. The window before cutting is Window A. It is diamond-shaped twelve inches high and twelve wide. Students sigh in relief and insight.

This story illustrates the frustrations people feel when they know they are not understanding each other. One person has an image which is not equivalent to another's. The two must find some common set of symbols for translating the images. In this case the common language is a drawing. I suggested in chapter 5 that illustrations can help make images more concrete and thus help people to see what others are saying.

Maier offers the following additional suggestions for talk which facilitates understanding:

1. "Hear the person out, with an attitude of withholding judgment." (Do not decide he must be crazy because you cannot see what he is saying.)

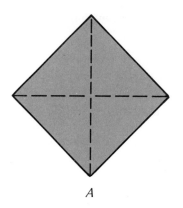
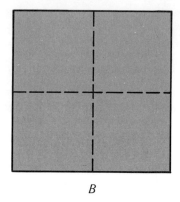

A   B

FIGURE 6.5
Two Windows of Same Height and Width (From Norman
Maier. *Problem-Solving Discussions and Conferences: Leadership Methods and Skills.* New York: McGraw-Hill, 1963,
p. 111.)

2. *"Ask other people if they understand."* *(Other people may be able
   to provide the "common vocabulary" needed to translate ideas.)*
3. *"Ask the person whose idea you do not understand to elaborate."*
   *(Some questions which could be used are: "How do you mean
   that?" "Can you enlarge on that?" "I'm not sure I understand.")*[32]

*If people with different backgrounds are to negotiate a collective
decision, they face a continuing problem of comprehending what is
being said. At the simplest level this is a problem of comprehending
how another person is using particular words. It is not likely that group
members will arrive at a consensus solution to a problem if there is
little consensus over how important terms are being used.*

*In group discussion there is an additional problem of understand-
ing or equivalence. The process of group discussion involves many
tasks. Some of these are suggested by the theories of decision building
discussed above. For example, the problem must be defined, information shared, possible solutions must be presented, criteria for evaluating
solutions must be presented, evaluated, and selected. Possible solutions must be evaluated according to a set of values and a collective
decision on the solution must be chosen.*

*In a group discussion some people may be working on defining
the problem while others are suggesting solutions. That is, you may
misunderstand what I am saying if I intend my remark to be a definition of the problem and you interpret it as a possible solution. So, in
a problem-solving group people must understand how each other's
remarks relate to the process of finding an acceptable solution. The*

rationale behind the "reflective thinking agenda" (see Figure 6.1) was to keep all group members focused on items of the agenda or kind of talk at a time. All group members, for example, would discuss the statement of the problem and then all would move to the next step on the agenda. In this way the agenda helps people to understand each others's intentions.

Maier suggests some other agenda-type methods which can help group members focus on one issue or task at a time. In this way, the discussion is more "organized" because members know what the topic of conversation is. They can coordinate their actions with one another because there is an agenda which helps them to know when to introduce what kinds of ideas. Maier calls these three methods: "Posting Problems," "Two-Column Method," and "Developmental Discussion."

POSTING PROBLEMS. This method is appropriate when people have many ideas or problems they want to raise. It is likely in such cases that the discussion will wander chaotically over the range of problems with little resolution. The problems will not be tackled in an orderly fashion.

The "Posting Problems" method provides the opportunity for order. The chairperson asks people to indicate problems they want to discuss. Instead of handling each as it is suggested, he or she "posts" the problem on the blackboard. Notice that the leader does not evaluate ideas at this stage, it is his or her job merely to record them in words acceptable to the suggester. After the list has been constructed, everyone can see the range of topics to be discussed. This overview helps everyone to orient themselves to one another's perspective. Then an agenda can be constructed. Some problems might be combined; others deleted. During the discussion which follows, members can follow what others are saying because they know the topic being discussed and they have a sense of what will be discussed later.

TWO-COLUMN METHOD. The two-column method is a technique for avoiding group debate. It can help a group use conflict for creative ends. In a debate, people line up on two sides of an issue. A group of people, for example, may be "discussing" whether a highway should be built around the commercial part of town. Residents object to the road crossing through their neighborhood. Merchants want the road built to increase their business. People on each side are unable to see any logic in the other's position. They only offer arguments on their own side. There is no chance for consensus. The two-column method is designed to help each side appreciate the strengths and weaknesses of both sides.

As with the Posting procedure, the use of a blackboard is essential. The chairperson draws two columns on the board. One is called "Favorable to A"; the other "Favorable to B." For example, "Favorable to Building the New Road" and "Favorable to Continuing Present Road System." The leader then asks for arguments favorable to building the new road. In particular, the leader encourages those against the road to contribute to this column. By establishing the expectation that everyone speaks in favor of both sides of an issues, the factions cannot break into heated arguments with one another, nor can they avoid the controversy altogether.

Once the list of arguments for each side is displayed for all to see, the group can proceed to measure the advantages of one against another. The two-column method does not guarantee that conflicts over values will disappear. That is neither possible nor desirable. It is a way of clarifying what values are in conflict and of securing consensus about the information to be used in making a decision. Most important, it can help group members understand somewhat the perspective of the other because each must speak for both sides of the issue.

DEVELOPMENTAL DISCUSSION. This is a technique for organizing a discussion in which many variables must be weighed and somehow "added up" to a single collective decision. This is a useful method for improving rationality in those well-structured situations (like cattle judging) where the alternatives are all known in advance and the criteria may be listed early in the discussion. For example, a company needs additional space and has decided to relocate. The group charged with deciding on a new location must make a number of different kinds of evaluations before announcing the final choice. These evaluations might include cost of site, municipal services provided (and their cost), cost of moving personnel and equipment, desirability of new location to personnel (available housing, quality of schools, cost of living, access to shopping areas).

A group using a "Developmental Method" would break the problem (of finding a new location) into subproblems. They would first decide on the subproblems or criteria for making the final decision. Next they would rank order the subtopics in order of importance to the overall decision. They would then evaluate all the sites under consideration on each subtopic (availability of land, cost, etc.). The possible sites can then be evaluated according to how well they measure up to the individual or subtopic criteria.

Maier suggests that the developmental method is particularly useful in personnel decisions such as hiring and promotion because it can help overcome biases and reveal mental sets:

A bias is the influence of the impression the candidate makes on the group either from knowing the person or from seeing his record and having a description of the person. . . . If all members of a group have a favorable impression, the bias performs its function without being noticed.[33]

Groups using a developmental method for a personnel decision would list and discuss the requirements for a job. Then they would consider the qualities of applicants in terms of job requirements. Thus, a bias toward an applicant who is personally impressive but not qualified for the job would be uncovered.

In one study Maier compared the simulated personnel decisions of groups using the developmental method with those using a "free" method where people did not have a set order of topics. He found that groups using the developmental method arrived at a higher-quality decision 39.7 percent of the time; the other groups, 18.9 percent of the time. Because group members attend to only one issue at a time, Maier suggests that they give more systematic attention to each issue and thus can deal with problems more objectively. Perhaps equally important, by reducing the complexity of the overall problem into simpler problems handled one at a time, group members can more easily understand each other's meanings.

Achieving Purpose

Collective decision building is a format in which people are consciously pursuing purpose. Motivating integration and achieving equivalence of meaning contribute to the end of achieving the group's purpose. Not much can be said in favor of a problem-solving group which does not solve any problems. In an earlier section I described "consensus" as the distinguishing characteristic of effective problem-solving groups. A group seeks a solution which has at least the tacit approval of all members based on explicit understanding of one another's perspective. Consensus represents the goal or purpose of a group.

USING REASONED DISCOURSE IN DECIDING. Jay Hall suggests the following communicative methods for achieving consensus. The suggestions relate reasoning to the accomplishment of group purpose:

1. Avoid arguing for your own position. Present it as lucidly and logically as possible, but be sensitive to and consider seriously the reactions of the group in any subsequent presentations of the same point.
2. Avoid "win-lose" stalemates in the discussion of opinions. Discard the notion that someone must win and someone must lose in the

discussion; when impasses occur, look for the next most acceptable alternative for all the parties involved.

3. *Avoid changing your mind only in order to avoid conflict and to reach agreement and harmony. Withstand pressures to yield which have no objective or logically, sound foundation. Strive for enlightened flexibility; but avoid outright capitulation.*
4. *Avoid conflict-reducing techniques such as the majority vote, averaging, bargaining, coin-flipping, trading out, and the like. Treat differences of opinion as indicative of an incomplete sharing of relevant information on someone's part, either about task issues, emotional data, or "gut level" intuitions.*
5. *View differences of opinion as both natural and helpful rather than as a hindrance in decision making. Generally, the more ideas expressed, the greater the likelihood of conflict; but the richer the array of resources as well.*
6. *View initial agreement as suspect. Explore the reasons underlying apparent agreements; make sure people have arrived at the same conclusions for either the same basic reasons or for complementary reasons before incorporating such opinions into the group decision.*
7. *Avoid subtle forms of influence and decision modification; e.g., when a dissenting member finally agrees, don't feel that he must be "rewarded" by having his own way on some subsequent point.*
8. *Be willing to entertain the possibility that your group can achieve all the foregoing and actually excel at its task; avoid doomsaying and negative predictions for group potential.*[34]

Notice that almost all of these suggestions insist upon reasoned talk as the means by which members achieve a collective position. Consider, for example, numbers 1, 3, and 4. Number 1 says that you should expose your reasoning to other people, but not bind yourself to your position. Do not put others in a position where they must reject you if they reject your argument. If you do tie yourself to your argument, then those who like you may accept the argument just to please you. (It may be a poor one which would have been rejected if considered seriously.) Those who dislike you may reject your idea just because you said it. (It may have been a good one which would have been accepted if considered seriously.) In neither case is the decision based upon what is said.

Suggestions 3 and 4 also insist that the basis for a collective decision be the ideas which are presented and evaluated. If I give in, average the difference, or flip a coin, I am not presenting or hearing evidence which may suggest a better collective position. Discussion groups should achieve their solutions through discussion, not through discussion-avoiding procedures such as majority vote. Methods which encourage reasoned talk rather than discourage sharing of ideas promote the group's purpose.

Using Justification in Deciding

The idea that groups should make decisions using "reasoned discourse" may appear to imply that there are standards of objective rationality which lie outside individual members of a group. If found and followed, these standards will lead to better decisions. I have denied this idea of "objective rationality" several places in this chapter and in chapter 2. Rather than an objective rationality, groups construct a "subjective rationality." In the process of using reasoned discourse to build a decision, a group constructs a rationale for its decisions which is acceptable to all group members. Thus, within the group the standard for what is "rational" is what the group members will accept as rational. A group's rationale for its decision is a large part of what I have called its collective intelligence.

In some cases the only measure of the quality of a decision is its acceptance by group members. The guys who are deciding whether to go to McDonald's or Hardy's for hamburgers must only please themselves. If they like their decision, then it was a good decision for them. But a lot of decisions will be judged by how "workable" they turned out to be in practice. A group wants to construct a "subjective rationale" which leads them to build a decision which will prove to be workable.

Another way of saying that groups work to construct decisions which are subjectively rational is to say that they seek justifiable decisions. I am defining justification here as "reasons applied to audience." A justifiable decision is one which appears reasonable to the audience to whom it is announced. The audience may only be the group making the decision. Or the group may be making a decision which affects outsiders and therefore must be justified to outsiders. In seeking to build a workable solution, it is helpful to think about the process of decision building as a process of building a justification.

If the group only has to justify its decision to itself then it must find methods for avoiding justifications which are found too quickly and therefore may not take into consideration enough ideas. According to Maier, groups have a psychological "rush" to find a solution. There is a "tendency to accept the first workable solution that is obtained."[35] That is to say, members of a group are searching for the first justifiable solution. Once the first solution is found which can be justified to all members, they assume that the solution is workable and they end the discussion.

A method which may improve the group's ability to find a work-

able solution is to search beyond the first justifiable solution. In this method, group members set aside the first decision they reach even though all members of the group agree that it is a reasonable solution. Experimental groups organized by Maier illustrate how this method works. The groups discussed and announced their solutions to test problems. Then the researcher instructed them to continue their discussion to arrive at another solution. The groups were then told to choose which one of their two solutions was the best. 11.1 percent of the groups arrived at the "high quality" solution for their first solution. 42.6 percent of these same groups obtained the "high quality" solution as their second solution.[36]

The procedure of searching for a second solution expands the creativity of a group by forcing members out of what might have been a narrow path to the first solution. Recall Jay Hall's description of groups with little conflict presented earlier in this chapter. If members begin their discussion with fairly similar ideas, they will arrive at a solution which is justifiable to all quickly wthout much real consideration of alternatives. When they continue to find a second solution which is also justifiable, they may think of new alternatives, new reasons, or critically examine previously accepted reasons. When a group is using a method of searching beyond the first justifiable solution, the mental set shifts to search for the better justifiable solution. It is more likely in such cases to find solutions which will prove to be workable ones.

Up to this point we have assumed that the members of a discussion group are the only ones to whom its decision must be justified. Quite often, especially in formal organizations, this is not the case. Justification as a process of deciding is especially useful when the decision will be judged by people outside the discussion group. As noted in quotations by Janis in an earlier section, often the workability of a decision depends on its acceptance by people outside the work because these other people must take action to implement the decision. When the President and the Council of Economic Advisers decide whether to continue or remove price controls from gasoline, they must announce and justify their decision to a set of more or less organized "publics" (gasoline buyers, sellers, the Congress, etc.). The quality of their decision will be based in part upon its reception by these audiences.

Discussion and clarification of "relevant audiences" for a decision is a method for improving the effectiveness of a group in achieving its purpose. By "relevant audiences" I mean those people to whom the decision must be announced and who therefore will judge the reasons for the decision. Relevant audiences are those people who must take action to implement the decision.

The process of discussing and clarifying relevant audiences in-

volves first deciding what people constitute the relevant audience for the decision. Second, it involves some explicit consideration of the values of the various audiences. This means talking about what kinds of reasons are likely to be acceptable. Subsequently, at each decision point in a discussion, the group members should consider whether the relevant audience will find the group's reasons to be reasonable. A decision to move a factory to a location where the land cost is low, but the residential crime rate is high will be difficult to justify to employees. The rationality of low land cost may make sense to stockholders; it probably will not make sense to employees.

The process of clarifying relevant audiences is a process of taking into account the expectations of people who are not actually members of the group. A great deal of this goes on in any discussion group which must present its decision to outsiders. Usually, however, others are taken into account in a rather haphazard fashion. Often there is no explicit discussion of what others expect in the decision. So, for example, one member of a workgroup may say, "We can't do that because the boss won't like it." Everyone else may drop the point without discussing explicitly what the bosses' expectations are and considering the proposal in light of a rational discussion of what the boss does expect.

The process of collective decision building involves discussion of expectations. When groups are using a method of clarifying relevant audiences, they not only talk about their expectations for one another in the discussion, they talk about the expectations of relevant people or groups who are not in the discussion group. They talk about (1) audiences to whom the decision must be justified, and (2) values which these audiences hold which will influence what they will accept as reasons for a decision. Thus, when a group is using justification as a process of deciding, it is concerned with developing reasons in light of the audiences for the decision.

ENDNOTES

1. Gerald M. Phillips, *Communication in the Small Group* (Indianapolis: Bobbs Merrill, 1973).

2. Harold Zelko, *The Business Conference: Leadership and Participation* (New York: McGraw-Hill, 1969).

3. James G. March and Hubert A. Simon, *Organizations* (New York: John Wiley & Sons, Inc., 1958), pp. 137–138.

4. Ibid., p. 151.

5. D. C. Dearborn and H. A. Simon, "Selecting Perception: A Note on the Departmental Identifications of Executives," *Sociometry* 21 (1958): 140–144.

6. Robert F. Bales, *Interaction Process Analysis* (Reading, Mass.: Addison-Wesley, 1951).

7. Kenneth D. Benne and Paul Sheats, "Functional Roles of Group Members," *Journal of Social Issues,* 4 (1948): 41–49.

8. Aubrey B. Fisher, *Small Group Decision Making: Communication and the Group Process* (New York: McGraw-Hill, 1974), p. 29.

9. Robert F. Bales and F. L. Strodbeck, "Phases of Group Problem Solving," *Journal of Abnormal and Social Psychology* 46 (1951): 485–495.

10. Irving Janis, *Victims of Groupthink* (Boston: Houghton Mifflin, 1972), p. 13.

11. Ibid.

12. Thomas Scheidel and Laura Crowell, "Idea Development in Small Discussion Groups," *Quarterly Journal of Speech* 50 (1964): 140–145.

13. Ibid., p. 143.

14. Fisher, *Small Group Decision Making,* p. 140.

15. Jay Hall, *Toward Group Effectiveness* (Conroe, Texas: Teleometrics International, 1971).

16. Ibid., p. 2.

17. Ibid.

18. Norman R. Maier and L. R. Hoffman, "Acceptance and Quality of Solutions as Related to Leaders' Attitudes Toward Disagreement in Group Problem Solving," *Journal of Applied Behavioral Science* 1 (1965): 373–386.

19. Hall, *Toward Group Effectiveness,* p. 4.

20. Jay Hall and M. Williams, "A Comparison of Decision-Making Performances in Established and Ad Hoc Groups," *Journal of Personality and Social Psychology* 3 (1966): 214–222.

21. Hall, *Toward Group Effectiveness,* p. 6.

22. Ibid.

23. Phillips, p. 15.

24. Daniel Katz and Robert L. Kahn, *The Social Psychology of Organization* (New York: John Wiley & Sons, Inc., 1966), p. 262.

25. Ibid., pp. 263–264.

26. Zelko, *The Business Conference.*

27. A more complete explanation of these principles is found in Noman R. F. Maier's *Problem-Solving Discussions and Conferences: Leadership Methods and Skills* (New York: McGraw-Hill, 1963), pp. 76–97.

28. Jay Hall, *Systems Maintenance: Gatekeeping and the Involvement Process* (Conroe, Texas: Teleometrics International, 1969).

29. Maier, *Problem-Solving Discussions and Conferences,* p. 110.

30. Two dimensions of motivation were suggested by the motivation theory of Frederick Herzberg. See "One More Time: How Do You Motivate Employers," *Harvard Business Review* 46 (Jan.–Feb. 1968): 53–62.

31. Maier, *Problem-Solving Discussions and Conferences,* p. 111.

32. Ibid.

33. Ibid., p. 189.

34. Hall, *Toward Group Effectiveness.*

35. Maier, *Problem-Solving Discussion and Conferences,* p. 119.

36. Ibid.

UNIT
III
Formalizing Social Systems

The next three chapters describe how formal organizations are accomplished. The purposes of this unit are: (1) to describe organizational documents as symbols, (2) to describe how the formal systems of hierarchy and specialization influence communication among people occupying different organizational positions, (3) to describe decision building in large, formal systems.

In chapter 7, I describe five kinds of organizational documents: organization charts, job descriptions, budgets, furnishings, and public relations messages. These are official statements about expectations. Documented communication is a fourth coordination format. In documented communication people create nonpersonal and relatively permanent messages about expectations. The application section provides some guidelines to use in interpreting how documents function as messages which formalize organizing processes.

The focus of chapter 8 is on integration in formalized systems. Documents create formal relationships among positions. The people who hold the positions communicate in order to establish human relationships. In chapter 8, I describe how formal positions influence that communication. In particular, I analyze some communication problems between supervisors and subordinates and among people of different organizational specialties, and suggest some methods for overcoming these problems.

Organizational intelligence is the focus of chapter 9. A group of people communicating face-to-face develop many common understandings without having to be explicit about those understandings. The process is much more difficult in complex organizations where people must coordinate their work with others whom they seldom see. Chapter 9 describes some integration methods for improving the development of organizational intelligence in order to accomplish large, complex organizations.

After finishing these three chapters readers should be able to distinguish documented communication from the three coordination formats described in Unit II. They should be able to identify how formal structures affect communication processes and human relationships; they should be able to identify some methods for improving communication among people with different organizational positions; and, they should be able to describe how formal structures affect the development of organizational intelligence and to identify some integration methods for improving collective decision building among people with little face-to-face contact.

CHAPTER
7

Documenting Social Structures

Documentation
Creating the Formal Structure
Entering the Formal Structure
Buying Structure
Staging Structure
Documenting the Public Image
Organizing Functions

APPLICATION: Analyzing Documents as Messages

In the previous unit, I discussed processes which organize all kinds of social systems—families, gangs, work groups, corporations. I described these processes as "evolutionary" or "learning" processes involving enactment, selection, and retention. Each of these processes functions somewhat differently in creating organizations. In this unit I describe processes by which "formal" social systems are organized. The process of organizing formal systems is a communication process, but the process functions somewhat differently in accomplishing enactment, selection, and retention.

The concept of a "formal organization" was popularized by the classical theorists. To them, any "organization" was one represented by the organization chart. Today "formal organization" is the term used to designate the system of deliberately planned roles and decision-making procedures. We can contrast the concept of "formal organization" with "small group." Of course, there is a difference in size. A small group is composed of a few people—perhaps as many as fifteen —who work together in a relatively coordinated way on some common task. Formal organizations are usually much larger. The principal difference lies in the explicitness of the role division.

In small groups there are few if any officially recognized roles (perhaps "chairperson" and "recorder"). In formal organizations the functional role division is highly visible. Each person in a formal organization has an explicitly assigned role; each person has a "title." In a small group, one person may regularly contribute information, and another crack jokes. Thus, members of the group may think of one as the "information giver" and another as the "clown."

Unless the members of the group have had a course in small group behavior, however, it is unlikely that they will be consciously aware of these informal roles. When one becomes a member of a formal organization, however, he or she is assigned a role and a title, for example, production manager, credit director, clerk-typist, mailboy. One person whose "title" is "clerk-typist" may function as an "information-giver-clerk-typist"; another may function as a "clown-clerk-typist," but only the title "clerk-typist" will be formally recognized or "documented." By assigning titles, by paying people with some titles more than others, by job descriptions and other means, an organization regulates individual behavior by documenting that individuals should coordinate their actions in certain ways. Functional role division is accomplished through deliberate creation of hierarchy and specialization.

In this chapter, we examine in detail the process of documentation or the process of making explicit hierarchical and specialized relationships. I describe documents as nonpersonal messages. An illustration of a nonpersonal message is a national law. Individual members of Congress make laws, but the laws are not personal messages. People act according to the intent of the law, not the personal intentions of individual law makers. Organizational charts, pay scales, and job descriptions are likewise nonpersonal messages or organizational documents. Documents are nonpersonal because they are addressed "to whom it may concern" and signed the "organization." Their purpose is to document role relationships and decision-making procedures.

In the following chapter, we examine the impact of documented relationships on personal communications in organizations. An example is a conversation between two men who work together; one's title is "foreman," the other's is "stoker." Whenever they talk about the work, they talk as "foreman" and "worker." Hierarchy is an important variable in their person-to-person communication processes. When an "internal auditor" talks to an "employment director," they are communicating across organizational specialties. Role specialization is an important variable in the communication. In chapter 9 I describe the processes of decision building in formal organizations. I describe how documentation affects formal decision-making procedures or how people collaborate on decisions with little or no oral communication.

DOCUMENTATION

The word "document" commonly refers to something written or printed which furnishes information or evidence. Organizational documents include such things as organization charts, standard operating procedures, goal statements, budgets, and plans of various kinds. We can also call such things as wages, furnishings, advertising, and public relations brochures "organizational documents." These seemingly different items all share three characteristics. First, they are nonpersonal. Though people create the documents, they do so in the name of the organization. By definition, "documents" are authoritative not because of the personal characteristics of the human author, but because they "speak" for the organization. Second, they all have relatively enduring physical structures. Most are written or printed. Some forms of documentation such as office furnishings are nonverbal messages, but unlike a smile which can change in an instant, office furnishings are relatively permanent insignia of one's status. Third, their primary function is to regulate relationships. They are "persuasive messages" about how people should relate to one another.

When I speak of documents as nonpersonal messages, I mean that documents are messages created by individuals acting for the organization. Very seldom do documents bear the name of their creators. Rather, they bear the name of the organization. In addition, documents are not addressed to individuals or even to particular groups. They are public communications to be seen by whoever has reason to see them. They are addressed "to whom it may concern." They are nonpersonal because by intent, they are nonadaptive.

When we communicate personally with another person, we attempt to adapt our message to the other. For example, watch an adult who is talking with another adult when a four-year-old comes up and demands attention. The speaker will turn his head, change the expression on his face, change his tone of voice, and change the level of his vocabulary. In short, he will adapt his messages to his new audience. Moreover, while he will, in part, adapt to his audience as "child," he will also adapt to this particular child at this particular time. If she is his child and he thinks she is unduly interrupting, he will probably scold her in a manner which he has found to be effective with her. Skillful communicators have often been characterized as those most able to adapt to particular others.

By contrast, the goal of documentation has often been described as absence of personal adaptation. The concept of documentation comes from the classical theorists. In their writings, documentation is the means of creating nonpersonal organizations. Warren Bennis has described the motivations of the classical theorists as the creation of nonpersonal human structures:

> Bureaucracy, as I refer to it here, is a useful social invention that was perfected during the industrial revolution to organize and direct the activities of a business firm. Most students of organizations would say that its anatomy consists of the following components: a well-defined chain of command; a system of procedures and rules for dealing with all contingencies relating to work activities; a division of labor based on specialization in human relations. It is the pyramidal arrangement we see on most organizations charts.
>
> The bureaucratic "machine model" was developed as a reaction against the personal subjugation, nepotism, cruelty, and capricious and subjective judgments which passed for managerial practices during the early days of the industrial revolution. Bureaucracy emerged out of the organizations' need for order and precision and the workers' demands for impartial treatment. It was an organization ideally suited to the values and demands of the Victorian era.[1]

The aim of bureaucracy is to replace personal decisions with non-personal rules so that personal factors of individual cases are not considered in decision making. Bureaucracies are created by document-ing what relationships are supposed to be and then enforcing these documents in a nonpersonal or nonpreferential manner. In this way, bureaucracies are created by nonpersonal messages.

For example, in Pennsylvania the Department of Public Welfare has a regulation that children under three cannot attend group day care center facilities where there are more than six children. The regulation "documents" certain relationships between children by forbidding more than six small children to be kept in the same place on a fee basis. When Jennifer was two and a half years old, she had been in a day care center since she was six months old (when the regulation was not enforced). When the child care authorities decided to enforce the bureaucratic regulation, they disregarded all the personal factors in the situation. (The child's brother was at the center; her friends were there; she was accustomed to that routine; her parents wanted her there; she was well adjusted emotionally and intellectually; she would soon be three years old.) They decided on the basis of the document, not on the basis of the personal circumstances, that she had to be moved. The document represents the "official" Public Welfare position and speaks "to whom it may concern" regardless of particular circumstances; officials were expected to enforce the regulation impartially.

Although documents are "nonpersonal" messages, they are responded to quite personally because people respond to the meaning they create out of the message and the situation or context within which they confront the document. In other words, though the source of a document issues the message "to whom it may concern" and does not adapt the message to the audience, individual members of the audience make personal adaptations when they interpret the message. Members of the audience interpret the meaning of the document and respond to it. Their response is influenced by their perception of the organization, its power over them, and the alternative courses of action open to them.

William Barrett[2] describes how one group of workers made personal adaptations to nonpersonal messages. Barrett was in charge of hiring and payroll for a gas company in the Southwestern United States. The employees of the plant were mostly recent Mexican immigrants. The official policy was to pay employees on the first and fifteenth days of the month. The Mexicans were not acculturated to the Anglican habit of stretching a paycheck over a two-week period. The men customarily appeared every three or four days for an advance on their paycheck until the "main office" sent down a memorandum that there would be no advances except for emergencies.

Soon, the workers began to appear at the payroll office with descriptions of sick children and stories of dying mothers. The payroll clerks gave them "emergency" advances. "Downtown" then sent out the regulation that there would be no advances even for emergencies. An employee could draw his earnings only on payday or the day he quit. The next afternoon after work, the men started resigning and drawing their pay. However, each one showed up the next morning to be hired again. Since these were highly skilled employees, there was no choice but to rehire them. Thereupon, another order came in: "Hereafter, no employee who resigns may be rehired within a period of thirty days." The workers read the announcement and walked out of the payroll office. The next morning they showed up to be rehired. Because of the formal rule, Barrett had to tell them no. "No dice, Juan," I said, "come back in thirty days." Barrett recounts what happened then:

His eyes looked straight into mine without a flicker. "There is some mistake, Señor," he said, "I am Manual Hernandez. I work as a stoker in Pueblo, in Santa Fe, in many places." . . . I knew that there was a gas plant in Pueblo, and that there wasn't in Santa Fe; but who was I to argue with a man about his own name? A stoker is a stoker. So I hired him. . . . Within a week our payroll read like a history of Latin America. . . . Finally Larry and I, growing weary of staring at familiar faces and writing infamiliar names, went to the Superintendent and told him the whole story. He tried not to grin, and said, "Damned nonsense." The next day the orders were taken down.

Documents, such as regulations, are issued nonpersonally. But, as is evident from Barrett's example, even nonpersonal messages function quite personally in communication processes. This is true because documents are interpreted by people. The immigrants in Barrett's story interpret the orders in terms of their own experiences. They were willing to risk dismissal to evade the regulations of the central office because of their personal interpretation of their situation in which the nonpersonal regulation was only one part. The workers knew that their particular skills were needed to run the power plant. They had some freedom to respond in their unique way to the payroll regulations. If they had been easily replaceable, they might have interpreted the message differently.

Part of the impersonality of documents results from their form. In unit II, I discussed symbolic "displays" as the messages which function to create social structures. Although it is possible to build and maintain a fine friendship through correspondence, such social systems are relatively rare. Informal social systems are organized principally through face-to-face communication. The messages in face-to-face communication are spoken words, gestures, body position. All these symbolic displays are ephemeral; they have brief physical duration. A smile may be remembered for a lifetime, but the actual physiological configuration exists for only a moment. Though they are brief, symbolic displays are numerous and complex. Social relationships are built through millions of smiles, frowns, words, and touches.

At any given moment we display to another hundreds of messages about our relationship. As the result of the brief duration, the number, and the complexity of symbolic displays, the messages by which we organize our social systems can be remarkably adaptable. We adapt our messages to each person or group with whom we communicate; we adapt our messages from one moment to the next.

By contrast, documents have relatively static physical structures. The organization chart is imprinted with paper and ink. The interpretation of a chart is, of course, a "living process." It is constantly changing, but in order to change the chart itself, people must agree to the change. Changing a document is an organizational decision. The teacher who is dissatisfied with the "curriculum guide," the personnel director who disagrees with the official hiring procedures, and the insurance salesman who is uncomfortable approaching a customer as he has been taught, all confront a similar problem. Like the stokers in Barrett's story, they face a choice situation. They must interpret the meaning of some organizational document (curriculum guide, job procedure manual) in terms of their own behavior. They literally must decide how to respond to the nonpersonal messages.

It is clear from these examples why the "informal organization" is so much more adaptative than the formal organization. A teacher who proposes a change in the curriculum guide must offer arguments about "why" and "how." He must assume the "burden of proof" to demonstrate what is wrong with the official policy and convince others that his alternative is better for everybody. Because changing documents involves organizational decisions, such changes are difficult to accomplish and may be threatening to those who propose the change. The easier alternative action is to ignore the document covertly. The tricks here are to do so quietly and to meet the organization's objectives as well (or better) than those who follow the procedures.[3]

The problem with covert subversion of documents is that relationships are created without official endorsement. Relationships which contradict the documented relationships are officially indefensible. The teacher who does not follow the curriculum guide may be dismissed because of his failure to meet his contractual obligations. This brings us to the third function of documents: they act as "persuasive messages" about how people should relate to one another.

Many social systems which we do not normally think of as "formal organizatons" have documents which regulate relationships of the people in them. Even marriages are based on documents. Marriage certificates document a certain legal, role-related relationship between a man and woman. Birth certificates document the relationship between a child and its parents and between the child and the collection of people known as a nation-state. Documents regulate relationships by creating obligations which may be enforced by the power of the document's source. If a husband fails to live up to the obligations of the marriage contract, his wife may sue him in the court—a branch of the governmental organization which documented their relationship. If a foreman fails to perform the duties of his position, his manager will fire him, thus evoking the power of the organization which specifies the duties of the position.

Documents formalize relationships in part by invoking the authority of the organization to enforce the relationships described by the documents. In a small group, for example, if the person who usually provides the comic relief for tensions does not perform his "role," others cannot say to him, "Let's shape up, there, Jim, you're not doing your job today." Informal roles are enforced much more subtly. Formal roles may be enforced directly. There is a similar distinction between norms and regulations. Small groups, as we have observed, have stable norms for regulating behavior, but these cannot be explicitly enforced. At best, people may say to someone who has violated a norm, "We don't usually do that." Typically a norm violator is "punished" by looks and perhaps silence.

When procedures are formalized they may be directly enforced. In fact, however, organizations rarely need to punish violators. Documents are not a means of direct coercion. Rather, documents symbolize the power of the organization in whose name they are issued. It is not a job description which persuades a person to perform certain duties; the individual responds to the authority represented by the organization. Thus, the effect of any document as a persuasive message about how a person should act depends upon what the person thinks (and feels) about the organization, what alternative acts he thinks are open to him, and how he judges the likelihood of certain actions by the organization. It acts as a "persuasive message" because it sends messages about expectations. When an organization promotes a person to the level of foreman, the declaration has a good deal of persuasive clout, but the relationship is not a "fact" unless the people involved are persuaded by the message. In the remainder of this chapter and the others in this unit, I describe in detail the complications of documentation as a communication process.

CREATING THE FORMAL STRUCTURE

Organizational charts are the focus of attention in this section. "Organizational charts" are those official messages about division of tasks such as actual line-and-box charts, job descriptions, and standard operating procedures and numerous policy derivatives reminding or informing members of formal procedures. The purpose of organizational charts is to document relationships among people. They document specialization by declaring functional task division; they document hierarchies by announcing who has authority over whom. Their intent is to communicate official expectations. By creating organizational charts, people document relationships; they create formal structures. Organization charts do not create relationships, but, because they symbolize official expectations, they formalize relationships.

The classical theorists regarded organizing as a process of creating organizational charts; for them the charts directly created the relation-ships. Today even the most enlightened management scientists tend to think of creating relationships by deliberate design. For example, they describe organizing as inevitably involving "dividing up the work into jobs, and at the same time, making sure that these separate clusters of work are linking together into a total team effort."[4]

Management texts discuss alternative ways to design patterns of formal organizational activity. Since this is not a management text, we are not concerned with standard patterns for organizational design, though general aspects of design are discussed in chapter 1 and chapter 9. We cannot ignore organization charts, however, because they are symbolic documents of organizational communications. They are "slices" of communication processes. For us the important questions to ask are not what are the standard patterns of division, but, how are charts constructed, by whom, for what purpose? And, how are they interpreted by various members of the organization?

In short, rather than taking the existence of organization charts as inevitable and asking what the charts should look like, we are going to focus on the process of organizing and consider "what" they are by examining how they come to be and how people respond to them. We could say that we want to examine the intentional meanings of organiza-tion charts—what the chart makers "intend" by their message—and the interpreted meaning—how people respond to the chart. Of course, there is no standard pattern by which all organizations construct their organization charts. However, let us examine two prototypical patterns and contrast the communication strategies for creating formal structures they illustrate.

A hypothetical corporation, we shall call the Smithson Corporation, was begun by Alexander Smithson forty years ago. During World War II Smithson was successful in securing government contracts for machine parts. Since that time, the corporation has diversified into electronics and textiles. Today there are twenty-seven different products in eight-een companies and twenty-one different manufacturing locations.

The corporation has mostly been run "out of the hip pocket" of Smithson. He personally started each company. He has close personal contact with the managers of all the operating companies. Over the past few years there has been a growing informal decentralization because Smithson is older and does not travel to the various plants as often and because the corporation has grown so large that one person cannot exercise close supervision of each operation. Smithson chose each manager personally and has come to trust their personal judgment in running their individual operations. The corporation has never had a printed organization chart. Rather, the organization has been run according to Smithson's intuitive and implicit ideas of how the work and authority should be divided. Smithson has communicated his ideas personally to each manager during many years of close but informal contact with them.

Smithson is almost seventy years old. Although he is in good health today, he knows that he will not be able to run the company much longer. In order to assure the continuation of the corporation, he feels that work relationships must be formalized. Two years ago he hired a prominent management consulting firm to investigate the corporation and make a recommendation about how to proceed with the formalization. The consulting organization recommended that the company be reorganized according to the chart shown in Figure 7.1.

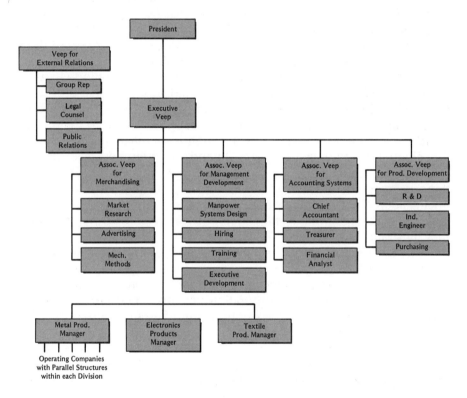

FIGURE 7.1
Consultants' Suggested Reorganization

When they heard about the hiring of management consultants, the managers of the various companies began to communicate with one another over the phone and through some informal meetings. They came up with an organization chart of their own, shown in Figure 7.2.

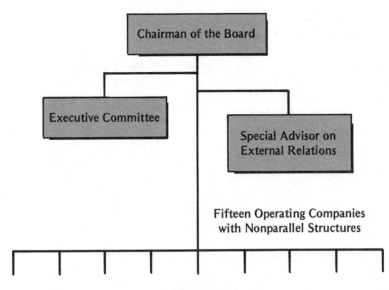

FIGURE 7.2
Managers' Suggested Reorganization

Stewart Jacobs, one of the managers and Smithson's closest friend, brought the managers' reorganization plan to Smithson.

With each chart came arguments for the adoption of that system of reorganization. The consultants argued that their reorganization would permit greater efficiency because of centralized data keeping in a modern accounting systems division. Purchasing, standards, and costing operations could be centralized for each product division, thus securing economies of scale. The system would retain the high degree of centralized decision making which had been Smithson's style. The department of research and development would insure the future of the corporation. It would bring a scientific approach to the activities at which Smithson himself had been most adept. By creating new products, this division would be the spearhead for new companies.

The consultants suggested that the first step in instituting the plan be the creation of the division of management development. This division would oversee the hiring and promotion of people for the new executive positions. It would communicate the new system regulations to employees. After the reorganization had been completed, it would institute regular procedures for personnel evaluation and training, thus insuring that the company benefited from the long range benefits of scientifically proven management principles and techniques. Finally, the consultants told Smithson that they were confident that their reorganization could secure the efficiency they promised because the plan was similar to the organizational design of many of the most important corporations in the world.

The managers argued that the consultants' plan was not well suited to the special needs of the organization. The chart, they said, looked "just like everybody else's" and did not reflect their special circumstances. For example, they pointed out that in the "metal products" division, all the companies would need to be reorganized from the foreman up to be parallel to one another. Such a reorganization would be costly and threatening to the individuals involved. According to the consultants, the purpose of the resulting parallel structure was to permit direct comparison of profits of the companies, but the companies operated in quite different market situations. Therefore, such comparisons, even of companies with parallel organizational structures, were unwise.

The managers argued that there was little need to coordinate the activities of various companies. What coordination was necessary could be accomplished by an Executive Committee composed of the fifteen presidents (they had decided that four small textile companies would better be consolidated into one, thus reducing the number of companies from eighteen to fifteen). The managers said that their work on the reorganization plan proved their ability to work together.

In private consultation with Smithson, Jacobs argued that the consultants' plan would result in taking away from the managers authority which they had been exercising for years. Those chosen to head the restructured organization would be reluctant to exercise their delegated authority, and those who were not promoted would be resentful of the authority "usurped" from them. Moreover, he said, all the managers were chosen by Smithson himself. They were all highly competent people who understood their particular operation. Each would run his or her own company better than anyone else. If the individual companies were run well, Jacobs argued, the corporation as a whole would prosper.

I suggested above that the first questions to be asked of an organizational chart are: how was it constructed, by whom, and for what purpose? The Smithson corporation example presents two ways an organization chart might be constructed. Many organization charts, of course, predate the organizations they represent. Those which are put onto paper after the organization exists may be entirely the product of members of the organization (almost always by the executives), or they may be largely the product of outside consultants. Outside consultants may vary a great deal in how much they study existing lines of communication and distribution of power and incorporate these into the chart.

The consultants in this Smithson example designed a chart based more on patterns of relationship successful in other companies than on the patterns of relationship already existing in the Smithson corporation.

They based the arguments in support of their design largely on the successes of others. The managers, on the other hand, did not investigate how similar corporations are organized. Rather, their design was extrapolated from their perceptions of relationships which already existed. Over the years, Smithson had left more and more decisions to the discretion of the managers. The managers' chart is an extension of that actual pattern. Their argument was that their past successes in taking over decision-making responsibility predicted their ability to be successful in a completely decentralized structure.

The president is confronted with two opposing arguments, neither of which is wholly convincing. The Smithson corporation is not entirely similar to other corporations, but Smithson cannot be too sure of the extent and significance of the difference. Moreover, the past is not always a good predictor of the future. There is, for example, a considerable difference between a manager having some authority and that person having virtually complete authority. With Smithson as president, each manager exercised his own judgment in doing what he thought Smithson would want. That is different than each manager doing what he thinks is best for his individual unit.

Up to this point we have assumed that Smithson would decide on the organization chart. In a formal sense, this is true, but Jacobs pointed out some crucial variables in the decision. The managers' cooperation would be necessary regardless of the organization plan chosen. The success of the reorganization depends upon how well it is put into practice, not how elegant it looked on paper or how well others have used the similar plans. Because the organization has been operated largely informally, each company is run according to the personal style of the manager. In such situations, the manager is not a "replaceable part."

The president is in a bind; he is dependent on each manager. This gives the managers power over what is officially only the president's decision. If the president decides that the consultants' plan should be implemented, many of the managers may leave (presumably the most talented ones who can most easily get other jobs); those who stay may subvert the reorganization. In making a decision about reorganizing, there are always crucial questions about how to get from here to there. Those people who will need to cooperate in getting the organization from here to there are "decision makers" regardless of whether their role is formally recognized or not. The president's dilemma is that if he accepts the managers' plan because he feels the people are indispensable to the company and does not want to alienate them, he exacerbates the problem. Under the managers' plan they become even more indispensable; future restructuring would be more difficult to carry out.

Any organizational chart reflects the values and the purposes of those who constructed it. The managers' plan reflects their entrepreneurial style—their desire to have independent authority over their own organizational units. They were each chosen by Smithson and so it is not surprising that they operate as he does and that, like him, they value independence and fluid structure. The consultants do not have to live in the organization; therefore, naturally their perspective is less directed toward the personalities of individuals and the social consequences of their plans. They work with many different organizations, and consequently, observe similarities among diverse types.

In other words, they have a broad perspective on organizational processes. They attend to gross features. Because they do not have to work in the organization, they do not have to be concerned with detailed matters. They see the organization through a wide-angle lens. They do not see details. Those who work in the organization often see only the details. The managers' problem is the opposite; they have difficulty obtaining sufficient perspective.[5]

Before an organizational chart is chosen, a decision will have to be made about whose values the chart will represent. We may expect, as we saw in chapter 6, that this important decision will not be the result of a group of rational people sitting around a table and discussing their own values and what values are good for the corporation. Instead, the "decision" will be the result of much compromise and implicit bargaining. Probably no one will know exactly when "the decision" is made because the decision will be built by many smaller decisions made by individuals and groups.

For example, Smithson might make some structural changes in the consultants' plan because of the managers' objections. He could announce the chart as official policy. But relationships will not automatically change as the result of Smithson's words. In the process of implementing the plan, there will, of course, be innumerable informal adjustments as each person interprets the chart in terms of his or her own behavior.

Seymour B. Sarason has written of the process of implementing organization charts and the relationship of that process to the continued existence of the organization. Sarason's point, like mine, is that it is the transactional process of "implementation" rather than the chart itself which is the crucial variable in organizing. Sarason points out that people who design organization charts forget that they are simply drawing relationships as they think they would like them to be, and not creating relationships:

> The organizational chart is based on the same assumption as that for a football play: if everyone carries out his assignment in the way he is supposed to—if the tackles throw the right block, if the guards pull out and provide the right interference, if the linebackers are taken care of, and so

on—we have a touchdown. Football coaches are infinitely more realistic than people who create settings [organizations] because they know that the great bulk of plays will not work; they indulge hope, but they plan realistically. In my experience those who create settings tend to come to regard the organizational chart as having a special power to compel people to do what they are supposed to do. As the leader becomes increasingly enamored with the chart as a "rational" statement of how to achieve a smooth-functioning setting he is no longer aware of something he once knew (but which football coaches never forget); the chances are that it will not work. And the chances are *very* high that it will not work.[6]

If organization charts do not "work," we have reason to question whether they are worth the bother they inevitably cause. But they do work as messages from the organization about how people are supposed to relate to one another. They have no "special power to compel people to do what they are to do." Organization charts serve as reference points for individual choices about how to act. Although they could subvert the consultants' plan, the managers of the Smithson Corporation could not choose to ignore it because the restructuring would necessarily affect their responsibilities, privileges and salaries. All organization charts are subverted to some degree, but the very existence of a formally documented structure means that interpersonal relationships are affected.

This discussion has centered on a hypothetical example which is not within the experience of most people. Our attention has focused on the organization chart of a large corporation and decision making at the levels of president and manager. The process of implementing a formal reorganization involves all members of an organization. All members of the Smithson corporation will take actions which affect the structure of the corporation. Many people will experience a reorganization process which has been designed by executives at the top of a formal structure.

However, the most direct experience most people are likely to have with reorganization is the reorganization of a small, usually voluntary organization. Such a reorganization might take place in a fraternity, the local chapter of Common Cause, a country club, or a welfare rights association. A recent experience of mine is much closer to the kind of experience most people have with the creation of organization charts.

The Women's Resource Center of Centre County, Pennsylvania, came into existence over two years ago as the result of the work of a few people. These people called themselves "coordinators." When they applied for tax-exempt status with the Internal Revenue Service, they had to present a written charter. They wrote a three page document establishing a formal structure. It reflected some of their work patterns, but mostly their hopes. For example, they described the operation of the Center as they thought it would be if there was a paid director. In fact, there was no money to pay a director. The structure represented in the chart bore little resemblance to how the organization functioned. Most people who worked with the Center knew little about what the charter said.

After two years, the Center faced a problem similar to that of the Smithson corporation: how to maintain its structure through changes in personnel. Just as Smithson ran his organization on the basis of the "structure" in his head, so the coordinators ran the Center with the structure in their heads. Now the last of the original coordinators was leaving town. It seemed reasonable that some expectations about how the organization functions should be written down. Moreover, some reorganization seemed necessary. The new coordinators wanted the "Advisory Board" to take on some policy-making responsibilities, but members of the board did not expect to do anything but advise.

Some members of the board asked me for help in creating an organization structure for the Center. They expected me to act as Smithson's consultants did and to present them with a structure like that of other women's centers or similar organizations. My answer was that I could not give them a structure, but that I would help them find one. I worked with a group of three members of the board and three coordinators. We planned a meeting with the full board and all the coordinators over which I was to preside. Figure 7.3 shows the questionnaire which all the coordinators and board members filled out at the beginning of the meeting.

The questionnaire assesses first the extent to which coordinators and board members have equivalent expectations (column I). I put the results of the questionnaires on the blackboard. We discussed first those instances of nonequivalence: board members thought coordinators had authority to make a policy, but coordinators thought the board had the authority. We discussed who should be responsible (using answers from column II). After there was a consensus about who should be responsible, we discussed how the organizational structure might be changed in order for that to be reasonable (column III).

This session had three purposes. First, it allowed the members of the organization to assess for themselves expectations on which they were operating the center. Second, it gave them the opportunity to discuss their values. They reached explicit consensus on what kind of coordination patterns they preferred. Finally, they had the opportunity to suggest forms of reorganization which were consistent with their values. Thus, all organizational members were involved in the process of formal restructuring of the organization. It was a process of collective decision building.

Circle one:

coordinator
board member

On the left are several hypothetical examples of situations that might come up at the Women's Resource Center.
Please consider each one and respond to it in the chart below.

	I What is the *current* state?				II Who do you think *should* do it?	III Does your answer to II imply any change in practice? Answer yes/no/ don't know
	Coordinator(s)	Board	No one	I don't know		
1. A board member must resign because she is leaving town. Who decides how (if at all) she will be replaced?						
2. The long range funding coordinator learns of government grants for experimental programs for rehabilitation of women ex-convicts. Who decides if she can apply for these funds in the name of the Center?						
3. Who has the primary responsibility for monitoring the legal implications of the Center's activities?						
4. Two coordinators are unhappy because they feel another coordinator is not doing the job she agreed to do. To whom should they take their concern?						
5. Who is responsible for creating the agenda and chairing board meetings?						

FIGURE 7.3

Women's Resource Center Working Session on Reorganization

The process functioned to secure commitment to the document which resulted. The document was actually written by a committee of coordinators and board members, but it had meaning for all the organizational members because it resulted from an orderly discussion in which all were involved in assessing the need for a change, creating the values of the new structure, and creating some of the form of the new structure. When the document was presented for ratification, it was everybody's document rather than a committee's document.

The process of formalizing a pattern of coordination is one which almost everyone is engaged in at sometime or another. It goes on in P.T.A. meetings as well as in expensive executive suites. Some of the elements in the process are the same regardless of what is being organized. It may not be necessary or desirable to use collective decision building to the extent that it was for the Women's Resource Center, but it is necessary to produce a document which will be meaningful to those who use it. The process of creating a formal organizational structure is putting down on paper coordination patterns which make sense to the people doing the coordinating and which make sense in terms of the work they are doing. The resulting pattern of coordination will result from how the people interpret, or make sense, of what the document says.

ENTERING THE FORMAL STRUCTURE

Organizations are "living systems" in which there is an ongoing process of bringing in new members and surviving the departure of any individual. This means that the process of enacting the formal structure is a continuous one. Standardization of jobs was the formal method devised by classical theorists to assure that the organizational structure could maintain its identity through changes in personnel. In this section we examine the job descriptions as formal messages whose purpose is to communicate official expectations to new members about how to act. I use the term "job description" rather broadly to refer to all the formal messages about how people occupying particular roles are expected to act.

Since managers abandoned the scientific management notion of completely describing all tasks, most have been content with more abstract definitions of jobs. A typical written job description is shown in Figure 7.4. The description is highly abstract. It provides little guidance about what the person who fills that job is supposed to do.

The job description was adapted from one brought to me by an advisee who had just been hired for the job. Her concern was typical of most people beginning her first job. I knew that she had the skills

TITLE: Employee Communications Specialist

REQUIREMENTS:

B.S. or B.A. in Communications, Industrial Relations, or the Behavioral Sciences. Some course work or experience in communications is desirable.

RESPONSIBILITIES:

1. Assists in evaluating, consulting and providing content to mass media communications (employee newsletter communications, film, management talks, etc.). This is the process through which employees are kept informed and understand "The what and why" concerning Company goals, problems, progress, competition, and customer positions, organization changes, compensation practices, personnel policies, etc.

2. Assists in defining the manager's role in communicating with subordinates (department meeting, individual performance appraisal interview, etc.).

3. Develops and encourages means whereby employees can express their opinions and concerns to upper management (such as complaint procedures, attitude surveys, rap sessions, etc.).

4. Recommends programs to expand the emphasis on face-to-face communications between employees and management throughout.

5. Assists in identifying attitudes and behavior patterns which inhibit effective communication between employee and boss, between interacting organizational elements, etc., and recommends action plans to correct them.

6. Keeps up-to-date practices in communications and relates to organization situations.

FIGURE 7.4
Job Description

described, but she was not sure. I was able to generate from the job description some fantasies about what she might actually be doing because I know people who do similar jobs. When I read the description, I thought of conversations with them and remembered their stories of frustration, foolishness, and achievement. In order to make her feel more confident of her ability to do the job, I retold the stories, concentrating on how people perceived particular situations and what specific actions they engaged in.

In other words, I tried to be as concrete as possible in describing what other people in similar jobs actually do. Her anxiety was a kind of fear of the unknown. She was not able to visualize herself in the new job. One reason that I knew she would do this job well was that she generally has great confidence in herself. She had put herself through college working as a dorm counselor and had much experience resolving interpersonal conflicts and facilitating problem solving. In talking with her about her new job, I tried to help her visualize new situations in terms of her past experiences so that she would know that indeed she did have the skills required. I wanted her to recognize that the new job was not totally new and unknown. The problems she encountered would be different, but not unrelated to her past experiences.

Perhaps the best job description would be thirty minute videotapes of people actually performing the jobs. The tapes would show people beginning work on a typical day; they would show machines breaking down; they would show what people talk about at coffee breaks; they would show people coordinating their work by talking with bosses, subordinates, and auxiliary specialists. A person being interviewed for the job could then "see" what the organization expected of the new employee. The interviewer could ask potential employees about how they would have handled particular situations. Thus, the interviewer could gain a much more specific image of how a person would perform the job. The concreteness of this visual job description should alleviate some of the fear-of-the-unknown anxiety on the part of the new employee; it could make hiring less like pure speculation, and it would standardize job performance much more effectively.

Job descriptions, like all organizational messages, are persuasive. Their intent is to influence people to act in particular ways. Job descriptions present images to new employees about what they are to do. Kenneth Boulding in *The Image* observed that "the whole art of persuasion is the act of perceiving the weak spots in the images of others and prying them apart with well-constructed symbolic messages."[7] New employees have extraordinarily "weak" images of their new roles. They are highly motivated to know exactly what is expected of them. We may say that new employees are highly persuasible audiences for messages about what they are to do on their new jobs.

Organizational policy planners can exercise some discretion about what kind of messages to use in persuading new employees. There are two general sources of messages which inform new employees about expectations: *formal messages* (the job description, job instructions from superiors, formal content of training program), and *informal messages* (casual conversations with co-workers, watching, activities, informal conversations with supervisors). Formal messages may be standardized or controlled by the organization. Informal messages are largely out of control of the organization. Policy planners must decide to what degree they want to attempt to influence individual action through formal messages.

Most of a new employee's instruction about what to do will inevitably come from informal messages because they are more concrete. Informal messages offer clearer images about what is to be done. When an employee joins a work group, he watches how his fellow workers spend their time. Over long periods of time watching actual behavior (rather than reading descriptions of what people do), the new employee develops images of what is acceptable behavior and what is not. Co-workers will also tell him what to do. Members of work groups, for example, are generally highly successful at setting their own work quotas regardless of what the "official" quotas are.

Moreover, informal messages are more persuasive because the new employee can check on the meaning of these messages more directly. New employees watch their fellow workers and imitate what they believe the others are doing. While they are imitating the others, they watch to see if their actions look like the actions of the others and if the others are responding to them as if they are acting "right." Formal messages are necessarily more abstract. Even a videotaped "job description" is a highly symbolic representation of the living process which constitutes the job. It represents in a few minutes actions which happen over hours and days. When new organizational members want to check to see if their own actions are satisfactory, they are much more likely to compare their actions to their fellow workers than they are to ask their supervisor.

Although most persuasion about what to do will result from informal messages, formal messages will have more or less effect depending upon how concrete they are. Policy planners can make formal messages more important as guides to individual action by making them more concrete. The employee who is given only an abstract written description will turn almost entirely to informal messages for images about what he is to do. By contrast, employees who are exposed to more complete job descriptions through videotapes, extensive job training, and close supervision during an initial learning period are much more likely to do things "the company way." In other words, representatives of an organization can approximate the influence of informal messages if they (1) construct formal messages which are relatively concrete and (2) present these messages in situations where the employees' responses can be closely monitored so that the employee can be told which of his behavioral responses are acceptable and which are not.

A crucial question for organizational policy planners is: to what extent is standardization of job description desirable? When an organization uses concrete formal messages to persuade an employee to behave in a certain way, it reduces the likelihood that the employee will find a creative way of behaving. That is the point, of course. The organization does not want the individual to behave creatively, but this is a trade off. The organization sacrifices the possibility of finding new methods for assurance that the old method will be employed.

An individual given an abstract job description will create an organizational role unique to him and his situation as he sees it. He may make better use of his individual skills. He can adapt to his image of the environment more easily. The individual who is offered a more concrete image of the job by formal messages will see the job more as "the organization" sees it. He may like the job more, at least initially, because he will be less anxious about what is expected of him.

The kind of formal messages an organization uses to persuade a new member about how to behave ultimately affects the whole organizing process. The "better" the messages—the more concrete, more specific and the closer the effect of the message is monitored—the more rigid the organization becomes. Conversely, the more general and abstract the job descriptions, the less control the policy planners have over the direction of the organization. Individuals who "create" their own jobs are likely to do so in more creative and adaptive ways. They are also likely to make the job unique to them so that if they leave the organization or move to another job, the organization cannot replace them with others who do the same job.

Organizational planners spend a great deal of time designating relationships among jobs—creating organizational charts and job descriptions. Charts and descriptions are not human relationships, however. Rather, they are symbolic messages about human relationships. As such the form of the message is a highly significant variable. When individuals construct the "meaning" of a job (when they predict what is expected of them in a job) the clarity of the formal message is important. The clearer the image it presents, the more suited it is to environments which are stable. But policy planners may not always want clear images. In highly unstable environments, the "best" job descriptions are general, not specific, ones.

BUYING STRUCTURE

Money talks, and nowhere does money talk like in organizations. Even the least structured, "voluntary" organizations like families must maintain themselves by "processing" money. In this section I describe how organizations use money to document human relationships. I describe budgets as symbols which document relationships between organizational activities and goals, and consider how organizations use money to document status among members, thus enforcing the formal hierarchy.

We learn the "power of the purse" early in life. Parents direct the activities of their children by the toys they buy them, the swimming or violin lessons they buy them, and later by the cars they buy (or do not buy) them. By the age of eight most children have learned that they must at least *appear* to obey parents because parents provide financial support. The relationship between money and authority is directly observable.

Budgets are the most direct means by which organizational policy planners enact their ideas about how the organization should be structured. If the planners decide that the organizational decision making should be decentralized, for example, this means that budget decisions are made lower in the organization. One east coast company whose top executives had been convinced of the wisdom of decentralization announced to its regional managers a new policy of "decentralization." The managers were to be given a wide range of discretionary powers to determine such things as salary levels, work schedules, and even product specifications. However, all new expenditures over $10,000 had to be cleared with the central office. This budgetary restriction, of course, negated all the verbal pronouncements about decentralization. The managers could not buy new equipment, hire new personnel, or increase their stockpile of raw materials without explaining to the central office. "Decentralization" became a joke among the managers because the policy had not been supported with money.

Budgets reflect the policy planners' values more than organization charts because they indicate where the organization is willing to spend money. Systems analysts who want to know what the real objective of an organization is look at how an organization spends its resources. C. West Churchman illustrates:

> If we look very carefully at certain cities we may come to expect that the real objective of the government of the city is to sustain the opportunities of the high income citizens by providing them with satisfactory living and satisfactory resources and space for their work. Thus, the claims that the city is trying to serve *all* the citizens are refuted by the city supervisors'

willingness to sacrifice these aims in favor of sustaining the opportunities of the higher-income bracket.[8]

To understand the values of the city policy planners, Churchman suggests, one does not need to know their verbal pronouncements. Rather, he looks for the patterns in how they allocate resources. Into what areas of the city are funds for improving sewers and roads spent? How much does a city spend on providing recreational facilities; does it spend more on golf courses or handball courts? In assessing the values reflected in a budget, you must make some assessments about what kinds of activities are not supported as well as what kinds of activities are supported. The National Urban Coalition attempted to uncover the priorities of national decision makers through analysis of the national budget. The result of their analysis was a "counterbudget." The counterbudget outlines national priorities and suggests how money would be spent if our government's real objectives were its announced objectives.

Budgets may be read as messages, but the messages are not easy to interpret. Budgets are in bizarre codes. The basic symbols are dollars and cents; amounts spent are arranged into some classification system. Most budgets show amounts spent by "object of expenditure." Casual observers are likely to learn little more than, for example, in 1974 an agency spent $5,492,770 on "personnel." Spies code their messages so that those who have no business reading them will be unable to do so. It is very tempting to believe that organizations do the same thing. By listing expenditures by abstract categories ("personnel," "capital equipment," "rentals") organizational policy planners can effectively keep secret information about what is actually being bought. The code restricts the information to a select group of people. In chapter 9, I discuss in more detail how the form of budgeting information influences decision-making process. I describe some ways of "demystifying" budgets so that they become public messages about organizational performance.

There is one part of an organizational budget which any member knows well—the line with his or her salary. Money is widely recognized as a form of motivation. Money is believed to motivate by encouraging people to work hard in order to obtain more money. It is also widely recognized that money motivates because it documents status relationships. Money is not simply financial remuneration for time spent. Rather, money is a means by which the organization communicates to individuals their personal value to the organization.

There are two major forms of remuneration: salaries and wages. Salaries have higher status than wages. The status is not a direct function of the amount of money. The wage-earning electrician earns more than the teacher, but the teacher earns a salary. Salaries have higher status because they symbolize the higher value of an individual's contribution.

The decision about whether there is a wage or salary associated with work is made by the policy planner. All people are paid by the "unit." One kind of unit is a product unit. In most manufacturing plants, assembly workers perform the same task repeatedly. It is convenient to pay these workers according to the number of parts they produce. Part-time secretaries may be paid by product units. Thesis typists are typically paid by the page. But the product-unit system would be inconvenient for staff clerk-typists who perform a number of different jobs.

Secretaries who had to keep records of everything they did (i.e., 370 pages typed; 72 letters filed; 500 stencils run) would spend a good deal of time simply reporting their "products." It is more convenient to pay them by hourly units. One assumption of pay by hourly units is that people who perform such jobs are fairly replaceable. When a plumber is repairing a leak or a secretary is typing a letter, the person can leave at the end of an hour and some other similarly trained person will complete the job about the same as the original person would have. Another assumption is that a person paid by the hour does the work during that hour; there is no specific "preparation" time involved (education or skill development is not considered "preparation" time). Payment by product-unit and by hourly-unit is called a wage. Wage-earners are presumed to make standardized contributions and to be paid only for their work.

Salaries are paid to people who are considered relatively "nonreplaceable." Teachers, for example, are hired by the year or the semester. If a teacher leaves in the middle of the semester, a replacement will be hired, but the replacement will not finish the semester as the first would have. Teaching a course is not like fixing a faucet; it is performed in a unique way by each person. Executives are hired "to manage." A manager could not stop at the end of an hour and have others complete the job.

People on salaries, moreover, are expected to work "all the time." If a machine breaks down on the graveyard shift and four people are called back to work, three hourly workers will receive overtime pay, the supervisor will get nothing. The presumption here is that the company had to buy more of the hourly workers' time, but the supervisor is "always" at work.

Fees and commissions are the high-status equivalents of product units. Doctors and lawyers are paid by the job. Again, the presumption is that the employee is nonreplaceable. He or she contracts for the whole job and works until the job is finished regardless of time. The kind of remuneration a person receives for his or her services is a message about how the organization values the particular person. Salaries, fees, and commissions are "high-status" pay not because the amount is higher than wages (though, of course, the average salary is higher than the average wage), but because in paying a person a salary the organization is declaring that the person is important to the organization. The job is not highly standardized; the pay is for creating as well as doing the job.

The amount of the remuneration is also important, of course. If the amount a person receives is known, it is a source of status. Donald Roy in describing a work group of punch press operators observed that there was a decided "ranking system" in the group of four. "George not only had top seniority for the group, but functioned as a sort of leadman. His supervisor status was marked in the fact that he received five cents more per hour, put in the longest work day, made daily contact outside the workroom."[9] Even in the depression five cents an hour was not a great monetary difference in pay, but it was enough to symbolize a status difference between George and the rest of the workers which allowed George to play a fatherly role in the group.

Abraham Maslow, in explaining his need hierarchy, stated that basic needs such as material comforts cease to be motivators when satisfied, but that the ego needs are never satiated. Understanding money as ego satisfaction helps us to understand the motivation of tycoons who work eighteen hours a day to earn money they never have time to spend. Money in our society documents status and declares success. Crawford Greenwald, at the time president of Du Pont, put it this way,

> Money is about the only form of recognition the business community has devised. If Du Pont's board of directors came to me tomorow and said, "You don't need the dough, why don't you work for nothing for the next five years?" I'd be let down. Money is a symbol in the same way that a Nobel Prize is a symbol to the scientist.

Greenwald valued his salary not just for what the money could buy him, but for what it told him about his value to the organization. His large salary was a symbol of his personal uniqueness—his nonreplaceability in the organization.

In describing some institutional changes which could make organizations more responsive to their environment, Victor Thompson suggests that

> a beginning might be made in the redefinition of "success" if organizations were to establish two equal salary scales, one for specialists and one for hierarchy. Many persons would then feel that they could "get ahead" by earning esteem rather than acquiring status. Some of the enormous waste of our country's technical and professional skill might thereby be

avoided.   It is noteworthy that in organizations where the success of the organization itself is obviously dependent upon esteem won by its functional specialists, as in sports or in other entertainment fields, such a double salary scale exists.[10]

With this suggestion Thompson was concluding an argument that specialists in organizations—researchers, accountants, and so on—are not rewarded by typical organizational salary practices.   In order to achieve recognition in the form of a "big" salary, the specialists have to leave their professional specialties and become managers.   It is, of course, the president and vice-presidents who receive the highest pay in most organizations.   This system of documenting status works to the disadvantage of organizations because many talented specialists accept "promotions" out of their specialties.   To alleviate this problem, Thompson suggests that specialists be put on a parallel salary system so that specialists can be paid as well as managers.   Thompson is not concerned with starving specialists.   They are paid a "living wage," but not a "status wage."   By changing the formal procedures for paying employees, Thompson feels that organizations can change individuals' decisions which affect organizational accomplishment.   By paying specialists more, the organization documents a higher status for these occupations and encourages talented people to enter and remain in them.

Research by Edward E. Lawler confirms this idea of money operating as a motivator.   Managers regard money as a form of recognition for a job well done and as a mark of achievement.[11]   Lawler describes a newly selected company president whose income from securities was about $125,000 a year.   The president asked for a salary of $100,000.   When asked why he did not take $50,000 and defer the rest until retirement, thus saving appreciable salary, he replied, "I want my salary to be six figures when it appears in the proxy statement."[12]   Salary is thus a proclamation of status.   It documents the worth of an individual within an organization.   Salary and wage decisions literally "buy" structure in an organization.

STAGING STRUCTURE

Organizations also buy structure as they buy buildings and furnishings. In large organizations there are sometimes policies about the kinds of furnishings people at different levels of the hierarchy may have.   This is to prevent a staff specialist inadvertently acquiring an office which is more luxurious than an obscure vice-president.

The notion of "staging structure" refers to more than luxuriousness of furnishings.   Interpersonal structure is "staged" by the way offices and furnishings are arranged.   The concept of "office landscaping" refers to office designs in which many people have their desks in a very large room instead of each one being cramped into a tiny, but private office. The large room is literally "landscaped" with furnishings. The idea is to encourage more interaction among coworkers. They pass each other's desk frequently. They look at one another whenever they look up. The "landscaped office" creates more opportunity for speech communication than the "eggcrate" office in which people are hidden from one another until they actively seek contact with one another.

However, employees are not usually happy with the way landscaped offices "structure" their interactions. Brian Wells has conducted extensive investigations of attitudes toward small, private and large, open offices. Four times as many people reported feeling that "larger offices make one feel unimportant" as reported that "a large office is better than a small one." When given a choice, people chose desks in small offices. Most important, workers in small offices tended to have more contact than those in a large office. Wells reports that small offices are more conducive to cohesiveness among workers.[13] For these reasons, architects Alexander, Ishikawa, and Silverstein recommend against "landscaped offices."[14]

Alexander, Ishikawa, and Silverstein's discussion of reception areas exemplifies the relationship of staging to formal structure. For example, they recommend that receptionists sit on a platform twenty inches above ground level:

> The best kinds of public interactions of this sort (client-receptionist interactions) are at eye-to-eye level. Since a client approaching a receptionist is on his feet, the receptionist should also be standing or on a high stool. If the receptionist is working behind a typical desk, the client has to bend down to speak to her; and the receptionist has to crane her neck to reply. This is an unnatural position, and establishes an air of formality to the meeting.[15]

If an organization wants to establish a casual or friendly relationship with its clients, it should start with their reception. A twenty-inch platform allows the receptionist to be comfortably seated. He or she can be engaged in other work and turn to greet a client at eye level without getting up. Thus, the "stage" tells receptionists to greet clients face-to-face; it puts the client at ease by suggesting a kind of direct access to the organization.

DOCUMENTING THE PUBLIC IMAGE

For a series of coordinated activities to be considered an "organization," there must be a "public image" which results from the activity.[16] By public image I do not mean a disembodied image common to the collectivity. A public image is not a property of a "group mind." There are two defining characteristics of a "public image" of an organization.

First, a public image is an image of the overall organization. The "public image" of Harvard University is not simply an image of a single department or of the buildings; it is the organized composite which the term "Harvard University" brings to mind. It is the meaning of Harvard University. A public image, however, it is not a set of individually idiosyncratic images. Rather, the public image consists of equivalent individual images. This is the second defining characteristic. To say that the Federal Government has a "public image" means that there is a fairly large number of people who construct equivalent meanings for the term "Federal Government." Kenneth Boulding explains the process by which public images are created:

> A public image is a product of a universe of discourse, that is, a process of sharing messages and experiences. The shared messages which build up the public image come both from nature and from other men. A group of people talking around a table do not receive the same messages. Indeed, each perceives the situation from his own position. Nevertheless, the image of the situation which is built up in each of the individuals is highly similar.[16]

Of course, informal social systems result in public images. Two people may decide to get married without realizing that a big factor in that decision was the fact that they and their friends had begun to look upon the two as a "couple." By being together often they acquired a "public image." They decide they are a couple because of "how they look together walking." The marriage ceremony was just a ritual to document the existence of the relationship.

Any formal organization undertakes to document its public image for people within and without. A message which documents a public image says, "To whom it may concern: 'This' is the organization." Organization charts, budgets, salaries, and staging are devices used by organizations to describe themselves to their own members. In addition there are many forms of "public relations" messages which document the image to outsiders. Our principal concern here is with messages which document the image to those on the outside.

The concept of an organization as an open system helps us to understand the importance of the image documenting process to the continued existence of an organization. Organizations are constantly interacting with elements of their environments to obtain resources (both personnel and material), to "sell" the product, and to obtain general support. Organizations are substantially dependent on their environments. The organizational response to this dependence is the creation of internal structures or subsystems whose mission it is to secure environmental support.

These sub-systems differ in the kinds of support they seek. For example, purchasing and personnel obtain resources; merchandising, sales, and advertising dispose of products; and public or "external relations" secures general support. Purchasing, merchandising, and sales all deal with the "product." The activities of people in these divisions involve handling a relatively concrete, measurable item. Personnel departments "process" people which may be counted. Advertising and public relations deal almost exclusively in images. Their objective is to secure public support for the organization by creating a "universe of discourse" favorable to the organization. Their work is highly elusive and not directly measurable.

Advertising divisions are generally concerned with creating messages aimed at a favorable image of the product rather than of the organization as a whole. Product identification is so closely tied to the organizational image that this line of division is rather vague. General Electric used the phrase "Progress is our most important product" in its product advertising for many years. The purpose was to tie a favorable image of the company to the product. Customers who were satisfied with the products were thus encouraged to think well of the company; the company used its public image to create favorable images of individual products. Until 1973, gasoline manufacturing companies advertised the quality of their products and services. When gasoline became scarce in the winter of 1974, these companies did not reduce their advertising budgets, but they did switch their message from the product to the company itself. Their new messages became how much the companies are spending to develop new sources of fuel.

An organization's budget usually reveals how important policy planners believe the public image to be. An organization which is dependent upon government contracts usually supports a large lobbying function. Organizations which market products across the country spend a great deal on advertising. Organizations made up of professional employees with a fairly rapid turnover may spend a good bit of money describing themselves in elaborate brochures or advertising in professional journals.

The line between personal and nonpersonal messages about the public image is not always easy to draw. For the most part, the image is "documented." That is, the "communicator" is the whole organization; the human(s) who devises the message does so in the name of the organization. The message is addressed "to whom it may concern": cigar smokers, automobile drivers, cheesecake bakers, or whomever. When "mass media" channels—radio, television, and newspapers—are used, nonpersonal messages are almost inevitable. Advertisers and public relations specialists recognize that personal communications which come from specific people and are addressed to specific audiences are often more effective. Therefore, they use a variety of gimmicks to simulate personal communication about the public image. Frequently celebrities or experts give "personal testimony" on television about organizations and their products. This is an attempt to personalize the message source.

Many organizations have speaker's bureaus which offer the services of their employees to tell community groups about the organization. The speaker's bureau of Smith, Kline and French (pharmaceutical) Laboratories of Philadelphia includes more than 500 employees who travel across the country without extra compensation giving speeches to build good will for their organization. Since 1959, more than 20,000 speeches have been given to audiences totalling over 1,000,000 people. The cost of these speeches has averaged less than $3.[18] The advantage of public speaking over mass media is that the human message source can be directly observed. Political candidates know that if they can get uncommitted candidates to hear them in person, they are much more likely to get the vote. Even a public speaker addressing 1000 people is a much more personal communication than the same person giving a televised address.

Moreover, the public speaker can adapt his or her message to a particular audience. A good speaker will not address members of the Chamber of Commerce as he would members of Common Cause. The occasion for the address, the organizational affiliation of the people in the audience, their age, sex and socioeconomic status all provide speakers with information about their expertise on the subject, their interests, and their vocabulary. Public speakers adapt their messages accordingly. Moreover, unlike the source of mass media messages, the public speaker can adapt to his or her audience while presenting the message.

Lobbying is a means by which public relations specialists attempt to use even more adapted messages to build a favorable public image. The expression "lobbying" originally referred only to the actions of people who stood in the lobbies outside of legislative halls trying to influence politicians to vote in particular ways. Politicians are still prime "audiences" for the lobbyist, but the activities of lobbyists are now used by other public relations and sales people. By taking the "audience" to lunch, by performing small favors or perhaps giving them gifts, the lobbyists attempt to ingratiate themselves into a friendly relationship which then becomes the basis for communicating a favorable image of the lobbyist's organization. The ultimate motivation is to document a favorable public image, but instead of addressing a mass audience in an impersonal way, the policy planners of the organization select certain important people in the "public." They attempt to influence these people by means of communications based on personal relationships.

Organizations differ in their zeal to become actively involved in creating favorable public images. For example, there is a marked difference between industrial and university organizations in their attitudes toward public relations. "Industry knows it must communicate with the general public in order to create a favorable climate in which to market its products."[19] Universities are equally dependent upon public support. Student protests of the late 1960s rebounded into public skepticism about the value of universities and led to a decline of financial support by legislatures and alumni. In the face of such obvious dependence of these organizations upon their environments, we should expect increased internal support for those subsystems which deal with the legislature and the public. However, this had not happened, by the early 1970's. As Dedmon observes, "Public relations work is generally viewed by the academician and a large segment of the administration as both degrading and inappropriate in an academic institution."[20]

The explanation for this anomaly of organizations which are dependent on public support and yet consider "communicating with the public a kind of necessary evil" may lie in the influence of the "public image" which members have of their own organization. Industrial corporations are avowedly competitive. Members of such organizations value competition. Though they may believe that "what is good for General Motors is good for the country," they recognize that General Motors is in no way sacred, nor will its value to society "speak for itself."

By contrast, in America, the value of education has been as widely recognized as the value of motherhood. To admit that a university must hire someone to tell others of the value of education is to admit that someone might be in doubt. The tradition of academics has always been that if a university is offering a "quality education," then the substance of that quality will "speak for itself." If a university has to persuade the public or the legislature that it is good, then its quality is suspect. This kind of attitude is behind the Code of the American Medical Profession which declares that advertising is an unethical practice for doctors. Thus, the public image of members of an organization will influence how they portray the image of the organization to outsiders.

There are other ways in which images persented to outsiders and images presented to members confound one another. Outsiders often obtain inside documents. Budgets and financial statements are not simply internal regulatory devices when funding is directly dependent upon outside agencies. For example, social services agencies such as the YMCA are autonomous but depend upon the United Fund for a large part of their financial support. This means that the United Fund oversees the YMCA budget. The budget is a message to the United Fund which tells it what the YMCA is doing with the money it receives. The financial statement of a public corporation is used not only to inform stockholders of the fiscal health of the organization, but it may also be used as a persuasive message to convince new stockholders to invest.

ORGANIZING FUNCTIONS

Documents are used by an organization's members as information from which they construct images of the organization and their roles in it. Documents declare what relationships are as a means of persuading people about what they ought to be. In chapter 2, I described meaning as retrospective. People turn their attention to their behaviors seen as a completed whole. Documents declare "how things are" in an organization. The message of the document is not, "We should do things like this"; rather, it says, "We do things like this."

Documents act as persuasive messages for individuals when they interpret their situation in order to take action. I have talked about the importance of expectations in the regulation of human action. Documents are a source from which individuals draw expectations. They are persuasive precisely because they do not suggest what people might do, rather they tell people what they are doing.

In interpreting their own behavior, then, people match their observations of their behavior with the descriptions of the organizational document. If a person perceives a discrepancy, he or she may choose to continue to act in a discrepant manner. Or he may adjust in an attempt to conform to his perception of the official description. Of course, people will interpret the official description differently and will act differently even when they try to conform. Moreover, because documents are symbols, they are necessarily abstract; they can never offer a complete description of behavior. But as the "official" description of human relationships, organizational documents are inevitably reference points which people use in constructing their own interpretation of their relationships.

In chapter 3, I described four differences between speech communication—symbolic display—and documentation. These four differences were: "personal richness," "adaptiveness," "informativeness," and "editing." All four concern rigidity. Speech is more "fluid" than documentation. Speech constantly changes as our "moods" change, as we adapt to the changing of the other, as we get more information about the other, as we attempt to adjust what we are saying because we are dissatisfied with how it is "coming out."

Those organizations which are created almost totally by speech are very fluid. They have a great capacity to adapt because members cannot hold one another to account to behave in accordance with written rules. The rules of interaction are potentially being renegotiated all the time. When members of an organization begin writing down their expectations they stabilize the patterns of interaction by introducing some rigidity. The message form—the document—stays the same, though of course, individuals still interpret the same overt messages differently.

There are several differences in function which are more or less related to the difference in rigidity. Use of documents permits much larger systems of coordination. Organizations such as we have today would be impossible if there were no documents to provide rigidity across large numbers of people. A second and related function is centralized control. The more organizing takes place through programmed and planned interaction and through face-to-face collective decision building, the more groups of people will develop idiosyncratic systems of expectations. Since these expectations are learned through speech, they will vary from one group to another. Use of documents brings some uniformity among different groups because they provide a single focus for interpretation. The more specific the document in describing who is to do what and when, the more uniformity there may be.

Documents are not means of mindless control. However, because central authorities do not observe first hand the responses to their messages, there is less reciprocity in control by documentation than in control through speech. This is another way of saying documents are less adaptive than speech and consequently the organizations they create are less adaptive. Organizing through documentation functions to permit a kind of blind impartiality. When they communicate through documents, members of an organization respond to each other not as live personalities, but as paper categories. Individuals may receive the same treatment as everyone else in their category. Such decision rules permit quick decisions as well as a kind of "fairness."

Documentation also permits the creation of what Elton Mayo called a "blackboard logic" in human relationships. "The organization" may appear to exist on paper (or on the blackboard). If the organization is represented on paper, then it may be redesigned on paper. Thus, managers and planners "change" organizations to be more rational. They "edit" the structure. Of course, they can directly change only the symbolic representation of the organization. The process of formalizing involves creating constraints so that interpersonal structures are "rationalized" in accordance with a paper design of human coordination.

Informal groups have great difficulty changing their structure, because members' expectations of one another have developed over many exchanges of symbolic display. Usually their expectations are entirely implicit. Members act without conscious awareness of the rules governing their actions. Because they are unstated, they are difficult to change through direct, purposeful action. Implicit rules govern human relationships in formal organization as well, but one of the implicit rules in a formal organization is that there will be documents which regulate the interaction. Changing formal regulations results in different information to members with which they construct the meaning of their own behavior. Thus, changing the formal regulation acts to change human relationships. Documentation alone is not organizing, but it is one process of communication which functions to organize.

SUMMARY

The process of formalizing a social structure is accomplished by creating documents. Documents are messages addressed "to whom it may concern" and signed "the organization." Documents are not speech communications. Rather, they have relatively permanent forms. Examples of written documents are organization charts, job descriptions and budgets. Money is a document. The physical facility and its furnishings constitute documentation. Documents are the means by which formal structure—hierarchy and specialization, in particular—are accomplished.

Although documents are nonpersonal messages, their meaning is constructed personally in relationship to other features of the organizational environment. Thus, the meaning of an organization chart does not reside on the paper on which it is printed. Understanding documents such as organization charts involves understanding their role in the sequential development of an organization—for example, how the chart was constructed and by whom. It also means understanding how it is interpreted by people with different perspectives—for example, how is the president's image of the chart different from the foreman's. Job descriptions, budgets, salary structure, and furnishings are all documents which act as "persuasive messages" influencing how people act in organizations by offering information about how people are expected to act.

Formal organizations, as well as many informal organizations, have "public images." A public image represents consensus about what the organization "is." A formal organization often charges particular people with the responsibility for communicating to its "public" a favorable image of the organization. People in the formal role of public relations representative often try to make the impersonal documents they construct about the organization's image as personal as they can by having speaker's bureaus or by having well-known people speak for the organization.

Documented organizations are more rigid than informal organizations. Documents make large face-to-face organizations possible. They also function to create one-way centralized control. Organizational change may be facilitated by changing documents. The structure on paper may be made more rational by changing the paper design, but a change on paper does not change organized relationships. At best changing a document creates a focus around which people change their own relationships.

APPLICATION: Analyzing Documents as Messages

When talking about documents such as organizational charts, job descriptions, and public relations brochures, it is tempting to speak of the difference between what is portrayed in the document and what "really" exists. Thus, we frequently hear about "the organization that is not on the chart" and the facades created by "public relations boys." In this chapter I have not even discussed whether documents reflect what "really" happens in an organization. Public accountants must ask whether money is actually spent as the financial statement declares. But for the analyst who is concerned with matters other than financial fraud, there are other important questions.

I have described documents as organizational messages and have suggested that people can learn about any organization by investigating how these messages function to formalize organizing processes. Instead of asking whether an organizational chart "really" represents the distribution of power and authority, one asks: who constructs the chart, how, for what purpose? And, how do various members of the organization interpret the chart?

Answers to the questions about "real power" may only reveal a static picture of the "informal organization." Answers to questions about how the organizational chart functions as a message in the organizing process can lead to explanations of the dynamics of organizing.

Actors must be identified, along with their motives, their actions, and the interrelationships of their actions. Moreover, instead of artificially separating the "formal" organization (the one on the chart) from the "informal" organization, questions about charts as messages lead to considerations of the mutual interdependence of spontaneous (informal) and documented (formal) relationships.

Instead of asking if a job description "really" reflects the activities of the person who fills the role, one may ask: when new members read a job description, what images of the priorities of the organization do they construct? Are these priorities equivalent to those envisioned by the policy planners? Are job descriptions sufficiently concrete that new members can construct images of their new roles, or are they so vague that the role is threatening because the expectations are unclear? On the other hand, does the organization communicate the activities required by a role so concretely that the new members have very similar ideas and are less able to adapt to new contingencies or otherwise be creative in constructing their organizational role?

Are the policy planners' avowed objectives supported by the distribution of resources in the budget? If not, how do members of the organization interpret the difference between the verbal statement of purpose and the budget document? Who has access to the budget? How clearly does it indicate organizational purposes and measures of accomplishment? Does the organization undertake to explain the budget document to members in its decision making? The more democratic an organization, the more public its resource allocation decisions. Not many organizations—even voluntary organizations run exclusively for the benefit of members—are very democratic by these standards. Other lines of investigation into the relationship of money to organizational structure are: Who is "successful" by organizational standards? (Who gets the most money?) What means of documenting success other than money does the organization use? Do members of the organization recognize these other means?

Instead of considering staging to be an organization facade, the use of staging to create organizational structure may be examined. For example, how does the organization document roles through its insistence on certain costumes and props? What is the response of organizational members to the staging of organizational roles? (Is the organization successful in using staging to create certain images or is there a boomerang effect of resentment?) What kinds of interpersonal relationships are encouraged by the arrangement of rooms and furniture? A description of how these general questions may be turned into research questions and hence may be turned into a research project is found in the Appendix.

ENDNOTES

1. Warren Bennis and Philip Stater, *The Temporary Society* (New York: Harper and Row, 1968), p. 55.

2. William Barrett, "Señor Payroll," *Southwest Review* 29 (1943): 25–29. Reprinted in Walter R. Nord, ed., *Concepts and Controversy in Organizational Behavior* (Pacific Palisades, Calif.: Goodyear, 1972), pp. 319–322.

3. Many organizations recognize that the whole organization operates not because the people follow official procedures, but because they accomplish sub-objectives which contribute to over-all organizational objectives. "Management-by-objectives" is the name given to the strategy of officially permitting idiosyncratic procedures and documenting only the relationship among unit objectives. Management-by-objectives is discussed more in chapter 9.

4. William H. Newman, Charles E. Summer, and E. Kirby Warren, *The Process of Management Concepts, Behavior, and Practices* (Englewood Cliffs: Prentice-Hall, 1967), p. 40.

5. This is the planner's perpetual dilemma: how to "see" enough detail to plan realistically while having enough perspective to plan at all.

6. Seymour B. Sarason, *The Creation of Settings and the Future Societies* (San Francisco: Jossey-Bass, 1972), p. 152.

7. Kenneth Boulding, *The Image* (Ann Arbor, Mich.: Univ. of Michigan, 1956), p. 134.

8. C. West Churchman, *The Systems Approach* (New York: Dell, 1968), p. 32.

9. Donald Roy, "Banana Time Job Satisfaction and Informal Interaction," *Human Organization* 18 (1959–1960): 159.

10. Victor Thompson, *Modern Organization* (New York: Knopf, 1961), p. 196.

11. E. E. Lawler and Lyman W. Porter, "Perceptions Regarding Management Compensation," *Industrial Relations* 3 (1963): 41–49.

12. E. E. Lawler, "Managers' Attitudes Toward How Their Pay Is and Should Be Determined," *Journal of Applied Psychology* 50 (1966): 273–279.

13. Brian Wells, Pilkington Research Unit, *Office Design: A Study of Environment* (Dept. of Building Science, Univ. of Liverpool, 1965).

14. Su Christopher Alexander, Sata Ishikawa, and Murray Silverstein, *A Pattern Language Which Generates Multiservice Centers* (Berkeley: Centers for Environmental Structure, 1968).

15. Ibid., p. 259.

16. Boulding, *The Image,* 1956.

17. Ibid., p. 132.

18. Gerald Goldhaber, *Organizational Communication* (Dubuque, Iowa: Wm. C. Brown, Co., 1974), p. 205.

19. Donald Dedmon, "A Comparison of University and Business Communication Practices," *Journal of Communication* 29 (1970): 316.

20. Ibid., p. 316–317.

CHAPTER

8

Interpersonal Communication in Formalized Systems

Documents which prescribe the formal structure of an organization provide a context for all the communication within the organization. In this chapter, we examine the process of constructing human relationships within the context of a formal structure. The first section considers how documents act as contexts or metamessages for communication in formal organizations. The next four sections consider communication in "supervisory relationships." A supervisory relationship is that which is created by a supervisor and his or her immediate subordinate. The last section describes how the division of people into organizational specializations influences the communication and hence the work relationships among them.

Documents are nonpersonal because they are addressed "to whom it may concern" and signed "the organization." People who are working with one another, however, cannot communicate "to whom it may concern." They see each other daily; they know one another. Often, therefore, they personalize even formal messages when communicating with one another.

Troops:
Now hear this!

Policy on smoking stated

The following policy regarding smoking in University facilities concurs with the recommendations to President John W. Oswald by the University Council. The policy takes effect September 1, 1975.

The policy on smoking is applicable to all facilities of the Pennsylvania State University except the Milton S. Hershey Teaching Hospital, the Ritenour Health Center, the J. Orvis Keller Building, and the Nittany Lion Inn, each of which has special smoking regulations.

The general purpose of the University policy on smoking is to protect the rights of nonsmokers, to provide ample arrangements for smokers, and to take into consideration the appearance and maintenance of University facilities. In order to achieve this purpose, it is necessary to prohibit smoking on certain premises while at the same time providing designated areas in public facilities where a person can engage in smoking as set forth in the following regulations:

Yes Smoking is permitted in the following areas: (1.) Hallways where receptacles have been provided and where no contrary instructions have been posted. (2.) Specially designated study areas, dining facilities and public lounges. (3.) Private offices and private laboratories, at the discretion of the assigned occupant(s). (4.) Designated foyers and lobbies.

No Smoking is not permitted in the following areas: (1.) Classrooms and seminar rooms. (2.) Study areas, dining facilities, and public lounges except in special segregated areas provided for smokers. (3.) Auditoriums, museums, and exhibition galleries. (4.) Laboratories. (5.) Elevators and stairwells. (6.) Indoor recreation areas. (7.) Committee meeting and conference rooms.

Violations of the University Policy on Smoking are to be submitted to the scheduling officer of the campus concerned who will route the information to the administrative officer or to the academic dean of the unit against which the complaint is lodged. It is the responsibility of the appropriate administrative officer or academic dean to ensure that the policy on smoking is observed and to take corrective actions where violations occur.

Smoking is now a no-no except in offices (and, presumably, behind the barn) hallways and the mailroom. If you don't want smoking in your office, post a sign to that effect.

FIGURE 8.1
Personalizing a Document

Figure 8.1 shows the way my supervisor humanizes messages in the Speech Communication Department of the Pennsylvania State University. The printed message appeared in the official faculty newsletter. Note how "official" it looks. My department head, Robert Brubaker, cut it out and added his own comments. It is a nice illustration of what can be done to personalize nonpersonal communication forms. It is more personal to me than to you because I interpret it within the context of the Robert Brubaker I know. Note, he is communicating that he expects us to live with the no-smoking expectations of the university. Here he is acting within his formal role as department head. He is at the same time reminding the faculty indirectly that he likes to be rather casual or informal in his relationship to us. This is also a message sent from him in his role as "head," but it is his style of enacting that role. The message may also be interpreted as saying that the no-smoking rule will be hard on him. Here he is not communicating within his formal organizational role; he is communicating person-to-person.

One message is thus three messages. It is a formal message sent from one organizational role to another. It is also what William Jones has termed a "subformal" message.[1] Subformal communication takes place among organizational roles (such as department head and faculty member). It concerns organizational performance, but it is "off the record." The casual, unplanned talk that goes on between supervisors and subordinates is subformal communication. Finally, the message in Figure 8.1 is nonformal communication because it is communication from one person to another without regard to organizational role.

Subformal communication is the focus of this chapter. Mostly our concern is with talk, but some communication of this kind goes on in written form such as that shown in Figure 8.1. Interpersonal communication in formalized systems is communication between people in formal organizational roles which has direct influence on the functioning of the organization. It is more personal than documentary communications because it creates relationships between specific people. We examine, here, those relationships and the communication which creates them.

FORMAL SYSTEMS AS METAMESSAGES

All communication contains not only content, but also claims about the relationship between communicators. Claims about the relationship are frequently called "metacommunication." According to Thayer:

> Metacommunication is a term which is useful to refer to anything which a person takes into account as a help in interpreting what another is say-

ing, the import of the situation, how to comprehend what is going on, etc. . . . We must necessarily take into account a great deal more than the "content" of what another is saying if we want to comprehend him as he expects or intends us to. There is the matter of who he is and what we see as the purpose of his attempt to communicate to us and how we orient ourselves to those conditions. There is the place, the time, and the manner. There are his inflections, his tempo, his pitch, his gestures, his countenance and facial expressions (if we can see him). There is our understanding and our feeling about the history of previous encounters with him. . . . There are the roles we enact and expect, and the rules by which we attempt to regulate the encounter.

The kinds of metamessages Thayer uses as examples are largely those I have described as expectations—roles, rules or norms, history of relationship or agenda, and motive or intention. In interpersonal relationships expectations are products of the personal communication between people. In formalized relationships, people must take into account factors beyond the present cues (such as facial expressions) and history of the relationship. They must also take into consideration formalized or officially "established" roles, rules, agendas, and goals. Thus, documents about formal expectations such as job descriptions are metamessages in the subformal talk which goes on between organizational members.

There are two ways in which formal structures as metamessages influence interpersonal communication. One way is through the creation of relationships which exist "beyond" the communication which takes place between the people involved. The second way is through the creation of non-face-to-face relationships in which people have to look for nonpersonal clues such as the language and form of messages to interpret the other's meaning. Let us examine each of these two ways.

Formal roles, rules, agendas, and goals give a relationship between two people an existence outside or beyond the communication which takes place between the two. Nonformal interpersonal relationships are "bounded by" communication between those in the relationship. Such relationships begin when people start to communicate with one another (the first encounter). If the talk is intense and serious, the relationship is intense and serious. Roles, rules, agendas, and intentions are created by the participants as the necessary and inevitable result of their interaction. When the people in such a relationship stop communicating with one another, the relationship ceases.

Take, for example, two people—Sid and Marty—who meet near a tennis court. Each is looking for a tennis opponent. They find that they play a fairly even match, and so they play on several other occasions. They like each other and enjoy improvised talk before and after each game for several months. They become friends. A casual relationship or social system is constructed of casual talk. After a year or so Sid grows somewhat tired of Marty's jokes, and Sid's extravagant life style makes Marty self-conscious. Their contact becomes less frequent. Then they cease playing tennis together at all. The relationship is "over." The relationship was created by common interests and communication. It dissolved when the communication ceased. Thus, the interpersonal relationship was bounded by the communication between them. The characteristics of the relationship were those of the talk which created the relationship.

Contrast this example with a parallel example in which there are formal metamessages. Suppose that Sid and Marty have met in an office instead of on the tennis court. The two men are new assistant personnel managers. Sid is in charge of hiring; Marty is in charge of training. Each has information which the other needs from time to time to do his job. In this case, their relationship has an existence beyond their personal communication with one another. They occupy formal roles which are related in the organizational structure. Their relationship is subject to rights and obligations which they did not create. Even though Sid gets tired of Marty's jokes, he is not free to discontinue communication unless he leaves the organization entirely.

Because of the existence of formal organizational roles and obligations, the relationship is not bounded by personal communication between Sid and Marty. The formal interconnection of responsibilities (Sid needs organizational information from Marty and vice versa) forces the two to maintain some communication with one another. Because the two must have some relationship with one another, we can expect that they will try to keep their encounters at least "polite" and "pleasant."

The existence of rights and obligations beyond those constructed by the participants means that there are metamessages which inevitably accompany every message in the relationship. The formal role relationship must be taken into account. One metamessage which Sid always "sends" to Marty is: "I'm in charge of hiring, you need me to do your job, and I need you to do mine." The metamessage, "We have to communicate with one another," carried by the formal position puts each person in a "No Exit" situation (see chapter 2). If one were to avoid communicating with another, the act of avoidance would in itself be a message.

"We have to communicate with one another" is but one metamessage of formal structure. In supervisor-subordinate relationships, the supervisor's metamessage is always, "You must be influenced by what I say." The subordinate's metamessage is always, "If I want to keep my job I must be influenced by what you say (or pretend to be), no matter how illogical or absurd it may be." When the representative of one organizational division speaks with the representative of another division, each message carries the metamessage, "I'm acting for the benefit of my division." Each person takes into account the organizational obligations of the other. The expectations of the relationship are not entirely negotiated by the people involved. Some of them are imposed by the formal structure.

A second way in which formal structures influence people is by creating relationships among people who do not have regular face-to-face contact. The relationship between a first-line foreman and the central office policy makers (such as the organizational president, vice-president, manager, and so forth) is an example of a non-face-to-face relationship. Except for occasional exchanges of talk when the president tours the plant, the foreman and president "know" each other only through the documents one sends to the other. There is minimum opportunity for coorientation. Neither can have a direct sense of the other's perspective. So how is each able to interpret the messages which are sent by the other? Obviously, the principal cue to interpretation is the formal role of the other. A message from any "unknown" foreman is interpreted in the same manner. There are additional cues. Spence and O'Connor describe some of these:

> In a large organization such cues (as posture and gestures) are not available to us and we are forced to rely on formal aspects of messages for guides to interpretation. Thus the written language—bureaucratic or casual; the form—order, request or advisory; the channel source—official or grapevine, must be relied on to discern the sender's intention. Likewise, the timing of messages, the volume of messages, or the promptness with which messages are responded to are all utilized by receivers to interpret the formal message.[2]

In a formalized system people who must coordinate their activities often have no personal contact with one another. A field representative may see his or her supervisor for a brief period every week—or every month. Much of the supervisory relationship is constructed through correspondence. In such cases, as Spence and O'Connor observe, the form of the correspondence—the timing, the choice of language, the acknowledging of previous communications—becomes critical as cues which the people take into account in interpreting the other's message.

In this section I have introduced the concept of a metamessage. The concept helps to explain how formal structures influence actual behaviors of people in organizations. The formal structure is a source of cues which people use in interpreting messages. The formal structure creates rights and obligations which influence how people interpret one another's communication. Formal structures make possible non-face-to-face relationships.

SUPERVISORY RELATIONSHIPS

In any social system where people are organized into hierarchies, there are no more important relationships than those which exist between subordinates and their immediate superiors. The subordinate may be a vice-president or a newly hired, unskilled laborer. Formal relationships described on paper become human relationships in the contact between supervisor and subordinate. For the subordinate, the authority of the organization is personalized in the superior. The superior must "get things done through people"; his or her subordinates are those people. Fritz Roethlisberger has observed: "It is in the relationship between a superior and a subordinate that more breakdowns of coordination and communication between various parts of the industrial structure finally show up. It is here that distortions of personal attitude and emotional disturbance become more pronounced."[3]

The existence of a relationship between a subordinate and a supervisor is degreed by the organizational structure. Enormous pressures can be placed on that relationship by organizational forces (for example, demands for production, cut-backs in production, relocation) over which neither subordinate nor supervisor has control. The larger organization sets a context for the personal communication by which a subordinate and a supervisor negotiate the character of their relationship. The larger organization provides metamessages which supervisors and subordinates take into account.

COORIENTATION IN SUPERVISORY RELATIONSHIPS

The formal system provides the framework within which supervisors and subordinates work out expectations unique to their relationship. As in any relationship some resemblance of "equivalence" expectations develops. The term "coorientation" refers to the process by which people learn others' expectations and meanings for issues and objects in their shared situation.

Some communication researchers have examined states of consensus between supervisors and subordinates as an indication of their communication and as a predictor of the satisfaction in these relationships. Unfortunately, most research has been concerned with the level of "agreement" between supervisors and subordinates. Agreement refers to a state in which both members of the pair hold the same belief or have the same perception of a situation. Very little research has been done on levels of "understanding." Understanding refers to the state in which each member of the pair knows the belief or perception of the other.

The basic procedure for studying agreement between supervisors and subordinates is to ask each member of the pair his or her opinion about issues of some importance in the coordination of work. Triandis, one of the chief developers of this methodology, asked supervisors and subordinates to describe five jobs (such as vice-president, clerk) and six people (such as the personnel director, the supervisor) using pairs of adjectives (for example: cooperative—uncooperative). The more the supervisor and subordinates agreed on their descriptions, the more "syndetically similar" they were judged to be. Pairs which were similar tended to report that their communication was more effective than pairs which did not. Triandis did not attempt to assess communicative effectiveness directly, for example by observing their interaction.[4]

W. H. Read[5] asked supervisory pairs to rank order a list of job-related problems in the order in which they caused problems for the subordinate. The results of such investigations is usually that there is disagreement about perceptions of supervisors and subordinates. Generally, researchers ascribe differences in perception to "communication breakdowns," but this is not a necessary conclusion. Supervisors and subordinates communicate from different perspectives. Each has a different cognitive map of the organization. The plant supervisor whose job it is to control overall costs may "naturally" believe that a foundry foreman's biggest problem is scheduling workers to avoid paying overtime. The foreman who has just had two furnaces break down is likely to see his most important problem as maintenance. The differences in perception simply reflect differences in how the people's cognitive maps are influenced by their formal position in the organization. No amount of "communication" will resolve the disagreement. Moreover, this kind of disagreement is far from undesirable in an organization. If the foundry foreman "saw the world" as the plant manager does, he would in fact be another plant manager. That is not his job. Doing his own job in the organization means that he must see the world as a foundry foreman. Seeing the world from the perspective of his formal role means that inevitably he will have some disagreements with his supervisor. No amount of communication could or should bring about consensus at the level of "agreement" on such issues.

Boyd and Jensen[6] investigated the agreement about a more critical issue—role expectations which supervisors and subordinates have for the subordinate. They found that 44 percent of the time the supervisor disagreed with the subordinate about whether the subordinate had the authority (formal role responsibility) to purchase new materials. Fifty-nine percent of the time there was disagreement about the extent to which the subordinate has authority for maintenance of equipment. Again, some disagreement is inevitable. A foreman has first hand knowledge of how many routine maintenance decisions he has to make as part of his job. The manager who supervises him is unlikely to realize how important those "little" decisions are in the working of the organization. His perspective is attuned to larger decisions, but disagreement on role expectations may indicate some failure to develop a social formula adequate for the interaction. Farace, Russell, and Monge cite Boyd and Jensen's research as an indication of disagreement on "communication rules" between supervisors and subordinates. Rules are systems of expectations. Farace, Russell, and Monge note the following about the consequences of disagreements about communication rules:

> It seems likely that in instances where these problems arise [lack of consensus on rules], individuals may well be penalized in one form or another, with an accompanying impact on their self-esteem and organizational performance. They may truly become victims of "the system," i.e., victims of the operation of a rules system where both supervisor and subordinate may be unaware of what is happening.[7]

A disagreement on expectations is more serious in an organization than a disagreement about attitudes because expectations are the basis of coordination. The more organizational members have disagreements on expectations, the more unorganized they are.

Russell[8] has conducted research on the consensus state of understanding between supervisors and subordinates. Through questionnaires, he gathered information about one hundred field representatives of a social service agency and their immediate supervisors. He was interested in consensus about four areas of communication rules:

1. Innovation—involvement in bringing up new ideas and modifying programs to meet particular situations.
2. Maintenance—bringing nonwork and family matters into discussions.
3. Sequencing—involvement and responsibility for seeing things through to completion.
4. Initiation—responsibility for seeing that tasks are actually undertaken.

He found some disagreement about rules. For example, supervisors reported that their communication was less frequent than subordinates reported it to be. "Each group saw the other as more concerned with

getting the job done while they saw themselves as having a more balanced interest in nonwork communication and communication about
new ideas as well." This finding is not particularly surprising. We all
"see" more of ourselves, and thus are likely to think of ourselves as
having "more balanced interests." Because supervisors and subordinates communicate with one another largely "within" their formal roles,
naturally they think of the other in terms of that role. This is part of the
significance of the formal system as a "metamessage."

Russell found a relatively high level of understanding about communication rules between members of supervisory pairs. That is,
superiors tended to know how subordinates viewed communication
rules and vice versa. Over one-half of the responses were "consensual"
in this way. However, between one-third to one-half indicated some
kind of misunderstanding. Many individuals believed that the other
shared their own perspective when, in fact, the other did not share that
perspective.

According to Farace, Russell, and Monge, this kind of misunderstanding is the most serious for communication. "If we disagree and
know it we can both make allowances for the other's point of view, but
if we are inaccurate about the other person's viewpoint and expect it to
be the same as our own then the stage is set for some potentially serious
misunderstanding."[9] Russell's research provides some indication that
indeed misunderstanding is undesirable in relationships between supervisors and subordinates. The higher the level of understanding, the
higher subordinate morale, the higher the supervisors' evaluations of
subordinates tended to be, and the more informal, or casual, the relationship was. Conversely, when there was misunderstanding, there
tended to be lower morale, lower evaluations, and more formalized
relationships.

SUPERVISION AND COMMUNICATION PROBLEMS

Communication between people in formalized relationships is subject
to the same kinds of communication problems discussed in previous
chapters. There are systemic problems in developing equivalent meanings. Self-fulfilling prophesies, multiple systems, serial transmission,
no-exit, concealed distortion, and information overload problems plague
communication between superiors and subordinates. In addition, there
are three kinds of problems which arise from peculiarities of formal
structure and potentially interfere with all relationships between superiors and subordinates.

Formal structures establish a system of authority in relationships among people. People have responsibilities for which they are held to account. Likewise, they have legitimate claims against the time and performances of others. The formal structure establishes some common purposes for the relationships. The talk which goes on among people must help to accomplish (or at least not prevent accomplishment of) that common purpose. In this setting we can identify problems which almost inevitably characterize communication to some extent. The first is an imbalance of concern for people vs. production. In any formalized relationship people must work together to produce, whether it is "goods" or "services." The communication may be so directed toward improving production that little concern for people is evident. Conversely, the people may be enjoying their talk so much that their production suffers.

A second kind of problem is clarity. People in formalized relationships give instructions and information to one another so that work may be done. Clear instructions and information, therefore, are obviously necessary. When this communication is muddled, there is a problem of clarity. Not only must instructions and information be clear, they must be consistent. When people send contradictory messages to one another, they do not know what is expected of them. Without expectations, of course, there cannot be coordination. Not only must explicit messages be consistent, but metamessages must be consistent with report messages. Problems of contradiction, therefore, are the third kind of communication problem we shall consider.

Concern

In chapter 5, I suggested that skillful communicators are simultaneously concerned with their plan for an interaction and concerned with the interaction itself (regarding the others as people whose goals and feelings must be attended to). This idea of the necessity of two simultaneous concerns is applicable to communication in formalized systems with minor alterations. A supervisor and a subordinate talking to one another could be engaging in "planned interaction." Each would have his or her private purposes for the interaction. Because their talk is part of their work activity, however, the formalized organizational goals influence their personal goals.

The importance of simultaneous concern for people and for production was established in very early research on organizational leadership. In 1945 a group of researchers at Ohio State University began a series of investigations into the effects of various leadership styles. They administered questionnaires to Air Force bomber crew members which asked them to describe their commanders. Typical items were:

He makes his attitudes clear to the crew.

He maintains definite standards of performance.

He finds time to listen to crew members.

He is friendly and approachable.[10]

From their analysis of 150 such items, the Ohio State Researchers concluded that there are two dimensions of leader behavior. The first they called "initiating structure." It is measured by items such as the first two listed above. A leader who initiates structure "tends to define the role which he expects each member of the crew to assume, and endeavors to establish well-defined patterns of organization, channels of communication, and ways of getting jobs done."[11] In "initiating structure" a leader's intentions are in accordance with the formalized organizational goals. The leader acts for the benefit of the organization as defined by the formal organizational goals. He or she is "concerned with production." The reader may recognize that this dimension is similar to the "intelligence" function of communication and the "task" dimension of group behavior.

A second dimension of organizational leadership, according to the Ohio State researchers, is "consideration." This dimension concerns the quality of "friendship, mutual trust, respect, and warmth in the relations between the aircraft commander and his crew."[12] Leaders who are motivated toward establishing relationships with subordinates which have high trust and warmth are "concerned with people." This dimension is similar to the "integration" function of communication and the socioemotional dimension of group behavior.

The researchers correlated leaders' scores on the dimensions of initiating structure and consideration with ratings of effectiveness by the commanders' supervisors and by their subordinates. They found that supervisors rated as effective those men who scored high on initiating structure but not necessarily on consideration. The implication we can draw from this is that the representatives of formal systems (in this case commanders' supervisors) expect people to be concerned about production. Formalizing relationships creates the expectation that people will act on concerns for production. In the actual relationship between an organizational leader and subordinates, however, there must also be concern for people. When the researchers asked subordinates to evaluate the effectiveness of their crew commanders, they found that only those judged high on both initiating structure and consideration were considered to be effective. These findings led the researchers to conclude that satisfactory work relationships between superiors and subordinates require supervisors who show by their actions that they are concerned for the organization's objectives and activities (production) and also that they are concerned with subordinates as people.

The work of Fred Fiedler suggests that the relationship between a superior and a subordinate need not be characterized by simultaneous concern for production and concern for people. Rather, that particular sets of constraints make one or the other kind of concern appropriate. Fiedler proposes a "contingency theory of leadership effectiveness." In some situations or "contingencies" concern for production is associated with effective leadership while under others, concern for people is related to effectiveness.

Fiedler measured what I am calling "concern" in terms of the leaders' "esteem for his least preferred coworker (LPC)." The leader is asked to imagine the coworker with whom he least prefers to work. The leader then describes this coworker using a series of eighteen to twenty sets of bi-polar scales such as these:

Pleasant   8 : 7 : 6 : 5 : 4 : 3 : 2 : 1   Unpleasant
Friendly   8 : 7 : 6 : 5 : 4 : 3 : 2 : 1   Unfriendly

The LPC score is computed by adding up the item scores. People who describe their least preferred coworker in relatively favorable terms are called "high LPC" leaders. Those who describe their coworkers in unfavorable terms are called "low LPC" leaders. In one study Merrwise and Fiedler found that LPC is quite similar to what we have been calling "concern."[13]

Fiedler described effective leaders as successful "influencers," though he did not directly measure influence. Instead he measures the output of the whole group. In supermarkets and factories objective productivity measures were used. Expert evaluations of the work of research chemists and shop craftsmen were used. His assumption is that whatever leaders actually do, their success is determined by the success of the people they lead.

Fiedler measured three contingencies. The first is "leader-member relations." Simply stated, this is a measure of how well a superior and a subordinate "get along" with one another. The second is "task structure." The pilot of an airplane flying under routine conditions leads a crew with a highly structured task. What is to be done, how, by whom, and in what order are known to all the crew members. By contrast, a college students affairs committee has an unstructured task. There is no clear set of procedures to be followed. The committee must decide what jobs they will take on, who will do what, when, and how.

A third kind of contingency is the power position of the leader vis-à-vis the other members of the group. A foreman who has complete control over hiring and firing of a nonunion shop during a recession has an extremely high power position. If jobs become available in other places, his or her power position is reduced. If the shop unionizes, the power position of the foreman is reduced. College professors usually have much less power over students than employees, but if a student is dependent upon the recommendation of a well-known professor for a job, that professor's power position may be higher than many employers. The head of a voluntary association or committee has relatively little power over workers for that association.

According to Fiedler, there is no one "best" style of supervision. Rather the best style (the most effective) is dependent upon the mix of contingent variables. Fiedler arranged the three contingency variables along a single continuum of eight cells which he calls "favorableness for leadership" (see Figure 8.2). The most favorable situation is one in which member-leader relations are good, the task is highly structured, and the leader has power over subordinates. Under this highly favorable condition Fiedler's theory predicts that the most effective leader is the one who is concerned with production. The least favorable situation is one in which the leader has poor relationship with subordinates, low task structure, and little power. Under these conditions, the most effective leader is also concerned with production.

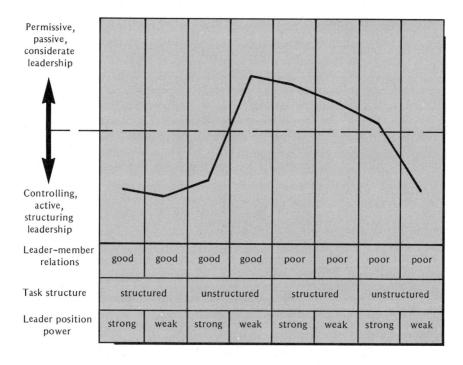

FIGURE 8.2
The Style of Effective Leadership Varies with the Situation
(From Fred E. Fielder. "Fit the Job to Fit the Manager."
Harvard Business Review 43 [1965]: 115–22.)

At moderate levels of favorableness, however, the effective leaders are those who are concerned with people. For example, if (1) leader-member relations are good, but (2) the task is not well structured, and (3) the leader's power position is low, the leader who shows concern for the people rather than driving for task accomplishment is more effective. The chairperson of a student affairs committee, for example, might find himself in such a position. He would be showing concern for the people, using his good relationship with them, in order to secure their commitment to a task which is ambiguous and where he has no authority to force their participation.

Another moderate situation is where the relationship between a leader and members is poor but the task is highly structured and the leader's position is high. In this instance also, the more effective leaders are concerned primarily with people rather than production. The fore-man on an assembly line might find himself or herself in such a position. The assembly line regulates the flow of work so that the task is highly structured. The foreman is the sole supervisor of the workers, giving that foreman a high amount of power over the workers (if they desire to keep their jobs). If the relationship between foreman and workers is a poor one, then the best foremen in such a position are those with high LPC, that is, those who evaluate their least preferred subordinate rather well. According to Fiedler, in such situations, the foreman had best attend to the workers—show concern for workers. Fiedler illustrates the predictions of contingency theory with Figure 8.2.

Fiedler suggests that training leaders to be either high LPC or low LPC according to what job conditions require is not very effective. Instead, he contends that organizations should either choose personnel to fit the job or engineer the job to fit the behavioral tendencies of the person filling the role. He calls this principle "organization engineering."

The "concern" which influences the relationship between a superior and a subordinate is not the concern they only "feel." It is the concern that one communicates to the other. Katz, in interpreting data about leader style and productivity, emphasizes this point:

> Supervisors who have actually achieved high levels of productivity have done so in part by making such behavior on the part of the employee a path to supervisory approval and a condition for the exertion of supervisory influence. For example, among employees in a tractor factory, those in the high-producing groups were more likely to say that their foreman considered high productivity one of the most important things on the job. Employees in low-producing groups more often said that other things were equally or more important to their foreman. The implication of such a finding is that the high-producing supervisor not only wants to attain high productivity but has successfully communicated to his

employees that at least one of the paths to supervisory approval is to produce at a high rate.[14]

The amount of concern supervisors and subordinates have for one
another and for the task cannot be easily isolated in specific instances of
communication. Concern is best communicated through metamessages.
Does the supervisor acknowledge suggestions made by subordinates?
If so, does he or she do so promptly? When the subordinate is talking,
is the supervisor looking at the subordinate or doodling or doing something else which detracts some attention? If the unit falls behind in
production, does the supervisor overlook it as long as possible or does
he or she talk to the subordinates about it? If he does not take notice
at all, the subordinates may decide that he is not concerned about production. Do subtle signs of approval (smiles, nods, "good work") go to
those who are high producers, or does a supervisor appear to give approval to both productive and nonproductive workers in about the same
quality and amount? Concern is communicated through very subtle
forms, but as Katz points out, it is communicated to subordinates.
Arthur Turner's investigation of "what makes a 'good' foreman" emphasizes the importance of how a supervisor communicates concern for
subordinates and for production. Turner quotes one autoworker:

> The average foreman in that plant is an "I-know-it-all-guy." We've had
> foremen that realize that they never were on the motor line, and they'll
> talk it over with you, but that is one in every 100. . . . [My present fore-
> man] don't know how to approach the men, don't know how to talk with
> them. He's got the attitude of an I-know-it-all-guy. . . . It shows up in
> the quality of the work. If he's a pretty good guy, you try to protect his
> job, or you try to do it a little better.[15]

The way in which we talk with others provides them with metamessages
about our concerns.

Clarity

Subordinates are dependent upon the approval of superiors for the work
they do. If they do not understand what the supervisor wants from
them, they are likely to be frustrated. This suggests that communication
between superiors and subordinates needs to be clear if their relationship is to be good. One way to increase clarity is to have observable
indicators of the meaning of important symbols. In deciding on what
grounds a subordinate is to be evaluated, superiors and subordinates
may strive to construct observable indicators of satisfactory subordinate
performance. This approach is basic to the managerial strategy usually
called "management by objectives." The management of people is in

terms of specific objectives; subordinates may choose how to achieve the agreed upon objectives. Meyer, Kay, and French have found that performance appraisal is associated with improved performance of subordinates only when it is based on observable objectives for measuring performance.[16] Such findings seem to suggest that clear references for "subordinate performance" lead to good superior-subordinate relationships in cases where the measure of the relationship is the performance of the subordinate.

However, many jobs are difficult to describe in observable terms. To be successful, the employee must do many jobs which are relatively nonmeasurable. For superiors and subordinates to communicate successfully about what is expected, each must have some idea of how the other sees the job. As we saw in the preceding section, they must co-orient about the nature of the job and successful performance of it. Drucker, in describing successful managers, described the general process of coorientation, though he did not use that term:

> The third thing I'd say managers need is probably communication skill—but I don't mean that. It is very largely a realization that unless they take responsibility for making themselves understood they won't be. It is not primarily a matter of skill. It is primarily a matter of being willing to see who needs to know—and have I really told him. It is an understanding of organization, what a human group really is rather than communication skill. . . . It is organizational responsibility—that's what it is.[17]

The important part of what Drucker is saying is his implication that the successful communicator in a manager's position attempts to find out what subordinates need to know from their perspective. He or she does not just tell them what they need to know from the manager's perspective. No communication is clear to everyone who may hear or see it. A philosophical treatise may be perfectly clear to some scholars and be absolutely incomprehensible to most of the world. Clear communications between supervisors and subordinates are those which meet the informational needs of both parties. That means that each party must take the responsibility to find out what the informational needs of the other are and must determine how particular communications are received by the other. This means communicating in such a way that each is revealing how he or she is interpreting messages.

Seen from this perspective, clarity is not a characteristic of the message itself. There are no messages which are necessarily "clear" to everyone. Clarity is an outcome of a communication process in which communicators actively seek information about how others are interpreting messages. The key term here is "actively seeking." Drucker uses the expression "responsibility." Communication between supervisors and subordinates becomes clear when coorientation is taking place in the sense that both are attending to what the other needs to know (from the other's perspective) and what the other is being told (from the other's perspective). Communication is not likely to be clear when one or both people assume that if they have said it (or written it), the message will be understood. Neither is there a guarantee of clarity if a message is "clear" to one person.

Contradiction

Obviously if one person is sending contradictory messages, the intent of those messages cannot be clear. Contradiction in explicit messages is not the only problem. A more vicious problem lies in the contradiction between the explicit message and the implicit message or metamessage. A typical contradiction of this kind is when a person is assigned a certain job, but not given the resources to do the job. The job description says, "do it"; the message implicit in the resources made available to the person is, "don't do it." One of the classic descriptions of the problem of contradiction is Fritz Roethlisberger's "The Foreman: Master and Victim of Double Talk." Many of the problems encountered by foremen are similar to those faced by all subordinates.

> The crux of the foreman's problem is that he is constantly faced with a dilemma of (1) having to keep his superior informed with what is happening at the work level (in many cases so that his superior may prepare in turn for the unfavorable reaction of his superior and so on up the line) and (2) needing to communicate his information in such a way that it does not bring unfavorable criticism on himself for not doing his job correctly or adequately. Discrepancies between the way things are at the work level and the way they are represented to be by management cannot be overlooked, and yet the foreman feels obliged to overlook them when talking to his boss. This makes the foreman's job particularly "tough" and encourages him to talk out of both sides of his mouth at the same time—to become a master of double talk.[18]

Thus, contradiction in the foreman's position also results from the metamessages of responsibility and authority. Foremen are told to get results—turn out production, maintain quality, hold costs down, keep their employees satisfied—yet they cannot hire or fire employees, set production standards, transfer employees, adjust wage inequalities, promote deserving men, develop better machines, methods, or products, or plan the work of their departments. At one level the message is, "produce," at another level the organization says, "do not produce" by making it impossible for them to do what they have been told to do.

In order to learn to play their many roles ("manager, cost accountant, engineer, lawyer, teacher, leader, inspector, disciplinarian, counselor, friend, and above all, example") foremen are sent to training sessions. The message here would seem to be that they should use what they learn. That is not the only message, however. Typically the foreman "is worried in particular by what the boss will think if he takes the time to do the many things his many training courses tell him to do. And in 99 cases out of 100 what the boss thinks, or what the foreman thinks the boss thinks, will determine what the foreman does. . . . For the most part, he does his best to perform by hook or by crook the one function clearly left him, the one function for which there is no definite staff counterpart, . . . namely getting the workers to turn the work out on time." Here again is a contradiction between the implicit message of the formal structure (in providing training courses) and the implicit or explicit messages of the superior which make it impossible for the foreman to do what he has learned.

Communication between supervisors and subordinates is not solely a function of the skills and intentions of the people. It is greatly influenced by the formal structure. This formal structure acts as a source of metamessages which individuals take into account when communicating. The formal structure which puts a superior in charge of evaluating a subordinate's performance is in effect "saying" to the subordinate that he should not communicate information which would reflect negatively on his performance. At the same time it says that the superior needs accurate information about how well the organization is functioning. A supervisor may say to subordinates that his or her "door is open" for them to come in and discuss personal or organizational problems. But if the superior receives urgent telephone calls every ten minutes and is otherwise loaded with information which requires immediate processing, the metamessage will contradict the explicit message that "my door is open."

MOTIVE ASSUMPTIONS IN SUPERVISORY RELATIONSHIPS

The process of communication between a supervisor and a subordinate is "coorientation." Because of the necessity of doing common work, the differential authority which one person has over another, and the inevitably different perspectives of each party, problems of concern, clarity, and contraction characterize communication in supervisory pairs. Another way of understanding communication between supervisors and subordinates is to understand the taken-for-granted assumptions about why the relationship exists or, why people assume that they are communicating with one another. Let us examine three common motive assumptions underlying communication and their influence in supervisory relationships.

Survival

Supervisors and subordinates are thrown together by virtue of their organizational roles. They must exchange some kinds of information. Each person may be doing no more than going through the routine of talking. Each may just be trying to "get through the day" with a minimum of hassle or threat. Each person's assumption about the motive of the talk is "survival."

When there is no threat, the communication between supervisors and subordinates may be characterized as "phatic" communication. This is ritual-like communication such as "Hello," "Nice day today," etc. The talk may serve important functions of defining the situation and structuring time so that there is at least some interest in the job. A retired chief engineer of an ocean freighter described his interactions with subordinates: "They knew what to do. I didn't have to tell them. I talked to them because I'd have gone crazy if I didn't talk to somebody. They were my friends." The chief engineer on a three-month ocean voyage has special "survival" needs that a factory foreman does not have. Nevertheless, everybody "needs" to talk. Some people like to talk more than others. Some of the communication between superior and subordinates can be explained by a need to talk. In other cases the topics of conversation can be explained as having "survival" value within the organization. Students who eagerly volunteer answers in class are trying to "survive" in the relationship with the teacher (and hence the organization).

When "survival" becomes problematic for members of an organization, then the talk may become more than "routine" or "phatic." When a subordinate is threatened with dismissal, or when a supervisor's supervisor threatens him or her with dismissal, then talk between supervisors and subordinates may be based on survival assumptions, but may not be routine. It may become what Jack Gibb has termed "defensive." He states:

> Defensive behavior is defined as that behavior which occurs when an individual perceives threat or anticipates threat in the group. The person who behaves defensively, even though he also gives some attention to the common task, devotes an appreciable portion of his energy to defending himself. Besides talking about the topic, he thinks about how he appears to others, how he may be seen more favorably, how he may win, dominate, impress, or escape punishment and/or how he may avoid or mitigate a perceived or an anticipated attack.[19]

Defensive communication is a kind of planned communication, but the planned goal is not a healthy one. Gibb examined tape recorded discussions of groups operating on defensive motive assumptions. In such groups, the talk was evaluative. Expression, manner of speech, tone of voice, and verbal content were used by people to evaluate one another. People reacted by blaming one another for problems, fitting each other into categories of good or bad, making moral judgments of each other, and questioning others' values and motives. When people are planning their attacks on others or their own defense, they have difficulty in concentrating on one another's messages. One result, of course, is personal discomfort. The overall functioning of the groups becomes inefficient because members devote their attention to themselves instead of to the common task.

The implication of Gibb's findings for supervisory relationships is fairly straightforward. Personal threat must be minimized if collective work is to be accomplished efficiently. The metacommunicational cues of the situation (such as that the supervisor is responsible for evaluating the subordinate's performance) constrain both to think of the relationship as a threatening one. Therefore, the talk itself should include a minimum amount of threat-provoking content. This means avoiding evaluation and claims of superiority in particular.

Influence

The most obvious reason why supervisors and subordinates talk to one another is to "influence." Supervisors and subordinates talk so that supervisors may influence what subordinates do. Early researchers in the area of leadership accepted this as the taken-for-granted assumption about motives for talk in supervisory pairs. They directed their research to finding ways of maximizing the influence of the supervisor on the subordinates. For them, as for many supervisors, "successful communication" must be judged by the extent to which subordinates do what the superior wants them to do. An analysis of training manuals developed by organizations to teach employees leadership skills recently revealed that many training directors still assume that the reason for talk between supervisors and subordinates is one-way influence. The manuals expressly taught supervisors ways to talk so as to influence subordinates.[20]

More recently, leadership researchers have emphasized that it is important for formal leaders to be influenced by their subordinates. This view is called "reciprocal influence." Hollander and Julian, for example, write:

> Because leadership embodies a two-way influence relationship, recipients of influence assertions may respond by asserting influence in return, that

is, by making demands on the leader. The very sustenance of the relationship depends upon some yielding to influence on both sides. As Homans put it, "influence over others is purchased at the price of allowing one's self to be influenced by others [p. 286]." . . . By granting esteem itself, or symbolic manifestations of it, one may in turn activate leadership, in terms of a person taking on the leader role."[21]

Communications which have influence as the underlying motive assumption have an "ulterior" quality to them. Each person is planning his or her communication with the hope of achieving some predetermined goal. This is not necessarily undesirable. If a leader is giving precise instructions, he or she should plan exactly what to say and how. If he "plays it by ear," he may leave out important details. But if the supervisor does not have adequate information to solve a problem, then "influence" assumptions are inappropriate to the situation.

Problem Solving

A third kind of expectation about why supervisors and subordinates talk is "problem solving." In situations where the assumption is "influence," the two people expect that the supervisor "owns" the problem and all the information to solve the problem. The supervisor decides on a solution and then "sells" the solution to subordinates. When "problem solving" is the motive assumption of their communication, both parties view the problem as their own. A slow assembly line is not the "super's problem"; it is everybody's problem. The supervisor does not have all the information needed to speed up the line. Rather, information about causes and cures for the slow line is distributed among supervisor and subordinates. Successful communication occurs when they share their information, concur on a diagnosis, and jointly plan for a remedy.

Chris Argyris describes the need for talk which he calls "experimenting." He says that experimenting is one of the rarest kinds of behavior among executives.[22] "Experimenting with feelings" talk is exemplified by the statement, "This is not easy for me to talk about. I feel my whole life has been a shambles."[23] An example of "experimenting with ideas" talk is, "Could we try this out for a few days before we evaluate it?" Experimenting talk carries with it the intentional meaning "I don't know." It is rare in supervisor-subordinate relationships because the supervisor is expected to know. Experimenting may be interpreted as a sign of weakness or poor job performance. But the first step toward learning together is knowing what each other does not know.

There is no one kind of assumption (and consequently talk) which is best. Survival talk can be as desirable as "phatic" communication, or as undesirable as "defensiveness." Influence talk can be as desirable as "leadership" or as undesirable as "manipulation." Problem solving can be as desirable as "experimentation" or as undesirable as "floundering." Part of the difference is the attitudes of the people involved. The more people are attempting to keep their concern for production and for people balanced, the more likely talk is to be desirable, whether it is based on assumptions of survival, influence, or problem solving. The more people are actively trying to be clear, the more desirable their communication is likely to be. The less communication is characterized by contradictions between report messages and metamessages, the more desirable the talk is likely to be.

One cannot determine how desirable or successful communication is solely on the basis of the attitudes of the communicators. Successful communication must be adapted to the situation. In situations where the coordination is largely routine, the most desirable kind of assumption is likely to be survival. Here, phatic communication provides a definition of the routine situation. People enjoy one another's company. There is neither change nor need for change. Communication is efficient, if unexciting. Where there is a moderate level of uncertainty, contingency theorists such as James Thompson predict that integration will be based on plans.[24] This suggests that in moderately innovative conditions influence is the appropriate assumption about why people are communicating. Supervisors are attempting to influence subordinates to act in accordance with the organization's plan. Subordinates are communicating in order to influence the construction of the organization's plan. In situations where there is a great amount of organizational uncertainty, problem solving is the appropriate assumption. In such situations no one knows what is best. Therefore, people can best deal with their situation when they admit that they do not know. The best guess is likely to be the result of collaboration. It is an attitude of "I don't have all the answers, and you don't have all the answers, let's see what kind of answers we can come up with together."

Communication problems can occur when people are making inappropriate assumptions about why they are communicating. In routine situations if people attempt to "problem solve," they are likely to be frustrated by the lack of problems to solve. Their efforts may result in inventing more problems than they "solve." Likewise, if they are so concerned with defending their own survival that they cannot attend to problems of coordination, the coordinated activity may not "survive." Successful communication between supervisors and subordinates in part depends upon communicators having assumptions which are appropriate to their situation.

Successful communication also depends upon a state of consensus on motive assumptions. Consider, for example, the subordinate who needs direction in his work. In effect he comes to an interaction with his supervisor expecting to be influenced. If the supervisor does not understand this, the supervisor may just be attending to his own survival. He may fail, therefore, to give the subordinate the direction he needs. The two are in a nonreciprocal or nonconsensus state with regard to intentions. See Figure 8.3.

In another case a subordinate may seek a supervisor's help for a work-related problem, expecting that she will still have some say in how the problem is resolved. She is thus intending to engage in "problem-solving" communication. The supervisor may mistake her request for assistance for a request for direction. The supervisor may then instruct her in what to do. Thus, the supervisor is acting as if the communication intention is one of influence. The subordinate may be angry with the supervisor for "taking over." If the subordinate chooses to ignore what the supervisor has said, the supervisor may become angry with her for asking for directions and then ignoring them.

In these two cases there is lack of agreement on the social formula of the situation. The best communication would occur if the two parties could agree on intentions underlying the interaction, but even without agreement, if they had a state of "understanding," the interaction could be improved. If the subordinate in the case above understood that her supervisor was operating on an assumption of influence, then she could take this intention into account in her interpretation of the supervisor's actions. A state of agreement between supervisors and subordinates on expectations is desirable, but a state of understanding is essential.

I have discussed situations and consensus separately here, but of course "situations" are defined through coorientation. Situational defi-

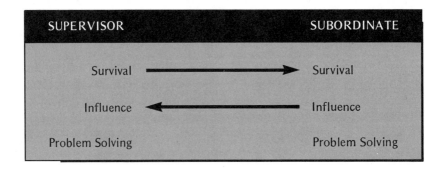

FIGURE 8.3
Nonconsensus of Motive Assumptions

nitions represent consensus of communicators. This is particularly true in informal relationships. By their actions, two friends may make their mutual situation routine or highly uncertain. Their "environment" is not given, but created through their interaction. The greater the degree of formalization, however, the less communicators create their own environment. Assembly-line workers are limited in the extent to which they can define their situation as novel. The point here is that consensus on motive assumptions and situational appropriateness of motive assumptions both influence communication. And to some extent they influence each other. In particular, the "situation" is not a feature which exists outside a relationship. The definition of a situation is in part the creation of the communicators' actions.

COMMUNICATION ACROSS ORGANIZATIONAL SPECIALIZATION

Each position in an organization is linked with several other positions. The linking of two roles—a pair of roles—is called a "role set." For example, a superior and a subordinate together constitute one role set. Lower level employees may have formalized interpersonal relationships only with their immediate supervisors. They may have interpersonal relationships with any number of "friends" in the organization, but have no formalized relationships with them on the organization chart. Conversely, all employees are formally related to the chief executive of the organization, but the only direct communication they have with him or her may be policy announcements and the "President's Message" in the organization's newsletter. Thus, they have no interpersonal relationship with the chief executive.

Organizational members from the foreman to the president are in "role sets" with a number of people throughout the organization. Wickesberg, for example, found that 80 percent of manager contacts were outside their immediate organizational unit. Eighty-five percent of nonmanager contacts were outside their unit.[25] A foreman, for example, engages in official face-to-face communications with union representatives, industrial engineers, personnel directors, and other foremen. These people are doing other *kinds* of jobs. Their work environments are different. Their perspective on the organizations and organizational priorities is different. Yet for them to do their jobs, they must communicate with one another. They must, in short, communicate across the differentiation or departmentalization of the organization. In this section I describe some of the differences among managers which derive from the formal structure and have an impact on the possibilities for their interpersonal communication.

Differences in Orientation

Lawrence and Lorsch define differentiation as "the difference in cognitive and emotional orientation among managers in different functional departments."[26] In particular, their research pointed to three differences in cognitive and emotional orientation: goal orientation, time orientation, and interpersonal orientation. In addition, they investigated a fourth kind of differentiation among units—formality of organization structure.

Lawrence and Lorsch posit a contingency theory in which there is no single set of principles or structure which is best for all organizations or for all units within a single organization. Rather, organizations are "complex" because they make differentiated responses to their complex environments. In one study, they examined six organizations in the plastics industry. They were interested in the differentiation among four departments in each of these organizations: sales, production, applied research, and basic research.

Each of these departments dealt with a different kind of environment. The scientific environments of the research divisions were extremely uncertain. As one research manager said, "The development of plastics is more of an art than a science. We don't fully understand what is needed to meet a customer's requirements, and if we do, we don't know how to process it." The environment of the sales division was somewhat more certain (there were specific customer orders to be filled) but there was a good deal of uncertainty about how to generate new orders. Moreover, the markets were numerous. As one sales manager put it, "We have a hundred markets each different in requirements because of the customers' processing needs." By contrast, "environment" of the production units was fairly certain.[27] Cost, time, chemical compositions were known by the time the product design reached the production stage. One production manager stated: "In production, life is really plain as it is geared to running the kind of plant and equipment which they currently have and where most of the decisions are built in.

Lawrence and Lorsch predicted that to be successful in the plastics industry an organization must be organized to allow each functional division (research, sales, production) to make an appropriate kind of response to its environment. Each unit should have a different kind of formal structure. Along with the differences in formal structure there should be differences in the manager's orientation toward goals of the division and the organization, toward time, and toward what kind of interpersonal relationships are useful in work organizations. They found consistent evidence of the differences in orientation. Let us examine the differences and consider how they might influence the potential for communication among managers of different divisions.

Orientation Toward Formalization. The researchers analyzed organizational manuals and charts and interviewed managers for data about the formal structuring of each department. They found that, as expected, the production units had the most rigid formal structures. They had more levels of managerial hierarchy. They had a higher ratio of supervisors to subordinates, suggesting the probability of closer supervision by the supervisors. They had more frequent and more specific reviews of performance by the managers and of the managers. They relied more on formal rules and procedures than did sales or research departments.

By contrast, the basic research departments, which dealt with the uncertain environments, had least reliance on formal structure. The span of control by supervisors was large; that is, each supervisor had a large number of persons reporting to him or her so that close supervision was impossible. The managerial hierarchy was relatively "flat"; there were few levels. Performance reviews were infrequent and general. There seemed to be little reliance on written regulations for guidance in how to do particular jobs. The applied research departments and the sales departments fell between these two extremes. They dealt with moderate levels of uncertainty and were organized by a moderately rigid formal structure.

Consider the possibilities for communication when managers from different departments come together to discuss mutual problems. The production managers, for example, must meet with the applied research managers in order to discuss the production of new products. The production managers are seeking exact information about manpower requirements. They need this information in order to write exact procedures for their workers. The applied research managers cannot fully comprehend the importance which these written procedures have for the production people because they do not work much with such documents. Similarly, if the production managers are unhappy with the work being done by sales personnel, they may attribute the blame to the "sloppy" managerial techniques used by sales managers. They may believe that sales managers let their subordinates do whatever they want to do with too little direction. Each kind of manager lives in a world which is structured somewhat differently than the others. The way they produce their own work is different. Managers tend to see their division's way as "natural." The "best" way to work is the way which works best in their division. If other divisions do not work that same way, they are at least suspect of working the wrong way. When deciding how to solve problems, each will try to get others to do things the way which works best in his or her department.

Time Orientation. The way the work is structured and the amount of uncertainty in the environment of different departments leads managers to have different orientations toward time. The researchers measured time orientation by asking managers "how much of their time was devoted to activities that contributed to company profits in different future time periods—one month or less; one to three months; three months to one year; and one year or longer."[28] The managers' answers confirmed their hypotheses that managers in production and sales were most concerned about short-range problems, often less than one month. Those in the research departments were concerned with problems often several years in the future.

Differences in time orientation interfere with communication among managers in different departments. When production managers complain to research managers about problems occurring right now, the research managers may be unable to see that the problems are serious unless they appear likely to continue to be problems for a year or more. For the researcher, the real problems are the long-range problems. For the production or sales managers, the future problems belong to the future. They must take care of what is happening in the present and what is likely to happen in the next few days or weeks.

Interpersonal Orientation. Perhaps most critical to the communication among managers in different units are differences in orientation toward interpersonal relationships. Building on the research of Fred Fiedler (described in the previous section), Lawrence and Lorsch predicted that "members of different departments would find it necessary, if they were to be effective, to develop different interpersonal orientations related to the nature of their task. Earlier research had suggested that members of units engaged in either highly certain or highly uncertain tasks would develop task-oriented interpersonal styles. Members of units with moderately uncertain tasks would develop relationship-oriented styles."[29] Production managers, dealing with certain tasks, would prefer to concentrate on the tasks and believe that interpersonal relationships are not particularly important to how well they do their job. Basic research scientists dealing with highly uncertain tasks were also predicted to care very little about maintaining good interpersonal relationships and to confine their contacts to task matters. Between these two extremes, the applied research division managers and the sales managers were expected to believe that maintaining good interpersonal relationships is very important to accomplishing work.

The researchers measured interpersonal orientation with a questionnaire which asked about the managers' preference for relationship-oriented or task-oriented interactions. Their data confirmed their predictions. For example, the managers of production and to a somewhat lesser degree the managers of research divisions indicated that when they found it "difficult to work with a particular colleague, their attitude was to get on with the job without special regard to maintaining positive relationships."[30]

Consider interdepartmental meetings with managers of all four kinds of units. The production managers will push for concern only with the immediate job at hand. They will be bored or annoyed by the sales managers' attempts to build closer interpersonal relationships. At the same time the fundamental research managers will be annoyed by both the sales managers' interpersonal talk and the production managers' myopic views that the only problems to be discussed are those which are occurring right now. They will want to discuss "real" (as opposed to "people") problems, but will want the group to look at problems from a larger perspective than the here and now. The managers from the applied research departments are likely to agree with their basic research colleagues that they must look to the future of the organization but are more likely to emphasize maintaining good interpersonal relationships as a principal means of preventing future problems. These descriptions are, of course, caricatures. Any individual manager may not fit these stereotypes. But these are the orientations which the formal differentiation of the organization encourages.

Goal Orientation. Like other researchers, Lawrence and Lorsch found that managers in different departments had different goal orientations. Differences in goal orientation are related not to differences in uncertainty, but to the fact that the different managers were pursuing different kinds of goals. "If these managers were to be effective in doing their specialized tasks, they must focus their attention clearly on objectives and goals directly related to them."[31] They found that, indeed, sales managers were primarily concerned with customer problems, competitive activities, and other events of the market place." Manufacturing personnel were concerned with cost reduction and process efficiency. Research scientists were concerned with technological improvements related to cost reduction and quality control. This surprised the researchers at first; later they realized that this was not too surprising because the research divisions were interested in long-run improvements in the manufacturing process.

When managers from different divisions come together to discuss organizational problems and organizational goals, they tend to find solutions which are related to their own goal orientations. Thus, researchers have found that when presented with case studies in which the "problem" facing an organization is presented in relatively ambiguous terms, the sales personnel define the problem as a sales problem, production people see it as a production problem, personnel staff describe it as a people problem (see description of research in chapter 6).

Although differentiation causes conflict orientations among managers, this conflict in itself is not detrimental to the organization. Quite the contrary, Lawrence and Lorsch's research indicates that differentiation within an organization is fundamental to a successful organization. To attempt to reduce differentiation in order to prevent these conflicts would be in effect "throwing out the baby with the bathwater." However, conflicts among managers may prevent the possibility of integrating the organization so that it functions as a single unit. Organizations need both differentiation and integration.

Communication as Conflict Resolution

One way to achieve integration among differentiated units is through design of the organization so that there are conflict resolvers to integrate. Integration as a design concept is discussed in chapter 9. Creating formal structures for integration is not enough, however. Conflict arises at an interpersonal level among people of differentiated units. It must be at least partially resolved at that level. Lawrence and Lorsch put it this way:

> When people live day in and day out in a specialized role, they tend to see their environment in terms of that role. The more personally involved in their jobs they become, the more this is true. Such involvement leads them to personalize the conflicts that arise with representatives of other organizational units. Of course they know logically that an organization needs different kinds of specialists, but they forget the full meaning of this when they run into a particular person who is "impossible to work with." Then they all too readily turn to an explanation based on personality traits that writes off the individual as an oddball and justifies their own withdrawal from or forcing of the conflict.[32]

One approach they offer to mediating the undesirable effects of differentiation is through personnel training. "Training cannot erase the basic antagonism between differentiation and integration, but it can relax the tension somewhat." Trainers could describe the theory of differentiation and integration and present some of the research findings which suggest the necessity for differentiation. Managers could be taught to understand, at least on a verbal level, that differentiation naturally leads to differences in orientation. The organizational structure and managerial style which works best in one department will not work best in another. The idea of this training is to legitimate differences between departments.

The kind of training suggested by Lawrence and Lorsch is what I have been describing as "coorientation." They state: "As various specialists sit together and exchange firsthand information about their respective ways of working, the insights begin to appear. . . . The marketing managers are surprised to learn that an offhand response to a question from a basic researcher about the market potential of an idea might start the latter off on a six-month inquiry." In other words, through such exchanges, people are describing how they respond to objects (ideas, people, etc.) in their common situation. The researcher tells the marketing manager, "Here is what your remark meant to me." ("Here is what I did because of your remark.") The marketing manager replies with, "Here is what my remark meant to me; I did not realize that it meant that to you." In the future, each person is more likely to be able to see their situation not simply from their own perspective, but to take the role of the other and imagine how the other might be seeing the situation. There will still be differences in goals, time concerns, and interpersonal styles, but at least there is the possibility for mediation of differences through understanding or coorientation.

SUMMARY

In this chapter I have discussed the communication process through which formal relationships become human relationships. In particular I have described some of the ways the formal structure of hierarchy and specialization influences interpersonal communication.

Even when people are communicating personally with one another, the documented expectations influence meaning and expectations. Formal rules, roles, agendas, and goals act as metamessages which individuals take in account. Organizational documents give formalized relationships an existence "beyond" the personal talk which goes on. It also makes possible relationships between people who never—or almost never—talk directly to one another. In such relationships, message forms such as language, stationery, speed of response become very important as clues about what is intended by a message.

In the relationship between a supervisor and a subordinate, the hierarchy of an organization takes on life. The process of developing expectations between supervisors and subordinates is coorientation. There is evidence of considerable disagreement within supervisory pairs about important issues in their work situation. Such disagreements are inevitable in role divisions. For the most part, they are necessary if supervisors are to perform their organizational role and subordinates are to perform theirs.

Disagreement about expectations may be undesirable, for expectations are the basis for organizing. Even more serious is a lack of understanding in which a subordinate does not know what a supervisor expects of him and vice versa. If each member of a supervisory pair believes he or she understands what the other expects, but in fact each does not, then severe problems in coordination may result.

Three problems which almost inevitably plague supervisory relationships are: concern, clarity, and contradiction. Empirical research on leadership indicates that successful supervisors are perceived as being concerned about both production and people. Fiedler's research indicates that supervisors need not be simultaneously concerned with both production and people, but that their concern for production or people must be appropriate to the situation.

Supervisors' and subordinates' taken-for-granted assumptions about why they are communicating must likewise be appropriate for their situation. In routine situations, survival intentions may be appropriate. People attempting to survive may simply be improvising their talk. If they perceive the situation as threatening, they may respond with defensive communication. In situations with some uncertainty, "influence" may be the appropriate taken-for-granted intention. People are planning their interactions. The result may be a desirable mutual influence situation or an undesirable exploitative one. In highly uncertain environments, the most appropriate motive assumption is "problem solving." People are engaged in sharing information to build collective decisions.

Not only must people have assumptions which are "appropriate" to their situation, they also must have consensus on the assumptions of their interaction. When communicators are operating on different assumptions and especially when there is little understanding of one another's intentions, problems are likely to occur.

Specialized roles, like hierarchical roles, inevitably create communicative problems. Research by Lawrence and Lorsch identified four differences in orientation among different units of an organization. These differences were: formalization, time orientation, interpersonal orientation, and goal orientation. Communication between people across lines of organizational specialty is difficult because people do not understand the orientations of others. Training people to improve communication across specialization largely involves helping them to appreciate the perspective which is "natural" in other units. Thus, it is aimed at improving people's ability to coorient.

ENDNOTES

1. William M. Jones, *On Decision-Making in Large Organizations* (Santa Monica, Calif.: The Rand Corp., 1964).

2. Larry Spence and Robert O'Connor, *Communication Disturbances and Their Consequences: Information Flow in the Welfare Delivery Systems of the Pennsylvania Department of Public Welfare* (University Park, Pa.: College of Human Development, Pennsylvania State University, 1974), p. 4.

3. Fritz Roethlisberger, "The Foreman: Master and Victim of Double Talk," *Harvard Business Review* 23 (Spring 45): 283–298, republished in vol. 43 (Sept. 65): 22–64.

4. Harry C. Triandis, "Cognitive Similarity and Interpersonal Communication in Industry," *Journal of Applied Psychology* 43 (1959): 321–326.

5. W. H. Read, "Upward Communication in Organizational Hierarchies," *Human Relations* 15 (1962): 3–15.

6. B. B. Boyd and J. M. Jensen, "Perceptions of the First-Line Supervisor's Authority: A Study in Superior-Subordinate Communication," *Academy of Management Journal* 15 (1972): 331–342.

7. Richard Y. Farace, Hamish M. Russell, and Peter R. Monge, *Communicating . . . and Organizing* (Reading, Mass.: Addison-Wesley, 1977).

8. Hamish M. Russell, "The Importance of Coorientation Toward the Procedural Aspects of Communication: A Study of Supervisor/Subordinate Communication," mimeographed (Michigan State University, Dept. of Communication, 1972).

9. Farace, Russell, and Monge, *Communicating . . . and Organizing*.

10. J. Hemphill and A. Coons, "Development of the Leader Behavior Description Questionnaire," in R. Stoghill and A. Coons, eds., *Leader Behavior: Its Description and Measurement* (Columbus, Ohio: Bureau of Business Research, Ohio State University, 1957), pp. 6–38.

11. A. Halpin and B. Winer, "A Factional Study of the Leader's Behavior Description," in Stoghill and Coons, *Leader Behavior: Its Description and Measurement*, p. 43.

12. Ibid., p. 42.

13. W. Merrwise and F. E. Fiedler, "Leadership and Group Creativity Under Varying Degrees of Stress" (Urbana, Ill.: Group Effectiveness Research Lab, Univ. of Illinois, 1966).

14. R. L. Kahn, "Human Relations on the Shop Floor," in E. M. Hugh-Jones, ed., *Human Relations and Modern Management* (Amsterdam: North-Holland, 1958), p. 69.

15. Arthur Turner, "What Makes a 'Good' Foreman," *Personnel* (1955): 382–392.

16. Hubert H. Meyer, Emanuel Kay, and John R. French, Jr., "Split Roles in Performance Appraisal," *Harvard Business Review* 43 (1965): 123–129.

17. Peter Drucker, "Interview," in Tony H. Bonaparte and John E. Flaherty, eds., *Peter Drucker: Contributions to Business Enterprise* (New York: N.Y. University Press, 1970), p. 326.

18. Fritz Roethlisberger, "The Foreman: Master and Victim of Double Talk," reprinted in R. T. Golembiewski and Frank Gibson, *Managerial Behavior and Organizational Demands* (Chicago: Rand McNally, 1967), p. 137.

19. Jack Gibb, "Defensive Communication," *Journal of Communication* 2 (1961): 141–148.

20. Barbara A. Pilla, "Two Perspectives on Leadership," *Personnel Journal* (1976): 304–306.

21. Edwin P. Hollander and James W. Julian, "Contemporary Trends in the Analysis of Leadership Processes," *Psychological Bulletin* 71 (1969): 387–397.

22. Chris Argyris, *Management and Organizational Development* (New York: McGraw-Hill, 1971), p. 133.

23. Ibid., p. 12.

24. James Thompson, *Organizations in Action* (New York: McGraw-Hill, 1967).

25. A. K. Wickesberg, "Communication Networks in the Business Organization Structure," Academy of Management Journal (1968): 253–262.

26. Paul R. Lawrence and Jay W. Lorsch, *Organization and Environment Managing Differentiation and Integration* (Boston: Harvard University Press, 1967), p. 11.

27. Lawrence and Lorsch's use of "environment" of production units is rather unusual. The environment of the nonhuman aspects of production is often called the "production task" by others. The Lawrence and Lorsch usage is justified because: "Production executives must draw information from this equipment's performance and analyze it in terms of costs, yield, and quality, just as they must also draw information from outside the physical boundaries of the firm about newly available equipment and alternative processes. It is this information . . . we are characterizing as certain." Ibid., p. 27.

28. Ibid., p. 35.

29. Ibid., p. 33.

30. Ibid., p. 34.

31. Ibid., p. 37.

32. Ibid., p. 217.

CHAPTER
9

Decision Building in Formalized Systems

> Structuring Organizational Intelligence
> Differentiation and Information
> Structuring Formal Integration

According to Daniel Katz and Robert Kahn, "A voluntary group becomes an organization when it acquires systematic methods for regulating its activities on the basis of information about its functioning." Minimally, this information concerns members, finances, and historical records. Katz and Kahn continue, "The systematic use of information to guide organizational functioning is the sine qua non of an organization." It is what makes an organization an *organization*.[1]

The subject of this chapter is the use of information to construct organizational decisions. The framework for understanding "decisions" was discussed in chapter 6. The essence of that discussion was that decisions are not made at a single "point in time." Rather, collective decision building is a process of reducing uncertainty about what "we" shall do. It involves both constructing a set of symbols which a group of people announces as their collective decision and interpreting those symbols in action. The focus of chapter 6 was on how several people use face-to-face communication to construct a set of symbols called a decision. The emphasis was on interpersonal processes and how they are used to construct decisions. Discussed in this chapter are more formal processes of decision building. We will be concerned with organizational documents and formal systems of coordination which are used to build decisions announced in the name of the whole organization. Our two specific concerns in this chapter are the same as those in other chapters: organizational intelligence and integration.

The concern of organizational intelligence centers here on the issue of how an organization collects and stores what it calls "information." Information is collected and stored in some kind of structure. The information gathered about job applicants is "structured" on the application form. The information about how much an organization is spending is structured on a budgeting form. Decisions about how to structure information constitute part of a process of decision building. Decisions about information structures are particularly important because the people who make such decisions may have little, if any, face-to-face contact with the people who use that information. The first section, then, is directly concerned with the "intelligence issue" in organizational decision building in that it addresses the question of how the structure of information influences decision building.

The second concern of this chapter is the integration of various groups within the formalized decision-building process. The organizational decisions of interest here are intergroup decisions. They are made "collectively" by so many people that it is impractical for all of them to attempt face-to-face decision making such as that described in chapter 6. The central question here is how to create formal structures of people to maximize intelligence in organizational decision building.

An example of a formalized decision-building process is the appointment of a new person to an executive position. One crucial part of the process may be the deliberations of a "search committee" appointed for the purpose of screening candidates and recommending a few names. The interaction among members of the search committee is face-to-face decision building of the kind described in chapter 6. The members of the committee have some knowledge of the skills required for the position. They discuss some of these skills as criteria for selecting their candidate, but some other skills are simply assumed without discussion to be criteria. A number of such a committee recently told me that he found it difficult to explain many of the selection criteria used by his committee. "We all know what we need," he said, "and we each know that the others also know."

Face-to-face groups can operate on some unstated assumptions about criteria and information because through their talk with one another they come to know each other pretty well. People making collective decisions in face-to-face groups usually develop interpersonal trust in one another so that many issues do not need to be discussed. Through face-to-face communication people develop equivalent cognitive maps relevant to their decisions. Because of this equivalency, it is unnecessary to discuss everything of concern. If the results of the committee's deliberation concerned only the members of that committee, criteria could be left largely understood or unstated. If the members are satisfied with the decision itself, the procedures by which information is gathered and processed (the process of creating the group's intelligence) may be irrelevant to anyone outside the group.

In formal organizations there are frequently "rational" procedures for making decisions which affect the whole organization. These are formal or documented procedures. The reasons are easy to understand. There is usually more "stake" in the collective decisions made in the name of formal organizations. The results of a bad decision such as appointment of an unqualified executive can be very costly. Therefore, for many organizational decisions it is worth spending several weeks or months collecting information and weighing alternatives. Formal organizations establish regular procedures for gathering and transmitting information about costs and consequences.

Personal decisions may be judged by the satisfaction of the decision maker. Small group decisions likewise may be judged by the satisfaction of members with the decisions, but when decisions are made in the name of a formalized organization, the decisions must be judged by more than the psychological satisfaction of the decision makers. This means that there must be formal standards for judging the quality of decisions.

In informal or face-to-face groups such standards may be unstated. Members of face-to-face groups come to trust one another because they communicate directly and therefore have opportunities to see each others' values. In formal organizations, decision building is not limited to face-to-face processes. Therefore, there must be a substitute for the trust which develops through face-to-face contact. Collective decisions in formal organizations are usually judged against how well they promote the documented objectives of the organization as well as how closely the process followed the prescribed agenda or procedures.

There is, of course, face-to-face communication in any organizational decision. Face-to-face groups are often charged with "making" decisions in the name of a formal organization. But such groups do not, in fact, "make" decisions. Rather, the face-to-face deliberations of such groups are but part of the communications which build the organizational decision. This is true because, for example, a group bases its decision on information it receives from others in the organization. This information reflects decisions made by others about what is relevant and useful to record and transmit.

The search committee I spoke of above illustrates decisionbuilding by a face-to-face group at a middle level of formal hierarchy. An upper level manager charges the search committee with the responsibility for recommending candidates for an executive position. The committee reports its recommendations to the manager. He, in turn, is charged with the responsibility for making the decision by the president of the organization. The people on the search committee were selected from members of the department that the new executive will head. The search committee has no face-to-face contact with the president. Members of the committee have relatively little face-to-face contact with the upper-level manager and with the other members of the department.

Much of the information about candidates is from letters of recommendation. Typically such letters are written by people no member of the committee has ever met. The members of the committee talk face-to-face, but the process of selecting a new executive extends beyond the committee. The committee must evaluate information given to them in written form by strangers. Since there is no basis for interpersonal trust with strangers, the committee must have formal procedures for evaluating this information. The committee must justify its recommendation to outsiders. The less face-to-face contact members of the committee have with "outsiders"—such as managers and department members—the more they must document their procedures so that the outsiders can judge those procedures for themselves.

Formality or documented procedure is the substitute for interpersonal trust in social systems where the process of collective decision building involves so many people that face-to-face communication is impossible. Thus, the procedure serve both "intelligence" and "integrative" functions. In the section below I describe some structures and procedures associated with formal or organizational decision building. The general question of concern is one of "intelligence": How does the form or structure of information influence decisions based on that information? Two ways of organizing data are illustrated: "cost structures" which are typically found in product-making organizations, and "program structures" which are increasingly common in nonproduct organizations.

The second section of this chapter describes problems of integration among various groups in an organization who are engaged in collective decision building. The third section considers the question: How can an organization achieve sufficient differentiation to collect information along with enough integration to share information to construct intergroup decisions? It describes six formal structures for integrating organizational decision-builders and evaluates them as methods for facilitating the development of organizational intelligence.

STRUCTURING ORGANIZATIONAL INTELLIGENCE

"Information structures" are the formal organizational equivalents of cognitive maps. Individuals selectively perceive the world and organize their individual perceptions into "sensible" wholes. Likewise, organizations have maps to guide how they perceive and store stimuli. The difference is that an individual's cognitive map is implicit. An individual may be largely unaware of his map. Even when members of face-to-face groups develop equivalent maps, these are largely unstated. Formal organizations create standard coding systems for structuring information. Standard forms for budget requests and expenditure rationales are examples of such coding structures. These codes represent the organization's formal "map" of the world. Together, all an organization's information structures serve as the bases for making formal decisions in somewhat the same way that an individual's cognitive map is the basis for his or her action. Together the information structures are the formalized organizational intelligence. Let us look at three kinds of information structure.

Information Structures in Product-Making Organizations

One example of an information structure used by almost any product-making corporation is a "cost structure." This is not an accounting text. It is not my purpose to describe how to design a cost structure, but examining the concept of cost structure provides a good illustration of the symbolic nature of such documents and their impact on the collective decisions of organizations.

For most executives, the important "information generators" in an organization are the people who analyze costs—people such as accountants, industrial engineers, methods analysts, and operations researchers. Methods of cost analysis and cost control fill textbooks of business administration. The sheer volume and variety of methods of analyzing costs are evidence that "cost" is not a simple and directly observable fact. Rather, the figures identified as "costs" in an organization are symbolic documents. People chose particular formulas for computing costs. If they had chosen other formulas, the resulting cost figures would have been different. Different cost figures would have resulted in different judgments about the organization's "productivity." This in turn might result in different organizational decisions such as whether or not to enter a new product line.

A similar structure is the profit-loss structure. The relative nature of organizational symbols is exemplified by how automotive manufacturers cut recession losses. During the first quarter of 1975 Ford reduced a 105.8 million dollar loss to 10.8 million dollars by changing its accounting method. Chrysler Corp. reduced a 116.9 million dollar loss to 94.1 million dollars. William Bousquette gave the following public account of how the reduction was made by switching to the "flow through" method of accounting:

> You can buy equipment worth $1,000 on which you can claim a 10 per cent investment tax credit. When you put it into service you get a $100 tax credit, because on "flow through" the credit is included as income when it is received. On the old, deferred basis, which has been followed by Ford, that $100 tax credit would have been taken into income over the life of the asset.[2]

In this case there may have been little effect on decisions made by the auto companies or potential investors. Bousquette further explained that Ford "clearly showed what our losses would have been without this change." Nonetheless, controllers and other policy makers found it reasonable to change the announcement of the corporation's profit or loss. Their purpose in wanting to show a smaller loss may have influenced their choice of an accounting system. Thus, even so obvious and objective a "fact" as profits (loss) is relative because it is symbolic. It changes with how you "look" at it and how you choose to count it. The people who made the change made a public justification of it.

Another example of the relativity of meaning of cost is pointed out by ecologists. Until a few years ago consumers computed the cost of owning an automobile by adding the price they paid for the car, the price of insurance, and the price of gasoline, oil, and maintenance. Recently we have learned that the cost of owning (and driving) a car should include the cost of cleaning up the air polluted by auto fumes.

Even more recently, we have realized that the cost must include the drain of natural resources in this country and a drain of our monetary resources to oil exporting countries. The question of "how much" it costs to drive a car 50,000 miles is not a simple, direct calculation. It is relative to one's values. To a person who values the aesthetics of clear air, the cost of driving an automobile is greater than the cost to a person who is only interested in reduced medical bills from air which is not only murky, but harmful.

To look at information structure such as profit and cost structures as symbolic documents means to ask the following kinds of questions:

1. What are the values which have been incorporated into the information structure?
2. What comparisons does this structure encourage?

The values and purposes which are included in a structure will usually be those of the people who construct it. Of course, their values will be considerably influenced by their perception of the formal values or stated goals of the organization. Thus, cost of "raw materials" will show up in a cost structure no matter who designs it. On the other hand, whether a special cost category such as "decorating and maintaining executive offices" shows up as a separate item on the document will depend considerably on the values of the people involved. The design of a cost structure is not simply a matter of "personal taste," however. The cost structure itself is the result of somebody's decision.

For example, the board of directors of a pharmaceutical company was in the process of finding a location for a new research laboratory. They asked accountants and industrial engineers to prepare documents comparing the "costs" of moves to the two sites under consideration. One site was in an older neighborhood. The schools in the area had a poor reputation. The other site was in an industrial park with easy access to an attractive neighborhood known for its good schools. How were the accountants to measure the costs of locating in a site where employees would be reluctant to live? How could they estimate the number of bright researchers who would refuse employment because of the location? What would be the cost to the employees of driving thirty miles to work? Would a "commuting personnel" be costly to the organization? To figure the costs, either the accountants or executives had to answer such questions. The documented costs of the move inevitably reflected the values of those who did the estimating.

An equally important question is, "What comparisons does the structure encourage?" The purpose of a cost structure is to provide information for decision building. By encouraging decision makers to compare certain costs rather than others, the cost structure has a substantial influence on the content of decisions.

In industry, probably the most common systematic procedure for structuring information for decisions is "cost accounting." The cost accountant is charged with the responsibility of showing decision makers how much it costs to produce each product. Cost accounting is expressly for the purpose of allowing decision makers to compare the costs of producing various products in their line as a proportion of the profitability of the various products. Peter Drucker, in *Managing for Results,* criticizes the typical practice of cost accounting because while it claims to document comparisons it does not, in fact, provide decision makers actual comparative figures. Rather, most of the costs are actually the accountants' estimates because most of the cost of a product is indirect.

Another way of arranging costs for comparison is the typical line-item budget. There, budgets show the output of money for each structural unit of the organization. Such arrangements encourage people to compare the costs of operating the manufacturing equipment with the costs of operating the warehouse. This kind of information system is simpler than cost accounting since it requires less approximating of costs. The difficulty is that comparisons between structural units may be meaningless. There are seldom decisions to be made which require comparing the costs of production machines with the costs of warehouses. Moreover, even comparing the past and present cost of each operating unit may be meaningless with this system. Costs are reduced in one place simply by being pushed somewhere else.[4]

Drucker's alternative to traditional cost accounting and budgeting by operational unit is a system which identifies "cost points." He states that there are four cost points in any operation: productive costs, support costs, policing costs, and waste.[5] Though Drucker's system of structuring costs may enable managers to make better comparisons, it will not reduce the relativity of cost figures as symbols in decision-building processes.

For example, Drucker describes how one shipping company "polices" its operation. The company does not use a quality control system which involves investigating a random sample of shipments. Instead it uses the complaints it receives. In one sense the company could cut "costs" by investigating only the five percent of claims which have a questionable basis. Thus, it would reduce costs in one part of the structure, but total costs might be increased. By investigating all claims, the company gathers detailed information about operational failures. It can locate trouble spots faster with a smaller sample size than a random test procedure.[6] Thus the company saves money which would be spent on a quality control division and on future claims resulting from operational failures.

The point of this example is that even such straightforward messages as information about the costs of products cannot be obtained by observation alone. Members of an organization must decide what to observe and what to record. The form of the report encourages decision makers to make certain comparisons. Other comparisons are either discouraged or impossible. Decisions about what information to collect and how to store it become part of the decisions made on the basis of the information.

Information Structures in Nonproduct-Making Organizations

Organizations which produce identifiable products—automobiles, sewing machines, televisions—can compare costs and "outputs" in relatively straightforward ways. This is not to say that the only "products" of such organizations are those which roll off of their assembly lines. Companies like General Motors must be concerned with a nonmeasurable phenomenon called public image as well as with Chevrolets.

However, most of the people in America today do not work for organizations which produce any product which can be observed directly and counted. These organizations include governments, public social service organizations such as schools, hospitals, and nursing homes, and private service organizations such as Girl Scouts and the Y.M.C.A. Even organizations such as G.M. contain substantial research and development units which do not manufacture products. They have large staff units, such as personnel and public relations, which do not have "products." The policy makers in these organizations, however, have informational needs similar to those who make policy in product-making organizations. They need to know what the organization is doing, how much it is doing, and how well it is doing it. They need to know the relative cost of various activities.

Policy makers in product companies set production goals and then measure the accomplishment of such goals. In order to be similarly goal oriented, policy makers in other organizations are beginning to use "program structures." A "program" is a symbolically constructed or artificial product. Program structuring allows nonproduct-making organizations to set goals and measure goal accomplishment.

In describing governmental program structures, Lee and Johnson state: "[Program] structure is a classification scheme which makes the crucial linkage between social aspiration and governmental activities. Broad societal goals are identified, and each in turn is subdivided and further subdivided. Going down the structure, each succeeding level focuses less upon general values and more upon specific functions and operations of government. . . . Program structures to some extent set priorities and therefore is essentially a part of the decision making process."[7]

The key concepts in this definition are that program structures show linkages between aspirations and activities and that the expressed purpose of the structures is to facilitate decision making. The people who design program structures begin by stipulating societal goals which the organization aspires to accomplish. The program structure of the Commonwealth of Pennsylvania, for example, states seven goals in general or abstract terms. One of these goals is "the protection of persons and property." The program structure documents what is being done by governmental agencies in Pennsylvania to protect persons and properties. The idea of a program structure is to arrange information about activities according to the goals of those activities. A program budget documents how much is spent for each activity. Decision makers are thus provided with information about the extent to which an organization is devoting monetary resources to accomplish its goals.

To be most helpful for decision makers, however, a program structure must do more than show the functional relationship among activities and the resource allocation by function. It should allow for comparisons of expenditures with goal accomplishment. This means that there must be measures of goal accomplishment. Since the organizations which use program structures seldom produce products, there must be other ways to observe and record accomplishment. Some organizations are content to measure the direct "outputs" of their programs or activities. Universities, for example, report the number of student credit-hours produced in a year. Measures of direct output are usually fairly easy to obtain. They may be readily quantified, but do student credit-hours really reflect the goal accomplishment of universities? Many program planners (as well as many students) think not. Some organizations, therefore, attempt to measure the *impact* of its programs on the people it serves. An impact measure of a vocational training program, for example, might be the increase in wages earned by students in the program. Such impact measures are obviously much more relative and more difficult to obtain.

Program structuring is an attempt to rationalize the process of collective decision building in nonproduct organizations. Program structuring is analogous to interpersonal planning discussed in chapter 5. It permits collective planning by formal organizations. An individual's interaction goals are typically vague and continuously changing. Such goals are fine for informal communication because interaction through symbolic displays is fluid and highly adaptable to the changing goal states of the communicators.

Formal organizations are much more rigid than informal groups, however. The use of symbolic documents for much organizational communication, of course, contributes to the rigidity. Since much important communication is documentary, it makes sense that the goals should likewise be put on paper. When goals are not documented, each person in the organization has his or her own idea about what should be happening. In face-to-face groups, people come to understand one another's goals and develop some implicit consensus about collective goals. When people cannot communicate face-to-face there is little opportunity for implicit consensus about goals to develop.

A program structure provides members of an organization with a common set of symbolic objectives. Each member of an organization should be able to see how his or her activities contribute to the overall objective. The structure should direct attention to comparisons between how much money is spent on various subgoals. It should also show to what extent the goals are being accomplished.

Slogans

Technical information structures such as cost structures and program structures are not the only kinds which influence decisions in organization. Harold Wilensky, in *Organizational Intelligence*, emphasizes the importance of diffuse "verbal environments" created by organizational slogans. A slogan captures how members of an organization see their world. It is a kind of shorthand map of their world. It identifies what is in the world and what is not. It is the "reality of the world" for organizational members. One of Wilensky's examples concerns how slogans influence governmental decision makers:

> In foreign policy, staff experts invent slogans that reinforce policymakers' adherence to a wartime myth of the single enemy, thereby blinding the vision and reducing the number of recognized opinions. For instance, the image of the "Sino-Soviet bloc" fostered so much rigidity in the State Department and its publics in the 1950's and early 1960's that President Kennedy, seeking very minor modifications of our China policy to fit dramatic signs of the Sino-Soviet split, felt himself a captive of both his foreign office and the mass media.[7]

Slogans as "information structures" are not the systematic orderings of information discussed above. Unlike cost structures or program structures, slogans are often genuine products of the folk culture in an organization. That is, no one person or group is the "author" of the slogan. Rather, slogans are learned as any pattern of behavior is learned. Someone "emitted" the slogan. Someone thought up the slogan "spontaneously" and introduced it into casual conversation. Other people liked the "feel" of the slogan. It made sense to them as a way of understanding the world. They used it; still more people learned the slogan and thus it became part of the shared wisdom of the organization. As shared wisdom, it unconsciously influences conscious choices in the organization.

In this section I have described one dimension of the intelligence function of communication in formal organizations. In order to make collective decisions, people who are not in regular, face-to-face communication use "information structures" to share what they know. The production foreman shares information about what he has done with the operations manager using forms for reporting output and costs. In this section I have emphasized that such forms (part of the "management information system") are necessarily relative. Information structures, like cognitive maps, reflect only part of what is available for people to know. The selection process is not random. In the following section, I describe some of the implications of limited information on how organizations accomplish integration.

DIFFERENTIATION AND INFORMATION

Organizations collect and process information for the purpose of taking collective action. We have seen in the previous section that there can be no simple formulas for determining the one best way to structure information so that its form is meaningful or useful to others. An information structure reflects the purposes and values of its designers. An information structure, after all, is but a "cognitive map" of how an organization is doing.

The best information structures, like the best maps, reflect most closely the territory they represent. The map is not the territory, but the more knowledge the map makers have of the territory, the better the map they can make. The more time map makers have spent learning the territory and the more direct their contact with the territory, then the more closely their map can reflect that territory. Following this analogy, the best information should be generated by those most familiar with the phenomena represented by the information. It is this line of reasoning which suggests that information in highly differentiated organizations is potentially better than information in less differentiated organizations.

The concept of differentiation was defined in chapter 8 as differences in orientation among managers in different functional departments of an organization. These differences come about precisely because each manager is attempting to be a good "map maker" of his or her department and of the environments of that department. Lawrence and Lorsch state:

As organizations deal with their external environments, they become segmented into units, each of which has as its major task the problem of dealing with a part of the conditions outside the firm (or in the case of the production environment, inside the firm). This is a result of the fact that any one group of managers has a limited span of surveillance. Each one has the capacity to deal with only a portion of the total environment. If we take as an example either a division of a large, diversified corporation or a medium-sized manufacturing firm, we readily observe sales, production, and design units, each of which is coping with a portion of the organization's external environment. The sales unit faces problems associated with the market, the customers, the competitors, and so on. The production unit deals with production equipment sources, raw materials sources, labor markets, and the like. Such external conditions as the state of scientific knowledge and opportunities for expanding knowledge and applying it are in the most general sense the purview of the design unit. These parts together also have to be linked together toward the accomplishment of the organization's overall purpose.[8]

Managers in sales units are mapping the market, the customers, the competitors. They are generating information about these "territories" both for themselves and for the whole organization. The more they concern themselves only with this territory, not with production territory, for example, the more likely they are to produce a map which closely reflects the marketing territory. It is important for an organization to be differentiated so that people can direct their attention to particular segments of the organizational environment and produce good maps of that environment.

There is another reason why an organization should be differentiated. The assignment of people to specific roles supplies them with the expectation that they are to become "experts" in particular areas of interest to the organization. Assigning people to be production managers acts as the basis for the expectation that they are to generate and transmit information relevant to production. Social clubs will typically organize committees (such as the social committee, the publicity committee, etc.) in order to charge particular people with the responsibility to collect and/or to distribute certain kinds of information relevant to the whole club's activities.

Differentiation within an organization promotes good intergroup or organizational decision building in two ways. First, it produces more "accurate" information (information which reflects more exactly the phenomena it represents). It is necessary to have people who are specialists producing and transmitting information because all information is relative. No information structure can accurately reflect all organizational environments. Since there is no universally "best" way to structure information, it is necessary to have people who "know the situation" very well because they have a lot of firsthand experience with the situation.

A second reason why differentiation promotes better intergroup decision building is that when people are charged with the responsibility of reporting information on certain topics, decision makers can be more confident that they are not overlooking important information by mistake. Information generation is planned rather than random. The chairpeople of committees often assign certain people to gather and report information on particular topics. In such cases, they are using the device of formal structure to augment their face-to-face communication methods.

Differentiation thus contributes to "overall effectiveness" of organizations. But, state Lawrence and Lorsch, "there is another side. . . . [Differentiation also means] that when it becomes necessary to make joint decisions, managers from different departments will approach the problem from different frames of references and may have difficulty in collaborating effectively."[9] With differentiation comes specialization, and with specialization the possibility of rivalry between diversified groups.

Harold L. Wilensky suggests that specialization may be the most powerful source of information blockage and distortion in organizations. He states:

> The organization of the armed forces and industry alike encourages rivalry and restriction of information. Each service, each division, indeed every sub-unit, becomes a guardian of its own mission, standards and skills; lines of organization become lines of loyalty and secrecy. In industry, the personnel department defends its control over selection and training; accounting, its standards of reporting; production, its schedules of output; sales, its interests in product design and customer service—each restricting information that might advance the competing interests of others. . . . While information can also be used to persuade potential allies and to facilitate accommodations with rivals, it is more commonly hoarded for selective use in less collaborative struggles for power and position. . . . In 1941, the signals of the impending attack on Pearl Harbor lay scattered in a number of rival agencies; communication lines linked them, but essential messages never flowed across the lines. . . . In the Bay of Pigs fiasco of 1961, the intelligence branch of the CIA was out of touch with the operations branch which was planning the adventure; operations was only loosely in touch with the Joint Chiefs, who went along.[10]

Thus, differentiation which potentially contributes to better information for organizational decision building, may also contribute to blocking the flow of information and lead to inadequate information. In order to make effective organizational decisions, there must be not only differentiation, but also integration.

Integration is used in the formal sense here. Thus, for example, Lawrence and Lorsch define integration as "the quality of the state of collaboration that exists among departments that are required to achieve unity of effort."[11] They use the term to refer to the relatively formal processes and methods which are used to achieve unity of effort or collective decisions. In the following section I describe various methods which may be used to integrate diversified groups or departments for the purpose of making collective, intergroup decisions. The chief problem to be solved by any formal integrative method is how to share information collected by differentiated units among those who need the information to make decisions.

STRUCTURING FORMAL INTEGRATION

Hierarchy

The classical approach to integration is the "scalar chain" or organizational hierarchy. One achieves coordination among units by designing information and authority to flow along the same lines. Managers of diversified units would have the same superior. Theoretically each would send information about what is happening in his or her unit to the supervisor, who would put the information together from the different units and make decisions about what each of the managers is to do. The supervisor would then transmit instructions to the managers, who would follow them because of the supervisor's authority. In a strict scalar chain organization there would not be a need for the members of different departments to communicate with one another. Only Luther Gulick among the classical theorists (such as Fayol, Urwick, and Gracunias) admitted the possibility for coordination other than hierarchy.

Whether or not there are other means of integration sometimes employed in an organization, the use of hierarchy as the principal means has definite disadvantages from the perspective of information transmission for decision building. Wilensky explains:

> Information is a resource that symbolizes status, enhances authority, and shapes careers. In reporting at every level, hierarchy is conducive to concealment and misrepresentation. Subordinates are asked to transmit information that can be used to evaluate their performance. Their motive for "making it look good," for "playing it safe" is obvious. . . . Restriction of problem information is motivated by the desire not only to please but also to preserve comfortable routines of work: if the subordinate alerts the boss to pending trouble, the former is apt to find himself on a committee to solve the problem. The aphorism "Never volunteer for anything" is not confined to the Army; it is part of folk wisdom.[12]

One of the most frequently cited studies of the effects of hierarchy on information transmission was conducted by William H. Read. Read investigated the motivational and attitudinal factors which affect the accuracy with which members at one administrative level communicate upward to a higher level. Read's major hypothesis was that the more employees wanted to be promoted, the less accurately they would communicate to their superior information which might reflect negatively on their job performance. They would "withhold, restrict, or distort information about the problems, current and unsolved, which they experience in their day-to-day work."[13]

Read also predicted that this tendency to distort negative information could be modified by the extent of interpersonal trust between a superior and a subordinate and by how influential a subordinate thought his or her superior was with those in higher levels of the organization. One hundred four middle-managers (52 superiors and 52 subordinates) participated in the study. Read measured accuracy of upward communication by the "degree of agreement between superior and subordinate about the relative degree of difficulty these problems caused the subordinate, i.e., the degree to which they were problems to subordinates. Low agreement was taken to indicate relatively poor or inaccurate communication of this type of information; high agreement indicated the reverse." Subordinates' desire or "need" to be promoted was measured by asking them to choose between pairs of hypothetical alternatives. One alternative was a promotion to a rather unpleasant job situation. The other was a lateral transfer to a position with pleasant conditions. The more often the subject chose the promotion alternative, the more "need for advancement" he was presumed to have.

Read found a statistically significant correlation between the subordinate's desire for advancement and inaccuracy of his upward communication to his superior. A low amount of interpersonal trust and, to some extent, a perception of the superior as being influential with his superiors exaggerated the effect of desire for advancement and distortion of communication. That is, Read confirmed his hypothesis that the more a person wants to be promoted, the less he trusts his superior, and the more influence he believes his superior has with organizational decision makers, the more distorted the person's communication with that superior. Even when there is high trust between superiors and subordinates, Read cautions, a subordinate will tend to distort information which unfavorably reflects on his job performance.

The conclusion we can draw here is that interpersonal variables (in this case trust) can influence communication between superiors and subordinates, but the more powerful influencer is the formal organization structure. Hierarchical structure is a metamessage which subordinates take into account in choosing what information they will pass along to a superior and what information they will not pass along. Hierarchy is thus theoretically a method of integrating information for the purpose of organizational decision building. In practice, the pressures on people not to pass along information which reflects negatively on their job performance will restrict this method of integration.

System 4 Organization

Rensis Likert and others of the Michigan Survey Research Center advocate an alternative to the strict hierarchy of classical design. The idea of System 4 was to design a structure in which communication might flow throughout the organization, not simply down and up the chain of command. According to Likert, an organizational design must implement three concepts: (1) the principle of supportive relationships, (2) group decisionmaking and group methods of supervision, and (3) high performance goals.[14] The organizational design involves sets of groups linked by managers instead of people linked through hierarchy on a one-to-one basis.

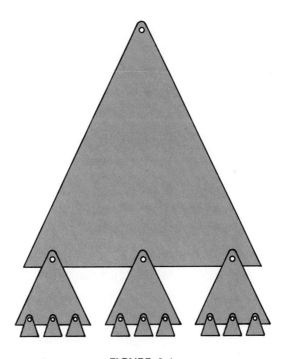

FIGURE 9.1
The System 4 Organization (From Rensis Likert. *The Human Organization*. New York: McGraw-Hill Book Co., 1967, p. 50.)

Likert's illustration of the concept of System 4 design is shown in Figure 9.1. Managers serve as "linking pins." Likert claims a number of interpersonal distinctions from classical hierarchy. For example: subordinates are supposed to be freer to discuss job problems; the interaction process is supposed to be "open and extensive"; there are supposed to be greater perceived confidence and trust. Organizational processes of control are supposed to be decentralized; performance goals are supposed to be high. These differences result from (1) training in interpersonal relations and group problem-solving methods, and from (2) the System 4 structure in which group problem-solving sessions are used for sharing information at each level of the organization.[15]

System 4 represents an improved design for integration in that it encourages contact among people at the same organizational level (horizontal communication), which classical hierarchy does not. But the system depends upon groups composed of a manager and several subordinates. Because the manager is still in charge of the promotion of the subordinates, this system does not overcome the problems of distortion of upward communication discussed in the last section.

Moreover, the group discussions which constitute the means of integration at higher levels have a good deal of pressure on them because the subordinates come from different groups and thus have different orientations which make it difficult for them to see the other points of view. Whether, in fact, System 4 promotes better interaction than classical hierarchy depends upon the skill of managers and subordinates in interpersonal processes and collective decision making. Read's findings suggest that even where interpersonal trust exists, the structural features of hierarchy place severe limits on the free transmission of information. System 4 design is one way to begin restructuring for the purposes of improving integration, but it does not eliminate information distortion due to hierarchy.

Management by Objectives

Management by objectives is often conceptualized as a method for improving motivation of individual workers in an organization. For example, Odiorne, in describing MBO, states that it is

> a process whereby the superior and subordinate managers of an organization jointly identify its common goals, define each individual's major areas of responsibility in terms of the results expected of him, and use these measures as guides for operating the unit and assessing the contribution of each of its members.[16]

When managers and subordinates have a clear understanding about the subordinate's job areas of responsibility, what will constitute an acceptable level of performance, and what needs to be done to improve performance, then improved motivation should result. This point was made in the discussion of MBO in the last chapter.

Management by Objectives is also a way of improving the coordination of units of an organization. It may serve as a means of decentralization. According to Drucker, who introduced the concept,

> the objectives of the district manager's job should be defined by the contribution he and his district sales force have to make to the sales department, the objectives of the project engineer's job by the contribution he, his engineers, and draftsmen make to the engineering department.[17]

When each organizational unit has its own objectives, the departments can be coordinated on the basis of the objectives. Each unit is thus free to accomplish its objectives in its own way. This means that the only kind of information for decision making which goes out of a department may be information about the extent to which that department achieved its objectives. The form of this information is rather prescribed by the goals or objectives which the manager of the department negotiated with higher level decision makers and may be relatively free of the kind of distortion to which Read refers. Because important decisions are "decentralized"—made within each department—information is not subject as much to distortion in serial transmission up the hierarchy.

Management by Objectives, like System 4 design, depends upon the skills of the managers who implement it. Meyer, Kay, and French, for example, found that attitudes toward goal-setting programs depend upon (1) the extent to which subordinate managers made use of their experiences, (2) managers' ability to plan, (3) the extent to which managers were receptive to new ideas, and (4) the extent to which managers believed and accepted their goals.[18] Decentralized organizational decision making through management by objectives is no guarantee of better decisions. The managers in charge of decisions at their level must be capable of making the decisions.

One problem frequently cited in regard to Management by Objectives is that it increases the paperwork of managers. After four years of operation in the Purex Corporation, managers reported negative attitudes toward the program because they claimed that higher management was using it as a "whip" and because of the increased amount of paperwork.[19] Tosi and Carroll's investigation of MBO in another large manufacturing plant revealed similar findings. Managers cited as the major problem the increased amount of documentation required of them. They were required constantly to send exact written information about objectives and progress to the coordinator of the program.[20]

The most serious criticism of MBO as a method of nonface-to-face decision making is that the information which must be shared across differentiated lines is not limited to measures of output. People in one unit need all kinds of information from other units. To adopt an MBO approach to interunit decision making makes each unit autonomous or isolated from others with only the smallest amount of integration among units. Many organizations will not find this satisfactory as an integration method.

Organizational Joint Problem Solving

Robert Swinth offers a model for integrating information for organizational decision making for "complex novel problems such as the creation and development of a new component or product, or the creation of a regional plan for a metropolitan area." A complex novel problem is one which: (1) must serve a variety of organizational and subunit objectives, (2) involves a high degree of interdependence of units in solving and implementing a solution, (3) is too complex to be understood by one person or group, and (4) arises because of changes in the organization or its environment so that a solution may require knowledge which no one has. Swinth states that urban planning is a good example because solutions require that the skills of architects, economists, and others be combined in unusual or unknown ways.[21]

Swinth's model or procedure for "organizational joint problem solving" is essentially an agenda which suggests what kinds of groups should be involved in solving a problem at which stages of the decision-building process. Stage One is the establishment of "centers" which are "linked" together. There is one overall head, but coordination is not done through the head alone. Rather, centers or groups are also linked to one another. The participants in each center relate to one another as peers. That is, the groups or centers are not arranged into a hierarchy. The centers do not necessarily replace an organizational hierarchy which may run routine matters in an organization. Rather, they may be ad hoc or temporary groups which coordinate information and decisions for a particular problem. The centers do not have to be equally involved in the decision building. Some may be central, others brought in on a consultant basis. Swinth observes that the role of a legal team in a regional planning process may be somewhat minor compared to others.

An important determinant of success of the decision building in such an organization is the way in which the structure is "bought." If the members of each team are rewarded (pay increases, promotions) on the basis of the performance of their individual center, then their loyalty will be to that center. Rewards have to be geared to the performance of the overall cooperative systems in order to motivate individuals to seek cooperation with other centers.

Stage Two is the initial setting of general goals for the effort. This general goal setting should be done in terms of the overall goal to be accomplished. Although the centers are not hierarchically arranged, a complex problem will usually have a number of levels of concern. Lower levels provide output into higher levels (though the same center may be responsible for some lower levels and some higher levels). At the conclusion of Stage Two there should be some specification of the overall mission to provide individual centers with some direction to pursue in attempting to solve the problem.

Stage Three is conducted within each center. There is a search made at the level of each center to produce a temporary solution which fits the needs of that particular center. During Stage Three each center works independently of one another. Thus, there is the possibility of creativity, because centers are not initially constraining one another's problem-search. Also the initial plans or solutions are suited to the needs as perceived by those most capable of understanding the "local" problem. This allows for the benefits of specialization in accumulating information (discussed in the subsection on "Differentiation and Information").

Stage Four is the sharing of information and proposed solutions between centers. Swinth suggests that as much information be sent to other centers as they can process without overloading them. Information is sent directly to other centers (without being sent to a coordinator). Although the general recommendation is to send information to everyone, if the members of one center know that only certain other centers can use the information, they can send information only to them.

Stage Five is the analysis of the temporary solutions and plans designed by centers for inconsistencies across centers. Two centers may work together to find a way in which their plans may be interrelated, but it is not expected that each center will understand completely the plans of the other center. Swinth uses the example of designing a tape recorder:

> The amplifier center develops a subplan in which a transistor of a certain type is to be used, but an input of a certain characteristic is presumed from the center responsible for the speaker. Yet the center designing the speaker has decided upon a component which has a different output characteristic. By using the communication technique they find this inconsistency, and then work together to reconcile. This approach differs from traditional group search techniques in that neither center to an interdependency necessarily understands the whole problem or even the proportion that encompasses both of them. Whereas traditionally one

of the centers would have enough information and understanding to decide on all the questions for both, here each is only aware of the other's portion of the task in the immediate vicinity of the interdependence.[22]

Note that Swinth is describing the concept of "equivalence." The centers do not have to have identical "cognitive maps" of their common task. Each center does not need to know everything that the other center knows. Rather, each has to understand only the "immediate vicinity of the interdependence." They have to have equivalent concepts of their common task. The output of one center has to be acceptable as input into the other center.

Stage Six is the repetition of the process of coordinating individual centers creating ever larger consistent plans. Swinth's conception of a plan is consistent with the conception of plans described in chapter 5 in that he is concerned with reflective rather than projective nature of planning. He notes, "In the early passes through the problem both the within and between component decisions will be unacceptable in many ways. But by a series of revisions and changes, each built upon the previous steps, it is possible to obtain an acceptable closure." The essential part of the planning process is not the original proposing of plans, but refinement after specific proposed plans have been found. Note that this notion of collective refinement of proposals is similar to the process of collecting decision building described in chapter 6.

Organizational joint problem solving is a procedure for ordering coordination among centers concerned with common problems. That is, it may help those involved in a cooperative task to determine when units should coordinate. It provides an alternative to a system approach in which goals are sent down from the top level of hierarchy and made more specific at each level. The chief difference is that after some general goals are set at the top, the work is shifted to the "bottom." The first real work on problems is carried out by centers most concerned with narrow problems. The overall solution is "built up" by coordinating individual solutions rather than created by making a general solution more specific as it moves down an organizational hierarchy. The centers may be thought of as the "bottom," but really there are at best two levels: the level of an overall coordinator, who in fact may have little formal decision-making power, and the level of the centers, which have a "peer" relationship to each other.

Although the OJPS procedure provides guidelines about when to coordinate, it leaves unresolved two important questions in coordinating information and decisions across several differentiated units (centers). One is the question of "how": how are inevitable conflicts between differentiated units to be resolved? The other is a question of "who": which members of centers communicate with members of other centers to work out the conflicts? Lawrence and Lorsch's research on contingency design offers some guidance in answering these two questions.

Contingency Design

The concept of contingency design is based on the premise that there is no one best way to organize all kinds of organizations. Rather, the "best" organizational design for some purposes is not a good way for other purposes. In particular, organizations which are productive in stable or certain environments are not as productive in unstable or dynamic environments.

Not only do whole organizations require different kinds of designs, but different units require different kinds of organization since they are dealing with different segments of the environment. Some differences which Lawrence and Lorsch found among research, marketing, and sales divisions in the plastics industry were discussed in the previous section. The more effective organizations were those which had both differentiation and integration. Lawrence and Lorsch offer some guidance about designs which best facilitate decision making in which different organizational units must contribute information and arrive at common solutions.

According to their theory, the process of making a joint decision is the process of resolving inevitable conflict. Effective organizations were different from ineffective organizations because of the manner in which they resolved conflicts among units. Effective organizations more often made decisions on the basis of expertise. But when a number of divisions or units are making collaborative decisions, who has the greatest expertise? To determine this, the researchers devised a concept called the "dominant competitive issue." In each industry, there is an area of competition among companies which largely determines which companies will have a large share of the market. This area of competition is the "dominant competitive issue."

In the plastics industry, the dominant competitive issue is innovation. Their research indicated that in the food industry innovation is likewise the dominant competitive issue. For example, one food company executive stated, "The big thing in this industry is the almost fanatical desire for new, new, new. This has become the life blood of the business. . . . Prices don't make any difference, and they have no relationship to volume, costs, or anything."

In contrast, executives in the container industry claimed that delivery schedules were the most important area of competition for them. One stated, "The only way you can make dollars is to keep moving the product out the door. . . . The big issue is scheduling, and it is a matter

of every day, all day.   We either have too much product or too little."[23]
In making joint decisions, those units with the most information about
the dominant competitive issue (research in food and plastics; production in containers) have the most expertise.   The effective organizations
were those in which the units with information about the dominant
competitive issue had the most influence in joint decision making.

The "rule" about the unit with the most information about the
dominant competitive issue is rather abstract to apply to specific cases.
After all, decisions are made by people.   The people who are involved
in making joint decisions and sharing information across boundaries of
integrated units are called "integrators."   An integrator may or may not
have a title such as "liaison officer."   Lawrence and Lorsch outline
several guidelines to effective uses of integrators for sharing information
among differentiated units and building joint decisions.

To be most effective, the integrator must be in an intermediate
position among those units being "integrated."   One reason for this is
so that the integrator will have orientations which are "equidistant" from
the units being integrated.   They offer the following example of an
integrator in a low-performing organization:

> This manager complained that the integrators were constantly coming to
> him about matters that should be handled several levels higher up the
> production hierarchy.   From the point of view of the integrators, accus-
> tomed in their own department to emphasis on direct contact among
> managers at lower levels, this seemed appropriate.   But to this produc-
> tion manager, in a highly structured department where rules and proce-
> dures specified who did what, the integrators' behavior was an irritant,
> which reduced his effectiveness in working with the plant manager on
> matters that he could handle.   The plant manager did not realize the
> difference in structure that created his problem, but to us this seemed to
> be the case.[24]

The integrators must live in a structured situation which is somewhat
similar to the situation of those he or she is attempting to integrate.
The more dissimilar the structures, the more difficult it will be for the
integrator to understand the constraints of those in the other units.   If
those in the units to be integrated must perceive that the integrators do
not understand their situation, the integrator will not have much opportunity to influence them.   In short, the integrator may lose credibility.
The following comment from a manager is typical of a reaction to an
integrator who does not have influence or credibility because he does
not have an orientation which is appropriate for the units he is integrating: "I am no integrator, but I can see that one of our troubles is that the
integrators are so tied up in day-to-day detail that they can't look to the
future.   They are still concerned with [this year's] materials when they
should be concerned with [next year's] markets."[25]

We see here a process described in the previous chapter. The formal structure of the organization places limitations on the communication which occurs between people. In this case, the effect of those limitations is that the integrator is not able to coordinate information and mediate conflicts so that effective joint decisions can be built. In designing integrators, some attention must be paid to the most likely time, goal, and interpersonal orientations of the integrators as well as to the kind of organizational structure with which they are going to be most familiar. The more an integrator differs in these orientations from those of managers in the units to be integrated, the more difficult will be communication and integration.

A second guideline to what makes for successful integrators is the basis of power of the integrator. Integrators in both high performing and low performing organizations were seen by managers as having a good deal of influence. The difference between the two was that the managers in low-performing organizations saw the integrators as having power only because of their formal position in the organization. For example:

> A good [integrator] is a guy with a red hot bayonet. He doesn't take "no" for an answer on anything. He is also in an enviable position, since he reports to the general manager and finds very little opposition to what he wants to do.[26]

By contrast, integrators in high performing organizations were seen as influential largely because of their information and expertise. To quote a manager in such an organization:

> The [integrators] are the kingpins. They have a good feel of our [researcher's] ability, and they know the needs of the market. They will work back and forth with us and the others.[27]

Lawrence and Lorsch emphasize that it is important in designing a formal structure for the integrator's positions to be given formal decision-making authority. But that formal or documented authority is not enough. It must be supplemented by the perception on the part of organizational members that the integrators have the knowledge to make good decisions. This knowledge might result from the fact that the integrators were in a formal position to understand the time and goal orientations of the units they were integrating. In less effective organizations, integrators did not understand the orientations of at least one of the units they were supposed to integrate. Also in these organizations, members of the units perceived that higher management used those in the integrators' positions to force decisions which they wanted. In these cases, we can say that rather than a contingency design, what was operating was an hierarchy under the guise of contingency design, for the decision was made on the basis of hierarchical position rather than information and bargaining.

A third determinant of successful design for integration is the reward system for the integrators. High performing organizations tie rewards of the integrators to the overall performance of the units they are charged with integrating. Suppose that a person is responsible for integration between production and research units. The person might hold a formal position within the research unit. If salary and other benefits are based on that person's work in the research unit, then the organization is sending a message to him or her that the most valuable work that person performs for the organization is the research work. If the person is supposed to mediate conflicts between production and research, we can predict that he or she will have little incentive to find resolutions which are satisfactory to both units. After all, he or she is being paid by the research unit.

That formal structure will act as a metamessage which will be taken into consideration by the integrator, the research unit, and the production unit. The reward system will be part of the message whenever there is communication between the integrator and representatives of the units. The alternative is to reward the integrator on the basis of his or her success in integrating. In such a situation, benefits would be based on the combined performance of the research and production units. Now the reward system acts as a metamessage to both integrator and to representatives that the integrator has a stake in successful integration for the benefit of both units, not just one.

A fourth guideline to successful use of integrators is concerned with where influence is concentrated within individual units. To be effective an integrator must have direct contact with those people who are most influential in any individual unit. The temptation is to have integrators contact the top manager in each department, but the top manager is not always and should not always be the person with the most influence in a department. Rather, influence, according to Lawrence and Lorsch, should be "concentrated at the managerial level where knowledge to make decisions was available."

In research divisions, the important "work" of the organization is the research done by scientists. The scientists—the people at the "bottom"—have the knowledge to make decisions. Therefore, it is appropriate for decisions to be made at lower levels in these divisions. Analogously, the knowledge to make decisions is found in the middle level in sales divisions, and at upper levels in production units. Lawrence and Lorsch found decisions concentrated in upper levels in applied research departments in one low-performing organization; decision-making influence was concentrated in low levels of a production unit in another low-performing organization. In deciding how to design integration, then, one must consider what kinds of decisions are made within each individual unit and who has the knowledge to make those decisions. Integrators should have most contact with those who have most information pertinent to integrative decisions.

Although Lawrence and Lorsch are interested in formal design as one means of successful integration, they emphasize that design alone will not guarantee integration. Also important is the interpersonal skill of the integrators. In particular, they distinguished three methods of handling conflict. One method is "smoothing over." Here is how one manager described relationships among units:

> The relations are wonderful. We are happy—we are friendly and happy as larks. We chew each other out and are happy and go about our business. I've never run into more cooperative people. I think they think we are cooperative also, but nothing happens.

The smoothing over method is "groupthink" described in chapter 6. It is a method of compromise, of trading "wins" among group members so that no one is unhappy, but this method does not use "hashing out" or reasoned talk to consider what is the most logical course of action. It is a methd of integration which sacrifices intelligence.

A second method of resolving differences is "forcing" decisions by taking them to authorities higher in the hierarchy. For example, one manager described how conflicts are resolved in his organization:

> If I want something very badly and I am confronted by a roadblock, I go to top management to get the decision made. If the research managers are willing to go ahead [my way], there is no problem. If there is a conflict, then I take the decision to somebody higher up.[29]

The forcing method of conflict resolution uses hierarchy as an integrative method. Like smoothing over, little or no reasoned discourse is involved.

The third method is "confrontation." A manager describes confrontation:

> Our problems get thrashed out in our committees. We work them over until everybody agrees this is the best effort you can make. We may decide this isn't good enough. Then we decide to ask for more plant, more people, etc. We all have to be realistic and take a modification sometimes and say this is the best we can do.[30]

Confrontation uses conflict among group members as a resource for making better decisions. Opinions are aired and reasoned discourse is the method by which a group decision is made.

One result of confrontation as a method of conflict resolution is that everyone feels like he or she had had a part in making the decision. Lawrence and Lorsch found that in high-performing organizations where confrontation was the method of resolution, everyone felt that his or her department had great influence in the decision-making process. They point out that "influence" is not a fixed commodity which some people must "lose" if others gain. Rather, influence is an expandable commodity. When people feel like they have had their say and that their opinions have been considered, then they have influenced the decision. When conflicts are smoothed over or when a higher level manager is brought in to force the decision, then both units' influence is diminished.

Contingency design does not provide a universal structure for integration. It does, however, provide a set of guidelines for particular organizations to use in deciding what kind of formal design is most likely to be useful. The philosophy behind the design is that organizations are not static entities. The design must allow for maximum adaptation to the environment. High performing organizations are those in which units are integrated without losing their ability to understand and respond to their environments. This means achieving both differentiation (required for intelligence) and integration. The key to effective contingency design is the use of integrators.

In order for integrators to be effective conflict resolvers, they must: (1) be in an intermediate position among those units being "integrated"; (2) have power based on perceived knowledge as well as formal authority; (3) be rewarded for the collaborative work of the units they integrate; (4) be integrated into a unit at the point where there is knowledge appropriate to make decisions. Integrators must encourage conflict resolution by confrontation rather than smoothing over or forcing so that members of each unit feel they have influence on joint decisions.

Project Management

All of the methods of organizational decision making described above assume some kind of hierarchical organization; though most modify the effect of hierarchy with group decision making. In some organizations there is a move away from hierarchy, at least in "pockets" such as executive teams. Some organizations which operate in extremely uncertain environments have teams of executives in which there is no hierarchical organization. Instead, people form project groups to work on individual tasks. Any individual may work on more than one project at a time. Project management groups are temporary. Groups are dissolved after the project is completed.

One advantage of project management design is the informal communication network it encourages. Because of overlapping memberships and temporary groups, most of the members of the entire pool of people know one another. There are no formal barriers to securing information from people who are not members of a particular project group. A second advantage of project management design is that the project groups can be organized to suit the needs of a particular task. Andre Delbecq describes three typical tasks and suggests organizational features which are appropriate for groups doing those tasks.[31]

Routine decisions are the first kind of task. If a group is in charge of making a large number of routine decisions, Delbecq suggests that it should have the following characteristics:

1. The norms of the group should emphasize professionalism. By professionalism he means that individuals should feel a good deal of commitment to their individual jobs. Values of economy and efficiency should be stressed.
2. Group members should be specialists. They should work relatively independent of one another. Their leader should be a coordinator of information.
3. The agenda of the group should begin with an initial planning period in which the specialists and the coordinator specify objectives. After that, people work independently. The coordinator works with the group members individually.
4. The climate of such a group is likely to be one of high stress. The stress is the result of time constraints and individual commitments.

A second kind of decision is creative. In this kind of decision making (or decision building) people are working with unstructured problems. According to Delbecq, "the central element . . . is the lack of an agreed-upon method of dealing with the problem." Group members are dealing with an "uncertain environment" and naturally, their way of generating information and of integrating with one another should be more open than in routine situations where people are dealing with a certain environment. Characteristics of decision building are:

1. The norms of the group support originality and even eccentricity. People tend to hold and encourage relativistic views of life and independence in judgment. Humor and undisciplined exploration of viewpoints are the norm.
2. Group members are heterogeneous. They do not act as specialists, but rather as generalists. They work together; all people explore all ideas. Their leader is a facilitator of communication within the group setting. In contrast with the coordinator in routine situations who engages in one-to-one communication with group members, the facilitator communicates with the whole group.
3. The agenda is characterized by separation of problem definition from generation of solutions, separation of idea generation from idea

evaluation, suspension of judgment, and avoidance of early concern with solutions. Full participation of all members is encouraged. People communicate directly with one another instead of trying to direct their comments through the leader.

4. The climate of the group is relaxed and nonstressful. "Behavior is motivated by interest in the problem, rather than concern with short-run payoff."

A third kind of decision task is negotiated decisions. These are decisions in which there is a genuine conflict of interest among members of the group. As we observed in chapter 6 and in the discussion of contingency design, it is important that conflicts be confronted. One method for confronting and resolving a conflict is the "Two Column Method" which was discussed in chapter 6. Delbecq offers the following guidelines about organizing groups such as negotiating teams which deal with conflicts of interest:

1. Norms of the group must support individual freedom and freedom to disagree within the group. People must be encouraged to reach agreement. There must be an openness to new approaches to compromise. The norm must support conflict as healthy and natural rather than pathological.
2. The group should consist of proportional representatives of each faction with at least two people representing each faction. Each individual must be simultaneously committed to his or her own group (each must indeed "represent" his group's interests), and at the same time, each must be committed to negotiating an acceptable collective decision. The leader of the group must be impartial.
3. The agenda of the group should be formal, including formalized procedures for handling who speaks and for how long, and for voting. Each side should have a veto, however, so that the decisions are consensual.
4. The climate of a group should be frank without emotional hostility and aggression. People should assume that commitment to due process as a principal motivator.

Delbecq's categories of decision are consistent with the description of decision building in chapter 6 and in the early portions of this chapter and at the same time consistent with the contingency approach described throughout the book. The key concept is that groups operate in different decision environments. Effective decision building is a function of the organized response for gathering information and taking collective action in that environment. His research indicates that managers and group members can successfully redefine their own expectations and hence their decision methods. They can change the expectations with which they coordinate to gather information and take action. At an organizational level, a project management design facilitates this kind of change or adaptation because it allows groups to "begin" their existence with each new set of environmental task conditions. At the beginning they can discuss their expectations and decide on appropriate norms, roles, agendas, intentions, and climate in their task environment.

SUMMARY

Decision building in large, formalized organizations requires sharing of information among people who do not have face-to-face communication with one another. In this chapter, structures useful for achieving contact are discussed.

Information which is shared across group boundaries is typically in the form of documents. There is no "right way" to decide what should be included in the documents called information structures and how the material should be arranged. Information is relative to the values and perceptions of those designing the information structure.

In product-making organizations there are typically information structures which relate costs to production. Even such straightforward questions as "how much does it cost to produce one automobile?" are not straightforward. The answer "depends." It depends, for example, upon how you allocate labor costs and costs of capital. A question such as "how much does it cost to operate a car?" is more murky because one's values determine what should be included in the cost figure. The values included are not personal values. Rather, cost structure should be devised to show comparisons which are important to decision makers. If decision makers do not have to decide whether to allocate money either to storage facilities or production facilities, the information structure should not encourage this comparison.

Information structures in nonproduct organizations are even more relative because there is no "product" to which costs may be allocated. In order to gather information for cost comparisons, many nonproduct organizations create "artificial" products called "programs." A program structure is a classification scheme of observable objectives and related activities of an organization. A program budget relates expenditures to objectives as a way of rationalizing allocation decisions.

In addition to rationally determined schemes for structuring information, organizational decision makers are influenced by "wisdom" captured in slogans. The way people talk to one another and to outsiders creates a verbal environment which makes some collective decisions more probable than others.

Because of the relative nature of any information structure, the "best" structures are those which map details of the territory they represent. Thus, differentiation among organizational units contributes to organizational intelligence. At the same time, for collective decisions there must be integration among units. Six methods for achieving integration among nonface-to-face groups are described. Each is assessed for its potential as a means of creating integration. These six are: hierarchy, System 4 design, management-by-objectives, organizational joint problem solving, contingency design, and project management.

ENDNOTES

1. Daniel Katz and Robert Kahn, *The Social Psychology of Organizations* (New York: John Wiley and Sons, Inc., 1957), p. 43.

2. William Boresquette, "Business Mirror: Varying Accounting Methods Noted," AP release, April 29, 1975.

3. Peter Drucker, *Managing for Results* (New York: Harper & Row, 1964), p. 28.

4. Ibid., p. 70.

5. Ibid., p. 83.

6. Ibid., p. 87.

7. Harold Wilensky, *Organizational Intelligence* (New York: Basic Books, 1967), pp. 19–20.

8. Paul R. Lawrence and Jay W. Lorsch, *Organization and Environmental Managing Differentiation and Integration* (Boston: Harvard University Press, 1967).

9. Ibid., p. 44.

10. Wilensky, *Organizational Intelligence,* p. 48.

11. Lawrence and Lorsch, *Organization and Environmental Managing Differentiation and Integration,* p. 11.

12. Wilensky, *Organizational Intelligence,* p. 43.

13. William H. Read, "Upward Communication in Industrial Hierarchies," *Human Relations* 15 (1962): 3–15.

14. Rensis Likert, *The Human Organization* (New York: McGraw-Hill, 1967), p. 47.

15. Ibid., pp. 197–211.

16. George Odiorne, *Management by Objectives* (New York: Pitman Publishing Co., 1965), p. 26.

17. Drucker, *Managing for Results,* pp. 128–129.

18. Herbert H. Meyer, Emanuel Kay, and John R. French, Jr., "Split Roles in Performance Appraisal," *Harvard Business Review* 43 (1965): 123–129.

19. Anthony P. Raia, "A Second Look at Management Goals and Controls," *California Management Review* 8 (Summer 1966): 49–58.

20. Henry L. Tosi and Stephen J. Carroll, "Management Reaction to Management by Objectives," *Academy of Management Journal* 11 (1968): 415–426.

21. Robert L. Swinth, "Organizational Joint Problem-Solving," *Management Science* (October 1971): 68–79.

22. Ibid., p. 78.

23. Lawrence and Lorsch, *Organization and Environmental Managing Differentiation and Integration,* p. 89.

24. Ibid., pp. 61–62.

25. Ibid., p. 60.

26. Ibid., p. 65.

27. Ibid., p. 64.

28. Ibid., p. 75.

29. Ibid.

30. Ibid., p. 74.

31. Andre Delbecq, "Managerial Leadership Styles in Problem-Solving Conferences: Research Findings on Role Flexibility," *Academy of Management Journal* 8 (March 1965).

Conclusion:
Communication and Change

> **Change Function of Communication**
> **Planned Change**
> **Organizational Development**
> **The Interventionist Role**

Every age develops an organizational form and life style most appropriate to the genius of that age. Most organizations reflect the uneasiness of transition for they were built upon certain assumptions about man and his environment. The environment was thought to be placid, predictable, and uncomplicated. Man was thought to be placid, predictable, and uncomplicated. Organizations based on these assumptions will fail, if not today, then tomorrow. They will fail for the very same reasons that dinosaurs failed: the environment changed suddenly at the peak of their success.

The environment now is busy, clogged, and dense with opportunities and threats; it is turbulent, uncertain and dynamic. The people who work for organizations are more complicated than ever before. They have needs, motives, anxieties, and to make matters even more complicated, they bring higher expectations than ever before to our institutions. The institutions themselves are changing, through the press of environmental challenges and the internal demands of its people. Organizational development is a response to these complex challenges, an educational strategy which aims to bring about a better fit between the human beings who work in and expect things from organizations and the busy, unrelenting environment with its insistence on adapting to changing times.

Warren G. Bennis, *Organizational Development: Its Nature, Origins, and Prospects*

This chapter draws together the perspective on organizing which has been developed throughout the book and applies that perspective to the process called organizational change. In the first section I describe change as a function (a necessary and inevitable consequence) of communication. Inevitable change can be seen to have direction or pattern only in retrospect. That is, looking back on the history of a family, a social group, or a corporation, one can detect patterns in its development. In the second section, I describe change which is guided by some kind of forethought. In this section we look at planned change and consider why people in an organization plan a systematic change. We will consider how planned interactions, collective decision building, and documentation act as methods for accomplishing planned change.

In the third section is described the method of organizational intervention and change known as "organizational development." Examples of planned change through programs of organizational development are discussed. Finally, there is a section about the role of the interventionist in planned change.

CHANGE FUNCTION OF COMMUNICATION

Throughout the book I have described inevitable consequences of communication. In chapter 2, for example, communication problems such as self-fulfilling prophecy and multiple systems were described as inevitable (or nearly so). These problems are inevitable because they result from the nature of communication as dynamic, ever-changing, and continuous. The two principal functions of communication described throughout the book are intelligence and integration. Both of these functions are learning processes. That is, intelligence is not a static state; rather, it is a process of learning. Likewise, integration is not a static state, it is also constantly evolving. Integration is the process of learning to integrate. Learning is change. It takes place because of the nature of communication as dynamic, ever-changing, and continuous.

In one sense any set of objects which together comprise a larger object may be thought of as an "organization." Kenneth Boulding notes that "the jig-saw puzzle, the statue, the picture . . . are examples of this [simplest] level of organization." A slightly more advanced level of organization is the "clockwork" in which there is a "predetermined structure repeating its movements because of some simple law of connectedness among its parts."[1] Organizations at neither of these levels can change unless that change is introduced by forces on the outside. A human being can change the parts of a jigsaw. A jigsaw cannot change itself. Though the parts of a clock move, they move only as some person has determined that they will move, and then only in accordance with immutable laws of mechanics.

The capacity for change is a direct result of the capacity for communication. The simple thermostat has a limited capacity to change itself. It can turn on its heater and turn it off again. Its capacity is limited by its ability to communicate among its moving parts. It has the ability to sense its environment in a limited way (it senses temperature). It can send a message to itself which says, "turn off the heater" or, "turn on the heater." At a more complex level, animals can change their organization because they possess a greater ability to sense their environments and to send messages.

At the most advanced level, human organization is made possible by our ability to sense our environment and to send messages appropriate to changes in that environment. Boulding notes, "because of his capacity for abstract communication and his ability to enter in imagination into the lives of others, man is able to build organizations of a size and complexity far beyond those of the lower animals, even of the social insects."[2] Communication makes organization possible because communication is the process of organizing. Thus, any organization necessarily has these same characteristics of communication. Organizations are necessarily dynamic, ever-changing, and continuous.

PLANNED CHANGE

Communication is the process by which organizations change. Most of the change is "unplanned." It is a learning process by which people respond to their environment, but communication also gives people the capacity to predetermine or plan how they will change. Change in human systems may be purposeful or deliberate.

The reasons for planned change are the same as the forces which produce unplanned change. One reason is change in the environment. The environment of an organization is anything which is relevant to the operation of the organization, but over which the managers of the system have no direct control. The invention of the automobile changed the environment of wagon wheel manufacturing organizations. The migration of middle class families from center city areas has changed the environment of the families who remain there. A court decision that a telephone company may not have a monopoly over the manufacture of telephone instruments used with their lines changes the environment of the telephone company. Any such change raises in the minds of organizational decision makers: what are we going to do now? One organizational response, of course, is to attempt to change the environment. Another way is to change the formal and/or informal organizational structure to adapt to the environment.

Another reason for planned change is dissatisfaction with the consensual expectations of members of the organization and the climate those expectations create. Expectations (hence organizational climates) are always evolving slowly. As the result of unplanned change, the expectations of people in an organization may come to be "unsatisfactory." They may be demoralizing people and hence creating job dissatisfaction. They may not support high production goals, and hence result in lower productivity. Expectations may result from assumptions about human beings which were acceptable many years ago, but are no longer acceptable. That is, they may be unsatisfactory because (though they change some) they tend to be conservative. Collective expectations do not change as rapidly as individuals—hence creating that "uneasiness of transition" which Bennis describes in the quotation at the beginning of this chapter.

The reason for planning change is that organizations based on largely unstated expectations (and resulting patterns of behavior) do not naturally change as rapidly as environmental conditions and individual demands change at certain times. When the environment and the individuals within an organization are changing slowly it is likely that organizing patterns will respond "naturally." A slow learning or adaptation will take place. But at other times, dramatic—even traumatic—events will occur which make necessary a planned response. Or, an organization may be so unresponsive to changes in its environment or its personnel over a long period of time that the effect of its lack of adaptation will accumulate until organizational decision makers can no longer ignore the extent to which the organization is "out of sync." At this point they may decide on a dramatic response to what has been a growing change in their environment or personnel.

There are several methods for planned or purposeful change in an organization. At the conclusion of chapter 4 there is a discussion of coordination formats as methods of organizational change. Let us review that discussion in light of some of the material about the formats presented in later chapters of the book.

One method of planned change is planned interaction among individuals. With this method only one person has to be dissatisfied with the organizational process. That individual diagnoses the problem, sets change goals, and determines his or her own strategies for accomplishing those goals. Planned interaction is the least collaborative kind of planned change because the "planning" is an intrapersonal process. It takes place within the minds of individuals. Several individuals may be simultaneously engaged in planning (this is typically the case), but there is no collaboration on the plan. This method is often used by leaders who want to change their organization. The leader diagnoses problems among a group of subordinates. The subordinates may or may not be brought in to "discuss" the problem. Even if there is discussion, it is the leader's definition of the problem which guides the direction of the change. Although this change strategy is most likely to be used by formal leaders, it may also be used by subordinates.

Total Woman[3] is a book which describes how subordinates (remaining in the role of subordinates) can influence their "superiors" and thus change the whole character of their social system. It is a book about how housewives can change their marriages without even discussing "change" with their husbands.

The chief advantage of the planned change strategy over the "wait and see" strategy of unplanned change is that the direction of the change has some deliberate direction. The disadvantage of this method is that it represents less than full coordination on change. The direction of change is either that determined by only one person, or the uncoordinated result of different people attempting to change the organization in different directions. It is difficult to believe that a program of systematic change of a large organization could be successful if it were the result of planned interaction of one individual or even many individuals who were not collaborating.

When the individuals are collaborating, then collective decision building is the method of planned change. In collective decision building individuals talk about the reason for the change. They construct a collaborative definition of the problem. They set collaborative goals for the change. They achieve consensus on strategies for achieving the goal. With collective decision building there is purposefulness at the collective level. The direction of the change is the result of consensus. The principal advantage of collective decision building as a method of change is that it generates commitment on the part of organizational members for the change. In the classic study by Coch and French on overcoming resistance to change, collective decision building was established as the means by which to involve organizational members in a process of change (see discussion in chapter 1).

The problem with using collective decision building as the means of organizational change is that collective decision building itself may be the desired goal of a program of change. For example, an organization may find that its market environment has become much more uncertain over a period of a few years. As the result, the bureaucratic design of the sales staff is no longer appropriate to the contingencies of the situation. Some people on the staff and higher levels of management may think that a design which encourages more participation is needed. They may want to use collective decision building for making more organizational decisions, but the salesmen expect key decisions to be made higher up in the organization. Sales staff members are unaccustomed to making decisions. People lower in the organization have no established norms to use in constructing collaborative decisions. Their norms encourage them to "wait until you are told" to do something. Collective decision-building methods of interaction are the *goal* of the change. Of course, one cannot get such methods by fiat. Because the members of this group do not have expectations which lead them to workable group methods, their attempts at change will be difficult. They cannot easily describe the goal because they are not familiar with what collective decision building "looks like."

Chris Argyris describes the lack of knowledge about what effective decision building looks like as a major problem in organizational change aimed toward increased participative management. He describes one organization where he was a consultant in a program of planned change or organizational development (OD):

> Vacillation and testing began with the president, who was one of the most dedicated adherents to change and development. He was not always clear as to how he should react; how to design new managerial methods, new structures, new rewards and penalty systems; how to respond to elation as well as to depression, his own or others'. Nor were the OD specialists able to make suggestions that satisfied even their own aspirations. Again and again we come smack up against the barrier of lack of tested knowledge.[4]

In chapters 6 and 9 I presented a good deal of the known information about how collective decision building can be made to work. But those descriptions are necessarily incomplete. The problem, as Argyris points out, is for group members to work out their own cognitive maps and expectations. This is difficult enough in a situation where people are committed to this kind of change, as the statement above indicates. It is even more difficult when not all are convinced that collective decision building is a worthwhile goal for making organizational decisions. Those supporting more participative decision-building methods are disadvantaged when they must argue for their preferred methods because they lack cognitive maps to explain clearly what the new methods will be like[5] and because they are trying to change the typical approach of "selling" an idea. This means that they are reluctant to engage in selling as a means of getting to a nonselling norm of interaction.[6] There can be no description of what the goal of the change will be before it is accomplished. The goal is clarified as it is accomplished. It is retrospective.

The goal is clarified as it is accomplished through a joint learning process. In Argyris's words:

It can be said with a good degree of safety that change will not come through the constant input of information or the mechanics of persuasion [planned interaction]. Change will come slowly as a result of the members in problem-solving or decision-making conferences being permitted to confront the new values, their superiors, their peers, and their subordinates; constantly monitoring and correcting every move; periodically reacting with frustrations, anger, and withdrawal at the difficulties involved.

The goal of such a change in organizing cannot be specified beforehand in much detail. Note how similar this description is to the phases of organizing discussed in chapter 3.

Documentation is a third method of planned change. In some situations documentation may be combined with either planned interaction or collective decision building. That is, in autocratic organizations, the chief executive may determine individually that there should be some kind of organizational change and then announce the change to the other organizational members via a document. In most organizations, a change in formal policy is the announcement of some kind of collective decision. The difference between this kind of documentation as a change and collective decision building discussed above is that in documentation the people who decide that there should be a change are not the people who are involved in the change. A team of managers may decide that the interactions among their subordinates should change and then attempt to force the change they want through changing the formal job descriptions of their subordinates.

When documentation is the method of change, the direction of the change is likely to be more "logical" than in the methods described before. Community planners are more likely to create logical plans about how a community should be developed than is a group of people who actually live in the community because residents each have their own stake in the future. They are likely to compromise and negotiate with one another and come up with a plan which is suited to their interests, but does not reflect any rational "planning concept." The larger and more complex the organization, the more it may make sense to have some rational planning for change in an organization.

The problem with documented or formal plans for change is that they are "paper and pencil" creations. They are not human creations. They have a rigidity which human behavior (the goal of the plan) does not have. Therefore, there will always be differences between the documented plan and the enacted plan. The difference is inevitable because organizations are oral cultures. People cannot live as rules on paper say they could or should live. Therefore, people in interpreting the rigid plan, will "humanize" it. They will interpret the plan in terms of what they can do and what they think they should do.

A fourth method of change is to "call in a change agent." This method involves at least one of the other methods. A change agent works through planned interaction, collective decision building, documentation, or some combination of these. In recent years human relations specialists who act as change agents in organizations have come to be called "organizational developers" or "organization development interventionists." In the following sections I describe organizational development and the role of the interventionist in facilitating organizational change.

ORGANIZATIONAL DEVELOPMENT

Organizational development is a term widely used in management circles. As with any term widely used, it has an imprecise referent. In its broadest sense, it refers to any process of preparing for and managing change.[7] More narrowly, it has been defined as:

> A normative, re-education strategy intended to affect systems of beliefs, values, and attitudes within the organization so that it can adapt better to the accelerated rate of change in technology, in our industrial environment, and society, in general. It also includes formal organizational restructuring which is frequently initiated, facilitated and reinforced by the normative and behavioral changes.[8]

Or:

> A long-range effort to improve an organization's problem-solving and renewal processes, particularly through a more effective and collaborative management of organization culture—with special emphasis on the culture of formal work teams—with the assistance of a change agent or catalyst and the use of the theory and technology of applied behavioral science.[9]

These quotations reflect differences in descriptions of what constitutes organizational development, but they also reflect some basic similarities in the assumptions, goals, and methods of "O.D."

One goal of a program of planned change through organizational development is an improved problem-solving or learning capability of the organization. An important assumption of the O.D. theorists is that organizations exist in turbulent environments and that those who survive have the capacity to learn about and adapt to their environments. Thus, O.D. is an attempt to improve the "intelligence function" of an organization. *This means their goal is to change the structure of integration in order to improve collective decision building or problem solving within an organization.*

When the president of American Airlines hired a team of O.D. consultants in 1968 he articulated objectives of the program: "We've got to learn to combine [employees'] talents in a manner that will enable us to plan effectively, to secure maximum cooperation between varying disciplines in an inherently complex business, and to experiment and adapt to the challenges that lie ahead." Notice the relationship between the two objectives. He wanted the members of the organization to learn to combine their talents (integration) in order to plan effectively (intelligence). More specifically, integration was conceptualized as:

> The creation of an atmosphere that will provide every employee with a satisfying experience at work. This means among other things
> (a) A democratic organization
> (b) A free exchange of ideas—up, down, and sideways—and the fostering of constructive dissent
> (c) Group participation in decision making.[10]

Chris Argyris, in describing the objectives of organizational development, outlines three. The goal is to create and maintain a quality of life within an organization so that participants:

1. Produce valid and useful information especially about their more important problems.
2. Make effective decisions.
3. Generate a high degree of human energy and commitment to their decisions in order to diligently monitor and effectively implement them.[11]

Organizational intelligence and integration are inseparable goals. Integration, valuable in its own right, is also necessary to accomplish organizational intelligence. Changing the way in which organizational members construct their collective knowledge, means changing the expectations among members of the organization.

A plan of systematic change begins with a diagnosis of the problems of a particular organization and setting goals for that organization. Each organization's plan is unique. However, there are some general expectations which O.D. researchers are more likely to establish as goals of the change. Blake and Mouton's plan of organizational development as the "Piedmont Corporation" (a fictitious name) illustrates the typical goal. The kind of group norms discouraged were:

1. Members giving more importance to maintaining friendly relations than to solving work problems.

2. Members preferring to keep their opinions to themselves rather than to laying their cards on the table.
3. Members preferring to do a job by themselves rather than with other members of the group.
4. Members often compromising when disagreement arises.[12]

These attitudes or norms are similar to those described in the section of chapter 6 pertaining to characteristics of ineffective groups.

Argyris tries to promote the following norms in his plans for organizational development:

1. Self-acceptance, feels of essentiality, and valid confirmation of group members.
2. Experiences of psychological success rather than psychological failure.
3. Communicating relevant information in directly verifiable or observable categories rather than inferential categories. "This means that whenever possible (i.e., in human relationships, policy statements, directives) evaluative, attributive, and mutually contradictory information should be minimized."
4. Leadership assigned on the basis of expertise and the needs of members.
5. A feeling of internal commitment to effective management of the group ("e.g., keeping it 'on target,' concern about providing climate for open exchange of views, high trust among members, etc.).[13]

The process of organizational development has been described as an "organic" one. That is, the development must grow as part of what I call an "oral culture" of organizational members. Organizational development is in part dependent upon some changes in the formal restructuring of the organization. But formal restructuring alone will not produce organizational development. Blake and Mouton's Piedmont program illustrates the process of "organic growth" in an organizational development plan.

The first two phases were really "manager development." The organization was hierarchically ordered. Through the change, the company would become more "System 4" in orientation, but the hierarchy of supervisors and subordinates would remain an important part of the structure. Therefore, the first two phases were to help individual employees learn improved concepts for relating to one another, to their supervisors, and to their subordinates. The first phase was "laboratory-seminar training." The O.D. specialists formed teams which were composed of people from "diagonal slices" of the organization. That is, there were different levels of the organization in each "team," but the people in a team were from different organizational departments. The people filled out managerial grid questionnaires to determine their typical managerial styles. (A discussion of Blake and Mouton's Managerial grid is found in chapter 6.) In fifty hours of intensive training, the people participated in simulated problems and discussed their interpersonal behavior and its effect on their task performance. Team members gave one another feedback on their managerial styles. The idea here was to learn new ways of interacting in a situation which was largely "protected" from the routine concerns of one's work environment.

Phase two was "team development." After members of the organization were trained as individuals, teams were formed among those people who worked together. Members talked about their expectations in these teams. That is, they talked about their "ground rules" and their relationship. Usually these teams began by talking about their supervisor-subordinate communication. Norms of openness and candor were discussed and encouraged. The idea in this phase was to work out new expectations for interaction in everyday working conditions. According to Blake and Mouton, one objective was to: "Make managers more critical of outworn practices and precedents while extending their problem-solving capacities in interdependent situations. Words like 'involvement' and 'commitment' became real in terms of day-to-day tasks." The skills worked on in this phase were those discussed in chapter 6 (face-to-face decision building) and part of chapter 8 (interpersonal communication between superiors and subordinates).

The change at Piedmont, however, was intended to develop the capacity of the whole organization to make better decisions, not just to improve climate and decision making within groups in which members had regular contact. The last four phases were "organizational development" in the broader sense of improved intelligence and integration among people who did not regularly talk together. Phase three was concerned with intergroup development. The objective was to have group members learn better expectations for coordinating their work with other groups. Group members and/or their representatives sat down with members of other groups and discussed situations where intergroup tension was interfering with their group level cooperating. According to Blake and Mouton, the groups worked at creating assumptions which supported joint problem solving rather than the typical assumption of "win-loss."

Phase four was "organizational goal setting." Broad problems such as cost control, union-management relations, safety, promotion policies, and overall profit improvement were discussed by special task groups which represented a "diagonal slice" of the organizations. Phase five used methods similar to phase one, except with real organizational problems determined in phase four. There were task groups set up to discuss and recommend solutions to organizational problems. These teams recommended corrective steps and assigned responsibility for carrying these out. They monitored the actions taken. Thus this phase was "Goal Attainment." The leaders of these task teams were "neither line nor staff in the conventional sense." The idea was for the teams to "seek action based on understanding and agreement, not because of any formal authority" of an individual or individuals. Blake and Mouton admit that this approach is more difficult than forcing decisions through formal authority. But it reduces resistance. The final phase is stabilization. In this phase the trial behaviors became part of the regular routine of the organization.

This process of organizational development is by no means universal, but it is a fairly common procedure. Important elements of this model are:

(1) learning new patterns of relationship outside one's typical place in the organization.
(2) group discussion and collective decision building among teams of people who work together.
(3) talk among people who work for different teams to reduce intergroup tensions associated with differentiation into specialized groups.
(4) teams of people from across the organization who set organizational goals and coordinate the accomplishment of those goals.

THE INTERVENTIONIST ROLE

The role of interventionist or change agent in an organizational development process is somewhat disguised in this discussion. It is a critical, but difficult role. One of the more simple tasks of change agents is to assess attitudes of organizational members to the problems of the organization. At American Airlines, for example, the consultants used questionnaires to assess members' perceptions of the organization, its policies and practices, and the style and effectiveness of the management.[14] A more difficult role is the designing of the overall plan for an organizational change while keeping that change an "organic" one, not a documented or imposed one.

Argyris summarizes the three primary tasks of the interventionist:

(1) Generating and helping the clients to generate valid information that they can understand about their problems.
(2) Creating opportunities for the clients to search effectively for solutions to their problems, to make free choices.

(3) Creating conditions for internal commitment to these choices and apparatus for the continual monitoring of the action taken.

In the process of generating information and creating opportunities for clients to search for solutions, it is likely that conflicts will emerge between the interventionist and the client. The interventionist, after all, is an employee of the client. But he or she is a peculiar kind of employee. Interventionists cannot do their jobs if they do everything the client would have them do. At the most general level they have been brought in to facilitate change, but obviously, someone in an organization wants change. Probably not everyone wants change. Any major change is disrupting. The model of change presented in chapter 4 illustrates that things get worse before they "bottom out" and get better in the process of change. Thus, even those responsible for bringing in the interventionist will likely be uncomfortable in the process and hold the interventionist responsible. Argyris outlines four causes of possible difficulty for the relationship between change agent and client:

(a) There is a tendency toward an underlying discrepancy between the interventionist's and the client's behavior, values, and criteria which each uses to judge effectiveness. Discrepancies tend to exist regarding the causes of problems, new designs necessary to remedy the situation, and the behavior that is necessary on the part of the interventionist and client.
(b) The interventionists' actions are likely to be or appear to be different from his own ideas. Interventionists are in "marginal roles" between two worlds, their own and the clients. They must somehow act in both roles and this can cause inconsistent actions.
(c) Clients are likely to feel and talk about their confusion, frustration, and mistrust of the interventionist. They will not soon understand "the order and trust the interventionists are attempting to establish."
(d) Clients will tend to give the interventionist insufficient feedback about his effectiveness. That is, they will protect him from information about his own ineffectiveness even though he is telling them about the importance of open sharing of information.

There are two conflicting kinds of roles typically played by an interventionist, both of which must be played to some extent. One role is "source of certainty"; the other role is "source of uncertainty."

As a source of certainty, the interventionist provides a model of the desired actions. He or she shows the client different kinds of actions. Argyris notes that the interventionist cannot be a consistently good model because the interventionist is not a member of the organization. He cannot act as both the interventionist and the client. Note the necessary contradiction: the role both requires the interventionist to be a model and prevents him or her from being a model.

One apparent way out of this contradiction is for the interventionist to be a "trainer." A trainer describes for the clients (via lectures or other direct methods) the actions he wants them to learn. The trainer models the actions for brief periods of time in simulated situations. The trainer calls attention to his actions in modeling desired actions. Thus, the trainer is a "source of certainty." The interventionist uses demonstration as a method of clarifying or making desired actions observable to the organization members.[15] But the modeling is limited to relatively brief periods of time and categories of activity.

An alternative role is that of source of uncertainty. Recall that collective decision building is one response to unpredictability. Recall also that it is, relative to programmed and planned interactions, an unpredictable process. This suggests that if collective decision building is the goal, it's helpful to introduce uncertainty. The interventionist can introduce unfamiliar information into the client's decision-building system. The client must then interpret the meaning of the information and decide what to do with it. In the process of introducing uncertainty, clients are likely to feel confusion and frustration and accurately to ascribe the cause of their confusion to the interventionist. Thus, acting as a source of confusion is often a necessary prerequisite to the change process. If clients treat the intervention as routine, no intervention is possible.

To some extent, all interventionists must act both as sources of certainty and sources of uncertainty. But any individual or team will choose which is to be the predominant mode of interaction with the client. The two roles proceed from different philosophies. A basic dilemma underlying this entire book is evident in the philosophical differences of these two roles.

In playing the role of certainty, the interventionist is implicitly stating, "I know what's best for this organization." Trainers (sources of certainty) establish prospective goals, or goals determined prior to interaction. Experienced trainers usually set up precise behavioral objectives for trainees. Such planned interaction on the part of the trainer brings direction and predetermined rationality into the change process. However, the assumption that the trainer knows what is good for an organization is questionable. Trainers generally sell a "package" of skills which may not be exactly appropriate to any particular organization. Interventionists acting as trainers bring in some preset ideas about what is "good," but their biases may not allow them to see if, in fact, it is good in the particular social system with which they are working. Even adaptable interventionists such as Argyris and Blake tend to promote a particular perspective on what constitutes "good" interpersonal relations.

The idea of having predetermined learning objectives is also open to question, given the notion that goals are retrospective. The trainer who attempts to describe in precise terms how to improve communication within a work group will not be able to describe beforehand all the features of what "improved communication" will look like. We see here the basic problem encountered by anyone who is seeking to obtain a rational change in human behavior by planning that change. There are limits on the extent to which we can know what we want before we get it.

The alternative role is source of uncertainty. In playing this role, the interventionists emphasize their role as outsiders. Leonard Hawes describes the "cultural stranger" perspective of the interventionist in the role of "source of uncertainty":

> Listening and reading done from the perspective of a cultural stranger perspective enables one to hear and see activities and objects uninfluenced by excessive familiarity assumptions. . . . The obvious analogy I have been using is cultural anthropological. Before prescribing agricultural techniques to non-literate agrarians, learn the culture into which the techniques must be assimilated. At the same time, the agricultural consultant is no good to the client culture if he/she "goes native."[16]

The interventionist must learn the cultural "map" without forsaking his/her own map. Hawes defines his role as an interventionist as one of feeding back his outsider's perspective on how members of the organization accomplish summaries of their work called "reports," "policy statements," "decisions," etc. In particular, Hawes seeks to account for how such "objects" relate to past talking and writing and to subsequent talking and writing. Members of the organization are given this "outsider's" account of their work. They must make sense of the outsider's report (note this process involves subsequent talking and writing about the report). The report represents "uncertainty" from which the client must draw some sense. In this self-reflexive decision-building process, organizational members must discuss their expectations. The direction of the process of change is left to the organizational members, not mandated by the interventionist. At best, the interventionist invites organizational members to look retrospectively at their goals and processes.

SUMMARY

Organizational change is a constant feature of organizations. Organizations are dynamic, ever-changing, and continuous because they are constantly accomplished by communication which is dynamic, ever-changing, and continuous.

Organizational change may be speeded up and deliberatively directed through planning. Usually a planned change is undertaken because of dissatisfaction with the internal climate of an organization and/or its relationship to its environment. Planned change may be accomplished by planned interaction, collective decision building, documentation, or some combination of these. Change agents or interventionists are people who are hired for the expressed purpose of facilitating a change process.

Organizational development is a planned change aimed at improving organizational performance by improving interpersonal skills and organizational climate. That is, its aim is to improve organizational intelligence and action through improved integration. Blake and Mouton's six-phase program of organizational development is discussed.

The interventionist's role in organizational development is critical. Beyond assessing the need for a change and planning the overall strategy, the interventionist performs three tasks: (1) generating with the client valid information about the client's problems; (2) creating opportunities for the client to search for solutions, (3) creating conditions for internal commitment to his or her solutions and for monitoring the effectiveness of the solutions.

Interventionists have different styles with which they generate information, create opportunities, and create conditions. At one end of a style continuum, the interventionist may presume to know the client's problems and solutions. The interventionist acts as a "source of certainty." He/she is a trainer who tells the client what is wrong and teaches the client new ways of acting. At the other end of the continuum, the interventionist acts as a "cultural stranger" who offers information, but no evaluation or direction. The clients use the ambiguous information provided by the interventionist to arrive at their own conclusions and solutions. This second role is more consistent with the dynamic quality of communication and with the commitment function of collective decision building. But the first role—source of certainty—is consistent with most organizational members' desire for rationality and deliberation in creating organizations.

The problem of the interventionist is thus like the problem of all organizers: How can one accomplish rationality and deliberate purpose in collective action given inevitable limitations on the accomplishment of collective intelligence and integration? Or, from another perspective: given our human capacity to achieve collective intelligence and integration without rationality or deliberate purpose, under what condition is rational change desirable at all?

ENDNOTES

1. Kenneth Boulding, *The Image* (Ann Arbor, Mich.: Univ. of Michigan Press, 1956), p. 20.

2. Ibid., pp. 26–27.

3. Marabel Morgan, *Total Woman* (Old Tappan, N.J.: Fleming H. Revell Co., 1973).

4. Chris Argyris, *Management and Organizational Development* (New York: Mc-Graw-Hill, 1971), p. 150.

5. Ibid., p. 86.

6. Ibid., pp. 32–33.

7. James L. Gibson, John M. Ivanovich, and James H. Donnelly, *Organizations: Structure, Process, and Behavior* (Dallas: Business Publications, 1973), p. 340.

8. Alexander Winn as quoted in Gibson et al., *Organizations*, p. 341.

9. Wendell L. French and Cecil H. Bell, "A Definition and History of Organizational Development: Some Comments," Proceedings of the Thirty-first Annual Meeting, Academy of Management, Boston, 1972, reprinted in Keith Davis, *Organizational Behavior: A Book of Readings* (New York: McGraw-Hill, 1969).

10. National Industrial Conference Board, " 'American Airlines' Behavioral Science: Concepts and Management Application," reprinted in Gibson, Ivanovich, and Donnelly, *Organizations*, p. 430.

11. Argyris, *Management and Organizational Development*.

12. Robert R. Blake and Jane S. Mouton, *The Managerial Grid* (Houston: Gulf Publishing Co., 1964).

13. Argyris, *Management and Organizational Development*, pp. 21–22.

14. National Industrial Conference Board, in Gibson et al., *Organizations*, p. 447.

15. See Irwin L. Goldstein, *Training Program: Development and Evaluation* (Monterey, Calif.: Brooks/Cole, 1974).

16. Leonard C. Hawes, "Displaying 'Evaluating' Procedures: A Study of the Pragmatics of Talk and Writing in Organizations," Paper presented to S.C.A. Post-Doctoral Program on Organizational Communication, San Marcos, Texas, 1976, pp. 5–6.

Appendix: Investigating Organizing Processes

From Hunch to Research Question
From Question to Evidence
From Evidence to Inference

The intent of this section is to provide the reader with some guidelines to research on organizational communication. It may be read before any of the text. The suggestions provided here are consistent with, but not dependent upon, the ideas in the text. Obviously, this section cannot describe all methodologies available to researchers. Nor can it prescribe the one best way to conduct organizational research. Like several of the regular chapters, this one provides the reader with a way of conceptualizing a process. It describes three tasks to be accomplished in conducting an investigation of organizational communication. It suggests methods for accomplishing each task. These three tasks involve moving (1) from "hunch to research question," (2) from "question to data," and (3) from "data to inference."

FROM HUNCH TO RESEARCH QUESTION

The process of investigating almost always begins in an unscientific way: someone has a hunch. The "hunch" may be a dissatisfaction with "the way things are in this organization."   One student who was a resident assistant in a university dormitory conducted an investigation of the screening procedure used to select resident assistants.   The motivation for his study was a dissatisfaction shared by many in the residence assistant hierarchy (from "RA's" to the Dean of Student Affairs) who felt that the present system of interviewing and selection was cumbersome and ineffective.   Another student began an investigation of written communication between the central office of a retail food chain and store employees because of his frustration as a store employee in interpreting the memos from the central office.

Much research is begun with simple curiosities rather than dissatisfactions.   For example, a researcher may be curious about how the introduction of automated technology will affect social relationships among workers.   The researcher's curiosity is like that of a small child who takes apart a toy just to find out how it works.   Competent researchers, of course, will find out "how it works" without destroying "it."

Whether one begins with a dissatisfaction or a curiosity, researchers almost always begin by thinking in relatively common-sensical terms. Typical hunches or curiosities are that "memos" in this organization are "bad."   The "workers" in this office are "lazy."   The "job" that I do is "boring."   I get more "reports" than I have "time to read."   The nouns in each of these sentences refer to common-sense objects.   The adjectives—such as bad, lazy, boring—are our "everyday language" terms and as such they are imprecise.   In order to proceed with research, concrete nouns and imprecise adjectives need to be clarified.   The researcher must substitute more precise language for the ordinary language in which he or she first thought about a problem.   Let us follow the example of the "bad memos" in the retail food chain to see the kinds of considerations a researcher must make in moving from hunch to research question.   If your hunch is that "memos are bad in this organization," you need a precise way to identify "memo" and a precise way of identifying what is "bad."   Then you may proceed to determine whether "the memos are bad" and, if so, why.

In the process of clarifying what you want to investigate, you will begin to see concrete objects in more abstract terms.   The question of what constitutes a "memo" may seem obvious at first.   On reflection, a researcher may decide that memos are a class of non-face-to-face communicative media.   Note that the concept of a class of non-face-to-face communication media implies the existence of other kinds of media. There must be (by implication) face-to-face as well as non-face-to-face media.   Within the non-face-to-face category there is more than one class.   The researcher has developed the idea (at least indirectly) that memos are one means (medium) of communication and that, at least theoretically, there are other media.   There must be some kind of choice involved in the use of memos. Whether consciously or not, communicators could choose other means of communication.

Now that the researcher has developed the idea of choice among communicative media, it occurs to him or her that the memo is used for some purpose. Different memos may be used for different purposes. Therefore, the researcher develops a list of the purposes of memos. The purpose of any particular memo may be to direct the reader to perform either specific tasks (Do not cash personal checks) or to perform general tasks (Keep the store clean). The purpose of other memos may be to provide information (Next month there will be a sale on Brand X toothpaste). Still others may serve an "integrative" purpose, that is, they may act to help the reader feel like part of the organization ("Mabel Smith, clerk at the Riverside Ave. store, just had a new baby"). The researcher thus develops a four-part category system or "typology" with which to sort the kinds of memos according to purpose. Such a typology might be: Instruction-Specific; Instruction-General; Information; Integration.[1] Memos are but one means by which these purposes may be accomplished.

The concept of memo may be further refined by considering the "components" of memos. The researcher creates categories for sorting the components of a memo, for example: length of entire memo, number of different subjects in a single memo, kind of subject, difficulty of vocabulary, sentence length, abstractness of words.

Notice that the researcher has now both broadened and refined his hunch. Memos have become "functional units" in a larger "social system." Memos are but one means of accomplishing certain purposes within the social system. Memos are a "chosen method." Other methods or media could be chosen by organizational members to accomplish the same purposes. Having chosen memos as a means for accomplishing a certain purpose, the user has other choices. These include the length of memo, number of topics, and language.

Now the researcher must clarify what constitutes "badness." The first consideration is the choice of a frame of reference for interpreting what is bad: Are the memos bad for individual readers or bad for the functioning of the organization? If the personal frame of reference is chosen, then "badness' might mean that the memos cause dissatisfaction (readers are bored). The researcher could legitimately end his investigation after he had determined under what conditions readers rated memos as "boring" or "confusing." For example, he might find longer memos to be more "boring" than shorter ones. Memos using abstract terms are more confusing than those with more concrete terms.

Such findings are hardly surprising or exciting. A more serious indictment of such findings is that they are simply summaries of what people say; they do not help us to understand *why* people say that long memos are boring. This is because the term "boring" is not an interesting or useful way of thinking of "badness" of organizational communications. The concept of "badness" in this instance may more usefully be conceived from the frame of reference of the organization. To do this, the researcher returns to his typology of purposes. A memo may be bad, from the perspective of the organization, if it is used for a particular purpose (to give specific instructions, for example) and does not succeed at that purpose (people do not understand the specific tasks they have been told to do). But a memo may be "bad" even if it succeeds at its specific purpose, if it also results in undesirable consequences. For example, a reader may correctly interpret a memo which instructs her to do a particular task; she may do the task. Yet, she may be insulted by the memo. She may feel less commitment to the organization as a result of believing that managers are "patronizing" her. If most of her job instruction comes from similar memos, she may quit. In order to understand these more subtle meanings of "bad" the researcher might develop a typology for describing possible unintended consequences—or dysfunctions—of communications.

In order to think of possible unintended consequences of messages in an organization, the researcher has to have some ideas about how organizations work and how communication is related to this "working." If the researcher has not been using the findings of other organizational researchers before, he or she will surely begin at this point to read and use what others have said on the subject of the research. He will need to develop or borrow from others an overall framework for understanding (and explaining) how communication functions in an organization. From this framework he can then derive an explanation for why memos (one class of communication) may be bad (harmful to the functioning of the organization). This explanation can then be turned into the specific questions to be investigated.

The process of going from hunch to research question thus may be summarized as the following general steps:

1. Stating hunch in writing.
2. Pulling out key terms for refinement into abstract categories and writing a more precise "problem."
3. Placing the particular problem for investigation within a larger theoretical framework.
4. Using the larger framework to derive explanations for how the concepts in the problem may be related to one another.

The most difficult part of the process of moving from hunch to question is placing the problem within an appropriate conceptual framework. In order to get a clearer image of the process, let us look at an extended illustration of how one group of researchers set their research question within a conceptual framework of communication and organization theory. Spence and O'Connor's investigation of communication within the Pennsylvania Department of Public Welfare began with a hunch similar to the one I have been using as an illustration ("memos in this organization are bad"). In the summary of their report they describe how they embedded their problem in a theoretical framework. Their work is a useful model for this difficult process. They begin by stating their "hunch."

> This is a report of a fact-finding study of that part of the communications network of the Department of Public Welfare concerned with income maintenance and the delivery of social services at the county level. Nearly everyone in the Department has judged communications in this area inadequate. We have tried to find out in what ways and why communications between workers in the county boards of assistance and the Harrisburg offices are blocked or disturbed.[2]

Their hunch was that the communications between the workers in county boards and the Harrisburg office are inadequate. (Memos are bad.) They developed this hunch into a more general problem by first defining what they meant by communication:

> This study is focused on the implicit aspects of communication. All human communication takes place on at least two levels. There is the explicit message conveyed by words and numbers and the implicit message conveyed by secondary aspects of the message exchange such as voice tones, gestures, vocabulary, style, etc. The implicit message provides us information about the intentions and constraints of the sender— it gives rules about how the explicit message is to be understood.[3]

Spence and O'Connor then describe the conceptual framework or theory from which they drew their explanations for *whether* communications were inadequate and, if so, why they were. Note that the theory described below allows the researchers to move from the frame of reference of the individual to the frame of the organization. They begin with the individual ("notice how you feel") and move to the frame of reference of the organization ("the results are damaging to the organization"):

> Implicit messages are of a primary and volatile quality. Notice how you feel when someone fails to respond to your direct address; or how you interpret the intentions of an acquaintance who bombards you with more talk than you can handle; or again what it means to you when others speak to you in a specialized, and little understood jargon. In each of the cases the hackles are raised because there is implied in such messages a lack of consideration for the receiver. We cannot help but understand such messages as meaning that our efforts and lives don't count, that they mean very little, that our own language is inferior and unimpor-

tant in the sender's view. These responses will then guide the way we interpret and understand what the sender has to say.

When the implicit message denies in some way the worth of the receiver or when the implicit message is incongruous with the explicit message it is likely that the words of the sender will be interpreted in surprising and hostile ways. The initial reaction to such situations is to call attention to the denial or the incongruity. But this is not always possible, especially in an organization where the originator of the message is hard to locate. The next reaction then is to defend against the implicit message by 1) filtering out the explicit message, 2) discounting the worth and competence of the sender, 3) ignoring or circumventing the explicit message, and 4) avoiding further exchanges as much as possible. These responses in a face to face situation will set off enough tension to force a change or an end to the situation. But again in a large organization they are likely to fail. . . . The end result of systematic communication denials in an organization is the near isolation of the individual worker. This is true whether the worker responds in the pattern we have sketched here or whether the denial or incongruity is simply ignored in the first place. In either case the results are damaging to individuals—they promote anomy, alienation, and probably severe behavioral disorders such as alcoholism, drug abuse and mental instability. Further the results are damaging to the organization. Communication becomes problematic at best and continuous evaluation leading to corrective measures and innovations becomes almost impossible.[4]

From this conceptual framework, Spence and O'Connor drew the following hypothesis or statement to be researched:

There is a relationship between communication disturbances and individual distortions and between remedial responses and individual distortions.

Their theory led them to measure four categories of communication distortion and four types of remedial responses. Measures of distortion were:

(1) lack of diversity or the selection of communication channels and media based on the sender's needs rather than receiver's requirements; (2) restricted coding or the use of in-group language to exclude others and promote solidarity; (3) impaired feedback capacity or the loss of ability to process information to improve performance; and (4) defective responses or the habitual disregard of explicit message content and intensive interpretation of implicit intentions.[5]

Measures of remedial response were:

(1) message filtration or the systematic disregard of certain types of communication; (2) rationalized avoidance of administration or the development of a set of beliefs and attitudes about management's ignorance, indifference, and unreliability that justifies workers following their own

dictates; (3) automatic horizontal control or the routine exchange of information, assertion of norms, and interpretation or violations of regulations among workers at the same organizational level; (4) restriction of upward communication or regular patterns of secrecy, dissembling, and outward compliance resulting in laundered and irrelevant messages to superiors.[6]

Most important for our purposes here is the understanding that a research hypothesis (a claim about what the researcher expects to find) or a research question is based upon the researcher's conceptual framework. It is based upon a more or less specific theory of how things work. The theory directs attention to what the researcher should look for and provides an explanation of how those "things" will probably be related to one another. Spence and O'Connor explain how a different theory of communication (one in which substantive content was the predominant concept) would have directed them to a different kind of investigation:

> Had we focused on the substantive aspects of communication we would have found, for example, that workers are poorly informed about Department goals, programs, structure and personnel. But such findings of themselves are misleading. They suggest that a quantitative increase in messages or stricter regulation of message transition would improve communication. That is wrong, since communications will remain blocked and tangled until the implicit messages of denial and incongruity are altered.[7]

The quality of a piece of research can be no better than the quality of the thinking which went into refining the hunch into a research question. One question which may be used to test the quality of a research question is: "Will I know anything of value if I answer this question?" If all you will know is that "people find long memos to be boring," your results are not likely to justify the effort you will expend. The first criterion for judging a research question is whether the question is worth answering.

The second criterion is whether the research question is answerable. The curiosity, "Are memos bad?" cannot be answered. They may be bad to you, but not to me. The terms of a research question must be clear enough to allow an answer which will satisfy reasonable people. Some researchers use the term "falsifiable" to label this criterion. A research question is falsifiable if it is possible to find that the relationship suspected by the researcher is false (for example, one can find that memos are not bad). Spence and O'Connor's definitions of communication distortion and remedial responses allowed for both the possibility of finding such phenomena and for not finding them. All research questions should be scrutinized to make sure they are answerable.

FROM QUESTION TO EVIDENCE

After the researcher has clarified a hunch into a precise question, he or she then proceeds to collect evidence pertinent to the question. If the question is stated as a hypothesis which predicts a certain directional relationship, the researcher attempts to collect evidence by which he or she draws inferences about whether the relationship is predicted. The aim is to provide enough evidence from which to draw a reasonable inference about the answer to the research question. This section discusses how researchers should begin their selection of a research method by considering how much they need to "intrude" into the phenomena they will investigate. By "intrusion" I mean a change in what is studied which is brought about by the researchers. If they are seeking to describe—for example to describe how managers do their work—then they do not want to interfere with how managers work. On the other hand if they want to determine the casual relationship between two variables, they may need to create a situation in which they can manipulate the variables to examine how one influences the other.

Three kinds of research are described below. In observational studies the researchers observe and record behavior. In survey studies the researchers ask people to describe their attitudes and/or actions. In experimental investigations the researchers change certain conditions and then, through observation or survey, assess how certain other conditions change.

Observational Investigations

Observational studies are the least intrusive approach because the researcher simply watches people. There is some intrusion, of course, because the researcher may be recognized as a stranger in the setting. If he or she records with pen, audiorecorder, or camera, those activities are sure to be noted by those being observed. But, after awhile, the activities of the researcher are likely to "fade into the background" of the setting because people have their own work to do.

Observational studies may take the form of "case studies." In a case study the researcher observes one person or group over an extended period of time. Donald Roy's study, "Banana Time," described in chapter 4 is a case study. Only one group of workers was studied, but Roy observed virtually all their behavior over a period of several months. Case studies produce data which is rich in descriptions of how people act. The researcher attempts to understand the world from the perspective of the research subject while remaining outside so that he does not take everyday events for granted. It is possible for the researcher to become a participant in the activities of the research subjects, as Roy did, but researchers strive to see a situation as an outsider even if he is a participant. The idea is for researchers to "map the world" being studied, not for them to adopt that world as their own. There is little or no "intrusion" by the researcher into the "normal" patterns to be observed. Research subjects may not even know that they are subjects.

There are some disadvantages which a researcher should consider before opting for this nonintrusive methodology. First, the information generated is so rich in details about a particular person or group, that it is hard to compare two or more cases. Readers of a research report may find it difficult to understand general principles exemplified in the case study. They may be skeptical that the case is representative of anyone. It is difficult to verify hypotheses through a case study. Because the case study involves detailed descriptions, the reports are generally longer, making them more difficult to publish or even to summarize.

On the other hand, the richness of detail of case studies make them particularly valuable as a source of information about how people communicate to organize. The researcher who can understand the perspective of the insider while remaining an outsider translates for others the nature of organizational life. Good examples of what can be learned from case studies are Alvin Gouldner's study of a gypsum plant[8], Walker and Guest's study of automobile manufacturing[9], and Whyte's study of organizing on street corners.[10]

Another kind of observational study is illustrated by Mintzberg's investigation of the work of managers.[11] Mintzberg observed the chief executives of five medium to large organizations for a period of one week each. Because he watched members of several organizations for a relatively brief period of time, this is not a "case study" in the strict sense. The executives were aware that they were research subjects. They cooperated with Mintzberg in making observations about the chronology of their activity, their mail (890 pieces of mail were examined to determine their purpose and format as well as the attention and action response they received), and their personal contacts (phone calls, scheduled and unscheduled meetings, tours).

Observational studies can provide reliable information about what people do. They can be used to test hypotheses about what people do. If the studies are conducted over a brief time span, as Mintzberg's was, they may not provide detailed accounts of why people act as they do from their own perspective. The danger is that a researcher will be able to describe only the "movement" of people around a setting, but will have little understanding of the meanings of people's actions because the researcher has not had an opportunity to learn those meanings (as in a case study) nor to ask the subjects (as in a survey investigation).

Survey Investigations

Investigations which use interviews are more "intrusive" than observational studies because subjects are asked to stop what they are doing and to talk about it. The interviewer is getting the information a subject has chosen to give (interviews are planned interactions). The observational researcher is more likely to get data about organizational routines. But interviews generate information about how subjects interpret their own actions and the actions of others. Interviews allow researchers to get data on interactions they may not be allowed to observe. Managers may be unwilling to allow a researcher to observe them interacting with subordinates for a week or more. The researchers may not have that much time. But managers may be willing to take an hour to tell the researcher about how they communicate with subordinates.

One of the greatest benefits of the interview over observational studies is that the data from an interview is relatively "compact." By contrast, the data from observations are "diffuse." I was a technical advisor to a filmmaker who made a series of films on "the meaning of work" for broadcast on public television. The films show people at several levels of the organizational hierarchy. We constantly wrestled with the problems of diffuseness. Activity of the general manager was ongoing; it was not his own activity, but related to activity of the accountants, secretaries, factory foremen, sales personnel, etc. The camera crew could not get into some key meetings. Even when they could, there was the problem of bringing together snatches of conversation[12] so that outsiders could have some sense of what was happening. Our solution was to mix scenes showing people doing their work with scenes of them being interviewed about their work. The interviews gave us both a clearer and more compact image of the meaning of their work as they saw it and provided contexts for the actions of individuals.

If a study needs a large number of research subjects, it may not be possible for researchers to use the "face-to-face" methods of gathering research such as observations or interviews. Instead they may have to rely on written communication in the form of a questionnaire. Questionnaires are more intrusive than open-ended interviews discussed above because they limit the respondent's potential answers. Questionnaires usually ask subjects to respond using a limited scale such as "strongly agree, agree, disagree, strongly disagree." Questionnaires do not allow the researchers to verify whether subjects have understood the responses. Questionnaires typically give very sparse information. But they yield data which can easily be converted to numbers and summarized. Thus, it is even more "compact" than interview data.

Researchers may attempt to develop their own questionnaires or they may find questionnaires which measure the processes in which they are interested. When "standardized questionnaires" are used, the researcher may be able to compare his findings with those of other researchers using the same questionnaire.

In an attempt to generate comparative data about communication in formal organizations, researchers who belong to the International Communication Association are collaborating in a project known as the "Communication Audit." An audit is more than a series of questionnaires. Goldhaber describes an audit as "a research procedure which assesses the effectiveness of the organizational communication system according to a set of standards."[13] The workplan for auditing an organization's communication system is presented in Table A.1. Note that assessing the effectiveness of both the overall system and specific communications activities begins with determining the formal objectives and policies. Gathering facts about communication activities is done both by interview and questionnaires. Interviewers use standard questions such as:

1. Kind of information received
2. Kind of information sent
3. Source of information
4. Modes of communication
5. Organization outcome.[14]

The questionnaire has six parts. Two parts are of particular interest here since they may be used in less comprehensive investigations than the audit.

One kind of questionnaire is the "critical incident technique." As the name implies, subjects are asked to identify important communication incidents they have directly observed. (Downs reports that the term "critical" has proved unfortunate with some subjects who believe they are being asked to report only negative incidents.) Subjects write about what happened in the incident and describe the outcome. From this information, coders interpret where people get information and what they do with it (how they act on it; whether and to whom they pass it along).

An ECCO analysis questionnaire is used in the ICA Audit to investi-

TABLE A.1
Workplan for a Communication System Appraisal
(From Gerald Goldhaber. *Organizational Communication*. Dubuque, Iowa:
Wm. C. Brown, Co., 1974, p. 298.)

Section A: Overall Communication System

Stage I: Fact-Finding
1. Determine organizational objectives, organizational policies, and communication policies.
2. Inventory the communication activities and classify in relation to specific communication policies.
3. Identify the nature of communication system controls, and the organization function vested with communication as a key responsibility.

Stage II: Analysis
1. Study the communication activities in terms of levels, objectives, functions, channels, and other class-types.
2. Utilize appropriate measurement techniques to judge the strengths and weaknesses of the overall communication system.
3. Note the strengths and weaknesses of the overall system in relation to organization situational factors including structure, processes and leadership.

Stage III: Evaluation
1. Summarize the data obtained and arrive at conclusions concerning the adequacy of existing activities to implement policies.
2. Recommend necessary changes and/or supportive communication programs; and furnish details as to implementation.

Section B: Specific Communication Activities

Stage I: Fact-Finding
1. Determine the nature and objectives of the activity.
2. Ascertain the procedural instructions for the activity with reference to applicable communication performance criteria.
3. Arrive at performance standards constituting satisfactory performance for each procedural instruction.

Stage II: Analysis
1. Employ appropriate measurement techniques to estimate actual performance and deviation from standards.
2. Study deviations representing important weaknesses in the communication activity and give attention to the activity situational factors influencing communication behavior.

Stage III: Evaluation
1. Summarize the data obtained and arrive at conclusions concerning the adequacy of the specific communication activity to meet the objectives set for that activity.
2. Recommend corrective measures furnishing details as to implementation; and/or report on the presence of organization situational factors preventing accomplishment of objectives.

Prior to receiving this questionnaire did you know the information in the box below or any part of it?

(Message)

Please Check One:
_____ Yes I knew all of it.
_____ Yes I knew part of it. If so please list the numbers of the parts you knew
_ _ _ _ _
_____ No I did not know any of it.

If your answer above was "Yes I knew all of it," or "Yes I knew part of it," please complete the questionnaire by providing the information requested below.

If your answer above was "No I did not know any of it" you have completed the questionnaire. Please return the questionnaire to me or drop it in the information box. Thank you very much for your cooperation.

If you had the information in the box but the facts you heard were different, please write the facts you heard next to the associated number.

1. _____
2. _____
3. _____
4. _____
5. _____

Question #1.

From whom did you first receive the information in the box? Please place the source's code number (from your code sheet) on this line _____. Remember that by using the code number you never identify the specific person who gave you the information because each code number is assigned to several persons (in the operator group).

Question #2.

Where were you when you first received the information in the box above? Please check one:

_____ At my desk-board or other location where I carry out my job duties.
_____ Elsewhere in the room where I work.
_____ Outside this room but still working.
_____ Away from my unit-department but still working.
_____ Away from my unit-department but not while working (coffee break, etc.).
_____ Away from the building and while not working for Mountain Bell.

Question #3.

How long ago did you first receive the information in the box? Please circle the approximate time:

Today   Yesterday   3 4 5 6 7   days ago
                       2 3 4 5 6   weeks ago

Question #4.

By what method did you first receive the information in the box above? Please check only one of the following methods:

Written or Visual Methods
_____ Personal letter from the Co.
_____ Letter, memo or Service Program
_____ Annual Report
_____ News Letter
_____ Company Magazines
_____ Company film
_____ Public newspaper or magazine

Talking or Sound Methods
_____ Talking with one other person in his presence
_____ Talking over the telephone
_____ Talking (and listening) in a small group of two or more
_____ Attending an organized meeting or conference
_____ Overhearing what someone else said
_____ Radio or television

Miscellaneous
_____ I did it or I originated the information or decision
_____ Other Please explain _____

FIGURE A.1
Example of an ECCO Analysis Instrument

gate communication networks. A sample questionnaire is found in Figure A.1. In the "critical incident" format the subject chooses what he will report about. In the ECCO procedure, the researcher selects the incident to be described. By finding out who had what information and from whom he had received it at a particular time, the researcher learns about diffusion of information among people. He may have some data about how members develop "organizational intelligence." Both Critical Incident and ECCO Analysis provide data about information transmission, but neither is likely to be very informative about the character of relationships which people develop as they pass information.

Part of the Michigan State coorientation questionnaire is presented in Figure A.2. This questionnaire may be used to assess the character of a relationship between a superior and a subordinate by measuring coorientation on communication rules. The theory explaining why coorientation on communication rules is important in superior-subordinate relationships is discussed in chapter 8. I have had students develop their own questionnaires similar to this model. They found significant relationships between answers to the questionnaire and measures of employee satisfaction. Remember that in order to use the coorientation, supervisory pairs must be identified. That is, the researcher must be able to match the questionnaire of a subordinate with the questionnaire of the subordinate's supervisor.

Experiments

The most intrusive method for generating evidence is the experiment. In the experiment, the researcher intrudes into the behavior and changes one or more conditions. The most famous organizational experiment was the Hawthorne Investigation. In the first Hawthorne studies, for example, the researchers took a group of workers out of their regular work situation and put them into a special room where the lighting conditions were controlled by the researchers. They manipulated the lighting conditions and measured any resulting changes in worker productivity.

Observational and interview methods can produce information about what conditions happen together. A researcher may observe that in six companies the more "relationship-oriented" the supervisor, the higher the production of workers. The condition of "high relationship-orientation of supervisor" occurs where the condition of high productivity occurs. But this correlation is not sufficient to conclude that high relationship-orientation causes high productivity. Indeed supervisors may have "high relationship orientation" because the workers in their departments are high producers and therefore they do not need to put task pressure on them. The data about a cooccurrence does not permit, in this case, inferences about what causes what.

Using an experimental design, the researcher is able to collect information about causality. Researchers attempt to "control" all the conditions except those they are investigating. In this case, the variables of interest are supervisory style and productivity. The hypothesis is that style causes productivity. This means that style is the "independent" variable; productivity, the "dependent" variable. The variations in productivity are dependent upon variations in style. The experimenters measure conditions before their intervention. They then manipulate the independent variable. Perhaps they "train" supervisors with low relationship-orientation to develop higher relationship orientation. Then they measure again. They measure to make sure they have indeed produced an "experimental effect"; that is that the supervisors are, indeed, more relationship-oriented. They measure the dependent variable. Has productivity risen along with relationship-orientation?

This is the simplest kind of experiment. It investigates only one independent and one dependent variable. A more sophisticated design would examine kinds of tasks the people do. Supervisors of high producing units with uncertain tasks may have a different style than managers of units with routine tasks. This investigation has two independent variables and one dependent variable. Researchers are hypothesizing that in order to predict high productivity one needs information about both supervisor style and kind of tasks.

Managers engaged in informal research tasks ("why is morale so low around here?") do not need to be concerned with the setting of their research. They do their investigating where they are. Often organizations will hire researchers to investigate certain specific problems. Independent researchers, however, must determine appropriate settings. In particular, researchers who intend to conduct an experiment must decide whether to attempt to "create" the variables they want to study in the laboratory or to attempt to find and manipulate them in an organization. Leavitt's original investigations of the effects of communication networks were done using college students in specially designed rooms which restricted their communication to the channels the investigator was studying.[15] Later investigators examined similar communication networks "in the field."[16]

The decision of whether to conduct experimental research "in the field" or "in the laboratory" usually involves a trade-off of control of variables to be researched (the lab usually permits more control) against the generality of findings (it is sometimes unconvincing to argue that organizational simulations in a lab are real). Goldhaber illustrates the

My perception: Supervisor would probably say:

5. When you and your immediate supervisor talk about work prob-   5.___
lems (getting the job done, scheduling, etc.), who usually
brings them up?

   A. He does.
   B. I do.
   C. It's split about evenly between us.
   D. We don't talk about work problems.

5a. How satisfied are you with the amount of talk you and he   5a.___
have about work problems?

   A. I'd like to talk more about work problems.
   B. I'd like to talk less about them.
   C. I'm satisfied now.

6. When you and your immediate supervisor talk about people   6.___
problems (interpersonal relations, counseling people, solving
personal problems, etc.) who usually brings them up?

   A. He does.
   B. I do.
   C. It's split about evenly between us.
   D. We don't talk about people problems.

6a. How satisfied are you with the amount of talk you and he   6a.___
have about people problems?

   A. I'd like to talk more about people problems.
   B. I'd like to talk less about them.
   C. I'm satisfied now.

7. When you and your immediate supervisor talk about new ideas   7.___
or new ways of doing things, who usually brings the subject
up?

   A. He does.
   B. I do.
   C. It's split about evenly between us.
   D. We don't talk about new ideas or new ways of doing things.

7a. How satisfied are you with the amount of talk you and he   7a.___
have about new ideas?

   A. I'd like to talk more about it.
   B. I'd like to talk less about it.
   C. I'm satisfied.

Indicate your impressions of how you conduct "talk" with your supervisor. In the
space on the right side, indicate your guess about how your supervisor would answer
the question.

My perception: Supervisor would probably say:

1. When two people begin to communicate, one of them has to ask   1.___
for it to happen. Over time, when you and your supervisor
communicate, who usually asks for the meeting to occur? Does
he usually suggest. . .do you usually suggest. . .or do you
suggest it about equally?

   A. I usually suggest the meeting.
   B. He usually suggests
   C. We suggest it about equally.

2. Of course, it takes two to communicate. Sometimes one person   2.___
suggests a meeting, but the other one delays it, or puts it
off, or says he can't get together, etc. Between you and your
supervisor, who is more likely to put off getting together?

   A. He is more likely to put it off.
   B. I'm more likely to put it off.
   C. We do it about equally.
   D. Neither one of us puts off or delays a meeting.

3. When two people get together, one of them has to decide what   3.___
they'll talk about. Generally, when you and your immediate
supervisor talk, who usually decides on the topics to be
discussed?

   A. He usually decides.
   B. I usually decide.
   C. It's split about evenly between us.

3a. How satisfied are you with this arrangement?   3a.___

   A. I'd like to have more to say about what we talk about.
   B. I'm satisfied.

4. When you and your immediate supervisor talk, whose problems   4.___
do you talk about for the most part. . .his problems or your
problems?

   A. We talk more about his problems.
   B. We talk more about my problems.
   C. It's split about evenly between his and my problems.

4a. How dissatisfied are you with this arrangement?   4a.___

   A. I'd like to talk more about problems I have.
   B. I'd like to talk more about problems he has.
   C. I'd like to talk more about both his and my problems.
   D. I'm satisfied the way it is now.

Source: Michigan State Communication Department Research Team directed by David K. Berlo.

Assessing communication rules, p. 4

My perception: Supervisor would probably say:

_____ 11a. How satisfied are you with this?   11a. _____

A. I'd like to do more of the talking.
B. I'd like to do less of the talking.
C. I'm satisfied.

_____ 12. On the average, aside from brief greetings, how often do you 12. _____
and your immediate supervisor communicate (face-to-face or
telephone?

A. Several times a day.
B. Once a day.
C. Once or twice a week.
D. Once or twice a month.

_____ 12a. How satisfied are you with the frequency with which you   12a. _____
and your supervisor communicate?

A. I'd like to get together more often.
B. I'd like to get together less often.
C. I'm satisfied.

_____ 13. When you and your immediate supervisor talk face-to-face,   13. _____
how long do your talks together usually last?

A. 5 minutes or less.
B. 6-10 minutes.
C. 11-20 minutes.
D. 21-30 minutes.
E. More than 30 minutes.

_____ 13a. How satisfied are you with the length of these conversa-   13a. _____
tions between you and your immediate supervisor?

A. I'd like to get together for longer periods of time.
B. I'd like to get together for shorter periods of time.
C. I'm satisfied.

Assessing communication rules, p. 3

My perception: Supervisor would probably say:

_____ 8. When two people talk, one or the other sometimes interrupts   8. _____
to change the subject. When you and your immediate super-
visor talk, who usually interrupts to change the subject?

A. He does.
B. I do.
C. It's split about evenly between us.
D. Neither one of us interrupts to change the subject.

_____ 8a. How dissatisfied are you with having your immediate super-   8a. _____
visor interrupt you?

A. I wish he'd let me finish things without having him
interrupt me.
B. I'm satisfied.

_____ 9. Sometimes communication is interrupted by outside inter-   9. _____
ference, e.g., phone calls, someone breaking into the conversation, etc. When this happens while you and your
immediate supervisor are talking, who are the outsiders
looking for usually?

A. They are usually looking for him.
B. They are usually looking for me.
C. It's split about evenly.
D. We aren't interrupted when we're talking to each other.

_____ 9a. How satisfied are you with the amount of these outside   9a. _____
interruptions?

A. I wish there were fewer of them.
B. I'm satisfied.

_____ 10. When two people are talking, somebody has to decide to end   10. _____
the conversation. Over time, when you and your immediate
supervisor communicate, who usually ends the conversation
. . . who decides when it is time to stop?

A. I usually end the conversation.
B. He usually ends it.
C. We do it about equally.

_____ 11. Overall, who would you say does most of the talking in your 11. _____
conversations with your immediate supervisor?

A. He talks a lot more than I do.
B. He talks a little more than I do.
C. We talk about the same amount of time.
D. I talk a little more than he does.
E. I talk a lot more than he does.

FIGURE A.2

Assessing Communication "Rules" Between You and Your Immediate Supervisor (From Michigan State Communication Dept. Research Team directed by David K. Berlo. Reprinted with the permission of David K. Berlo.

two sides of field experiment vs. lab experiment debate with the following conversation which he claims to have overheard at a convention:

Mr. X: "I'm sick and tired of these damn researchers reporting their trivial results which they got in some university research lab. I'll bet more of them have never been in a company in their lives! Why the hell should I believe what they say when they've never been involved in the real world!"

Mr. Y: "You may be right, Mr. X, but don't you think that research results derived in lab settings would be more valid than those obtained in sloppy field settings!"

Mr. X: "Sloppy? My company is in electronics—it's a clean industry!"

Mr. Y: "I mean that it's hard to control variables in the field, therefore your research isn't as clean as that done in a lab.

Mr. X: "Look, I'm only interested in what I can get out of the research. What will it do for me and my company? If you can't tell me that, then I don't care about your cleanliness habits!"[17]

Even when a field experiment would be a better methodological choice, researchers have to settle for a laboratory simulation because they cannot get access to an organization. That is, they may be unable to find an organization which is willing to permit them to change organizational conditions for the purpose of investigation, no matter how much the company might gain from the experiment. The independent researcher is much more likely to get permission merely to observe interaction or to interview organizational members.

The organizational researcher who gives up controlled settings for field settings is not necessarily gaining "reality." One does not have to study "organizing" in the context of a formal organization. At present, we know little about how a group of people in face-to-face communication organize their activity. Those who study the processes of developing equivalent expectations and cognitive maps are investigating organizational communications as the term is used in this book.

FROM EVIDENCE TO INFERENCE

Although researchers must ask answerable questions, no single study will provide a final answer to the research question. Instead, researchers aim to draw inferences about the answers to their questions. I discuss here three kinds of inferences researchers are likely to make.

Statistical Inference

When the data is quantitative or numerical, researchers often draw statistical inferences. Quantitative researchers usually study a sample of the whole population in which they are interested, but they wish to draw conclusions about the whole population. Procedures for drawing statistical inferences relate sample to population. Typically, quantitative researchers are looking for categorical relationships and/or categorical differences. A researcher may want to answer the question, "Do upwardly mobile subordinates communicate differently than subordinates who do not aspire for advancement?" To answer this question, researchers draw upon a sample of subordinates.

Obviously, they cannot study all subordinates. Subordinates in the sample must be classified into categories of "upwardly mobile" and "not upwardly mobile." Then researchers determine how subordinates communicate with their supervisor. The researchers look for a numerical association of upward aspiration and communication in the sample. In particular, they ask "Does knowing categories of aspiration help to predict differences in expectation?" Summarizing the data allows one to answer this question for those people actually observed (the sample), but, if they are interested in knowing about the population from which the sample was drawn, they must use their sample to make inferences about the population. Inferential tests such as a "chi-square test" or an "F-test" provide researchers with information about how likely it is that a difference or a relationship found in a sample will be found in the population.

Causal Inference

Many researchers seek to draw "causal inferences" from their data. A causal inference states that given an observed relationship between A and B, A caused B. Under certain conditions, researchers may draw causal inferences from survey data.[18] Typically, however, researchers who want to draw causal inferences use experimental designs. They manipulate or change certain conditions (independent variables) and then measure to determine if other conditions (dependent variables) change.

The simplest experimental design is called a "one shoter." It is represented by the symbols:

$$X \qquad O$$

X is the experimental manipulation of independent variables; O is the observation of dependent variables. Careful researchers usually avoid this design because it provides a very weak basis for inference. They have no way of making sure that differences in O, in fact, resulted from changes in X.

TABLE A.2

Factors Jeopardizing Causal Inferences from Experiments (Adapted from Donald T. Campbell and Julian C. Stanley. *Experimental and Quasi-experimental Designs for Research*. Chicago: Rand McNally, 1963, p. 5.)

History	Events occurring between first and second measure in addition to experimental treatment may cause the second measure to be different from the first.
Maturation	Passage of time (not particular events) such as growing old, growing hungrier, growing more tired, may cause second measure to be different from first.
Testing	Effects of taking a test the first time may influence what people report on subsequent tests.
Statistical regression	Changes between first and second observations may result from choosing subjects on the basis of extreme scores on the first measure. Subjects with extreme scores initially may have more moderate scores the second time because their first scores were not their typical responses.
Selection	The criteria on which subjects were selected may influence the difference between first and second observation.
Experimental mortality	Change in measures between observation one and two may result from some subjects tested the first time not being tested the second time.

Table A.2 summarizes potential "sources of error" in drawing causal inferences from experimental data. Each of the sources represents a "rival hypothesis." For example suppose a researcher observes a work group during the first week of November, institutes an organizational change, then observes the same group the third week of December. He may claim that the organizational change has resulted in improved "friendliness" in the organizational climate. A rival hypothesis is that the increase in friendliness has been caused by the Christmas season, not the experimenter's induced change. The potential source of error is "history." Even if the holidays or other "historical events" do not constitute a possible explanation, this experimental design could have problems. It is shown symbolically by:

$$O_1 \quad X \quad O_2$$

(O_1 = observation one; O_2 = observation two) Observed changes could result from "testing." If members of the work group filled out questionnaires or were interviewed at O_1 their behavior at O_2 might have changed because the questions drew their attention to their behavior.

The simplest design which avoids most of the rival hypotheses shown in Table A.2 is symbolized:

$$R \quad O_1 \quad X \quad O_2$$
$$R \quad O_1 \quad \quad O_2$$

People are randomly assigned to groups. Observations are made of both groups. Only one group receives the experimental treatment. Second observations are then made of both groups. If the two groups are different, then the researchers may reasonably make the inference that the experimental treatment, rather than the effect of "history," or "testing," or "selection," etc., was the causal factor

Fallacious Inferences

In its most general sense, inference refers to the process of thinking in which a person draws conclusions about the unknown based upon the known. Statistical inference and causal inference are special problems associated with the use of statistics and the intent to attribute causality. Even researchers who do not face these special problems of inferring should be alert to certain fallacies which may muddle their inferential thinking. Barzen and Graff[19] suggest four fallacies which are likely to plague the thinking of researchers who are seeking to draw reasonable inferences.

One fallacy is overgeneralization or generalization beyond the available evidence. Use of allness terms such as "all," "every," and "never" may be used in cases where there is little evidence that a proposition is universal. There are two frequent reasons for overgeneralization. One is simply carelessness in the use of such terms and a neglect of qualifying terms such as "almost," "nearly," and "perhaps." A second cause is a failure by researchers to search long enough to find cases which provide negative evidence for the generalization. Researchers may conclude, for example, that managers make extensive use of the phone in transacting their business. This seems to be the case for most mangers, but an adequate search could prove that is by no means a universal practice.

A second kind of fallacious inference involves reducing a complex phenomenon to a simple one. This is a "reductionist" fallacy. The phrase "nothing but" is a flag which often signals this fallacy. To describe a manager as "nothing but" an interpersonal manipulator reduces the complexity of the role beyond reason.

A third kind of fallacy is tautology. A tautological inference is one in which a research calls a single phenomenon two different names and claims to have "discovered" that they are related to one another. For example, a researcher may find a relationship between how a person describes his job and how satisfied he is with the job. But if the scale on which the worker described the job contained items on which the worker reflected his satisfaction, then the researcher has measured only one variable—satisfaction—not two. Since the two are the same, naturally they occur at the same time.

The fourth fallacy is misplaced literalism. This fallacy results from not taking into account the context of what is said. Verbal reports always take place within a sequence of events at a certain place, and in relationship to certain people. Barzen and Graff insist that it is the researcher's responsibility to "judge, in light of his wider knowledge. . . . If he remains boldly literal and contents himself with quoting extracts, he invariably ends by showing his human subject to have been a mass of contradictions."[20] In drawing inferences, researchers must take into account the content of their data and not simply the literal interpretation of what they have been told.

Turning the research inferences into a document called a "research report" is the final phase in most research processes. Research reports are persuasive communications in which the writer attempts to convince the reader of the reasonableness of his/her inferences. The typical research report contains the divisions discussed in Table A.3. The length of the different divisions will vary with whether the research was observational, survey, or experimental. This format does not always need to be followed. However, because it is a familiar format,

TABLE A.3
Format for Reporting Research

---

1. Problem statement — Explain the problem and its importance.
2. Related research — Summarize several sources of special relevance to the study. Provide the reader with a theoretical framework for the study.
3. Objectives — Clearly and briefly indicate the purpose of the study. State hypotheses, if any.
4. Procedure — Detail how the study was conducted. Indicate:
   a. population and sample
   b. design
   c. measures of variables (questionnaires, etc.) and how the data was gathered
   d. analysis — methods used to summarize and draw inferences
5. Results — Describe what was found in the sample and what statistical inferences are warranted.
6. Discussion — Relate the results to the statement of the problem and the theoretical framework. Present general inferences.
7. Conclusion — Indicate directions for further research and practical implications of the findings for how people should act.

---

the reader can go quickly to the researcher's inferences and judge them in light of the evidence provided. The principal advantage of the format is its efficiency as a form for communicating evidence and inference.

SUMMARY

Investigating organizing processes involves three tasks: (1) moving from hunch to research question, (2) moving from question to evidence, (3) moving from evidence to inference.

The hunch which stimulates a research question may be a vague dissatisfaction with a situation or a curiosity about how things work or how behaviors relate to one another. Hunches occur to people in common-sense terms. The task of moving from hunch to research question involves clarifying the vague hunch by (1) defining the meaning of terms and (2) embedding the question in the context of theory. The quality of a research question may be assessed by asking two questions: (1) Will I know anything of value if I answer this question? (2) Is it possible to find an answer to the question as it is stated?

Three ways of collecting evidence are described: (1) observational studies, (2) survey investigations, and (3) experiments. The three approaches are distinguished according to the extent the researchers "intrude" into the phenomena they are investigating. Advantages and disadvantages of each method are discussed. References to additional information on each method are provided.

The process of drawing inferences from data is making statements about the unknown based upon the known. Researchers usually seek to make claims about some general state of affairs based on less than complete observations of that "state of affairs." Statistical inferences are probability statements that relate observations of a sample to what may be true of the larger population. Causal inferences relate the observation of cooccurrence to a causal relationship. That is, in making a causal inference one goes from saying, "When *A* happens then *B* happens" to inferring that *"A* causes *B."*

Inferring is a process of thinking in which one moves from specific examples (the known) to generalizations (the unknown). In the process, the researchers' thinking may be fallacious in a number of ways. Four common fallacies in the research process are: overgeneralization, reductionism, overreduction tautology, and misplaced literalism.

The final step in most research is turning the process into a document called a research report. A format for such reports is suggested.

ENDNOTES

1. This typology is somewhat similar to the functional typology developed by Greenbaum: Legislative, innovative, integrative, and informative-instructive. See Howard H. Greenbaum, "The Audit of Organizational Communication," *Academy of Management Journal* 17 (1974): 739–754.

2. Larry Spence and Robert O'Connor, *Communication Disturbances and Their Consequences: Information Flow in the Welfare Delivery System of the Pennsylvania Department of Public Welfare*. (University Park, Pa.: College of Human Development, Pennsylvania State University, 1974).

3. Ibid.

4. Ibid.

5. Ibid., pp. 23–24.

6. Ibid., pp. 20–21.

7. Ibid.

8. Alvin Gouldner, *Patterns of Industrial Bureaucracy* (New York: The Free Press, 1954).

9. Charles R. Walker and Robert H. Guest, *The Man on the Assembly Line* (Cambridge: Harvard University Press, 1952).

10. W. F. Whyte, *Street Corner Society* (Chicago: University of Chicago Press, 1943).

11. Henry Mintzberg, "Managerial Work: Analysis from Observation," *Management Science* (1971): 97–110.

12. Mintzberg notes that managers in his study spent less than nine minutes on most of their activities. He quotes Guest's research that foremen spend about forty-eight seconds on each activity.

13. Gerald Goldhaber, *Organizational Communication* (Dubuque, Iowa: Wm. C. Brown, 1974), p. 295.

14. Cal Downs, "Research Methods," Paper presented to S.C.A. Post-Doctoral Program on Organizational Communication (San Marcos, Texas, 1976).

15. H. J. Leavitt, "Some Effects of Certain Communication Patterns on Group Performance," *Journal of Abnormal and Social Psychology* (1951): 38–50.

16. See Tom Burns, "The Direction of Activity and Communications in a Departmental Executive Group," *Human Relations* 7 (1954): 73–97, and A. K. Wickesberg, "Communication Networks in the Business Organizational Structure," *Academy of Management Journal* (July 1968): 253–262.

17. Goldhaber, *Organizational Communication*, p. 270.

18. For further information on causal influences from survey data see Herbert M. Blalock, *Causal Inferences in Non-Experimental Research* (Chapel Hill: Univ. of North Carolina, 1964).

19. Jacques Barzen and Henry F. Graff, *The Modern Researcher* (New York: Harcourt Brace Jovanovich, 1957).

20. Ibid., p. 128.

INDEX